THE NEW YORK TIMES LIVING HISTORY

WORLD WAR II

THE NEW YORK TIMES LISTING HISTORY

WORLD WAR II

The Allied Counteroffensive, 1942–1945

Douglas Brinkley,

General Editor

Edited and with chapter introductions by David Rubel

Times Books

Henry Holt and Company

New York

Times Books

Henry Holt and Company, LLC

Publishers since 1866

115 West 18th Street

New York, New York 10011

AN AGINCOURT PRESS BOOK

President: David Rubel

Senior Editor: Julia Rubel

Assistant Editor: Brooke Palmer

Proofreader: Laura Jorstad

Image Research: Erika Rubel

The Library of Congress has cataloged Volume I as follows:

LIBRARY OF CONGRESS CATALOGING-IN-PUBLICATION DATA

World War II / Douglas Brinkley, general editor ; edited and with chapter introductions by
David Rubel.

p. cm. — (The New York Times living history)

Includes index.

ISBN 0-8050-7246-2 (vol. 1)

1. World War, 1939–1945. I. Title: World War 2. II. Title: World War Two. III.
Brinkley, Douglas. IV. Rubel, David. V. Series.

D743.W6495 2003

813'.54—dc22   2003059658

ISBN: 0-8050-7247-0

First Edition 2004

Designed by Fritz Metsch

Printed in the United States of America

1 3 5 7 9 10 8 6 4 2

For text permissions, see pp. 393–394. For illustration credits, see pp. 395–396.

CONTENTS

INTRODUCTION

By Douglas Brinkley

In late December 1941, following the devastating Japanese attack on Pearl Harbor, Rear Adm. Chester Nimitz replaced Husband Kimmel as the commander in chief of the U.S. Pacific Fleet, a position that Nimitz would hold until the end of the war. "I'm the new commander in chief," he told his wife, Catherine, on the day that he learned of the appointment. As Nimitz spoke, however, he looked so downcast that his wife felt compelled to remind her husband of the fact that he had dreamed of obtaining this particular command nearly his entire life. "But, sweetheart," Nimitz countered, "all the ships are at the bottom."

Nimitz wasn't too far off in his assessment: The Japanese had indeed destroyed or badly damaged eleven of the Pacific Fleet's largest ships, and the imperial navy remained a significant offensive threat. During the first six months of 1942, it dominated the Pacific theater through occupation in the west and intimidation in the east. As a result, within the Pacific Fleet—or what was left of it—morale was low, and for the first time in a hundred years American sailors began thinking of themselves as underdogs in their own waters. In other branches of the armed forces, the situation was nearly as bad. In the army, for example, American soldiers had their own confidence shaken badly in February 1943 after taking a hard loss at the Kasserine Pass in North Africa.

No American had imagined that U.S. entry into World War II would be a breeze. Yet neither had many anticipated the dire situation that presented itself in 1942. As one Axis victory followed another, the idea that the United States would win the war, but not easily, transformed itself into a fear that the Allies might not win at all.

Even as Nimitz took stock of his crippled forces, the Japanese prepared for a new assault, which Nimitz's superiors in Washington believed would target Alaska, beginning with the Aleutian Islands. They pressured the admiral to deploy his remaining fleet there, but Nimitz, who was less sure of the target, resisted. Meanwhile, two factors worked in the Americans' favor. One was the familiar human tendency to ease up when things are going well. In the case of the Japanese, their security relaxed in the aftermath of their victories at Pearl Harbor and elsewhere. The task force that had been sent against Hawaii had enforced radio silence. But by May 1942, the Japanese were talking up a storm in the Pacific, albeit in code.

Fortunately for Nimitz, his other advantage was the small but talented group of cryptanalysts he had working for him at Pearl Harbor. Assigned to a windowless basement room outfitted with worktables made of planks and sawhorses, the staff of the Combat Intelligence Office (known as Station Hypo) had deciphered enough Japanese naval traffic by the spring of 1942 to recognize the surprising recurrence of the term *AF*. Station Hypo chief Joseph Rochefort, who padded around his uncomfortable cellar office in slippers and a red smoking jacket, quickly concluded that *AF* must be the name of the next major Japanese target, but where was it? The navy brass in Washington still insisted that *AF* must be Alaska, but Rochefort had a hunch that the target was actually a tiny island at the far end of the Hawaiian chain known as Midway. To test his theory, Rochefort arranged in early May for the small garrison on Midway to radio in the clear a message that it was running out of fresh water because its distillation plant had broken down. Two days later, Station Hypo decoded a Japanese intercept reporting that *AF* was running low on drinking water. This confirmation that *AF* was indeed Midway cleared the way for Nimitz to act.

Against the much larger Japanese fleet converging on Midway, Nimitz sent everything he had: his three aircraft carriers against their six, his eight cruisers against their fifteen, and so on. Overall, the U.S. fleet totaled just one-quarter the size and strength of the Japanese, but it was nevertheless much larger than any the Japanese had anticipated. As the battle unfolded early on June 4, the American aircraft carriers sent wave after wave of dive-bombers and torpedo bombers against the Japanese, decimating Adm. Yamamoto Isoroku's overconfident armada. It was the most important single victory of the entire Pacific war.

How do we know all these details of what happened? From the historical record, of course. From military orders and battle plans and ships' logs. From personal letters and diaries and memoirs. From transcripts of intercepted radio messages and briefings and memos and recalled conversations. And from newspaper reports such as those that appeared in *The New York Times* each day.

For *The Allied Counteroffensive*, as for all of the other volumes in the Living History series, *The New York Times* has made available its archives, containing some of the most detailed and insightful reportage on World War II, written as the major political and military events occurred, often from the scene of the action. These arti-

cles, the first drafts of history, provide modern readers with an unusually vivid sense of the war years, enabling us to imagine what it must have been like to live through that era without knowing how the fighting would end. Unlike the historians who followed them, the reporters of *The New York Times* accomplished their research as the war was still unfolding, and whatever their stories lack in hindsight is more than made up for in immediacy.

Like historians, however, these journalists based their reportage on the same fundamental source material—primary documents—that World War II historians use today. Following this logic, the Living History pairs with each *New York Times* article a related primary document, chosen for its unique voice and evocative perspective. For instance, accompanying a poignant *Times* editorial on the fighting for Guadalcanal, readers of this book will find a frank account of the struggle for Henderson Field penned by Sgt. Mitchell Paige, a marine who was later awarded the Congressional Medal of Honor for his heroism. Similarly, supplementing one of the first reports of the Warsaw Ghetto Uprising is an excerpt from the testimony given by Tsivye Lubetkin, a survivor of the uprising, at the 1961 trial of Adolf Eichmann in Jerusalem. Reading Lubetkin's recollection of his experience is probably as close as any of us would care to come to occupied Poland in 1943.

Perhaps the most important goal of the Living History series is to allow voices such as Lubetkin's to emerge from the clutter of the past and speak again. Among the many provocative offerings readers will find in *The Allied Counteroffensive* are a deposition given by a black Detroiter describing the June 1943 race riots there, an entry from the private diary of Nazi propaganda minister Joseph Goebbels recounting Adolf Hitler's reaction to the overthrow of Benito Mussolini, the text of George Patton's speech to elements of the Third Army on the eve of D day, Allen Dulles's intelligence dispatches concerning the development of Hitler's secret V-weapons, and a kamikaze pilot's farewell letter to his family.

Such accounts evidence the shift in popular sentiment that took place during the last three years of the war. The battle of Midway marked the end of the most frightening period for the American public—the six months following Pearl Harbor during which the prospect of Japanese mastery seemed all too real. The country was on the defensive, Allied morale was low, and U.S. government propaganda, never very extensive, was having little positive effect. With British and American successes in the Mediterranean theater, however, and the Soviet victory at Stalingrad, the military momentum changed, and civilian morale in the Axis nations began to fall. In Italy, an already war-weary public, tired of the alliance with Germany and a rationed diet that reduced their intake to nine hundred calories a day, cheered Mussolini's July 1943 ouster.

In Germany, morale was not much better, but the resentments that did exist were kept more carefully hidden—until July 1944, that is, when opposition within the German military attempted a well-planned coup d'état, scheduled to begin with Hitler's assassination because only violence could separate the Führer from his stranglehold on power. Unfortunately for all of those who died during the final year of the war, Hitler survived the explosion of the bomb planted beneath his conference table. It was a damned sort of miracle.

With Hitler's subsequent purge of the Wehrmacht and the military government equally entrenched in Japan, the Allies had little hope of an easy victory in 1944. Yet they were making substantial, if costly, progress. The most memorable surge came on June 6, D-day, when American, British, and Canadian troops established the long-awaited beachhead in France and began that country's liberation. Gen. Dwight D. Eisenhower, who oversaw the planning for D-day, left nothing to chance, mobilizing 1.5 million troops and the largest invasion fleet the world has ever seen.

Luck and a gust of strong wind blew part of the U.S. Army's Fourth Division to a quieter part of the Normandy coast than had originally been intended. Brig. Gen. Theodore Roosevelt Jr., the late president's son, commanded these troops, and after taking a moment to survey his relatively peaceful landing zone, he told his junior officers, "We'll start the war from here." In fact, the final phase of the European war did "start" from there, with the breakout at St. Lô leading to the liberation of Paris and thereafter the push into Germany.

Just before Christmas 1944, Hitler staged his last major offensive, attacking through the Ardennes forest in northeast France. Known as the Battle of the Bulge (because of the shape the incursion created in the Allied lines), the assault was, by some measures, the largest ever withstood by the U.S. Army. With the Germans fighting desperately to keep the advancing Allied troops from reaching the Rhine, the Americans in their path had some extremely rough going in frigid December weather. Yet the First and Third Armies handed the Wehrmacht a devastating defeat, ending all hope for an outcome other than Germany's unconditional surrender, which finally came in early May 1945.

Meanwhile, the Japanese made their own desperate stand at Iwo Jima—an island south of Tokyo that was considered part of the capital's prefecture and thus sacred imperial soil, requiring its defense to the last man. Iwo Jima also had strategic significance for the Japanese, who used it to refuel fighters challenging the B-29s raiding mainland Japan. It took three divisions of marines three weeks to wrest control of the island from its irrationally determined defenders. Some battalions reported casualties of 100 percent; none lost fewer than half of its men. After visiting the battlefield, war correspondent Robert Sherrod wrote, "Whether the dead were Japs or Americans, they had died with the greatest possible violence. Nowhere in the Pacific war had I seen such badly mangled bodies....Only the legs were easy to identify; they were Japanese if wrapped in khaki puttees, American if covered by canvas leggings. The smell of burning flesh was heavy."

It was this sort of gruesome fighting, which also took place on Okinawa and elsewhere, that revealed to Pres. Harry Truman the potentially enormous cost of invading the Japanese mainland. Any such operation would lead to an extended struggle resulting in perhaps two million casualties. For that reason—and, most likely, also to intimidate the Soviets and keep them out of the Pacific Rim—Truman ordered the use of atomic bombs on Hiroshima and Nagasaki. The consequences of this decision for the postwar world can only be acknowledged here but are well known to those who lived through even the winding down of the Cold War.

By August 1945, of course, the two men who had led the western Allies to victory had been removed from their respective seats of power—Franklin Roosevelt by death and Winston Churchill by an electoral defeat that shocked the world, if not the British public. Churchill felt especially resentful at having to leave the ongoing negotiations at Potsdam to the new prime minister, Clement Attlee. "My removal from the scene at the time when I still had much influence and power," he wrote later, "rendered it impossible for satisfactory solutions to be reached." Perhaps Churchill was right, yet his dismissal oddly underscored the ultimate triumph of his own democratic ideology. In victory, one can be sure, a dictator such as Hitler would never have stepped aside as Churchill did.

TURNING POINTS

1.

The Battle of Midway

June 1942

Japanese naval commander in chief Yamamoto Isoroku was convinced that his country's only chance to win the war in the Pacific lay in the quick elimination of the U.S. Pacific Fleet. Otherwise, the United States would have time to mobilize its vast productive capacities, thereafter dwarfing the output of Japan's own modest industrial base. The December 1941 attack on Pearl Harbor

had begun the admiral's task well, but the job wouldn't be completed, he knew, until the American aircraft carriers were also smashed.

Yamamoto's new plan called for a showdown battle off Midway, the westernmost of the Hawaiian Islands. The admiral correctly perceived that the Americans would have to commit all their resources to defend Midway because of its strategic importance as a potential staging area for an invasion of Oahu. What Yamamoto didn't realize was that U.S. naval cryptanalysts had broken the Japanese fleet code and knew in advance of his complex plan to entrap the American carriers.

Even so, the Japanese still had a considerably stronger fleet. The main Japanese task force, commanded by Pearl Harbor hero Nagumo Chuichi, featured four heavy carriers whose planes would begin the battle by attacking the air bases on Midway, thereby forcing the American carriers to intervene. Later, Yamamoto's own task force, lurking in the rear, would come up to join the fight and finish off the Americans. There were obvious flaws in the plan, which Nagumo and others pointed out, but the Japan-

ese were so confident in their ability to overcome all obstacles that they went ahead with the plan regardless.

In addition to the heavy carriers, the Japanese also had two light carriers, seven battleships, fifteen cruisers, and forty-four destroyers. To oppose them, the Americans had three carriers, eight cruisers, and fifteen destroyers. Rear Adm. Raymond A. Spruance was given operational control of Task Force 16, built around the *Enterprise* and the *Hornet*, while Rear Adm. Frank J. Fletcher led Task Force 17 and exercised overall command from his patched-up flagship *Yorktown*.

The three American carriers hid over the eastern horizon while Nagumo's task force approached Midway from the northwest. According to Japanese intelligence, only the *Enterprise* and the *Hornet* remained afloat, both last seen in the South Pacific. Therefore, Nagumo was surprised when one of his scout planes discovered early on June 4 a nearby American carrier. About 9 A.M., a still-confident Nagumo ordered his ships to close on the single enemy carrier. Within twenty-four hours, however, all four of Nagumo's own carriers would be gone.

This photograph of navy SBDs attacking the Japanese fleet at Midway was taken from a 16mm color motion picture. Below the planes, which are Douglas Dauntlesses, can be seen a burning Japanese ship.

2, PERHAPS 3, JAPANESE CARRIERS SUNK WITH ALL THEIR PLANES, NIMITZ REPORTS

Sea Fight Goes On; Momentous U. S. Victory in Midway Battle Is in View, Admiral Says

By ROBERT TRUMBULL

PEARL HARBOR, June 6—Admiral Chester W. Nimitz, Commander in Chief of the United States Pacific Fleet, announced today that two or three Japanese aircraft carriers had been destroyed and that "a momentous victory is in the making" in the great battle on the Midway Island sea front.

The admiral, who said in a communiqué that "Pearl Harbor has now been partially avenged," also announced that the United States forces had damaged one or two other carriers, as well as three battleships, four cruisers and three transports of the enemy invasion fleet that failed in its assault on Midway, which never got beyond the stage of aerial preparation.

Admiral Nimitz's communiqué, the third he has issued since the battle got under way on Thursday, follows:

Through the skill and devotion to duty of their armed forces of all branches in the Midway area, our citizens can now rejoice that a momentous victory is in the making.

It was on a Sunday just six months ago that the Japanese made their peacetime attack on our fleet and Army activities in Oahu. At that time they created heavy damage, it is true, but their act aroused the grim determination of our citizenry to avenge such treachery, and it raised, not lowered, the morale of our fighting men.

Pearl Harbor has now been partially avenged. Vengeance will not be complete until Japanese sea power has been reduced to impotence. We have made substantial progress in that direction. Perhaps we will be forgiven if we claim we are about midway to our objective.

The battle is not over. All returns have not yet been received. It is with full confidence, however, that for this phase of the action the following enemy losses are claimed:

Two or three carriers and all their aircraft destroyed, in addition to one or two carriers badly damaged and most of their aircraft lost.

Three battleships damaged, at least one badly.

Four cruisers damaged, two heavily.

Three transports damaged.

It is possible that some of these wounded ships will not be able to reach their bases.

One of our carriers was hit and some planes were lost. Our personnel casualties were light.

This is the balance sheet that the Army, Navy and Marine forces in this area offer their country this morning.

In a communiqué issued yesterday Admiral Nimitz said that the brunt of the action against the enemy's invasion force was being borne by airmen of the Navy, Marine Corps and Army. Today's communiqué disclosed that an American carrier had been in action, but nothing has been said about any other American surface ships.

"The terrifying scream of the dive-bombers reached me first."

An excerpt from Fuchida Mitsuo's account of the battle of Midway

Fuchida Mitsuo, the author of this account, was, like Nagumo, a hero of Pearl Harbor, having planned and led the air attack. He would have fulfilled a similar role at Midway had he not been recovering from appendicitis. Fuchida later called the June 1942 engagement "the battle that doomed Japan," and it is generally agreed that Midway was the turning point of the Pacific war. Before the battle, the Japanese had six heavy carriers operating in the Pacific, while the Americans had only three (not including the *Saratoga,* which was in port for repairs). Afterward, taking into account both sides' losses at Midway, the Japanese had only two carriers left, while the Americans (losing the *Yorktown* but regaining the *Saratoga*) still had three. More important, during the next two years, while Japan's shipyards splashed six new heavy carriers, America's turned out seventeen.

As the Nagumo Force proceeded northward, our four carriers feverishly prepared to attack the enemy ships. The attack force was to include 36 dive-bombers (18 "Vals" each from *Hiryu* and *Soryu*) and 54 torpedo bombers (18 "Kates" each from *Akagi* and *Kaga,* and nine each from *Hiryu* and *Soryu*). It proved impossible, however, to provide an adequate fighter escort because enemy air attacks began again shortly, and most of our Zeros had to be used to defend the Striking Force itself. As a result, only 12 Zeros (three from each carrier) could be assigned to protect the bomber groups. The 102-plane attack force was to be ready for take-off at 1030.

After *Tone*'s search plane reported the presence of a carrier in the enemy task force, we expected an attack momentarily and were puzzled that it took so long in coming. As we found out after the war, the enemy had long been awaiting our approach, was continuously informed of our movements by the flying boats from Midway, and was choosing the most advantageous time to pounce. Admiral Spruance, commanding the American force, planned to strike his first blow as our carriers were recovering and refueling their planes returned from Midway. His wait for the golden opportunity was rewarded at last. The quarry was at hand, and the patient hunter held every advantage.

Between 0702 and 0902 the enemy launched 131 dive-bombers and torpedo planes. At about 0920 our screening ships began reporting enemy carrier planes approaching. We were in for a concentrated attack, and the Nagumo Force faced the gravest crisis of its experience. Was there any escape? An electric thrill ran throughout the fleet as our interceptors took off amid the cheers of all who had time and opportunity to see them.

Reports of approaching enemy planes increased until it was quite evident that they were not from a single carrier. When the Admiral and his staff realized this, their optimism abruptly vanished. The only way to stave off disaster was to launch planes at once. The order went out: "Speed preparations for immediate take-off!" This command was almost superfluous. Aviation officers, maintenance crews, and pilots were all working frantically to complete launching preparations.

The first enemy carrier planes to attack were 15 torpedo bombers. When first spotted by our screening ships and combat air patrol, they were still not visible from the carriers, but they soon appeared as tiny dark specks in the blue sky, a little above the horizon, on *Akagi*'s starboard bow. The distant wings flashed in the sun. Occasionally one of the specks burst into a spark of flame and trailed black smoke as it fell into the water. Our fighters were on the job, and the enemy again seemed to be without fighter protection.

Presently a report came in from a Zero group leader: "All 15 enemy torpedo bombers shot down." Nearly 50 Zeros had gone to intercept the unprotected enemy formation! Small wonder that it did not get through.

Again at 0930 a lookout atop the bridge yelled: "Enemy torpedo bombers, 30 degrees to starboard, coming in low!" This was followed by another cry from a port lookout forward: "Enemy torpedo planes approaching 40 degrees to port!"

The raiders closed in from both sides, barely skimming over the water. Flying in single columns, they were within five miles and seemed to be aiming straight for *Akagi*. I watched in breathless suspense, thinking how impossible it would be to dodge all their torpedoes. But these raiders, too, without protective escorts, were already being engaged by our fighters. On *Akagi*'s flight deck all attention was fixed on the dramatic scene unfolding before us, and there was wild cheering and whistling as the raiders went down one after another.

Crew abandon the Yorktown *during the battle of Midway. The knotted lines in the foreground were used to evacuate the upper platforms.*

Of the 14 enemy torpedo bombers which came in from starboard, half were shot down, and only 5 remained of the original 12 planes to port. The survivors kept charging in as *Akagi* opened fire with antiaircraft machine guns.

Both enemy groups reached their release points, and we watched for the splash of torpedoes aimed at *Akagi*. But, to our surprise, no drops were made. At the last moment the planes appeared to forsake *Akagi*, zoomed overhead, and made for *Hiryu* to port and astern of us. As the enemy planes passed *Akagi*, her gunners regained their composure and opened a sweeping fire, in which *Hiryu* joined. Through all this deadly gunfire the Zeros kept after the Americans, continually reducing their number.

Seven enemy planes finally succeeded in launching their torpedoes at *Hiryu*, five from her starboard side and two from port. Our Zeros tenaciously pursued the retiring attackers as far as they could. *Hiryu* turned sharply to starboard to evade the torpedoes, and we watched anxiously to see if any would find their mark. A deep sigh of relief went up when no explosion occurred, and *Hiryu* soon turned her head to port and resumed her original course. A total of more than 40 enemy torpedo planes had been thrown against us in these attacks, but only seven American planes had survived long enough to release their missiles, and not a single hit had been scored. Nearly all of the raiding enemy planes were brought down.

Most of the credit for this success belonged to the brilliant interception of our fighters, whose swift and daring action was watched closely from the flagship. No less impressive was the dauntless courage shown by the American fliers, who carried out the attack despite heavy losses. Shipboard spectators of this thrilling drama watched spellbound, blissfully unaware that the worst was yet to come.

As our fighters ran out of ammunition during the fierce battle, they returned to the carriers for replenishment, but few ran low on fuel. Service crews cheered the returning pilots, patted them on the shoulder, and shouted words of encouragement. As soon as a plane was ready again, the pilot nodded, pushed forward the throttle, and roared back into the sky. This scene was repeated time and again as the desperate air struggle continued.

Preparations for a counter-strike against the enemy had continued on board our four carriers throughout the enemy torpedo attacks. One after another, planes were hoisted from the hangar and quickly arranged on the flight deck. There was no time to lose. At 1020 Admiral Nagumo gave the order to launch when ready. On *Akagi*'s flight deck all planes were in position with engines warming up. The big ship began turning into the wind. Within five minutes all her planes would be launched.

Five minutes! Who would have dreamed that the tide of battle would shift completely in that brief interval of time?

Visibility was good. Clouds were gathering at about 3,000 meters, however, and though there were occasional breaks, they afforded good concealment for approaching enemy planes. At 1024 the order to start launching came from the bridge by voice-tube. The Air Officer flapped a white flag, and the first Zero fighter gathered speed and whizzed off the deck. At that instant a lookout screamed: "Hell-divers!" I looked up to see three black enemy planes plummeting toward our ship. Some of our machine guns managed to fire a few frantic bursts at them, but it was too late. The plump silhouettes of the American "Dauntless" dive-bombers quickly grew larger, and then a number of black objects suddenly floated eerily from their wings. Bombs! Down they came straight toward me! I fell intuitively to the deck and crawled behind a command post mantelet.

The terrifying scream of the dive-bombers reached me first, followed by the crashing explosion of a direct hit. There was a blinding flash and then a second explosion, much louder than the first. I was shaken by a weird blast of warm air. There was still another shock, but less severe, apparently a near-miss. Then followed a startling quiet as the barking of guns suddenly ceased. I got up and looked at the sky. The enemy planes were already gone from sight.

The attackers had gotten in unimpeded because our fighters, which had engaged the preceding wave of torpedo planes only a few moments earlier, had not yet had time to regain altitude. Consequently, it may be said that the American dive-bombers' success was made possible by the earlier martyrdom of their torpedo planes. Also, our carriers had no time to evade because clouds hid the enemy's approach until he dove down to the attack. We had been caught flatfooted in the most vulnerable condition possible—decks loaded with planes armed and fueled for an attack.

Looking about, I was horrified at the destruction that had been wrought in a matter of seconds. There was a huge hole in the flight deck just behind the amidship elevator. The elevator itself, twisted like molten glass, was drooping into the hangar. Deck plates reeled upward in grotesque configurations. Planes stood tail up, belching livid flame and jet-black smoke. Reluctant tears streamed down my cheeks as I watched the fires spread, and I was terrified at the prospect of induced explosions which would surely doom the ship. I heard Masuda yelling, "Inside! Get inside! Everybody who isn't working! Get inside!"

Unable to help, I staggered down a ladder and into the ready room. It was already jammed with badly burned victims from the hangar deck. A new explosion was followed quickly by several more, each causing the bridge structure to tremble. Smoke from the burning hangar gushed through passageways and into the bridge and ready room, forcing us to seek other refuge. Climbing back to the bridge I could see that *Kaga* and *Soryu* had also been hit and were giving off heavy columns of black smoke. The scene was horrible to behold.

Akagi had taken two direct hits, one on the after rim of the amidship elevator, the other on the rear guard on the portside of the flight deck. Normally, neither would have been fatal to the giant carrier, but induced explosions of fuel and munitions devastated whole sections of the ship, shaking the bridge and filling the air with deadly splinters. As fire spread among the planes lined up wing to wing on the after flight deck, their torpedoes began to explode, making it impossible to bring the fires under control. The entire hangar area was a blazing inferno, and the flames moved swiftly toward the bridge.

Because of the spreading fire, our general loss of combat efficiency, and especially the severance of external communication facilities, Nagumo's Chief of Staff, Rear Admiral Kusaka, urged that the Flag be transferred at once to light cruiser *Nagara*. Admiral Nagumo gave only a half-hearted nod, but Kusaka patiently continued his entreaty: "Sir, most of our ships are still intact. You must command them."

The situation demanded immediate action, but Admiral Nagumo was reluctant to leave his beloved flagship. Most of all he was loathe to leave behind the officers and men of *Akagi*, with whom he had shared every joy and sorrow of war. With tears in his eyes, Captain Aoki spoke up: "Admiral, I will take care of the ship. Please, we all implore you, shift your flag to *Nagara* and resume command of the Force."

At this moment Lieutenant Commander Nishibayashi, the Flag Secretary, came up and reported to Kusaka: "All passages below are afire, Sir. The only means of escape is by rope from the forward window of the bridge down to the deck, then by the outboard passage to the anchor deck. *Nagara's* boat will come alongside the anchor deck port, and you can reach it by rope ladder."

Kusaka made a final plea to Admiral Nagumo to leave the doomed ship. At last convinced that there was no possibility of maintaining command from *Akagi*, Nagumo bade the Captain good-bye and climbed from the bridge window with the aid of Nishibayashi. The Chief of Staff and other staff and headquarters officers followed. The time was 1046.

On the bridge there remained only Captain Aoki, his Navigator, the Air Officer, a few enlisted men, and myself. Aoki was trying desperately to get in touch with the engine room. The Chief Navigator was struggling to see if anything could be done to regain rudder control. The others were gathered on the anchor deck fighting the raging fire as best they could. But the unchecked flames were already licking at the bridge. Hammock mantelets around the bridge structure were beginning to burn. The Air Officer looked back at me and said, "Fuchida, we won't be able to stay on the bridge much longer. You'd better get to the anchor deck before it is too late."

In my condition this was no easy task. Helped by some sailors, I managed to get out of the bridge window and slid down the already smoldering rope to the gun deck. There I was still ten feet above the flight deck. The connecting monkey ladder was red hot, as was the iron plate on which I stood. There was nothing to do but jump, which I did. At the same moment another explosion occurred in the hangar, and the resultant blast sent me sprawling. Luckily the deck on which I landed was not yet afire, for the force of the fall knocked me out momentarily. Returning to consciousness, I struggled to rise to my feet, but both of my ankles were broken.

Crewmen finally came to my assistance and took me to the anchor deck, which was already jammed. There I was strapped into a bamboo stretcher and lowered to a boat which carried me, along with other wounded, to light cruiser *Nagara*. The transfer of Nagumo's staff and of the wounded was completed at 1130. The cruiser got under way, flying Admiral Nagumo's flag at her mast.

Meanwhile, efforts to bring *Akagi*'s fires under control continued, but it became increasingly obvious that this was impossible. As the ship came to a halt, her bow was still pointed into the wind, and pilots and crew had retreated to the anchor deck to escape the flames, which were reaching down to the lower hangar deck. When the dynamos went out, the ship was deprived not only of illumination but of pumps for combatting the conflagration as well. The fireproof hangar doors had been destroyed, and in this dire emergency even the chemical fire extinguishers failed to work.

The valiant crew located several hand pumps, brought them to the anchor deck, and managed to force water through long hoses into the lower hangar and decks below. Firefighting parties, wearing gas masks, carried cumbersome pieces of equipment and fought the flames courageously. But every induced explosion overhead penetrated to the deck below, injuring men and interrupting their desperate efforts. Stepping over fallen comrades, another damage-control party would dash in to continue the struggle, only to be mowed down by the next explosion. Corpsmen and volunteers carried out dead and wounded from the lower first aid station, which was jammed with injured men. Doctors and surgeons worked like machines.

The engine rooms were still undamaged, but fires in the middle deck sections had cut off all communication between the bridge and the lower levels of the ship. Despite this the explosions, shocks, and crashes above, plus the telegraph indicator which had rung up "Stop," told the engine-room crews in the bowels of the ship that something must be wrong. Still, as long as the engines were undamaged and full propulsive power was available, they had no choice but to stay at General Quarters. Repeated efforts were made to communicate with the bridge, but every channel of contact, including the numerous auxiliary ones, had been knocked out.

The intensity of the spreading fires increased until the heat-laden air invaded the ship's lowest sections through the intakes, and men working there began falling from suffocation. In a desperate effort to save his men, the Chief Engineer, Commander K. Tampo, made his way up through the flaming decks until he was able to get a message to the Captain, reporting conditions below. An order was promptly given for all men in the engine spaces to come up on deck. But it was too late. The orderly who tried to carry the order down through the blazing hell never returned, and not a man escaped from the engine rooms.

As the number of dead and wounded increased and the fires got further out of control, Captain Aoki finally decided at 1800 that the ship must be abandoned. The injured were lowered into boats and cutters sent alongside by the screening destroyers. Many uninjured men leapt into the sea and swam away from the stricken ship. Destroyers *Arashi* and *Nowaki* picked up all survivors. When the rescue work was completed, Captain Aoki radioed to Admiral Nagumo at 1920 from one of the destroyers, asking permission to sink the crippled carrier. This inquiry was monitored by the Combined Fleet flagship, whence Admiral Yamamoto dispatched an order at 2225 to delay the carrier's disposition. Upon receipt of this instruction, the Captain returned to his carrier alone. He reached the anchor deck, which was still free from fire, and there lashed himself to an anchor to await the end.

Stand-by destroyer *Arashi* received word at midnight that an enemy force was 90 miles to the east of *Akagi*'s and her own position. One hour later a lookout sighted several warships through the darkness, and the commander of the destroyer division, Captain K. Ariga, gave chase with all four of his ships, *Arashi*, *Nowaki*, *Hagikaze*, and *Maikaze*. He failed to catch up with or identify these shadows, however, and returned to stand by the carrier. It later turned out that the mysterious ships belonged to Rear Admiral Tanaka's Destroyer Squadron.

When Admiral Yamamoto ordered the delay in disposing of *Akagi*, it was because he saw no need for haste in this action since his force was then proceeding eastward to make a night attack on the enemy. Now, however, as defeat became apparent and the prospect of a night engagement grew dim, a quick decision became necessary. At 0350 on 5 June, Admiral Yamamoto finally gave the fateful order to scuttle the great carrier. Admiral Nagumo relayed the order to Captain Ariga, directing him to rejoin the force when his mission had been accomplished. Ariga in turn ordered his four destroyers to fire torpedoes at the doomed ship. *Nowaki*'s skipper, Commander Magotaro Koga, later described how painful it was for him to fire the powerful new Type-93 torpedo into the carrier, which was his first target of the war. Within 20 minutes all four destroyers had fired. Seven minutes later the sea closed over the mighty ship, and a terrific underwater explosion occurred, sending out shocks that were felt in each destroyer. The carrier's final resting place was at latitude 30°30' N, longitude 179°08' W. The time was 0455, just minutes before sunrise.

All but 263 members of the carrier's crew survived this last of her great battles. Before the fatal torpedoes were fired, *Akagi*'s navigator, Commander Y. Miura, had boarded the carrier and persuaded Captain Aoki to give up his determination to go down with the ship. Both men finally moved safely to one of the destroyers.

2.

Churchill's Second Visit to Washington

June 1942

U.S. Army chief of staff George C. Marshall believed that the only way to win the war in Europe was to invade France. Once on the Continent, Allied troops could then conquer the industrial Ruhr, halt German arms production, and destroy the Wehrmacht (the German army). It was a typically American strategy: Strike at the enemy's strength, cripple his ability to wage war, and end the fighting as soon as

possible through the application of overwhelming, irresistible force. Ulysses S. Grant had used a similar approach to win the Civil War; and, like Grant, Marshall benefited from a nearly inexhaustible supply of men and matériel, which he was not afraid to use.

In early April 1942, Marshall traveled with presidential aide Harry Hopkins to London to present new American plans for the opening of a second front in Europe. First, there would be Bolero, the massive buildup of American forces in the British Isles. Then, in the spring of 1943, Roundup, the invasion of France, would follow. In the meantime, should either the Soviet Union or (less likely) Germany near the point of collapse, a contingency plan, Sledgehammer, would be put into effect. This option anticipated a smaller landing on the Continent within just a few months. Backing Marshall's plans enthusiastically, Pres. Franklin D. Roosevelt cabled British prime minister Winston Churchill, "What Harry and Geo. Marshall will tell you has my heart and *mind* in it."

For his part, Churchill believed that the only way to *lose* the war in Europe was to invade France prematurely. Although he went along with Marshall at first, not wanting to contradict his allies just yet, the prime minister had deep reservations about the opening of a second front in Europe. Unable to put the horrors of the last war out of his mind, he preferred to postpone any invasion of France until he was certain that Adolf Hitler's Germany was too weak to resist it.

In late May, however, Soviet foreign minister Vyacheslav M. Molotov visited Washington to plead for more help. Roosevelt responded with promises of a second front in 1942. Then, following Molotov's departure, FDR cabled Churchill, "I am more than ever anxious that Bolero proceed to definite action." Now Churchill had no choice but to express his reluctance to Roosevelt, deciding to do so face to face. On June 17, he boarded a Boeing flying boat at Stranraer, Scotland, and twenty-eight hours later arrived in Washington.

CHURCHILL HERE FOR TALKS ON SECOND FRONT

Premier's 2d Visit; Visitor to See President on 'Winning the War,' Says Early

By FRANK L. KLUCKHOHN

WASHINGTON, June 1—Prime Minister Winston Churchill of Great Britain arrived in the United States today for conferences with President Roosevelt on "the war—the conduct of the war and the winning of the war," the White House announced shortly after 8 o'clock tonight.

Speculation that the talks would cover the task of opening a second front in Europe would be "perfectly justified," a spokesman affirmed.

Mr. Churchill was scheduled to begin his conferences with President Roosevelt "immediately." It was said at the White House that no further statements on his visit should be expected this week.

The Prime Minister was accompanied by ranking British staff officers and two personal aides. It was apparent that considerable secrecy would be maintained until the talks were completed. No information was vouchsafed as to how Mr. Churchill reached here for his unannounced visit.

The arrival of the British Prime Minister, who had spent late December and early January in this country soon after its entry into the war, followed by only a few days the visit of Vyacheslaff M. Molotoff, Soviet Foreign Commissar. The latter led to a full understanding between the United States and Soviet Russia on "the urgent tasks of creating a second front in Europe in 1942."

It was thought natural here that the Roosevelt-Molotoff conferences would be followed by others between the President and Mr. Churchill. It was noted that the talks between the American and British leaders followed visits of ranking United States Army, Navy and Air officers to London and of British military and supply leaders here. It was thought in diplomatic circles that final policy might be determined in the talks that began today.

Although it had been known since early afternoon that Mr. Churchill was arriving, it was only about fifteen minutes before the announcement that reporters were called to the White House. Stephen Early, Presidential secretary, dictated the following informal statement to reporters in his office without referring to notes:

"Mr. Winston Churchill, Prime Minister of Great Britain, is again in the United States. The Prime Minister will confer while here with the President.

"The conferences will begin immediately. The subject of the conferences will be, very naturally, the war—the conduct of the war and the winning of the war.

"With the Prime Minister when he arrived were General Sir Alan Brooke [Chief of the British Imperial General Staff]; Major General Sir Hastings Ismay [Secretary of the Imperial Defense Council]; Brig. Gen. G. M. Stewart [Director of Plans of the War Office]; Sir Charles Wilson [Mr. Churchill's personal physician]; Commander C. V. R. Thompson, secretary and aide, and Mr. John Martin, private secretary to the Prime Minister.

"I do not anticipate any further statements by the President or Prime Minister this week."

A reporter asked Mr. Early whether the discussions would deal with the opening of a second front. The Presidential aide replied, "I think that conjecture is perfectly justified."

It was noted when the White House disclosed the Molotoff-Roosevelt agreement June 12, upon the Russian Foreign Minister's arrival in Moscow by way of London, that the accord did not flatly state that a second front would be opened in Europe this year. Since then press reports from London have reflected serious doubt that such a front actually could be opened during the next six and one-half months.

Whether a final decision upon this point will be taken by Mr. Roosevelt and Mr. Churchill is a matter of pure speculation. Some diplomats here, however, have seen signs that Washington is more inclined than London to believe the early opening of a second front is practicable.

The arrival of a third large American troop convoy in Northern Ireland was announced only last Saturday. Some observers have noted indications that American action might be planned to begin shortly. More United States troops will be called up in June and July than in any previous months, according to reports in usually reliable circles.

Under the agreement by which the Joint Staffs Councils were established, Mr. Roosevelt and Mr. Churchill have the final word on strategy. Conjecture, therefore, naturally will center upon the possibility that decisions with respect to a second front may be reached at the current conferences.

It also was regarded as only natural that the two leaders should desire to get together again for the type of conversations that determined strategy and proved so satisfactory soon after the United States entered the war.

Mr. Churchill's visit takes place at a moment when the British are being thrust back in Libya and the Germans are besieging Sevastopol in Russia and threatening a new major push near Leningrad. It also comes at a time when China's supply problem has become critical and only a trickle of supplies is reaching her by air.

It was regarded as obvious that the Prime Minister would not leave Britain at such a moment with such important members of his staff unless there were more than casual matters to discuss. Diplomats noted that it was soon after Mr. Churchill's last and equally dramatic visit to this country that a governmental crisis arose in London that led to the reshuffling of the War Cabinet. They surmised that the Prime Minister would not come here again unless major decisions of world importance were to be taken.

Mr. Early's remark that he did not look for further statements by the President or Prime Minister "this week" was taken as a clear indication that a statement might be expected after the visit was completed.

During his previous visit to this country Mr. Churchill addressed Congress, attended church publicly with the President, took part in one of Mr. Roosevelt's press conferences and was seen in public a great deal. This kind of program was not expected to be followed this time, at least until urgent business had been dealt with.

The press, which had known of Mr. Molotoff's visit well in advance and kept the secret until he returned home, did not even have a hint until today that Mr. Churchill was on his way. The veil of secrecy surrounding the British leader's trip was dropped, however, as soon as he was safely on American soil.

"Winston's buoyant temperament is a tremendous asset."

Entries from the diary of Winston Churchill's physician, Lord Moran

In May 1940, shortly after Churchill became prime minister, he accepted Charles Wilson, Lord Moran, as his personal physician. Later, Moran became Churchill's confidant as well. "Winston knew that if he was to help me he must not keep anything back, and it became my custom as I drove away from No. 10, or Chequers, or Chartwell to note, sometime on the back of an envelope, anything that he said which might help me to get to the bottom of his troubles," Moran recalled. "From these notes I wrote out the conversations with Winston the same night."

June 18, 1942

The P.M. is always a little apprehensive in the air and our "narrow squeak" flying back from Bermuda has not helped matters. He asked me whether I minded flying. But before I could answer, I saw that he was thinking of something else. Last night, when we were making our way along the quay at Stranraer to the launch which took us to the flying boat, I heard him humming: "We're here because we're here." I wondered if he was whistling to keep up his spirits. All the same, he is in good shape.

Once installed in the White House, the P.M. lost not a moment in beginning his campaign. It was not an easy task which he had set himself. Those whom the President trusted—Hopkins, Marshall and the rest—were of one mind: There was only one way to shorten the war, and that was to set up a Second Front in France. No one but Winston could have hoped for a hearing in such circumstances.

June 21, 1942

Went to the White House this afternoon when the P.M. sent for me. Found him pacing his room. He turned on me:

"Tobruk has fallen."

He said this as if I were responsible. With that, he began again striding up and down the room, glowering at the carpet:

"What matters is that it should happen when I am here."

He went to the window.

"I am ashamed. I cannot understand why Tobruk gave in. More than 30,000 of our men put their hands up. If they won't fight—" The P.M. stopped abruptly.

He forgot all about me, and kept crossing and recrossing the room with quick strides, lost in thought. After a little, he fell into a chair. He seemed to take a pull at himself.

"It was the President who told me; he was very kind. He only asked, 'What can we do to help?' And then, although they were already allocated, the President promised me Sherman tanks. Some of them must be sent at once to Alexandria to reinforce the army."

Only last week the Admiralty pressed that no ships should be sent through the Mediterranean, which is swarming with submarines and quite unsafe.

"I shall take the responsibility of sending them through the Mediterranean. If I give a direct order, they will carry it out."

The P.M. got up; there was vigour in all his movements. He found comfort in action.

June 23, 1942

Winston's buoyant temperament is a tremendous asset. The fall of Tobruk, like the loss of the Prince of Wales and the Repulse, has been a blow between the eyes. Not only Cairo and Alexandria, but the Suez Canal and all the oilfields of the Near East seem to be at the mercy of Rommel. And yet, before I left his bedroom on Sunday, Winston had refused to take the count; he got up a little dazed, but full of fight. I sat up on the night of Tobruk and last night till he went to bed, thinking he might want me. But he isn't made like that. There is never any danger of his folding up in dirty weather. My heart goes out to him. I do like a really full-sized man. With our military prestige at zero here, he has dominated the discussions.

All day and half the night, they have gone on since the news of Tobruk came through. Winston has battled with the Americans; he has not allowed the facts, damaging as they are, to handicap him. At this game, there is no one here of his own weight. He has made use of the crisis as an argument for postponing the Second Front; without any help from anyone, he has sustained the theme that only an invasion of North Africa can relieve the crisis. Marshall and Hopkins have not accepted the postponement of the Second Front, but they have agreed to divert tanks and other supplies to the Nile Valley, which is perhaps the same thing, since it means a revision of the shipping.

Harry Hopkins tells me what is happening: The big man on the American side in this dismal time is apparently the President. He reminds me of Lloyd George. Discerning people grieve over flaws in his character; they say, for instance, that he is not truthful. But now, when day after day he has to take big decisions, and the people around him are conscious of a crisis, his brain goes on working as if it were packed in ice. The stuff surely is in him; he is built for great occasions.

And if he needs a prop, there is Marshall. He has seen the British collapse in the Middle East end in the success of the P.M.'s efforts to postpone a Second Front. A smaller man would have turned sour. When our army has taken a bad knock, when its fighting spirit is suspect, Marshall has been driven to try to reassure the P.M. that the American infantry is better than the P.M. thinks. Winston has promised before he returns to England that he will go to see this infantry for himself, and it has been arranged that we are to go tonight in the President's train to South Carolina. However, the coach in which the P.M. was to have slept has collided with some railway carriages, and a worthy substitute cannot be provided at a moment's notice. So we are to dine at the White House while they search for rolling stock.

3.

The Fall of Tobruk
June 1942

The "sideshow" in North Africa, as Hitler called it, was entirely the creation of Italian dictator Benito Mussolini. Having failed to win glory during Germany's speedy spring 1940 conquest of France, Mussolini thought that he saw an opportunity in North Africa, where his Libyan army greatly outnumbered the British forces in neighboring Egypt. After some foot-dragging during the summer of 1940, Marshal

Rodolfo Graziani finally led his reluctant troops across the border on September 13. After just one week, however, Graziani halted his advance so that he could establish fortified camps and stockpile supplies. Meanwhile, Britain's commander in chief for the Middle East, Field Marshal Archibald Wavell, organized a counteroffensive that began on December 9. Using his superior armor to overcome Graziani's advantage in manpower, Wavell routed the Italians, capturing the port of Tobruk on January 22 and reaching El Agheila on February 9. No doubt he would have taken all of Libya had not the strength of his army been transferred in mid-February to Greece (where it ultimately failed to stop the April 1941 German invasion).

Just as Hitler chose to save the Italians in Greece, he also felt it necessary to clean up the mess Mussolini had made in North Africa. To that end, he sent Erwin Rommel and a Panzer division to Tripoli in mid-February 1941. Rommel's instructions were to remain on the defensive until more tanks could be sent, but the general ignored these orders and went quickly on the offensive. The surprised and weakened

British were pushed back into Egypt, yet Wavell left behind a sizable garrison at Tobruk, which Rommel bypassed during his advance. Several subsequent attempts to dislodge the British failed, however, and the situation became a stalemate, with Wavell's efforts to relieve Tobruk also falling short. Finally, Churchill replaced Wavell in July 1941 with Field Marshal Claude Auchinleck, who used the newly constituted British Eighth Army (under field commander Alan Cunningham) to launch Operation Crusader on November 18. After some initial setbacks resulting in Cunningham's dismissal, Auchinleck pushed the Afrika Korps back to El Agheila and thus relieved Tobruk.

Auchinleck's success, however, was short-lived. The surprise Japanese attacks on Hong Kong and Malaya in December necessitated the transfer of two Allied divisions and an armored brigade to Southeast Asia—after which Rommel, sensing an opportunity, struck back in late January 1942. He forced the British to retreat behind a fortified line running south from Gazala (about thirty-five miles west of Tobruk) and then regrouped for a new spring offensive.

A British brigadier commanding tank units near Tobruk uses a sand table to instruct subordinates during a planning session sometime in 1941.

TOBRUK FALLS, AXIS CLAIMS 25,000 PRISONERS

Nazis Near Egypt; British Are on Border as Rommel Presses On After Victory

By DAVID ANDERSON

LONDON, June 21—A smashing blow delivered yesterday by waves of German tanks, heavily supported from the air, crushed the defenses of Tobruk in Libya. The War Office tonight confirmed the loss of the town, already claimed by the enemy, who said 25,000 prisoners, including "several generals," had been captured.

The story of what happened, as given by both German and Italian sources, appears to cover the battle fairly fully, but the accuracy of these reports cannot be checked at present. Briefly, it can be said Field Marshal Erwin Rommel's armored units that had passed Tobruk in pursuit of the British Eighth Army did so to make certain whether the British showed any signs of preparing a counter-attack.

When the German Marshal was satisfied this was not the case he reversed his forces, bringing back tanks against Tobruk from the south, driving from the vicinity of Ed Duda, and did this fiercely with every ounce of power at his command. At the same time the Luftwaffe began intensive bombing of Tobruk's defenses. Within a matter of hours the battle was over.

Tobruk must have been softer in its last moments than during the many other attacks it beat off during the last seventeen months since it was captured from the Italians on Jan. 22, 1941. It has been on the fringe of the Libyan battlefield for some weeks with inevitable strain as strategy wavered between one of concentration of strength there and one of evacuation.

Despite the presence of a large garrison when Tobruk fell it is believed there was not time to lay minefields on its perimeter or otherwise strengthen its defenses to face an immediate storming.

A Cairo communiqué, released here at noon today, paved the way for the worst. It read:

"Yesterday the enemy attacked the perimeter of Tobruk in great strength. In spite of most determined resistance by our forces the enemy succeeded in penetrating the defenses and in occupying a considerable area inside them."

Twelve strong points in the defenses were taken by the first wave of enemy tanks, according to Berlin. This made a wedge two and a half miles wide, and German sources state the British defenders then realized that further resistance was useless.

But they had other reasons for weighing most seriously the advantages of carrying on the fight. The Germans said today that "numerous bombers' ceaseless attack wrought great destruction in the fortifications and other military works of the port and town."

It was not long after noon yesterday when large formations of German bombers swooped down on a group of four anti-aircraft batteries, all of which were silenced, it was reported by Berlin. Still more of the Luftwaffe's heavy aircraft, laden with high explosives, cruised over a column of twenty tanks, setting many of them ablaze.

Finally, the German radio said, "About 2 P.M. another great attack was made on Tobruk, which lasted three hours without interruption and caused numerous fires. The air above Tobruk was dominated by German fighters."

Italian troops were credited with playing a part in the capture of Tobruk in the German communiqué. It is thought they pinned down British forces in areas other than that selected for the decisive operation.

The Berlin communiqué stated that yesterday Marshal Rommel stormed Tobruk and this morning "a British officer, bearing a flag of truce, offered to surrender the town to the Italian corps staff."

It was added that Bir el-Gobi and Bardia also were taken. The British here believe they were not defended.

Fragments of information reaching London from Cairo, Berlin and Rome indicate that the defenses of Tobruk crumbled before the onslaught of Marshal Rommel's heavy tanks, striking along the ground while his air force pressed home the attack from above, the tanks forcing a breach in the lines through which the German infantry poured and then the tanks smashed on, followed by more infantry.

Bitter as it was to accept the fall of Tobruk, it must have added insult to injury to have to surrender to Italians, carrying a reminder of what the Germans did when they conquered Greece and then turned over the triumph to the Italians who still were feeling the sting of defeat.

Rome broadcast today the fact of the British surrender, adding:

"Axis troops have occupied the stronghold of the city and the port. Twenty-five thousand prisoners have been taken, among them several generals. The booty is overwhelming and cannot be given in detail."

The same source claimed late today that

British tanks patrol the outskirts of Tobruk in 1941.

Tobruk harbor was found to be in condition for immediate use by the Axis forces.

A British description of the last-ditch fighting was given by the Air Ministry in an account of operations in Libya preceding the fall of Tobruk. With German tanks only fifteen miles away Allied fighters and bombers not only stood firm but also struck back.

The enemy was within five minutes' flying time from one airport while squadrons were landing and taking off regularly like trains using a busy terminus. Most of them managed to withdraw successfully to new bases, it was added.

The Royal Air Force headquarters in Cairo announced tonight that enemy positions near Tobruk and Bengazi were bombed yesterday. British fighters were reported active over forward areas but this does not seem to include Tobruk, which already was effectively isolated by Marshal Rommel.

"Tobruk was a symbol of British resistance."

An excerpt from the memoirs of Erwin Rommel

When Erwin Rommel committed suicide in October 1944, he left behind a considerable number of official documents as well as his personal diary and other notes that he had dictated to his aides, often on a daily basis. "Whenever a lull allowed, he prepared a more considered appreciation of what had taken place," his son Manfred has written. "…As events took a less favourable turn, my father became all the more anxious that an objective account of his actions should survive his possible death so that his intentions could not be misinterpreted. On his return from Africa, he worked on his papers in great secrecy, dictating, or giving drafts for typing, only to my mother or one of his [aides]." This account of the capture of Tobruk was among those completed by the general before he was sent in early 1944 to prepare the German defenses in France for an Allied invasion.

Tobruk was one of the strongest fortresses in North Africa. In 1941, with magnificent troops in its garrison, it had presented us with immense difficulties. Many attacks had collapsed in its defences and much of its outer perimeter had literally been soaked in blood. Often the battle had raged round a square yard at a time. We were no strangers to Tobruk.

We intended this time to attack and storm the fortress according to the plan which we had finally evolved in 1941 but which had been forestalled by Cunningham's offensive. Under this plan a feint attack was first to be launched in the south-west to conceal our true design and pin down the garrison at that point. The formations assigned to make the main assault were to arrive on the scene unexpectedly. To this end they were to move on eastwards past Tobruk in order to give the impression that we intended to lay siege to the fortress as in 1941. Then they were to switch back suddenly to the south-eastern front of the fortress, deploy for the assault during the night and, after a heavy dive-bomber and artillery bombardment, launch their assault at dawn and overrun the surprised enemy.

To every man of us, Tobruk was a symbol of British resistance and we were now going to finish with it for good.

On the morning of the 16th June, I drove up to the Via Balbia and then along it to the west. Fighting at Gazala had finally ceased and another six thousand British troops had found their way into our prison camps. Evidence of the British defeat could be seen all along the road and verges. Vast quantities of material lay on all sides, burnt-out vehicles stood black and empty in the sand. Whole convoys of undamaged British lorries had fallen into our hands, some of which had been pressed into service immediately by the fighting troops, while others were now awaiting collection by the salvage squads. Apparently the British had taken off some of their units by sea. Soon we met our troops advancing eastwards from the Gazala line. They received orders to push on as fast as they could up to the western edge of Tobruk and were provided with lorry columns to carry their men up to the front by shuttle service. Quick regrouping for the investment of Tobruk was now the most urgent necessity.

One of the first lessons I had drawn from my experience of motorised warfare was that speed of manoeuvre in operations and quick reaction in command are decisive. Troops must he able to carry out operations at top speed and in complete co-ordination. To be satisfied with norms is fatal. One must constantly demand and strive for maximum performance, for the side which makes the greater effort is the faster—and the faster wins the battle. Officers and N.C.O.s must continually train their troops along these lines.

In my view the duties of a commander are not limited to his work with his staff. He must also concern himself with details of command and should pay frequent visits to the fighting line, for the following reasons:

(a) Accurate execution of the plans of the commander and his staff is of the highest importance. It is a mistake to assume that every unit officer will make all that there is to be made out of his situation; most of them soon succumb to a certain inertia. Then it is simply reported that for some reason or another this or that cannot be done—reasons are always easy enough to think up. People of this kind must be made to feel the authority of the commander and be shaken out of their apathy. The commander must be the prime mover of the battle and the troops must always have to reckon with his appearance in personal control.

(b) The commander must be at constant pains to keep his troops abreast of all the latest tactical experience and developments, and must insist on their practical application. He must see to it that his subordinates are trained in accordance with the latest requirements. The best form of "welfare" for the troops is first-class training, for this saves unnecessary casualties.

Erwin Rommel delivers orders from a jeep in the North African desert in early February 1942.

(c) It is also greatly in the commander's own interest to have a personal picture of the front and a clear idea of the problems his subordinates are having to face. It is the only way in which he can keep his ideas permanently up to date and adapted to changing conditions. If he fights his battles as a game of chess, he will become rigidly fixed in academic theory and admiration of his own ideas. Success comes most readily to the commander whose ideas have not been canalised into any one fixed channel, but can develop freely from the conditions around him.

(d) The commander must have contact with his men. He must be capable of feeling and thinking with them. The soldier must have confidence in him. There is one cardinal principle which must always be remembered: One must never make a show of false emotions to one's men. The ordinary soldier has a surprisingly good nose for what is true and what false....

Tobruk, hemmed in on its eastern and western sides by rocky and trackless country, extends out to the south into a flat and sandy plain. It had been extremely well fortified by the Italians under Balbo, and full account had been taken of the most modern weapons for the reduction of fortifications. The numerous defence positions running in a belt round the fortress were sunk in the ground in such a manner that they could only be located from the air. Each defence position consisted of an underground tunnel system leading into machine and anti-tank gun nests. These nests, of which most of the defence positions had a considerable number, waited until the moment of greatest danger before throwing off their camouflage and pouring a murderous fire into the attacking troops. Artillery could not take them under direct fire because of the lack of apertures on which to take aim. Each separate position was surrounded by an anti-tank ditch and deep wire entanglements. In addition the whole fortified zone was surrounded at all points passable to tanks by a deep anti-tank ditch.

Behind the outer belt of fortifications, most of which was several lines in depth, were powerful artillery concentrations, field positions and several forts. The majority of the defence works were protected by deep minefields.

The feint attack in the south-west was to be executed by XXI Italian Corps, who were provided with several tanks in support. The group making the main attack consisted of the Afrika Korps and XX Italian Corps. Before the attack was opened the main attack sector, south-east of the fortress, was to be bombed by the entire German-Italian Air Force in Africa. Once the infantry had succeeded in reducing the fortified lines, the Afrika Korps was to press on over the crossroads to the harbour and open up the Via Balbia to the west. Following up the Afrika Korps, XX Italian Corps was to capture the British defence works and thrust through to the Ras el Madauer in the rear of the South Africans.

My assault force moved into its assembly areas on the night of the 19th June. At 05.20 hours several hundred aircraft hammered their bombs on the break-in point south-east of the fortress. I watched the effect of this attack. Great fountains of dust plumed up out of the Indian positions, whirling entanglements and weapons high into the air. Bomb after bomb tore through the enemy wire.

As soon as the aircraft had finished, the infantry of the Afrika Korps (15th Rifle Brigade) and XX Italian Corps moved forward to the assault. Lanes had been cleared through the mines the night before. Two hours later the German storming parties had succeeded in driving a wedge into the British defences. One position after another was attacked by my "Africans" and captured in fiercest hand-to-hand combat.

The engineers had the anti-tank ditch bridged by 08.00 hours. The exploits of the engineers that day merited particular praise. It is difficult to conceive what it meant to do work of this kind under heavy British fire. Now the way was open and we unleashed the armour.

At about 08.00, I drove with my *Gefechtsstaffel* through the Ariete's sector and into the 15th Panzer Division's. Riding in an armoured troop-carrier, I went through as far as the lanes through the minefields, which lay under heavy British artillery fire. Considerable traffic jams were piling up as a result of this fire and I sent Lieut. Berndt up immediately to organise a smooth flow of traffic. Half an hour later, I crossed the anti-tank ditch with Bayerlein and examined two of the captured positions. Meanwhile, the Afrika Korps was becoming the target of British tank attacks from outside the fortress and a violent tank battle flared up, in which the artillery on both sides joined. Towards 11.00 hours, I ordered the Ariete and Trieste, who, after overcoming the anti-tank ditch, had come to a halt in the British defended zone, to follow up through the Afrika Korps's penetration. The German attack moved steadily on and the Afrika Korps, after a brief action in which 50 British tanks were shot up, reached the crossroad Sidi Mahmud at about midday. We held the key to Tobruk.

I now accompanied the Afrika Korps's advance onward from the crossroad. A furious fire beat into the attacking troops from the Fort Pilastrino area and several nests on the Jebel descent. Several British ships weighed anchor and made as if to leave harbour, apparently attempting to get their men away by sea. I at once directed the A.A. and artillery on to this target and six ships were sunk. Most of the men aboard them were picked up.

The advance continued and we soon reached the descent into the town, where we came up against a British strong-point which fought back with extraordinary stubbornness. I sent Lieut. von Schlippenbach with a summons to the garrison of 50 men to surrender. Their only answer was a withering fire on our vehicles. Eventually, our outrider, Corporal Huber, covered by six anti-aircraft men, succeeded in approaching the strong-point and putting the garrison out of action with hand grenades.

Pilastrino offered to capitulate in the evening and a Stuka attack on the fort was called off. Fort Solaro was stormed by my men and another gunboat sunk in the harbour. By nightfall two-thirds of the fortress was in our hands; the town and harbour had already been captured by the Afrika Korps in the afternoon.

At 05.00 hours on the 21st of June, I drove into the town of Tobruk. Practically every building of the dismal place was either flat or little more than a heap of rubble, mostly the result of our siege in 1941. Next I drove off along the Via Balbia to the west. The staff of the 32nd British Army Tank Brigade offered to surrender, which brought us 30 serviceable British tanks. Vehicles stood in flames on either side of the Via Balbia. Wherever one looked there was chaos and destruction.

4.

Nazi Saboteurs in America

June 1942

The term *fifth column* originated during the Spanish Civil War when Gen. Gonzalo Queipo de Llano y Sierro used it to describe militant fascists working to undermine the Republican government from within. As Queipo marched on Madrid with four columns of infantry, he reportedly quipped that such civilians within the capital were his "fifth column." More generally, fifth columnists were members of

clandestine groups whose goal it was to weaken an enemy's solidarity by weaving disruptive agents into its social fabric. These agents used methods such as rumor, misinformation, espionage, and sabotage to exploit public fears and lessen a nation's political resolve.

After Pearl Harbor, fears of fifth-column movements rose sharply in the United States. On the West Coast, Japanese Americans were the focus of public attention; elsewhere, it was the former German-American Bund. Founded in 1933 as Friends of the New Germany, the pro-Nazi, quasi-military Bund appealed primarily to German Americans but also reached out to non-Germans who shared its anti-Semitic views. Although the Bund disappeared as a public organization after Germany's declaration of war on the United States, some of its members remained active in espionage cells, and others, recruited by the Abwehr before the war, returned to America as saboteurs.

The Abwehr, the principal organ of German military intelligence, launched its most ambitious operation against the United States in June 1942, when U-boats landed eight saboteurs—four near Amagansett, Long Island, just after midnight on June 13 and four more on Ponte Vedra Beach near Jacksonville, Florida, on June 17. Their leader, thirty-nine-year-old George Dasch, had left the United States in 1939 to join the German military but had never quite accepted the Nazi rhetoric. Back in America, he faltered and on the evening of June 14 called the FBI in New York to confess. Using the name Pastorius, Dasch revealed that he was a saboteur and said that he would call again the following week when he was in Washington. On the morning of June 19, Dasch telephoned FBI headquarters from his Washington hotel and gave the agents, who had been expecting his call, the address. After his arrest, Dasch provided the FBI with the identities and probable whereabouts of his seven colleagues. All were apprehended before they could undertake any sabotage; and, as far as is known, no enemy-inspired acts of sabotage were ever committed in the United Sates during the war.

One of numerous posters produced by the federal government to boost morale and promote watchfulness, this design first appeared in 1943.

FBI SEIZES 8 SABOTEURS LANDED BY U-BOATS HERE AND IN FLORIDA TO BLOW UP WAR PLANTS

Invaders Confess; Had TNT to Blast Key Factories, Railroads and City Water System

By WILL LISSNER

Two groups of saboteurs, highly trained by direction of the German High Command at a special school for sabotage near Berlin, carrying cases of powerful explosives and nearly $150,000 in cash, were landed on the Long Island and the Florida coasts from submarines in the last fortnight with orders to blow up certain key plants and to cause panics in large cities, it was disclosed last night.

Despite their training the two gangs of four men each fell afoul of special agents of the Federal Bureau of Investigation almost immediately and the arrest of all eight was announced last evening by J. Edgar Hoover, director of the Bureau. They were in custody within a month after they had shipped on their expedition out of a submarine base on the French coast.

Mr. Hoover reported the arrests to President Roosevelt and released full biographies of the men, which showed that they were former waiters, machinists and German-American Bund agitators, long resident here and fluent in English, who were repatriated by the German Embassies in the United States and Mexico to be recruited for the sabotage school.

In the possession of the men was a list of special assignments of industrial plants they were to sabotage and department stores in which they were to create panics. The plants were the following:

Aluminum Corporation of America, Alcoa, Tenn.

Aluminum Corporation of America, Massena, N. Y.

Aluminum Corporation of America, East St. Louis, Ill.

Aluminum Corporation of America, Cryolite (aluminum base) plant, Philadelphia.

Chesapeake & Ohio Railroad (around industrial areas.)

Pennsylvania Railroad (at Newark, N. J.)

Hell Gate Bridge (railroad bridge from Astoria, Queens, to the Bronx.)

Canals and locks of the Ohio River from Cincinnati to St. Louis. (St. Louis, contrary to German geography, is not connected with the Ohio River.)

Specified department stores and railroad stations, in the lockers of which bombs were to be planted.

Water supply system of New York City and its conduits in Westchester County.

Hydroelectric power plants at Niagara Falls, N. Y.

Horseshoe curves of railroads at Altoona, Pa., in the coal district.

All the objectives singled out are heavily guarded and are vital to war production. The German High Command, which was charged directly with sending the men here, was more ingenious in preparing explosive materials than in directing its spies, it was said.

Under the cover of night the submarines came within 500 yards of the Long Island and

Florida coasts. The saboteurs changed from German Navy uniforms to civilian dress, dragged heavy cases of ingenious explosives ashore and buried them on the beach and then broke up.

But before the men could begin carrying out their orders the FBI was on their trail and the round-up began. One after another they fell into the special agents' net. Each confessed fully, providing information that will make repetition of the sabotage invasions difficult.

Two are United States citizens, and one of these was a member of the Reserve Officers Training Corps at a Chicago high school. Several of the others, during their residence here, had been in the process of naturalization.

All face the death penalty since their activities occurred in wartime.

The arrests disclosed that the German Embassy in Washington and the German consulates in New York and San Francisco were part of a pre-war set-up designed to bring home to Germany nationals who could be used for sabotage when war started. They recalled the activities of Franz von Papen and Captain Karl Boy-Ed, Germany attachés, in planning the Black Tom explosion and other acts of sabotage in the first World War.

The motive of Germany's solicitousness in bringing nationals home for trips and for repatriation was disclosed in the sabotage conspiracy, for several of the prisoners, on reaching their homeland, found themselves drafted as privates in the German Army and then ordered to "volunteer" for the sabotage school to carry on activities for which they would face odium and the death of a spy.

The first "invasion" of the saboteurs was at Amagansett Beach, Long Island, last June 13. The submarine reached the coast at night and surfaced. A rubber boat was put overside. Four men, now dressed in civilian clothes, clambered aboard and dragged with them heavy cases. When they reached shore they dug a hole above

the waterline and buried the cases for recovery later when their plans had matured.

The Long Island landing was made on a foggy night, along sixty-foot stretch of sandy beach flanked by high beach grass and further secluded by low dunes. Every five miles along the beach was a Coast Guard station, its complement maintaining constant patrols along the shore. Back off the dunes were settlements of fishermen's cottages and bungalows of summer residents, only half of them occupied at the time, and the vacant ones providing many hideaways. A quarter of a mile away from the beach the Montauk Highway stretches, giving ready access to New York if a car were waiting. The Long Island Railroad station is a half mile from the beach.

The cases contained packages of TNT, bombs of highly explosive chemicals resembling pieces of coal, bombs in the form of pen and pencil sets, including pistols, fuses and timing devices. The equipment, designed for the tasks set for the gang, was said to be especially destructive for its size.

There were four of these cases and each was large, so that enough material was brought ashore by the saboteurs to carry on a two-year campaign of terror. Mr. Hoover said the cases were the most modern and efficient outfit for sabotage known. All have been recovered.

With the cases buried, the crew of saboteurs came to New York and split up. They had been here a week when the FBI arrested three of them on June 20. Two, Heinrich Harm Heinck, 35 years old, and Robert Quirin, 34, were arrested in New York, and the third, Ernest Peter Burger, 36, at an undisclosed place. Last Monday their leader, George John Dasch, 39, was arrested in New York.

Both submarines involved in the "saboteurs' invasion" left Germany late in May. Four days after the Long Island group had made its landing, another group of four men was put ashore in Florida south of Jacksonville, at a place known as Ponte Vedra Beach.

The Florida group had virtually the same equipment as the Long Island group and apparently followed instructions on its disposal, since it also was hidden above the waterline on the beach for later recovery. However, of the nearly $150,000 in American currency—five, ten and twenty dollar bills and change—that was allotted to the two expeditions, the Long Island group received $90,806.15 and the Florida group $58,942.61.

The money was not the reward of the German spies. They were promised fabulous sums and high military honors—when they returned to Germany after accomplishing their assignments. They were also authorized to offer similar promises to win cooperation from subversive elements in the United States, their confessions disclosed.

Their instructions were to use the money to bribe Americans to permit them to carry on their work and to aid them and to buy the services of subversive persons here.

The Florida group went to Jacksonville, where it split up and its members soon were being captured, one by one, by the FBI. All its explosive equipment also was recovered.

Two of the group, Herbert Haupt, 22, and Hermann Neubauer, 32, went to Chicago. A third, Werner Thiel, 35, came to New York and registered at a large hotel as William Thomas. Their leader, Edward John Kerling, went to an undisclosed place, where he was arrested last Wednesday. On the same day, Thiel was caught. Haupt and Neubauer were captured in Chicago yesterday.

Almost from the moment the first group set foot on United States soil the special agents of the Federal Bureau of Investigation were on their trail. The FBI staged a series of arrests on June 20 and the last two members of the gangs were arrested yesterday in Chicago.

Mr. Hoover emphasized the training of the men for the destructive tasks to which they were assigned, which he said was under the direction of the German High Command. They had been selected carefully, apparently long before they were recruited, for several were permitted to work at the German People's Auto Works, a German Government project, until they were called for sabotage training.

All were English-speaking and had been in the United States long enough to feel at home here. All had been members of the German-American Bund and several had been leaders in it, so that their range of personal contacts with American residents was wide. All had returned to Germany only recently, between 1939 and 1941, and thus were not much out of touch with American affairs.

At the special training school for sabotage they received a thorough course in explosives and in the chemicals composing them, and also in incendiary bombs. They were taken to assembly lines of German factories that approximated American ones and were instructed by German experts how to put apparatus out of commission, at what points the plants were most vulnerable and where the most damage could be done.

They were required to study maps of transportation lines and of fuel and water supply systems and were shown their strategic points. They were also instructed how to find out where the bottlenecks of the systems were as they may have developed under the war program, so they could strike at these points.

To prevent any more successful landings by saboteur invaders, the Coast Guard has increased its shore patrols, the FBI director said.

"Cullen knew there were no clams for miles around."

An excerpt from the Coast Guard report describing the landing
of Nazi saboteurs on Long Island

John Cullen, a twenty-one-year-old member of the Coast Guard, was conducting a routine unarmed patrol of the beach near Amagansett on the night of June 12–13, 1942, when he came upon four suspicious men. This excerpt from the official Coast Guard report details their conversation. Fearing that he might be shot otherwise, Cullen took the bribe they offered, then hurried back to his station three miles away. "They're German," he breathlessly told the duty officer, who quickly sent an armed squad to investigate. The guardsmen searched the beach for the rest of the night but required the light of morning to locate the buried cache of explosives that proved Cullen's story. By that time, of course, the Germans were already on their way to New York City aboard the 6:57 A.M. train from Amagansett.

Cullen called out, "What's the trouble?" Nobody answered. The man on shore started toward Cullen. Cullen called again, "Who are you?" There was no answer. The man kept advancing.

Cullen reached to his hip pocket for a flashlight. The foremost man saw the motion, and apparently thinking the Coast Guardsman was reaching for a gun, cried out, "Wait a minute. Are you the Coast Guard?"

Cullen answered, "Yes. Who are you?"

"A couple of fishermen from Southampton who have run aground."

"Come up to the station and wait for daybreak."

Cullen recalled later that the weather seemed to get worse and the fog closed in.

The spokesman snapped, "Wait a minute—you don't know what's going on. How old are you? Have you a father and mother? I wouldn't want to have to kill you."

A fourth man in a bathing suit came up through the fog, dragging a bag. He started to speak in German. Cullen spoke up, "What's in the bag?"

"Clams."

Cullen knew there were no clams for miles around.

The man in civilian clothes said, "Yes, that's right."

Cullen's pretended gullibility appeared to influence him. In a friendly voice he said, "Why don't you forget the whole thing? Here is some money. One hundred dollars."

Cullen said, "I don't want it."

The man took some more bills out of his wallet. "Then take $300."

Cullen thought fast. He answered, "O.K."

The stranger gave him the money, saying, "Now look me in the eyes."

As Cullen explained to his superiors later, he said he was afraid he might be hypnotized. The stranger insisted. Cullen braced himself and looked directly at the man. Nothing happened, to Cullen's relief. As he looked at him, the stranger kept repeating, "Would you recognize me if you saw me again?"

When Cullen finally said "No," the man appeared satisfied.

5.

First Reports of a Holocaust
June 1942

It remains uncertain whether Hitler intended from the start to exterminate the Jews. By mid-1941, however, mass murder was clearly the path he had chosen. Even though the *Kristallnacht* riots of November 1938 had accelerated Jewish emigration from Germany and the former Austria, there were still some 350,000 Jews living in the Reich when the war began in September 1939. To this number

were soon added two million Jews living in Poland and, later, millions more in Western Europe and occupied Russia.

On July 31, 1941, just a month after the start of Operation Barbarossa (the German invasion of Russia), Reichsmarschall Hermann Göring ordered Reinhard Heydrich—then head of the Sicherheitdienst (SD), the security arm of the Schutzstaffel (SS)—"to carry out all preparations with regard to...a total solution of the Jewish question in those territories of Europe which are under German influence." To begin this task, Göring, who had been named Hitler's successor in 1939, wanted Heydrich to round up all the Jews in Europe and confine them to urban ghettos in Poland, where they could be closely monitored while means for their ultimate disposal were being arranged. Regarding these means, Göring told Heydrich "to submit to me as soon as possible a draft showing the...measures already taken for the intended final solution of the Jewish question."

Heydrich's plan, once approved, was presented to the Nazi bureaucracy on January 20, 1942, at a meeting in Wannsee, an upscale sub-

urb of Berlin. The fifteen officials present included representatives of the Ministry of Justice, the Ministry of the Interior, the Foreign Office, the Gestapo (the Nazi political police), and the governor-general of Poland. According to Heydrich, all 10.8 million Jews estimated to be living in Europe at the time would be "involved"—a euphemism typical of the language with which the Nazi elite described their "final solution." That day at Wannsee, in working out the practical details of Heydrich's plan, the Holocaust was formally launched.

In the meantime, special SS squads known as *Einsatzgruppen* ("task forces") were already killing hundreds of thousands of Jews in the East. Following in the wake of the advancing Wehrmacht, these units obviated the need to ghettoize Russian Jews by shooting them on the spot. In September 1941, for example, *Einsatzgruppen* massacred thirty-three thousand Kiev Jews beside the ravine at Baby Yar. By late 1942, when implementation of the "final solution" finally shifted to the largest Polish death camps, the SS had already killed an estimated 1.4 million Jews.

German soldiers line Polish Jews up against a wall in the Warsaw Ghetto and search them during a routine 1942 roundup. This photograph was found on the body of a German officer who apparently took part in the raid and was later killed near Moscow.

1,000,000 JEWS SLAIN BY NAZIS, REPORT SAYS

'Slaughterhouse' of Europe Under Hitler Described at London

LONDON, June 29 (UP)—The Germans have massacred more than 1,000,000 Jews since the war began in carrying out Adolf Hitler's proclaimed policy of exterminating the people, spokesmen for the World Jewish Congress charged today.

They said the Nazis had established a "vast slaughterhouse for Jews" in Eastern Europe and that reliable reports showed that 700,000 Jews already had been murdered in Lithuania and Poland, 125,000 in Rumania, 200,000 in Nazi-occupied parts of Russia and 100,000 in the rest of Europe. Thus about one-sixth of the pre-war Jewish population in Europe, estimated at 6,000,000 to 7,000,000 persons, had been wiped out in less than three years.

A report to the congress said that Jews, deported en masse to Central Poland from Germany, Austria, Czechoslovakia and the Netherlands, were being shot by firing squads at the rate of 1,000 daily.

Information received by the Polish Government in London confirmed that the Nazis had executed "several hundred thousand" Jews in Poland and that almost another million were imprisoned in ghettos.

A spokesman said 10,232 persons died in the Warsaw ghetto from hunger, disease and other causes between April and June last year and that 4,000 children between the ages of 12 and 15 recently were removed from there by the Gestapo to work on slave-labor farms.

The pre-Nazi Jewish population of Germany, totaling about 600,000 persons, was said to have been reduced to a little more than 100,000.

"Each bee must learn that the drones are a threat to us."

A Nazi children's fable

The same year, 1923, that Julius Streicher took part in the Beer Hall Putsch, he also founded *Der Stürmer,* a semiofficial Nazi periodical that specialized in scurrilous stories about Jews and Communists. One of the most ardent, crude, and corrupt early Nazis, Streicher also published anti-Semitic children's books. This story—written by Streicher's chief deputy, Ernst Hiemer—appeared in *Der Pudelmopsdackelpinscher (The Poodle-Pug-Dachshund-Pinscher),* published in 1940.

The Drones

Evening is coming. The sun slowly sinks in the west. The farmyard grows quiet. Only the bees are still at work. They fly from flower to flower and gather sweet honey and golden pollen.

Api, a little worker bee, returns. She quickly flies into the hive. She fills the honeycombs with all the honey that she has gathered with her hard work.

Her comrade Melli is next to her. She is usually a happy little creature and laughs the whole day. But now she is in a bad mood. Angrily her big eyes look to the honeycombs in the upper corner. Many bees who are much bigger and fatter than Api and Melli have gathered there. And these bees do not work. They can do only one thing: Eat, eat and eat!

Tears fill Melli's eyes.

"I have been slaving away from morning to night every day for eight weeks. I've filled two honeycombs all by myself so that we will be able to eat this winter. Now these fat lads come along and eat it all up!"

Little Api has been listening intently to her friend.

"You mean those drones up there? They are harmless animals. And they look silly! They are so fat and helpless. I have to laugh when I see the drones. They are really funny!"

Melli grows angry.

"Funny? Funny? Nonsense! Maybe you don't know the danger the drones are for our whole bee people?"

Api shakes her head.

"No! But tell me, please!"

Melli rubs her head with her legs a few times. Then she speaks:

"OK, listen carefully! We bees are an industrious people. We work our whole lives long. The sun is hardly up, and we are awake and searching for honey and pollen. We stop only when it is evening. We have to work hard so that we will be prepared for winter, when there are no flowers or blossoms. We have to work hard so that our children will have something to eat. We have to work hard to preserve our people. Do you understand?"

Little Api nods.

"Of course! But what does that have to do with the drones?"

"Pay attention," Melli says, "and I will tell you. The drones are bees, too, like us. But they do not help our people; they only harm it. They do not work. They laze away the whole day. The only thing they do is eat! Yes, eat! They eat everything that we have collected for ourselves, our people and our children. They make us poor, and they are absolutely insolent. Just yesterday, a drone punched me so that I fell and nearly broke a leg. That is how the drones are! They do not work. They live in luxury. They do nothing themselves but live from the work of others. They plunder us. They do not care if we starve over the winter or if our children die. The only thing they care about is that things go well for them. The main thing is that they can stuff their fat bellies. Api, listen to me: The drones are our misfortune!"

Little Api is thoughtful. For a long time she says nothing. Then she nods thoughtfully and says:

"Now I understand! You are right! The drones are our misfortune! But tell me, do the other bees know this?"

"No! They do not know. Most of them still believe that drones are harmless. They do not believe that drones hurt anyone. That is why we must educate our people. Each individual bee must learn that the drones are a threat to us. Then we have to ruthlessly destroy the drones. If we do not destroy them, they will destroy us and our children!"

Api is enthused.

"Yes! We must educate the whole bee people. We must call all our comrades to battle our people's enemy. I promise you that I will help. I will warn all the bees I know about the drones. I will tell them the truth. While working during the day and while resting at night, I will always say:

'Bees! Rise up against the drones before it is too late! Save us from the plague of drones to save our bee people!'"

Fourteen days have gone by. Api and Melli have educated the bees. At first the bees did not believe them. And when the drones learned that the truth about them was out, they roused the other bees against Api and Melli. But the two were not intimidated. Wherever they went, they spoke about the danger of the drones. Soon, ten other bees believed them and hated the drones. Then it was a hundred—then five hundred!—then a thousand and even more.

One night, the bee people, threatened by the drones, roused itself. The whole hive was in an uproar. Bees were running about, crying out:

"Wake up! The battle against the drones is beginning! Down with the deadly enemy of our people!"

The drones, who had until now been so impudent, gathered together and tried to look innocent. They acted as if they were the best animals on God's earth. They begged for pity. But they thought to themselves:

"Just wait until things quiet down again! Then we will devour you!"

But the bees could no longer be fooled. At Melli's command and under the leadership of Api, they attacked the drones. The battle was terrible. The drones were defeated. They were killed or driven out. Not one of them remained in the beehive.

The next morning, the sun was particularly bright. The thankful song of happy, liberated bees filled the hive. Many hundreds of voices joined their voices in singing to heaven:

"May you ever protect our people
From our destroyers, from robbers, drones!"

There are drones not only among the bees but also among people. They are the Jews!

Every nation has millions of workers, farmers, officials, and so on. They work hard, like the bees. The worker goes to the factory every day. The work is hard. But he does it gladly. He knows that his labor is necessary if his people are to live. The farmer works his whole life to grow what the nation needs—their daily bread! They are all "worker bees!" They work for the whole people. The farmer could not live without the worker, or the worker without the farmer. Without shoemakers, neither workers nor farmers would have shoes. If there were no teachers and inventors, who would discover things and build machines? Everyone depends on everyone else, regardless of whether they work with their minds or their hands.

But there are also "drones" who live among the peoples of the earth. Who are these drones? They are the Jews!

The Jews have a secret law book. It is the Talmud. In it, it is written:

"Work is very bad and not to be tolerated."

What does the Jew mean by that? He means that he hates work because it is hard and difficult.

Elsewhere in the Talmud it says:

"Non-Jews were created to serve the Jews. They must plow, sow, dig, reap, bind, weed and grind. The Jews are created to find everything ready."

What does this mean? It means that the Jews think only non-Jews must work. The Jew thinks that the non-Jews must work for him. He himself does not have to do anything.

The Jews do not want to work. They only want to live from the labor of others. They are just like the drones in the beehive. They are lazy. They do nothing. They create nothing. They rob the community. They exploit the people.

Julius Streicher (center) stands on a platform with other Nazi party leaders at a 1933 rally in Nuremberg.

These Jewish drones appear in various forms. For example, there is the Jewish tramp. A tramp is a person who never works. But he understands how to exploit those who do work and knows how to live an easy life through the work of others.

Then there is the Jewish fence. He buys goods that thieves have stolen. He earns a lot of money. But he creates nothing. He only swindles other people. He is harmful to the nation.

Then there is the Jewish farm swindler. He has no land, he does not sow, he does not tend a field. But through sneaky swindles he takes over many farms and throws whole families into misery.

And there is the Jewish merchant. He buys shoddy goods and sells them at enormous profit. The worker who has labored the whole week gives his money to the Jew in exchange for trash.

That is the Jew!

He is the drone of humanity. He is the exploiter of the labor of others. He is an enormous danger for all the nations. If one overlooks this danger, whole peoples can be destroyed. History is rich in examples that prove to us that the Jew has ruined millions of people.

But many do not know that the Jew is the drone among people. They see the Jew as an innocent and entirely harmless fellow citizen. They do not know that the Jewish danger for our people and for the whole world is the same as the danger of the drones to the bees. They do not know that the Jewish Question is the most important question in the world.

The bees recognized the danger of the drones. Therefore, they fought the bloodsuckers. Ruthlessly they cleansed their people of drones. Only then was there peace and order.

How is it with people? Until they have cleaned out the Jewish brood of drones, there will be no peace and no prosperity among the peoples.

6.

Convoy PQ 17 to Archangel

July 1942

Allied convoys to the Soviet Union began in August 1941, just two months after Hitler's surprise invasion of Russia. Because the Germans controlled the Baltic Sea and, with the Italians, made travel through the Mediterranean to the Black Sea dangerous, the Arctic Ocean became, by default, the obvious choice for shipments to the Soviets. (Later, the Allies developed an alternative supply route through

the Persian Gulf, thence overland across Iran.)

At first, the Germans paid little attention, but as the Wehrmacht prepared for its summer 1942 offensive in Russia, the High Command made the interdiction of Soviet supplies a high priority. It was decided that the navy and Luftwaffe (the German air force) would coordinate three-pronged attacks on the convoys as they passed through the Barents Sea in the narrow gap between Norway's North Cape and the Arctic ice pack. The first of these attacks came in late March, when Heinkel 111s and Junkers 88s, flying from bases in northern Norway, joined U-boats and surface ships in taking on convoy PQ 13. Bad weather limited Allied losses, but the attack persuaded First Sea Lord Dudley Pound that, as the Arctic days lengthened, the convoys would become dangerously vulnerable.

By the time convoy PQ 16 sailed in late May, however, the German surface fleet had become passive, and Pound's attention had shifted to air attacks. The Germans indeed came at PQ 16 principally from the air, with little success, maddening the German High Command. The Luftwaffe

flew 108 sorties but sank only six ships; U-boats, finding it difficult to operate in the prolonged daylight, added only one more. Thus, twenty-eight of PQ 16's thirty-five merchantmen reached Murmansk and Archangel safely.

Determined to stop PQ 17, the Germans decided to use their battleships again against the convoy's escorting warships. Fearing this, the admiralty objected to the mounting of PQ 17, but political considerations prevailed, and the convoy sailed on June 27. Air and undersea attacks began six days later, but the escort commander remained confident he could protect the merchantmen. Then, late on July 4, Pound called a meeting of his senior staff to discuss reports that the German battleships had sailed from Norway to attack PQ 17. Pound's decision to scatter the convoy, signaled at 9:23 P.M., proved immediately disastrous. Unescorted, the merchantmen became easy prey for the bombers and U-boats still in the area. During the next twenty-four hours, thirteen freighters were sunk. In the end, only nine of the thirty-three ships that dispersed on July 4 ever made it to port.

NAZIS LIST AS SUNK U.S. CRUISER, 28 SHIPS

Berlin Claims 'Large Number' of American Prisoners From Russia-Bound Convoy

BERLIN, July 7 (From German broadcasts recorded in New York)—German planes and submarines sank a heavy United States cruiser and twenty-eight out of thirty-eight merchant ships in a Russia-bound convoy off Northern Norway last week, the German High Command said today. "A large number of American sailors" were rescued and taken prisoner by German seaplanes, the communiqué said.

The Deutsche Allgemeine Zeitung said it was the "greatest catastrophe" suffered by a single convoy in the war and estimated that "at least 250,000 tons of precious war material" went to the bottom with the merchantmen.

"Remnants of the fully dispersed convoy are being pursued and attacked," the High Command said in a special communiqué.

The attack began last Thursday in waters between North Cape, Norway, and Spitsbergen, at a point 300 to 400 miles north of Norway, the communiqué said. [The distance from North Cape to Spitsbergen is roughly 500 miles.]

The convoy was carrying planes, tanks, munitions and food destined for the port of Archangel on the White Sea, about 750 miles eastward of the point where the attack is reported to have begun, and was heavily protected by strong naval units, destroyers and corvettes, the communiqué said.

The attack was a "large operation," with squadrons of bombers and U-boats working in cooperation, the High Command asserted. The planes destroyed nineteen merchantmen totaling 122,000 tons, and the submarines sank the other nine, which totaled 70,400 tons, and also accounted for the cruiser, the Germans asserted.

The German news agency, D. N. B., said that aircraft carriers protected by battleships formed part of the convoy and that four ships sunk were loaded with tanks, another carried planes and others spare parts for armored cars, motor vehicles and ammunition. D. N. B. quoted the High Command as saying it was the "most strongly protected convoy which ever sailed." D. N. B. said the convoy was bound for Murmansk rather than Archangel.

The Deutsche Allgemeine Zeitung said that "to give an idea of the dimensions of this disaster, during the entire siege of Sevastopol 30,000 tons of iron and twenty-five tons of bombs were dropped on the city," while more than eight times that amount of war equipment was lost in the convoy action.

"And then, slowly, terribly slowly, it went down to the sea."

The account of a journalist who crossed to Archangel with convoy PQ 16

War correspondent Alexander Werth, on his way to Moscow, took passage on the *Empire Baffin,* which sailed from Iceland as part of convoy PQ 16. Werth's book-length 1947 account of his four years in wartime Russia included this description of the journey. Further attacks by German bombers and U-boats ended the following day with the arrival of Russian-based British minesweepers, Soviet destroyers, and Hurricanes flying for the Red Air Force.

Wednesday, May 27

I am not likely ever to forget this day, and yet its exact sequence is hard to restore in one's mind, and what I remember, above all, is moments. I had had a good sleep; we had not been disturbed by anything all night, and one of the moments I remember is sitting on deck after breakfast, reading *Our Mutual Friend* and feeling wonderfully contented. Life on the *Empire Baffin* seemed to have returned to normal. Pushkov was again giving his Russian lesson to the R.A.F. boys in the smoke-room, and, after yesterday's feeble attempts, the Luftwaffe was clearly not as terrifying as people were apt to imagine. But then, at 10:30 the alarm bell went. From the gun-turret somebody shouted: "Here they come!" Again people rushed on deck, counting: three—three more, that's six—ten—twelve—fifteen. Now they came from all directions. Gun flashes and clouds of smoke came from the destroyers; then the barrage of the flak ship and the convoy ships went up; like a vulture pouncing on its prey, a dive-bomber swept down on to the submarine, right down to the water level, but she crash-dived, and the three pillars of water went high up in the air. For forty long minutes they attacked, usually in twos and threes, usually coming straight out of the sun, some diving low, others dropping their bombs from two hundred feet. From their yellow shark-like bellies, one could see the obscene yellow eggs dropping, and after a moment of suspense, one saw with relief the pillars of water leaping up. They were concentrating in that first attack on the forward part of the convoy, and we were, apparently, reserved for later. And then we saw the first casualty. The pale-blue and pale-green destroyer was smoking furiously, and signalling, signalling, signalling. What were those flashes saying? Was it the destroyer that had picked up those Huns on Monday? Somebody on board said: "They are all right. They are not going to abandon her." That didn't seem so bad. She was still smoking, but they seemed to have got the fire under control. Soon they put it out. The planes disappeared; the attack was over. That wasn't so bad, people said; and then we realised that it *was* bad. Not very far away from us was a Russian ship—I had realised for the first time that we had two or three Russian ships in the convoy—and her foredeck was enveloped in clouds of smoke, and flames were bursting out of the hold. "They're going to abandon her," somebody said. Were they? Yes, they were lowering their lifeboats. But no. She was still keeping up steam, still keeping up with the other ships, but the clouds of smoke rising from her were growing larger and larger, her whole fo'c'sle was in a cloud of black smoke—but she still went on, and through the cloud of smoke, one saw dim shapes of people running and doing something. I saw Alfred

Adolphus rushing past me; he was steaming with sweat, and there was a look of panic in his yellowish eyes. "Hullo, Alfred Adolphus!" I said. "I think I'll go mad! I think I'll go mad!" he cried.

So the destroyer had been hit, and the Russian ship had been hit, and both were fighting with the flames. And somebody said two more ships had been hit.

They came again in less than an hour. This was a short, sharp attack. They concentrated on the other end of the convoy. They dropped their bombs and disappeared. As we sailed on, I saw a ship that had stayed behind, with a corvette by her side, blazing furiously. We were already a mile or two away from her. And somebody said that another ship had received a direct hit and had blown up.

Then there was a lull. Dinner was served punctually at noon; Cook wasn't a minute late. Everybody was there, as usual: the lanky first mate, and the young second mate, and the long skinny engineer's mate with the fuzzy hair and the Hapsburg jaw, and our Flight-Lieutenant and the R.A.F. boys. Everybody gulped tea, but appetites were at a low level, and few words were exchanged. In their frames, the King and Queen were very calm. Like most of them, I drank a lot of tea, but the food seemed to stick to the palate. Pushkov, with a wan smile, said the lesson could, he hoped, be resumed tomorrow. I went out on deck. The Russian ship was still enveloped in smoke, though perhaps a little less than before. They had not abandoned ship. I saw Alfred Adolphus sauntering along the deck, now wearing his bright-blue suit with the red stripes and a new light-grey felt hat. "I'm through with it," he said defiantly. "I have refused to go down to the engine-room." "Why did you dress up like this?" "I want to save my clothes if we are torpedoed," he said. He was much calmer than in the morning. "It wouldn't matter," he suddenly cried, "but it's the *cargo*, the *cargo!*" With this remark, he slunk away. So that's what it is, I said to myself—T.N.T.? I had already heard somebody refer to it, but had taken no notice. The burning ship in the distance had now disappeared. Then the alarm bell went again. I forget what exactly happened at the beginning of that third attack, but this time they concentrated on our end of the convoy. The obscene yellow bellies were over us, and they dropped their eggs all round us. The bearded bank clerk with the Oxford accent was on one of the Oerlikons, and the man with the beret and the Soviet badge on another, and Steward was working a machine-gun, and the Flight-Lieutenant, his hair waving in the wind, was, I think, on an Oerlikon, and aft, the little R.A.F. sergeant was on one of the two Lewis guns. And then something happened which I shall never forget. I was standing amidships with the R.A.F. boys and Pushkov and several others, and we realised that something had happened to our sister ship, the *Empire Lawrence*, now without her Hurricane on board. She was no longer steering a straight course. Her bows were pointing towards us—was she moving at all? She was showing a slight list. And we realised that she was being abandoned. Already two of her lifeboats were bobbing on the water, and beside her was a little corvette, taking more men off. As we watched her, we heard all our guns fire like mad. Then one of the yellow bellies swept over us, but, perhaps unnerved by our fire, it dropped the bombs into the water some distance away, but immediately after, two more of the yellow bellies swept over us with roaring engines, almost touching our topmast, and—I could feel the ghoulish joy of the Nazis—they made a dead set at the helpless, dying ship. And suddenly from the yellow belly the five bombs detached themselves and went right into her. I don't think there was even a moment of suspense; there was an explosion that did not sound very loud, and a flash which, in the sun, was not very bright, and like a vomiting volcano a huge pillar of fire, smoke and wreckage shot two hundred feet into the air—and then, slowly, terribly slowly, it went down to the sea. The *Empire Lawrence* was gone. The surface of the water was littered with wreckage—planks, pieces of wood, and then, perhaps five seconds later, the black triangle of the bows, detached from the rest of the ship, came to the surface for a second, and sank forever again. The little white corvette was still there, seemingly intact, and perhaps looking for improbable survivors. What happened to the two lifeboats that had been near the *Empire Lawrence* only a few minutes before, I don't know. Nobody on board said anything at first. Faces were pale. I felt the blood pressing hard on my eardrums; it was horrible and fascinating. Poor *Empire Lawrence*, our sister ship! It was strange to think of it. They had that Hurricane pilot on board; they also had their Captain, and their steward, and perhaps another Geordie, and another Jumbo McGhee, and another Alfred Adolphus, and a smoke-room like ours, and cigarettes, and bottles of rum, and pictures of the King and Queen, and tea-cups and saucers, and lavatories, and a great big deep engine-room like ours, and a refrigerator with a lot of cheese and ham. And now it was all smashed, at the bottom of the sea, or some of it still floating about—and it was horrible to think of parts of human bodies floating about the ocean in life-jackets. "Chock full of T.N.T., so what d'you expect?" said little Harry with the blackheads. "Same here, isn't it?" I remarked. "You'd like to kn-aw, wouldn't ye?" he said, and winked his right eye. "Why don't you squeeze out those blackheads, Harry?" I said, trying to say something quite different. "Oh, no," he almost squealed at the suggestion. "It 'u-u-urts; I can only do it after a 'ot bath!" "What I'd like to do," said Harry, "is to kill a few of these Jerries. Leave them in the water; let them swim about and pop at them from a gun; don't hit 'em at once, but go nearer and nearer and nearer, in a circle, and then do them in after a while. But I'll tell you, I wouldn't like to be one of the Jerries on the destroyer that was hit this morning—Lord, no! I know what I'd like to do if I had some Jerry prisoners here."…

Germans bomb one of the merchant ships sailing in convoy PQ 17, the largest Allied convoy yet to the Soviet Union.

And then came another attack. This time they weren't merely dive-bombers, but torpedo-carriers as well. Again, as at the beginning of the first attack, I saw one of the dive-bombers pounce on the submarine, and amid large pillars of water she disappeared below the surface. Had she been hit? The next thing happened like a flash; I caught a glimpse of it darting along up and down the waves, and I felt our ship suddenly giving a sharp turn, and—the torpedo just missed our stern. Instead, it went right into the next ship. There was a not very loud explosion, and I saw her smoking at her stern, with a large gash just above the waterline, and in less than a minute I saw them taking to the lifeboats. She now stood at a right angle to the convoy; her engines had been knocked out. I knew some of the R.A.F. boys on board that ship; they had visited us when we were in Iceland. A corvette went up to her, to pick up the survivors; one felt they would be all right, provided the Germans did not strike at her, now that she was helpless, as they had struck at the *Empire Lawrence*. "Once she can't keep up speed with the convoy, the only thing is to abandon her," somebody said, "at least you've a chance of saving the crew." And somebody else remarked: "Our skipper has decided that we must abandon ship as soon as we are hit; there's no other way after what happened to the *Empire Lawrence*." And the bo'sun said to me: "It was horrible, horrible." He shuddered. "It's had a very depressing effect on our crew."

The ship that had received the torpedo meant for us, which we would have got but for Captain Dykes's extraordinary quickness, was left behind, with a heavy list. The destroyer was going to sink her, just in case the Germans took it into their heads to tow her, with all her tanks and other precious armaments, to Norway.

And then, as we looked back, we realised that this attack had perhaps been the deadliest of all. Far away, two of our ships were blazing, and some small vessel was picking up the survivors.

It was 8 o'clock, and welcome clouds were beginning to gather in the sky. But the visibility was still perfect, and for a long time we could watch the two bonfires burning far away on the grey sea. I think everybody felt that this was about as much as any human being could stand in one day. They did not come again that evening.

"I've never known anything like it," the bo'sun repeated. The crew were grim, tired, subdued; they were depressd by the *Empire Lawrence;* the bearded bank clerk with the Oxford accent was very calm, but the other man on the Oerlikon gun—the one with the beret and the Soviet badge—had a pinched look on his face, and long stubble on his chin, and red smarting eyes; he said he had not slept for seventy-five hours. Somebody said there had been only four survivors off the *Empire Lawrence;* others said that two lifeboats had got away, and that there must therefore have been many more survivors, except that the lifeboats had been machine-gunned; but nobody seemed to know anything definite. On the destroyer—the one that was hit in the first attack—twenty people were said to have been killed.

"What about a spot of grub now?" said the steward. We went to the smoke-room, which the R.A.F. boys had by now turned into their dormitory; they did not want to go down again to their dingy cabins without portholes and sleep "on the top of the T.N.T.," and the Flight-Lieutenant had supported them, much against the steward's wishes; for the steward "did not think this right." Cook produced tea and some cheese sandwiches, but we did not touch rum; since the Monday we had cut out alcohol completely. In the London blitz I used to like a double Scotch; here I didn't want it. Nobody else was having it, and a very clear head seemed an asset.

Pushkov had been very subdued all day. During the last attack, as we were watching one ship go down and three burning in the distance, I heard him say: "Slaughter of the Innocents." He was unhappy; he was thinking of his wife and children in Leningrad, but he was outwardly calm, though at supper I noticed how his hand trembled as he passed me a plate. And he was even more pale than usual.

The steward swore that several planes had been brought down during the day, and that he had certainly hit one, "right on the nozzle," and that it had reeled away with one engine on fire. It was strange to be back in the smoke-room, and to think of the other smoke-rooms now at the bottom of the sea. I confess we all enjoyed the peace of that supper hour, at the end of that dreadful day. Suddenly the steward, who had gone out for something, came rushing in: "Come out, quick! Do you want to see an Arctic Jewboy?" Good God, was this another kind of German plane? I thought for a moment. "What do you mean?" "Mr. Iceberg," the steward said, laughing like a ten-year-old. It was his first joke of the day. "Nearer, my God, to Thee," in the middle of the last great attack, hadn't quite come off. This time we all laughed.

For a long time after the last attack had ended, I still felt the blood trying to break through my ears—it was the physical sensation that had lasted all day. And now, after supper, and after we had had our little laugh, and had admired the beautiful "Mr. Iceberg" under the grey leaden Arctic sky, the haunting question arose: And what now?

It was clear that if the attacks continued on the same scale—and what was to stop them?—we were almost sure to be sunk. As I walked up and down the deck that evening, watching the convoy, and feeling that there was anguish at that moment in a thousand hearts, I wondered how many ships would be left afloat by to-morrow night—two-thirds of them, or one-third, or only a few perhaps? Or perhaps all would be unchanged—but that eventuality was the hardest of all to visualise. At the back of my mind I had a deep conviction that I'd get through, and that even the *Empire Baffin* probably would, though when I tried to rationalise it, on the basis of the day's experience, the chances seemed no better than two to one against getting through safely. The two other chances were: (a) being blown to pieces like the people on the *Empire Lawrence*, and (b) being torpedoed and picked up. The prospect of being badly wounded and lying in some gory inferno of a sickbay on one of the corvettes or destroyers was the most unpleasant of all, but I did not think of it. I tried to work out whether there would be any logic in my being killed just at this point, and came to the conclusion that it was not logical, and that it was, therefore, less likely to happen than if it were. Still, whatever was in store, the chances were that something pretty unpleasant would happen the next day. I wandered up to the Captain's bridge. I found the second mate there, a good-looking, open-faced little officer of about twenty-five. "What do you think our chances are?" I said, as casually as possible. He gave a faint smile. "Bad," he said. "But I'm sure we'll get through. You see, I'm psychic in these matters, and I just feel these things. However, I may be wrong; but I've got my own ideas and—I think we'll be all right." "What, Russian fighters?" "No, I don't think so. We are too far away. We've still nearly four days' sailing, and it'll be at least another twenty-four hours before the Russian fighters can get near us." Through the second mate's telescope I watched the icebergs in the distance; under the leaden sky, the air was transparent and in the Arctic twilight—it was about midnight now—the ships and all other objects had the precise outline of a line drawing. The sky and the calm sea and the ships were nearly all the same greenish-grey colour. The Fokke-Wulf was flying round and round as usual.

7

Marines Land on Guadalcanal
August 1942

The Japanese navy never recovered from the June 1942 battle of Midway, at which it lost a quartet of aircraft carriers, 253 planes, and nearly as many pilots. Thereafter, the imperial fleet remained formidable, but its offensive capability was gone and it spent the rest of World War II playing defense. On the other hand, in the months following the victory, the U.S. Pacific Fleet prepared for its first offensive

of the war: the invasions of Tulagi, Gavutu, Tanambogo, and Guadalcanal in the southern Solomon Islands. Commanded initially by Vice Adm. Robert L. Ghormley, the undertaking was dubbed Operation Shoestring because time and resources were so limited. The admiral had so few transports, in fact, that he had to leave half of the invasion supplies behind at Nouméa on the Free French island of New Caledonia, where his headquarters was located.

Ghormley's superiors in Washington ordered the hasty invasion after learning that the Japanese were building an airstrip on Guadalcanal from which they could attack the main shipping lanes between the United States and Australia. Therefore, at dawn on August 7, just two months after planning began, eleven thousand troops of the First Marine Division landed on Guadalcanal near the mouth of the Tenaru River, a few miles from the airstrip. When the surprised Japanese defenders withdrew into the jungle, the marines easily took control of the airstrip, which they renamed Henderson Field in honor of a marine flier killed at Midway. The

Japanese recovered quickly, however, and soon began landing reinforcements to challenge the marines vigorously for control of the island.

The fighting, which dragged on for six months, gradually became a struggle of supply—with each side trying to strengthen its own troops while cutting off the forces of the opposition. Typically, the Americans made their supply runs during the day, when the marine planes at Henderson Field could provide air cover. The Japanese navy, expert at night fighting, preferred the cover of darkness.

Ultimately, a series of major naval actions determined the outcome of the land battle. Nearly all took place at night in the body of water between Guadalcanal and Tulagi known as Ironbottom Sound because of the many sinkings there. Altogether, the Japanese came out slightly ahead, but both sides suffered such heavy losses that the Japanese decided they couldn't afford a final victory. As a result, in early February 1943, transports operating at night evacuated the remaining thirteen thousand Japanese soldiers, leaving behind twenty-five thousand dead.

*This newspaper cartoon from late 1942 illustrates the marines'
new "island-hopping" strategy.*

GUADALCANAL

Editorial

While the action at Guadalcanal hangs in suspense, and suspense fills the minds and hearts of all Americans as they wait for news of the fighting, one thing can be said of this battle that distinguishes it from Bataan and other last-ditch stands in the Philippines. This is a fight which we initiated. It can never be charged that Americans shrank from the great risks involved in challenging the enemy while our strength in the Western Pacific was still unequal to his. If this hand-to-hand encounter with the foe goes against us, it may be complained that we dared too much with too little, but not that we lacked the offensive spirit or the daring to strike hard with what we had. If it goes well, it will be a victory of audacity. We took long chances in landing in the Solomons, and the value and importance of the enterprise are underscored by the forces the Japanese are expending in the costly effort to drive us out.

However the battle goes, it is being fought with the fresh and inexhaustible courage that the American forces are pouring into this war. This week and last the streets of New York seem crowded with sailors and marines. Ready to embark for some unknown destination, they fill the town with laughter that the safe stay-at-homes have not the heart to answer. They remind us that a few weeks or months ago the boys who are now battling like demons in the jungle were also walking through Times Square and cheering us up with their friendly grins and casual gayety. Most of them had not even heard the name of Guadalcanal. All of them would have jeered at the idea that there was anything heroic in the job they were set to do. They were going where they were sent, full of faith in their own strength and the invincibility of their country.

Wherever they go, they take America with them. It is they—marines and pilots, soldiers and sailors of the ranks—who tell us more eloquently than all the war speeches what we are fighting for. Because they are there, Guadalcanal becomes as near to us as Staten Island. While they fight we all live in those unknown islands of the Pacific; they have become a suburb of all the towns of America. Watching and waiting for the outcome of the battle, we know that only something more precious than life itself could be worth so high a price.

"Smitty was pulling out pins as I threw the grenades."

A Congressional Medal of Honor winner's account of the defense of Henderson Field

The heaviest fighting on Guadalcanal took place along the defensive perimeter at Henderson Field. Sgt. Mitchell Paige—commanding a platoon of the Second Battalion, Seventh Marine Regiment—was on this line during the night of October 25–26 when the Japanese attacked. In his contemporaneous account, Paige describes the actions that won him a Congressional Medal of Honor for heroism. He also displays the tendency, rather common among American soldiers fighting in the Pacific, to dehumanize the Japanese. In this regard, Paige and his comrades were merely following the lead of their government, which used racist Japanese caricatures to sell war bonds yet eschewed such crudity when depicting Germans and Italians.

Before we could get set up darkness came and it started raining like hell. It was too black to see anything, so I crawled along the ridge-front until it seemed I had come to the nose. To make sure I felt around with my hands and the ridge seemed to drop away on all sides. There we set up.

With the guns set up and the watches arranged, it was time for chow. I passed the word along for the one can of "Spam" and the one can of "borrowed peaches" that we had with us. Then we found out some jerk had dropped the can of peaches and it had rolled down the ridge into the jungle. He had been too scared to tell us what he had done. I shared out the "Spam" by feeling for a hand in the darkness and dropping into it. The next morning I sent out a couple of scouts to "look over the terrain." So we got our peaches back.

That night Smitty and I crawled out towards the edge of the nose and lay on our backs with the rain driving into our faces. Every so often I would lift up and call some of the boys by name to see if they were still awake and to reassure myself as well as them.

It must have been two o'clock in the morning when I heard a low mumbling. At once I got Smitty up. A few minutes later we heard the same noise again. I crawled over to the men and told them to stand by. I started figuring. The Japs might not know we were on the nose, and we certainly didn't know where they were coming from or even how many there were. They might be preparing to charge us, or at any moment they might discover our positions. I decided to get it over with. As soon as the men heard the click of my pin coming out of the grenade, they let loose their grenades too.

Smitty was pulling out pins as I threw the grenades. The Japs screamed so we knew we had hit them. We threw a few more grenades and then there was silence.

All that second day we dug in. We had no entrenching tools so we used bayonets. As night came I told the men we would have a hundred percent watch and they were not to fire until they saw a Jap.

About the same time as the night before, we heard the Japs talking again. They were about a hundred yards from the nose. It was so damned quiet, you could hear anything. I crawled around to the men and told them to keep quiet, look forward and glue their ears to the ground. As the Japs advanced we could hear the bushes rustle. Suddenly all hell broke loose.

All of us must have seen the Japs at the same time. Grenades exploded everywhere on the ridge-nose, followed by shrieks and yells. It would have been death to fire the guns because muzzle flashes would have given away our positions and we could have been smothered and blasted by a hail of grenades. Stansbury, who was lying in the foxhole next to mine, was pulling out grenade-pins with his teeth and rolling the grenades down the side of the nose. Leipart, the smallest guy in the platoon, and my particular boy, was in his foxhole delivering grenades like a star pitcher.

Then I gave the word to fire. Machine guns and rifles let go and the whole line seemed to light up. Pettyjohn yelled down to me that his gun was out of action. In the light from the firing I could see several Japs a few feet away from Leipart. Apparently he had been hit because he was down on one knee. I knocked off two Japs with a rifle but a third drove his bayonet into Leipart. Leipart was dead; seconds later, so was the Jap. After a few minutes, I wouldn't swear to how long it was, the blitz became a hand-to-hand battle. Gaston was having trouble with a Jap officer, I remember that much. Although his leg was nearly hacked off and his rifle all cut up, Gaston finally connected his boot with the Jap's chin. The result was one slopehead with one broken neck.

Firing died down a little, so evidently the first wave was a flop. I crawled over to Pettyjohn, and while he and Faust covered me I worked to remove a ruptured cartridge and change the belt feed pawl. Just as I was getting ready to feed in a belt of ammo, I felt something hot on my hand and a sharp vibration. Some damned slopehead with a light machine gun had fired a full burst into the feeding mechanism and wrecked the gun.

Things got pretty bad on the second wave. The Japs penetrated our left flank, carried away all opposition and were possibly in a position to attack our ridge-nose from the rear. On the left, however, Grant, Payne and Hinson stood by. In the center, Lock, Swanek and McNabb got it and were carried to the rear by corpsmen. The Navy boys did a wonderful job and patched up all the casualties, but they were still bleeding like hell and you couldn't tell what was wrong with them so I sent them back. That

Marines hang out machine-gun belts to dry on humid, rainy Guadalcanal.

meant that all my men were casualties and I was on my own. It was lonely up there with nothing but dead slopeheads for company, but I couldn't tell you what I was thinking about. I guess I was really worrying about the guns, shooting as fast as I could, and getting a bead on the next and nearest Jap.

One of the guns I couldn't find because it wasn't firing. I figured the guys had been hit and had put the gun out of action before leaving. I was always very insistent that if for any reason they had to leave a gun they would put it out of action so that the Japs wouldn't be able to use it. Being without a gun myself, I dodged over to the unit on my right to get another gun and give them the word on what was going on. Kelly and Totman helped me bring the gun back towards the nose of the ridge and we zig-zagged under an enemy fire that never seemed to stop. While I was on the right flank I borrowed some of the riflemen to form a skirmish line. I told them to fix bayonets and follow me. Kelly and Totman fed ammo as I sprayed every inch of terrain free of Japs. Dawn was beginning to break and in the halflight I saw my own machine gun still near the center of the nose. It was still in working order and some Japs were crawling towards it. We got there just in time. I left Kelly and Totman and ran over to it.

For too many moments it seemed as though the whole Japanese Army was firing at me. Neverthe-less three men on the right flank thought I might be low on ammunition and volunteered to run it up to me. Stat brought one belt and he went down with a bullet in the stomach. Reilly came up with another belt. Just as he reached the gun, he was hit in the groin. His feet flew out and nearly knocked me off the gun. Then Jonjeck arrived with a belt and stopped a bullet in the shoulder. As I turned I saw a piece of flesh disappear from his neck. I told him to go back for medical aid, but he refused. He wanted to stay up there with me. There was no time to argue, so I tapped him on the chin, hard enough so that he went down. That convinced him that I wanted my order obeyed.

My ears rang when a Jap sighted in on me with his light machine gun but luckily he went away to my left. Anyway I decided it was too unhealthy to stay in any one place for too long, so I would fire a burst and then move. Each time I shifted, grenades fell just where I had been. Over the nose of the ridge in the tall grass, which was later burned for security, I thought I saw some movement. Right off the nose, in the grass, thirty Japs stood up. One of them was looking at me through field glasses. I let them have it with a full burst and they peeled off like grass under a mowing machine.

After that, I guess I was so wound up that I couldn't stop. I rounded up the skirmish line, told them I was going to charge off the nose and I wanted them to be right behind me. I picked up the machine gun, and without noticing the burning hot water jacket, cradled it in my arms. Two belts of ammo I threw around my shoulders. The total weight was about 150 pounds, but the way I felt I could have carried three more without noticing it. I fed one the belts off my shoulders into the gun, and then started forward. A colonel dropped about four feet in front of me with his yellow belly full of good American lead. In the meantime the skirmish line came over the nose, whooping like a bunch of wild Indians. We reached the edge of the clearing where the jungle began and there was nothing left either to holler at or shoot at. The battle was over with that strange sort of quietness that always follows.

The first thing I did was to sit down. I was soaked in perspiration and steam was rising in a cloud from my gun. My hand felt funny. I looked down and saw through my tattered shirt a blister which ran from my fingertips to my forearm. Captain Ditta came running up, slapped me on the back and gave me a drink from his canteen.

For three days after the battle, we camped around the nose. They estimated that there were 110 Japs dead in front of my sector. I don't know about that, but they started to smell so horribly that we had to bury them by blasting part of the ridge over on top of them. On the third day we marched twelve miles back to the airport. I never knew what day it was, and what's more I didn't care.

8.

The First Moscow Conference

August 1942

The initial American military response to Churchill's plan for a second front in North Africa was firmly negative. On July 11, 1942, less than three weeks after the prime minister's visit to Washington, army chief of staff Marshall and navy chief of staff Ernest J. King recommended to the president that he "assume a defensive attitude toward Germany...and use all available means in the Pacific" should the

British insist on "any other operation rather than forceful, unswerving adherence to full Bolero plans." Roosevelt, however, had no intention of abandoning his "Europe first" strategy and immediately sent the two chiefs to London to work things out with the British. When Churchill proved adamant, Marshall and King, following Roosevelt's instructions, acceded to the North African landing, now code-named Torch.

If the two chiefs of staff were perturbed by the shelving of Bolero, their agitation was niggling compared to Soviet premier Joseph Stalin's outrage. In the wake of the PQ 17 disaster, Churchill had already halted the Arctic convoys, and now the second front in France that had been promised for 1942 was also disappearing. Meanwhile, the Germans were once again on the move, advancing on Stalingrad and punishing the Soviets, who continued to bear by far the heaviest part of the fighting against Hitler. Unless the British and Americans became more actively involved and soon, Churchill feared, Stalin might well choose to seek a separate peace. Therefore,

the British prime minister decided to visit the Soviet leader personally and use his considerable diplomatic talents to improve, as best he could, Stalin's morale.

During his subsequent journey to Moscow, Churchill contemplated how he might mollify "this sullen, sinister Bolshevik state I had once tried so hard to strangle at its birth." In the end, there was little he could do. As he noted later, "Stalin observed that from our long talk it seemed that all we were going to do was no Sledgehammer, no Roundup, and pay our way by bombing Germany." The RAF had indeed intensified its area-bombing campaign during 1942, but this was hardly equivalent to the Soviet contribution and did nothing to distract the Nazis from their onslaught in the East. "Peering into that Kremlin gloom in August 1942," David M. Kennedy has written, "some historians have discerned the first shadows of the Cold War....Certainly the Soviets at this point had ample reason to doubt their Western partners."

Churchill and Stalin pose for photographers after one of their Kremlin meetings during Churchill's August 1942 visit to consult with the Soviet premier.

NEW STRATEGY SET, LONDON BELIEVES

Churchill Is Thought to Have Discussed Urgent Steps to Ease Dire Peril to Russia

By RAYMOND DANIELL

LONDON, Aug. 17—Prime Minister Winston Churchill went to Moscow via Cairo, according to a Cape Town report today, to synchronize United Nations strategy with Russian necessity.

At least that is the best opinion here following disclosure that the Prime Minister was in the Kremlin discussing the military situation with Premier Joseph Stalin and working out plans for combined action on the part of all the Allies to cheat Adolf Hitler of the victory he must win this Summer or lose the war.

It is a natural supposition that the crux of their conversations was that cryptic phrase in the London and Washington statements after the signing of the Anglo-Russian treaty that the United Nations agreed on the urgency of the task of opening a second front in Europe in 1942. When that statement was issued Russia was not in the same dire peril that she is now facing, with the German Army pressing upon Stalingrad and the Russian Southern Armies in danger of being cut off from the Northern Armies.

The time has come when something has got to be done quickly regardless of the risks involved, whether that means an offensive against Nazi-occupied Europe or reinforcement of the Russian forces in the Caucasus from Britain's Middle Eastern Armies or a mere redoubling of material assistance to the Soviets in the form of supplies, which can be sent only at great risk to precious shipping. The important thing—and one that, it is believed here, was settled at the Kremlin conference—was to work out a scheme whereby what forces the United Nations could muster could be applied with the greatest advantage and effect upon Nazi Germany.

That presupposes that the German forces in the East shall be fully occupied. At present they are not. Great and powerful as is the pressure in the southern sector of the great 1,800-mile front from Murmansk to Astrakhan, it is only a part of what the Germans can apply. So long as the battle line to the north of where the active fighting is now going on remains a quiescent or defensive one for the German generals it will be possible for them to shift enormous forces from the east to the west.

It is obvious that before Britain and the United States can undertake an offensive with anything like an assurance that it will affect materially the fate of Russia wherever it may be and whatever form it takes, the operation must be synchronized with the most powerful offensive that the Russians can launch themselves. In plain language, if the Russian High Command could attack the invaders from Leningrad to Moscow the Red Army would stand a better chance of cracking the enemy while American and British troops were at the same time containing large forces of German troops in the west. Likewise, any such Allied offensive would diminish in risk and effectiveness if it were timed to coincide with a Russian offensive in the north.

It is not meant to suggest that this was the plan on which Mr. Stalin and Mr. Churchill agreed.

That the discussions were of an essentially military nature was indicated by the presence of General Sir Archibald P. Wavell and General Sir Alan Brooke, British commander in India and

Chief of the Imperial Staff, respectively, at the talks with Marshal Klementy E. Voroshiloff. General Brooke would be the British leader of any second-front operation in Europe. General Wavell woud be concerned—and this may prove important—if it were decided that the Ninth British Army in Palestine and Iraq and the Tenth Army in Iran should go to help the Russians fighting north of them.

If this were the plan agreed upon, it would be highly important that the Russians should know exactly when and where this drive was to develop in order that, instead of spending their force north around Leningrad and Moscow, the Red Army could be concentrated back of Stalingrad to push westward in an attempt to cut off the German armies in the North Caucasus and liquidate them there.

It was the first meeting of Mr. Churchill and Mr. Stalin. Whatever differences of temperament and outlook may divide them academically, they are both realists. Their talks, it is believed here, will go farther toward cementing Anglo-Russian friendship and allaying any suspicions that remain than the Anglo-Russian treaty.

It is no secret any longer that the high hopes for mutual trust expressed on that historic occasion have not materialized to the extent that was expected here. It is the hope here that the two heads of States bound together in the common purpose of crushing Nazi Germany have overcome the doubts and dispelled the mysteries that have made complete coordination of effort difficult to attain.

In any case the British public will interpret the news of the meeting between Mr. Stalin and Mr. Churchill as a portent of action. Meanwhile the Axis is showing growing concern over the United Nations plans. This is becoming more apparent daily in references to them in the German press and on the radio, which either belittle the potentialities of an offensive or exaggerate the strength of Nazi defenses. The Axis line today was that Mr. Churchill had gone to see Mr. Stalin to explain why there could not be a second front in 1942 and had got into a quarrel with the Soviet leader. This was branded here as Goebbels twaddle.

However, there is one aspect of the Churchill visit to Moscow that is worth notice. Some time after the Prime Minister left London German radio stations announced that he had gone there. They said that William C. Bullitt, special assistant to United States Navy Secretary Frank Knox, was with him. Actually Mr. Bullitt was still in London then. Later it was said by the Nazis that Mr. Churchill was in Cairo when actually he was in Moscow.

However, today when the announcement was made of Mr. Churchill's visit to Moscow, there was a time fixed for cabling. Before that time had been reached the news was announced over the German radio. It was only after it had become apparent that the Germans knew all about it that the arbitrary release time was lifted. The implication of all these incidents is obvious. The Germans have pretty good sources of information in London and Washington.

"The Soviet Union is suffering far greater losses."

An exchange of cables between Winston Churchill and Joseph Stalin

These three messages form part of the correspondence between Churchill and Stalin during what the Soviets called the Great Patriotic War.

Received on July 18, 1942
W. Churchill to J. V. Stalin

We began running small convoys to North Russia in August 1941, and until December the Germans did not take any steps to interfere with them. From February 1942, the size of the convoys was increased, and the Germans then moved a considerable force of U-boats and a large number of aircraft to Northern Norway and made determined attacks on the convoys. By giving the convoys the strongest possible escort of destroyers and anti-submarine craft, the convoys got through with varying but not prohibitive losses. It is evident that the Germans were dissatisfied with the results which were being achieved by means of aircraft and U-boats alone, because they began to use their surface forces against the convoys. Luckily for us, however, at the outset they made use of their heavy surface forces to the westward of Bear Island and their submarines to the eastward.

The Home Fleet was thus in a position to prevent an attack by enemy surface forces. Before the May convoy was sent off, the Admiralty warned us that losses would be very severe if, as was expected, the Germans employed their surface forces to the eastward of Bear Island. We decided to sail the convoy. An attack by surface ships did not materialise, and the convoy got through with a loss of one-sixth, chiefly from air attack. In the case of the last convoy which is numbered P.Q. 17, however, the Germans at last used their forces in the manner we had always feared. They concentrated their U-boats to the westward of Bear Island and reserved their surface forces for attack to the eastward of Bear Island. The final story of P.Q. 17 convoy is not yet clear. At the moment only four ships have arrived at Archangel but six others are in Nova Zemlya harbours. The latter may however be attacked from the air separately. At the best therefore only one-third will have survived.

I must explain the dangers and difficulties of these convoy operations when the enemy battle squadron takes its station in the extreme North. We do not think it right to risk our Home Fleet eastward of Bear Island or where it can be brought under the attack of the airmen of German shore-based aircraft. If one or two of our very few most powerful types were to be lost or even seriously damaged while the *Tirpitz* and her consorts, soon to be joined by the *Scharnhorst*, remained in action, the whole command of the Atlantic would be lost. Besides affecting the food supplies by which we live, our war effort would be crippled; and, above all, the great convoys of American troops across the ocean, rising presently to as many as 80,000 in a month, would be prevented and the building up of a really strong second front in 1943 rendered impossible.

My naval advisers tell me that if they had the handling of the German surface, submarine and air forces in present circumstances, they would guarantee the complete destruction of any convoy to North Russia. They have not been able so far to hold out hopes that convoys attempting to make the passage in perpetual daylight would fare better than P.Q. 17. It is therefore with the greatest regret that we have reached the conclusion that to attempt to run the next convoy, P.Q. 18, would bring no benefit to you and would only involve a dead loss to the common cause. At the same time I give you my assurance that if we can devise arrangements which give a reasonable chance of at least a fair propor- tion of the contents of the convoys reaching you, we will start them again at once. The crux of the problem is to make the Barents Sea as dangerous for German warships as they make it for ourselves. This is what we should aim at doing with our joint resources. I should like to send a senior officer shortly to North Russia to confer with your officers and make a plan.

Meanwhile we are prepared to despatch immediately to the Persian Gulf some of the ships which were to have sailed in P.Q. convoy. The selection of ships would be made with the Soviet authorities in London, in order that priorities of cargo may be agreed. If fighter aircraft (Hurricanes and Aircobras) are selected, can you operate and maintain them on the Southern Front? We could undertake to assem- ble them at Basra. We hope to increase the through-clearance capacity of the Trans-Iranian routes so as to reach 75,000 tons monthly by October, and are making efforts to obtain a further increase. We are asking the United States Government to help us by expediting the despatch of rolling stock and trucks. An increased volume of traffic would be handled at once if you would agree to American trucks

Churchill and Soviet foreign minister V. M. Molotov (on the prime minister's right) review Soviet troops at the Moscow Civil Airport.

for the U.S.S.R., now being assembled in the Persian Gulf, being used as a shuttle service for transporting goods by road between the Gulf and the Caspian. In order to ensure the full use of capacity, we agree to raise the figure of loads due to arrive in September to 95,000 tons and October to 100,000 tons, both exclusive of trucks and aircraft.

Your telegram to me on June 20th referred to combined operations in the North. The obstacles to sending further convoys at the present time equally prevent our sending land forces and air forces for operations in Northern Norway. But our officers should forthwith consider together what combined operations may be possible in or after October when there is a reasonable amount of darkness. It would be better if you could send your officers here but if this is impossible ours will come to you.

In addition to a combined operation in the North, we are studying how to help on your southern flank. If we can beat back Rommel, we might be able to send powerful air forces in the autumn to operate on the left of your line. The difficulties of maintaining these forces over the Trans-Iranian route without reducing your supplies will clearly be considerable but I hope to put detailed proposals before you in the near future. We must first beat Rommel. The battle is now intense.

Let me once again express my thanks for the forty Bostons. The Germans are constantly sending more men and aircraft to Africa; but large reinforcements are approaching General Auchinleck and the impending arrival of strong British and American heavy bomber aircraft forces should give security to the Eastern Mediterranean as well as obstruct Rommel's supply ports of Tobruk and Benghazi.

I am sure it would be in our common interest, Premier Stalin, to have the three divisions of Poles you so kindly offered join their compatriots in Palestine, where we can arm them fully. These would play a most important part in the future fighting, as well as in keeping the Turks in good heart by a sense of growing numbers to the southward. I hope this project of yours, which we greatly value, will not fall to the ground on account of the Poles wanting to bring with the troops a considerable mass of their women and children, who are largely dependent on the rations of the Polish soldiers. The feeding of these dependents will be a considerable burden to us. We think it well while bearing that burden for the sake of forming this Polish army which will be used faithfully for our common advantage. We are very hard up for food ourselves in the Levant area, but there is enough in India if we can bring it there.

If we do not get the Poles we should have to fill their places by drawing on preparations now going forward on a vast scale for an Anglo-American mass invasion of the Continent. These preparations have already led the Germans to withdraw two heavy bomber groups from South Russia to France. Believe me, there is nothing that is useful and sensible that we and the Americans will not do to help you in your grand struggle. The President and I are ceaselessly searching for means of overcoming the extraordinary difficulties which the geography, sea-water and the enemy's air power interpose. I have shown this telegram to the President.

Sent on July 23, 1942
Message from Premier Stalin to Prime Minister Churchill

I have received your message of July 18.

I gather from the message, first, that the British Government refuses to go on supplying the Soviet Union with war materials by the northern route and, secondly, that despite the agreed Anglo-Soviet Communiqué on the adoption of urgent measures to open a second front in 1942, the British Government is putting off the operation till 1943.

According to our naval experts, the arguments of British naval experts on the necessity of stopping delivery of war supplies to the northern harbours of the U.S.S.R. are untenable. They are convinced that, given goodwill and readiness to honour obligations, steady deliveries could be effected, with heavy loss to the Germans. The British Admiralty's order to the P.Q. 17 convoy to abandon the supply ships and return to Britain, and to the supply ships to disperse and make for Soviet harbours singly, without escort, is, in the view of our experts, puzzling and inexplicable. Of course, I do not think steady deliveries to northern Soviet ports are possible without risk or loss. But then no major task can be carried out in wartime without risk or losses. You know, of course, that the Soviet Union is suffering far greater losses. Be that as it may, I never imagined that the British Government would deny us delivery of war materials precisely now, when the Soviet Union is badly in need of them in view of the grave situation on the Soviet-German front. It should be obvious that deliveries via Persian ports can in no way make up for the loss in the event of deliveries via the northern route being discontinued.

As to the second point, namely, that of opening a second front in Europe, I fear the matter is taking an improper turn. In view of the situation on the Soviet-German front, I state most emphatically that the Soviet Government cannot tolerate the second front in Europe being postponed till 1943.

I hope you will not take it amiss that I have seen fit to give you my frank and honest opinion and that of my colleagues on the points raised in your message.

J. Stalin

Received on July 31, 1942
Prime Minister to Premier Stalin

1. We are making preliminary arrangements for another effort to run a large convoy through to Archangel in the first week of September.

2. I am willing, if you invite me, to come myself to meet you in Astrakhan, the Caucasus, or similar convenient meeting place. We could then survey the war together and take decisions hand-in-hand. I could then tell you plans we have made with President Roosevelt for offensive action in 1942. I would bring the Chief of the Imperial General Staff with me.

3. I am starting for Cairo forthwith. I have serious business there, as you may imagine. From there I will, if you desire it, fix a convenient date for our meeting—which might, so far as I am concerned, be between August 10 and 13, all being well.

4. The War Cabinet have endorsed my proposals.

9

The Second Battle of El Alamein

October–November 1942

After the fall of Tobruk in June 1942, with Erwin Rommel's Afrika Korps advancing quickly into Egypt, Field Marshal Auchinleck decided to make a stand at El Alamein. Britain's commander in chief for the Middle East chose this spot sixty miles west of Alexandria because it occupied a bottleneck between the Mediterranean to the north and the soft sands of the impassable Qattara Depression to the south.

Rommel reached El Alamein on June 30 and attacked the British a day later. Led personally by Auchinleck, the Eighth Army held.

The first battle of El Alamein thus ended with an Allied victory, but it wasn't enough to overcome the preceding disaster at Tobruk, which persuaded Churchill to reshuffle his generals. In mid-August, the prime minister replaced Auchinleck with Harold Alexander, who had recently overseen the long British retreat from Burma into India, and made Lt. Gen. Bernard L. Montgomery field commander of the Eighth Army.

Churchill had received the news of Tobruk's capture while meeting at the White House with Franklin Roosevelt, who immediately offered to send more Sherman tanks to Alexandria. These soon began arriving in large numbers, while Rommel's own supply situation worsened as the Allied effort to suppress Axis shipping in the Mediterranean took hold. Rommel, therefore, was forced to act quickly, before Montgomery's advantage became overwhelming. On August 31, he tried to break through the

British lines at Alam Haifa, fifteen miles southeast of El Alamein, but Montgomery, using a plan originally devised by Auchinleck, drove him back.

A counterattack at this point might have devastated the Afrika Korps, but the ever-cautious Montgomery returned to the patient business of training and equipping his inexperienced troops, whom he regarded as "civilians in uniform." Although Churchill pressed for an attack, hoping that a victory would dissuade the Vichy French from opposing the upcoming Allied invasion of North Africa, Montgomery refused to move until satisfied that his preparations were complete. When the Eighth Army finally did open the second battle of El Alamein on October 23, Montgomery had nearly twice as many men, tanks, and airplanes as his opponent. On November 4, after nearly two weeks of fierce combat, the Eighth Army broke through the German lines and sent Rommel retreating back into Libya, with nearly half his army and most of his tanks either destroyed or in Allied hands.

Lt. Gen. Bernard L. Montgomery conducts a November 1942 inspection tour in North Africa.

EIGHTH ARMY PREPARED

New Commander Reported Happy Over Prospect of a Battle

WITH THE BRITISH EIGHTH ARMY, on the Front Near El Alamein, Egypt, Aug. 26—During the morning German shells have been bursting with their usual scream and dull thump along the screening ridges that hide the activities of the Australians in the coastal salient from the eyes of German artillery observers. One fell close enough to make correspondents duck when they climbed up one of those ridges to observe the enemy positions beyond the railway station of El Alamein and along the chalky-white rise of ground a few thousand yards west of Tel el-Eisa.

But the enemy gunners were not trying to eliminate correspondents. They were replying to the brisk barrage put up by well-concealed Australian 25-pounders that whanged metallically like oversize shotguns. The observers heard the scream of outgoing shells dwindling into No Man's Land, and, despite the heat haze, could see smoke burst out among German positions.

It was part of the Australian policy of making Jerry keep his head down—for brisk retaliation for any sniping or gunning by the enemy in the long run saves the lives of their own men and makes possible freer action, the Australians hold. At any event, that is how it works out on their part of the front.

All along the front there is an attitude different from that which prevailed in the last two weeks. Tenseness would not be the right word; it is rather an air of readiness. Whatever General Field Marshal Erwin Rommel may have in mind for this full moon, he will find the British Eighth Army ready. Nothing that the Germans could start now—even an attack carried out in conjunction with para-chute troops landed behind El Alamein, or troop landings on the coast—would be a surprise.

A dribble of Axis reinforcements seems to have filled the German Africa Corps to something like full strength, and there are many who think that the time has come—or is coming very soon—when a battle will break out.

It is known that German parachute troops are in the Western Desert, and the British Eighth Army is not making the mistake of ignoring the possibility that they will be used as such. An even more significant fact is that, as veteran outfits have been re-formed and rested, Marshal Rommel has been concentrating them, with armor, just behind his infantry and artillery screen—his usual way of preparing for an attack.

There are changes in the front-line atmosphere as a result of the new command. Lieut. Gen. Bernard L. Montgomery, the Eighth Army's commander, is now fully in charge of Allied operations and is reported to be happy over the prospect of a fight. General Montgomery, however, is said to be inclined toward the Russian plan of fighting much and announcing little, so the public will probably have to expect brief, noncommittal reports from the Eighth Army, even if a battle does begin.

The outlook on the front beyond El Alamein is good, despite the lowering battle clouds. The Eighth Army is well prepared and has been strengthened by the arrival of considerable amounts of United States equipment, including tanks, and by crack units of Scottish infantry.

Since the Eighth Army occupied its present positions it has staged almost nightly patrols to

Members of a British Eighth Army rifle brigade watch the burning of an ammunition dump at Hamra in November 1942.

check up on Axis activity. The Germans, on the other hand, seldom come out at all at night, and in a few areas have been withdrawn when they thought a big patrol was on the way.

That may mean that the Germans feel certain that they will begin the battle and do not care what the British Empire troops are doing. But it may also indicate a respect for their opponents, which may be apt to rob Marshal Rommel's forces of the fanatical optimism that encouraged them to smash on into Egypt with a badly depleted army.

"Nothing is ever hopeless so long as troops have stout hearts."

Orders issued by Bernard L. Montgomery as he prepared for the Second El Alamein

Churchill's first choice for field command of the Eighth Army was Lt. Gen. William "Strafer" Gott. But Gott died en route to Egypt—killed, ironically, by strafing after his plane crash-landed—leaving the position open for Montgomery. Better known to the public simply as Monty, Montgomery had a fondness for publicity, an ego the size of Douglas MacArthur's, and a similar penchant for distinctive headgear. Reprinted here are two sets of orders that he issued while preparing for the second battle of El Alamein. The first concerns morale; the second, leadership.

September 14, 1942

This battle for which we are preparing will be a real rough house and will involve a very great deal of hard fighting. If we are successful it will mean the end of the war in North Africa, apart from general 'clearing-up' operations; it will be the turning point of the whole war. Therefore we can take no chances.

Morale is the big thing in war. We must raise the morale of our soldiery to the highest pitch; they must be made enthusiastic, and must enter this battle with their tails high in the air and with the will to win. There must in fact be no weak links in our mental fitness.

But mental fitness will not stand up to the stress and strain of battle unless troops are also physically fit. This battle may go on for many days and the final issue may well depend on which side can best last out and stand up to the buffeting, the ups and downs, and the continuous strain of hard battle fighting.

I am not convinced that our soldiery are really tough and hard. They are sunburnt and brown, and look very well; but they seldom move anywhere on foot and they have led a static life for many weeks. During the next months, therefore, it is essential to make our officers and men really fit; ordinary fitness is not enough, they must be made tough and hard.

October 6, 1942

This battle will involve hard and prolonged fighting. Our troops must not think that, because we have a good tank and very powerful artillery support, the enemy will all surrender. The enemy will *not* surrender, and there will be bitter fighting.

The infantry must be prepared to fight and kill, and to continue doing so over a prolonged period.

It is essential to impress on all officers that determined leadership will be very vital in this battle, as in any battle. There have been far too many unwounded prisoners taken in this war. We must impress on our officers, n.c.o.s and men that when they are cut off or surrounded, and there appears to be no hope of survival, they must organise themselves into a defensive locality and hold out where they are. By doing so they will add enormously to the enemy's difficulties; they will

British soldiers lead Italian prisoners of war captured near El Alamein into a caged enclosure.

greatly assist the development of our own operations; and they will save themselves from spending the rest of the war in a prison camp.

Nothing is ever hopeless so long as troops have stout hearts, and have weapons and ammunition.

These points must be got across *now at once* to all officers and men, as being applicable to all fighting.

THE NAZI GRIP IS BROKEN

10.

Operation Torch

November 1942

Franklin Roosevelt was determined that American soldiers fight somewhere in the European theater of operations during 1942 so that the American public wouldn't lose interest in the war. Therefore, once it became clear that a cross-Channel invasion couldn't be mounted until 1943, the president began looking for an alternative. The North African invasion being pushed by the British seemed the obvious

choice—much to the displeasure of army chief of staff George C. Marshall, who preferred to concentrate Allied forces for an invasion of France in early 1943. What Marshall didn't grasp at the time was the political logic of Roosevelt's decision. "We failed to see," Marshall recalled later, "that the leader in a democracy has to keep the people entertained....The people demand action. We couldn't wait to be completely ready."

To command the invasion, code-named Torch, Marshall chose Lt. Gen. Dwight D. Eisenhower. Although Eisenhower was a relatively junior officer and had never held a field command, he had impressed Marshall not only with his excellent planning and organizational skills but also with his diplomacy and tact. The latter proved especially useful in dealing with the numerous British and American prima donnas under his command. "He merely has to smile at you," Field Marshal Montgomery wrote in his memoirs, "and you trust him at once."

The Torch landings, which began on November 8, were directed against Casablanca in Morocco and Oran and Algiers in Algeria. The question was, Would the soldiers in these French colonies resist? During October, American agents had conducted secret, high-level negotiations with the French colonial leaders, men ostensibly loyal to the collaborationist Vichy regime, yet extreme caution on both sides had prevented any agreement. Therefore, when the invasion began, the French defenders opened fire.

Algiers fell rather quickly on the first day, with Oran surrendering on November 10. Casablanca, however, proved much more troublesome, and Maj. Gen. George S. Patton Jr., commander of the Western Task Force, was preparing for a naval and air bombardment of the city when word came early on November 11 that a cease-fire had been signed. After two days of negotiation, Adm. François Darlan, commander in chief of the Vichy armed forces (who happened to be in Algiers on November 8), agreed to join the Allies in return for Eisenhower's recognition of Darlan as the French head of state. This conflicted with British support for Charles de Gaulle, but the problem vanished six weeks later when a fanatical Gaullist assassinated Darlan on Christmas Eve.

American soldiers off Oran await the order to leave their landing craft during Operation Torch.

AMERICAN FORCES LAND IN FRENCH AFRICA; BRITISH NAVAL, AIR UNITS ASSISTING THEM; EFFECTIVE SECOND FRONT, ROOSEVELT SAYS

U. S. Meets 'Threat'; Big Expeditions Invade North and West Africa to Forestall Axis

By C. P. TRUSSELL

WASHINGTON, Nov. 7—Powerful American forces, supported by British naval and air forces, landed simultaneously tonight at numerous points on the Mediterranean and Atlantic coasts of French North Africa, forestalling an anticipated invasion of Africa by Germany and Italy and launching effective second-front assistance to Russia, President Roosevelt announced tonight.

Lieut. Gen. Dwight D. Eisenhower is in command.

The President made the announcement even as the American forces, equipped with adequate weapons of modern warfare, he emphasized, were making the landings.

Soon he was speaking direct to the French Government and the French people by short-wave radio and in their own tongue, giving assurances that the Allies seek no territory and have no intention of interfering with friendly French, official or civilian. He called upon them to cooperate in repelling "the German and Italian international criminals."

By doing so, he said, they could help liberate France and the French Empire.

[United States and British planes dropped leaflets in France and French Africa containing messages to the people from President Roosevelt and General Eisenhower, London reported.]

General Eisenhower himself, the White House let it be known, also spoke by radio to the French people, explaining the purposes of the invasions.

His proclamation, delivered while the American troops were making their landings, gave specific directions to French land, sea and air forces in North Africa as to how they could avoid misunderstanding and prevent action against them by a system of signals. This is a military operation, General Eisenhower explained, that is directed against the Italian-German military forces there, and the only objective is to defeat the enemy and free France.

"We count on your friendship and we ask your aid," he said. "I have given formal orders that no offensive action shall be undertaken against you on condition that for your part you take the same attitude."

In telling the American people of the surprise action of large American forces under American command in this vital Vichy French region, apparently beginning, in effect, a pincer movement against the fleeing armies of General Field Marshal Erwin Rommel before the British Eighth Army at the western edge of Egypt, the President also gave assurances that "a considerable number of divisions" of the British Army would soon be brought up to reinforce our troops.

Invasion of Africa by Germany and Italy, President Roosevelt pointed out, would present a "direct threat" to America across the comparatively narrow sea from West Africa. The American invasion, he said, was designed to prevent Axis occupation of any part of either North or West Africa and thus deny to the enemy any starting point from which to move against the Atlantic coast of the Americas.

"In addition," his announcement asserted, "it provides an effective second-front assistance to our heroic Allies in Russia.

"This expedition will develop into a major effort by the Allied nations, and there is every expectation that it will be successful in repelling the planned German and Italian invasion of Africa and prove the first historic step to the liberation and restoration of France."

Simultaneously with the President's announcement, the War Department, in a communiqué, stated that landing operations by United States Army, Navy and air forces had begun "during the hours of darkness tonight" at "numerous points."

They were made necessary, the War Department said, by "the increasing Axis menace" to that territory. Both the radio and leaflets, it announced, were employed to apprise the French people of the landings.

General Eisenhower issued a proclamation to the French military, naval and air forces in North Africa, the War Department announced. In it he gave specific instructions as to signals these forces should make in order that there be no misunderstanding as to their peaceful intent.

By day, General Eisenhower said, such forces should fly the tricolor of France and the American Flag one above the other, or two tricolors, one above the other. By night, he said, a searchlight beam should be directed vertically into the sky.

Any refusal to comply with the orders of the proclamation, said General Eisenhower, who spoke in French over the air, will be interpreted as a proof of hostility. He ordered that all French naval and merchant marine units "stay where you are" and make no "attempt to scuttle your ships."

Speaking to the French people, President Roosevelt said that our armed forces had gone among them as Americans, with the aid of the United Nations, and were striving for their own safe future as well as the restoration of the ideals, liberties and democracy of France.

"We come among you," he said, "to repulse the cruel invaders who would remove forever your rights of self-government, your rights to religious freedom and your rights to live your own lives in peace and security.

"We come among you solely to defeat and rout your enemies. Have faith in our words. We do not want to cause you any harm. We assure you that once the menace of Germany and Italy is removed, we shall quit the territory at once."

Through the strict silence maintained by the United Nations, speculation as to possible Allied action against North Africa occupied considerable time on the German radio, intercepted broadcasts indicated. Early in the week Rear Admiral Luetzow, German radio commentator, was heard to discuss possibilities of an Allied operation against North Africa by Americans and a move against Casablanca, in French Morocco, from the Atlantic.

West French Africa, where Dakar has been the focal point of speculation about possible invasion operations for two years, and where General Charles de Gaulle, commander in chief of the Free French forces, was defeated in his attempt, was by-passed by tonight's Allied movement.

Just where the landings were made was not disclosed, but appeals to the people of Morocco and French North Africa appeared to give general locations, at least.

"The ultimate and greater aim is the liberation of France."

Franklin Roosevelt's message to Philippe Pétain concerning the Allied landings in North Africa and the Vichy leader's reply

The first of these documents is the message sent by President Roosevelt to Marshal Philippe Pétain, the head of state of unoccupied France, as U.S. and British troops landed in French North Africa. The second is Pétain's reply, sent from his capital at Vichy. Although Pétain strongly opposed the Allied invasion, Hitler responded immediately to Darlan's defection by sending German and Italian troops into those areas of France previously under Vichy rule.

Marshal Pétain:

I am sending this message to you as the Chef d'État of the United States to the Chef d'État of the Republic of France.

When your Government concluded the Armistice Convention in 1940, it was impossible for any of us to foresee the program of systematic plunder which the German Reich would inflict on the French people.

That program, implemented by blackmail and robbery, has deprived the French population of its means of subsistence, its savings; it has paralyzed French industry and transport; it has looted French factories and French farms—all for the benefit of a Nazi Reich and a Fascist Italy under whose Governments no liberty loving nation could long exist.

As an old friend of France and the people of France, my anger and sympathy grows with every passing day when I consider the misery, the want, and the absence from their homes of the flower of French manhood. Germany has neglected no opportunity to demoralize and degrade your great nation.

Today, with greedy eyes on that Empire which France so laboriously constructed, Germany and Italy are proposing to invade and occupy French North Africa in order that they may execute their schemes of domination and conquest over the whole of that continent.

I know you will realize that such a conquest of Africa would not stop there but would be the prelude to further attempts by Germany and Italy to threaten the conquest of large portions of the American Hemisphere, large dominations over the Near and Middle East, and a joining of hands in the Far East with those military leaders of Japan who seek to dominate the whole of the Pacific.

It is evident, of course, that an invasion and occupation of French North and West Africa would constitute for the United States and all of the American Republics the gravest kind of menace to their security—just as it would sound the death knell of the French Empire.

In the light of all the evidence of our enemy's intentions and plans, I have, therefore, decided to dispatch to North Africa powerful American armed forces to cooperate with the governing agencies of Algeria, Tunisia and Morocco in repelling this latest act in the long litany of German and Italian international crime.

These indomitable American forces are equipped with massive and adequate weapons of modern warfare which will be available for your compatriots in North Africa in our mutual fight against the common enemy.

I am making all of this clear to the French Authorities in North Africa, and I am calling them for their cooperation in repelling Axis threats. My clear purpose is to support and aid the French Authorities and their administrations. That is the immediate aim of these American armies.

I need not tell you that the ultimate and greater aim is the liberation of France and its Empire from the Axis yoke. In so doing we provide automatically for the security of the Americas.

I need not again affirm to you that the United States of America seeks no territories and remembers always the historic friendship and mutual aid which we have so greatly given to each other.

I send to you and, through you, to the people of France my deep hope and belief that we are all of us soon to enter into happier days.

Franklin D. Roosevelt

◆　◆　◆

President Roosevelt:

It is with stupor and sadness that I learned tonight of the aggression of your troops against North Africa.

I have read your message. You invoke pretexts which nothing justifies. You attribute to your enemies intentions which have not ever been manifested in acts. I have always declared that we would defend our Empire if it were attacked; you should know that we would defend it against any aggressor whoever he might be. You should know that I would keep my word.

In our misfortune I had, when requesting the armistice, protected our Empire and it is you who acting in the name of a country to which so many memories and ties bind us have taken such a cruel initiative.

France and her honor are at stake.

We are attacked; we shall defend ourselves; this is the order I am giving.

Philippe Pétain

11.

Counterattack at Stalingrad
November 1942

The Wehrmacht's failure to capture Moscow in 1941 produced a dramatic shakeup in Germany's military leadership. Soon after the Soviets began their counteroffensive that December, Hitler purged his top eastern-front field commanders—Gerd von Rundstedt, Fedor von Bock, and Wilhelm Ritter von Leeb—and simultaneously forced out army commander in chief Walther von Brauchitsch, whom he

blamed personally for the fiasco. This left in power only Franz Halder, chief of the German general staff, and solidified Hitler's control over all Wehrmacht operations.

Once a new stalemate developed in February 1942, Hitler began planning for a summer offensive that would focus on the oil-rich Caucasus region. Under the command of the reinstated Bock, Army Group South moved in June to the Don and then drove south along its western bank toward the industrial city of Stalingrad on the Volga. From there, Gen. Hermann Hoth's Fourth Panzer Army and Gen. Friedrich Paulus's Sixth Army were supposed to head farther south into the Caucasus. But an overly optimistic Hitler transferred Hoth's armor before the group's eastern flank at Stalingrad had been secured, leaving this task to Paulus alone. By the time the relatively slow Sixth Army reached Stalingrad in late August, the Red Army had already consolidated its forces there and arranged the city's defenses.

Although Marshal Semyon Timoshenko, the Red Army's southern commander, had con-

ducted the retreat to Stalingrad well, Stalin replaced him in late August with Marshal Georgi Zhukov, the "savior of Moscow," who had led the earlier defense of the capital. Zhukov's basic strategy was to keep pounding away at an objective until he achieved it, no matter the cost in lives. This approach was immediately applied to the situation at Stalingrad, where Gen. Vasili Chuikov prepared his Sixty-second Army for house-to-house fighting. Chuikov's tactics forced Paulus to take the city one block at a time, with heavy losses on both sides that only the Soviets could bear.

Gradually, the struggle became a test of wills: Hitler refused to accept defeat, and Stalin wouldn't surrender the city that bore his name. By early November, Paulus had taken nearly all of Stalingrad, but the effort had so weakened his army that Zhukov's counterattack, which began on November 19, easily cut off the German troops in the city and sealed their fate. Remarkably, Paulus, now isolated, held out for two months before surrendering on January 31.

A German soldier sits astride a motorcycle on the eastern front in February 1942. He is wearing a gas mask to protect his face from the bitter cold.

NAZIS' GRIP ON STALINGRAD BROKEN; 15,000 SLAIN AS SOVIET PUSH GAINS

12,000 More Taken; Russians Smash Ahead, Capture Many Places in Multiple Drive

MOSCOW, Wednesday, Nov. 25—The three-month-old Nazi grip on Stalingrad was weakening today after a swiftly advancing Red Army had killed 15,000 more Germans yesterday and captured 12,000, including three divisional generals, in a great Winter offensive rolling so fast that some Nazi units were cut down from behind in panicky retreat.

Russian official announcements raised the toll of Nazis to 77,000 dead or captured, not counting huge numbers of wounded who apparently are freezing to death on the frozen steppes, as did other German units last Winter in the rout from Moscow.

The Red Army's effort to encircle the entire Nazi army stalemated before Stalingrad, estimated at 300,000, clearly was gaining in power. Two communiqués told of vast stocks of war equipment falling to the Soviet tide, of at least one enemy airdrome being seized so swiftly that scores of German planes were unable to take to the air.

Inside Stalingrad the Russians in frontal assaults also were gaining against Nazi detachments whose rear communications had been slashed by Russian flanking armies sweeping across the Don River far to the west.

[The German High Command admitted the gravity of the situation by acknowledging the penetration of Nazi defenses southwest of Stalingrad. But it said "countermeasures" were under way and reported "savage battles" in the Don bend region. The London Express quoted a Stockholm report that the Germans had "begun to pull out of Stalingrad."]

The midnight Soviet comniuniqué said 900 Germans were killed and dozens of enemy blockhouses occupied in a slow but steady advance inside Stalingrad, while in the Caucasus Red Army units cut down additional hundreds of Nazis in successful stands in the Nalchik and Tuapse sectors.

This bulletin added some details to the striking Russian successes above and below Stalingrad and inside the Don River bend, as announced in a special communiqué. One Red Army unit captured a Nazi airdrome so swiftly, it said, that forty-two enemy planes did not have time to take to the air. Twenty-five of these planes were destroyed and the seventeen others were captured intact.

In some sectors there was evident Axis demoralization, because hundreds of fleeing Germans were being struck down from behind as the Red Army rolled onward.

This was the third special communiqué in three days and it told this story of increasing Red Army successes:

One Red Army gained twenty-five miles northwest of Stalingrad, another drove an additional twelve miles ahead to the southwest on a line paralleling the Stalingrad–Novorossiisk railroad in an apparent attempt to drive straight across the Northern Caucasus to the Black Sea and shatter communication lines of the German Mid-Caucasian army.

In the Don River elbow, directly west of Stalingrad, the Red Army already had cut direct Nazi army's communications with its faltering forces inside Stalingrad. It was inside the strategic Don loop that the three Nazi generals were seized. Twelve more Russian villages were taken in this huge pincer movement.

The Russians announced that in one day they had captured 1,164 guns of various caliber; 431 tanks, many in full working order; eighty-eight planes, many of them intact; 3,940 trucks, more than 5,000 horses, 3,000,000 shells, 18,000,000 cartridges and large numbers of infantry arms and other equipment and provisions, which "still are being counted."

In the twenty-five-mile advance northwest of Stalingrad a significant subsidiary action was mentioned by the Russians. One Red Army column driving straight down the western banks of the Volga captured the villages of Tomilin, Akatovka and Latashanka to link up directly with Red Army troops who for three months have held the northern factory district of Stalingrad.

This presaged an early rout of Nazi forces still entrenched in the ruins of that industrial city, in the opinion of observers. The greater arms of the offensive undoubtedly also will force an imminent decision on Nazi chieftains who have been told by Adolf Hitler to take Stalingrad at all costs. The Russians also had reached the town of Surovikino, seventy-five miles west of Stalingrad.

The central army, after slicing from the Volga to Kalach on the easternmost point of the Don bend, crossed that river, apparently to make a junction with other Red Army units crossing in the Kletskaya region, seventy-five miles northwest of Stalingrad.

With Nazi railroad arteries cut both above and below Stalingrad, these central armies now

Action on the Stalingrad front in November 1942.

were severing road links that ran straight eastward in the Don elbow and crossed that river by Nazi pontoons at a point only twenty-five miles short of Stalingrad.

A six-mile advance in the Don loop area found the Russians occupying the villages of Zimovaky, Trekh Ostrovyanskaya and Sirotinskaya.

The southern Red Army fanning out along the Stalingrad–Novorossiisk railway reached Sadovoe in a twelve-mile advance from Aksai. This village is more than fifty miles below beseiged Stalingrad. The villages of Umantsevo and Peregruzny also were taken in this advance.

The momentum of the Russian offensive and its direction suggested that the ultimate intent might be to drive clear across the top of the Caucasus peninsula to Rostov to trap Germans below the Don. At Chernyshevsk, the Russians were within 240 miles of Rostov.

"Hitler has left us in the lurch."

One of the last letters from Stalingrad

Late in January 1943, the last German plane out of Stalingrad carried with it seven sacks of mail that were never posted. Instead, the letters were impounded so that the German High Command could more closely gauge army morale on the eastern front. After officials in the army postal system's Central Censorship Bureau removed the names and addresses of each sender and recipient, their colleagues in the Bureau of Army Information read the letters and categorized them according to their "attitude toward the leadership." The results were 2 percent "positive," 4 percent "doubtful," 57 percent "negative," 3 percent "actively opposed," and 33 percent "indifferent." Like all the other "last letters," this one was never delivered.

This morning in the division command post, Hannes persuaded me to write to you after all. For a whole week I have avoided writing this letter; I kept thinking that uncertainty, painful though it is, still keeps a glimmer of hope alive. I was the same way in thinking about my own fate; every night I went to sleep not knowing how the scales might tip—whether we would get help here or would be destroyed. I didn't even try to come to any final conclusion, to resolve the doubt. Perhaps from cowardice. I might have been killed three times by now, but it would always have been suddenly, without my being prepared. Now things are different; since this morning I know how things stand; and since I feel freer this way, I want you also to be free from apprehension and uncertainty.

I was shocked when I saw the map. We are entirely alone, without help from outside. Hitler has left us in the lurch. If the airfield is still in our possession, this letter may still get out. Our position is to the north of the city. The men of my battery have some inkling of it, too, but they don't know it as clearly as I do. So this is what the end looks like. Hannes and I will not surrender; yesterday, after our infantry had retaken a position, I saw four men who had been taken prisoner by the Russians. No, we shall not go into captivity. When Stalingrad has fallen, you'll hear and read it. And then you'll know that I shall not come back.

12.

The Battle of the Atlantic at Its Height
November 1942

By early 1943, it had become clear that the enormous productive capacity of the United States would determine the outcome of the war. It seemed inevitable that, sooner or later, the Axis powers would drown in a flood of American planes, ships, tanks, and manpower. The Germans' only hope, therefore, lay in stemming the flow of these resources by disrupting the Allies' ability to ship them across the

North Atlantic. "The U-boat attack was our worst evil," Churchill later commented, "the only thing that ever really frightened me during the war."

Following the German declaration of war in December 1941, Hitler removed all restraints from Karl Dönitz's U-boat fleet and permitted the admiral to hunt at will. Initially, Dönitz focused on U.S. coastal shipping. Still considering the war to be far away, seaboard cities such as Miami and New York neglected to enforce blackouts—thereby rendering merchant ships, silhouetted against the bright urban glow, easy prey. In January 1942, a single *Unterseeboot* operating off New York Harbor sank eight ships in twelve hours; and by June 1942, Dönitz's subs had destroyed nearly five million tons of Allied shipping. "The losses by submarines off our Atlantic seaboard and in the Caribbean now threaten our entire war effort," George Marshall wrote to naval chief of staff Ernest J. King on June 19. Meanwhile, ending months of stubborn refusal, Admiral King finally established a convoy system for U.S. coastal waters.

The Interlocking Convoy System proved so effective that, in mid-July, Dönitz shifted his subs from the North American coast to the midocean "air gap" southeast of Greenland that lay beyond the reach of most Allied reconnaissance aircraft. Taking into account the replacement rate of Allied merchantmen, Dönitz calculated that, if his submarines could sink seven hundred thousand tons of Allied shipping each month, he would win the battle of the Atlantic. An intelligence blackout that began in February 1942 greatly aided his cause, and during the next eleven months, Allied losses mounted steadily, ultimately peaking at 729,000 tons in November 1942. Thereafter, however, Dönitz's success declined. The cracking of the new U-boat code—in combination with increasingly muscular escorts, new submarine-detection technology, and more reconnaissance aircraft—reduced the effectiveness of the German wolf packs dramatically. Finally, in May 1943, the second great U-boat campaign of the war ended with Dönitz's withdrawal from the North Atlantic.

ALLIES POOL RESOURCES TO WIN WAR ON U-BOATS

Air-Sea Might Coordination Believed Crux of Plans to Destroy Wolf Packs

By SIDNEY SHALETT

WASHINGTON, March 27—The latest news from the Atlantic—ominous but not at all unexpected—is that the Nazi U-boat wolf packs are prowling the seas again in what may be the dread harbinger of an all-out Spring offensive against Allied shipping.

The news from the home front, however, is that the Allies will pool their sea and air might, directed by their best available brains, to smash this menace and get the men and matériel across.

As the Nazis may figure it, it can be "win or lose" for them this year. Accordingly, they are reported to be preparing to hurl everything they have, which is considerable, into the U-boat war. United States and British leaders no longer discuss the possibility of defeat, but talk about the length of time it is going to take to achieve complete victory. They are determined that the U-boat threat must be met, countered and beaten.

This does not mean, however, that our leaders have any disposition to "talk away" the grave threat. From the highest authorities down, both in this country and in Britain, leaders have warned of the extreme seriousness of the situation. They have depicted the bitter cost that an all-out Axis underwater campaign undoubtedly will exact, despite our best defensive and counter-offensive methods.

Yet there is no defeatism here in Washington, where United States, British and Canadian leaders have been meeting to plot out a scientific, efficient, coordinated anti-U-boat campaign under the guidance of Admiral Ernest J. King, Commander in Chief of the United States Fleet.

At one time Secretary Knox told a Congressional committee it was expected that the Nazi underwater fleet would number 500 by January, 1943. This estimate now has been scaled down, however, and naval intelligence officers figure that Reichsfuehrer Hitler now has 300 to 400 submarines in his pig-boat pens from Norway to Sicily.

Barring disastrous losses, it is roughly estimated that Herr Hitler can keep one-third of these constantly in the fray. Fighting time of the total fleet is cut down by the necessity for repairs and overhauling, by the days consumed in getting to the hunting grounds, then back to base again to take on new supplies, fuel and torpedoes.

Herr Hitler is believed to have built furiously over the Winter. The fact that he does not—or may not—have 500 U-boats is undoubtedly a tribute to the zeal and efficiency with which the Royal Air Force, augmented by American bombers, pounded his great manufacturing centers, as well as his submarine lairs, through the Winter.

The Nazis have some giant U-boats, but naval experts here express the belief that they have concentrated on building 700-tonners, about 220 feet long. These are rather small craft compared with the 1,500-ton submarines on which the United States is concentrating. However, they are dangerous engines of destruction.

These 700-tonners are believed to pack twelve torpedoes—with an extra couple sometimes lashed topside—and by lying on the bottom or wallowing forward slowly during the day and

Crew on the deck of the Coast Guard cutter Spencer *watch the explosion of a depth charge in April 1943.*

coming to the surface to make greater speed under cover of night, they may be capable of cruising 12,000 miles. They can stay out six weeks or more—if their torpedoes hold out that long.

Although the U-boats of World War II are scientifically improved, infinitely stronger and much more difficult to sink with "ashcans" hurled from a destroyer, the actual tactics of U-boat warfare have not changed greatly. The ugly, cigarlike vessels still ambush their victims much as they did in World War I. Sometimes they go out to hunt singly; they sight their prey by periscope, or perhaps get the tip by radio from some far-off sub.

A sudden torpedo shot leaves a white wake through the water. If it hits, the U-boat commander chalks up another mark on his log; if it misses, he curses at the waste of the valuable tin fish, and if it is safe, as in the case of a defenseless merchantman, tries again.

If an Allied man-of-war is in the vicinity and picks up his trail, he usually crash dives and hopes to avoid a pattern of ashcans that will be laid on his head—and the sudden, horrible death that will result if one rips open the seams of his hull.

It is when the U-boats hunt in wolf packs that they are most dangerous. Six U-boats constitute a good pack; too many can be unwieldy. A favorite wolf pack trick, on picking up a convoy, is for one to get off a bit and let go a torpedo to draw out the escort vessels. Then, if the manoeuvre is successful, the other sea jackals close in and try to pick off what they can.

Over coastal waters on both sides of the Atlantic big planes and blimps fly patrol against the U-boats. Frequently they sighted subs and sank same, with the result that the U-boats grad-ually were driven out to mid-Atlantic. There destroyers, sometimes cruisers and the heroic little thin-skinned corvettes and cutters, took up the protective patrol. Before the end of the year America's new destroyer escorts are expected to be operating in force and may prove a decisive factor in winning the war against the U-boats.

Against this array the Nazis are expected to employ every trick they can muster. The opening of the North African front gave them new shipping lanes in which to hunt, but it also spread their strength somewhat thinner. One ruse they possibly may employ is to send a few U-boats to less critical areas in the hope of drawing off some of our patrol strength from busy areas.

At recent conferences in Washington representatives of the United States Navy, Army and Army Air Force, the British Navy and the Royal Air Force and the Canadian Navy and Air Force have been mapping out a plan of action.

The conferences have been going on for some time, and only the smallest inkling of the full story was told in the recent Navy announcement, which declared that "complete agreement" had been reached toward a coordinated campaign.

The question of who will head the Allied anti-submarine drive has been discussed. Rumors that one of America's ace submarine hunters would have the job have been heard, although Secretary Knox has denied emphatically that there will be any single head. It is known, however, that Admiral King has called in some of the best brains of this particular branch of the Navy to sit in with him on the conferences, and it is regarded as highly significant that the Commander in Chief himself presided over the discussions.

"We believe that you regard our work as important."
An appeal from Bletchley Park

The basis of all German military encryption was the Enigma machine. This typewriter-like device, which used a combination of thirteen plug-in cables and three rotating wheels, transformed plaintext into ciphertext that could be transmitted over open frequencies and then decrypted by the receiver. Beginning in 1941, U-boat radio intercepts, decrypted by the British code breakers at Bletchley Park (themselves code-named Ultra), allowed the sub trackers at the admiralty to reroute convoys around known U-boat positions. The Bletchley Park cryptanalysts were themselves able to accomplish this feat (as indicated by the letter reprinted here) through the use of "bombes," or mechanical calculating machines that quickly tested likely solutions for the ever-changing Enigma settings. On February 1, 1942, however, Dönitz ordered his U-boats to add a fourth wheel to their Enigmas, thus multiplying the number of possible settings and blinding Ultra for the rest of the year. On November 22, the British Operational Intelligence Center warned that the U-boat campaign was "the one campaign which Bletchley Park are not at present influencing to any marked extent—and it is the only one in which the war can be lost unless BP *do* help." First Sea Lord Dudley Pound was therefore greatly relieved to report to Admiral King on December 13 that the four-wheel Enigma code, known as Shark to the cryptanalysts, had finally been broken.

Hut 6 and Hut 8,
Bletchley Park

21st October 1941

Dear Prime Minister,

Some weeks ago you paid us the honour of a visit, and we believe that you regard our work as important. You will have seen that, thanks largely to the energy and foresight of Commander Travis, we have been well supplied with the 'bombes' for the breaking of the German Enigma codes. We think, however, that you ought to know that this work is being held up, and in some cases is not being done at all, principally because we cannot get sufficient staff to deal with it. Our reason for writing to you direct is that for months we have done everything that we possibly can through the normal channels, and that we despair of any early improvement without your intervention. No doubt in the long run these particular requirements will be met, but meanwhile still more precious months will have been wasted, and as our needs are continually expanding we see little hope of ever being adequately staffed.

We realise that there is a tremendous demand for labour of all kinds and that its allocation is a matter of priorities. The trouble to our mind is that as we are a very small section with numerically trivial requirements it is very difficult to bring home to the authorities finally responsible either the importance of what is done here or the urgent necessity of dealing promptly with our requests. At the same time we find it hard to believe that it is really impossible to produce quickly the additional staff that we need, even if this meant interfering with the normal machinery of allocations.

We do not wish to burden you with a detailed list of our difficulties, but the following are the bottlenecks which are causing us the most acute anxiety.

1. Breaking of Naval Enigma (Hut 8)

Owing to shortage of staff and the overworking of his present team the Hollerith section here under Mr Freeborn has had to stop working night shifts. The effect of this is that the finding of the naval keys is being delayed at least twelve hours every day. In order to enable him to start night shifts again Freeborn needs immediately about twenty more untrained Grade III women clerks. To put himself in a really adequate position to deal with any likely demands he will want a good many more.

A further serious danger now threatening us is that some of the skilled male staff, both with the British Tabulating Company at Letchworth and in Freeborn's section here, who have so far been exempt from military service, are now liable to be called up.

2. Military and Air Force Enigma (Hut 6)

We are intercepting quite a substantial proportion of wireless traffic in the Middle East which cannot be picked up by our intercepting stations here. This contains among other things a good deal of new 'Light Blue' intelligence. Owing to shortage of trained typists, however, and the fatigue of our present decoding staff, we cannot get all this traffic decoded. This has been the state of affairs since May. Yet all that we need to put matters right is about twenty trained typists.

3. Bombe testing, Hut 6 and Hut 8

In July we were promised that the testing of the 'stories' produced by the bombes would be taken over by the WRNS in the bombe hut and that sufficient WRNS would be provided for this purpose. It is now late in October and nothing has been done. We do not wish to stress this so strongly as the two preceding points, because it has not actually delayed us in delivering the goods. It has, however, meant that staff in Huts 6 and 8 who are needed for other jobs have had to do the testing themselves. We cannot help feeling that with a Service matter of this kind it should have been possible to detail a body of WRNS for this purpose, if sufficiently urgent instructions had been sent to the right quarters.

4. Apart altogether from staff matters, there are a number of other directions in which it seems to us that we have met with unnecessary impediments. It would take too long to set these out in full, and we realise that some of the matters involved are controversial. The cumulative effect, however, has been to drive us to the conviction that the importance of the work is not being impressed with sufficient force upon those outside authorities with whom we have to deal.

We have written this letter entirely on our own initiative. We do not know who or what is responsible for our difficulties, and most emphatically we do not want to be taken as criticising Commander Travis who has all along done his utmost to help us in every possible way. But if we are to do our job as well as it could and should be done it is absolutely vital that our wants, small as they are, should be promptly attended to. We have felt that we should be failing in our duty if we did not draw your attention to the facts and to the effects which they are having and must continue to have on our work, unless immediate action is taken.

We are, Sir, Your obedient servants,
A M Turing
W G Welchman
C H O'D Alexander
P S Milner-Barry

13.

The Casablanca Conference

January 1943

By the time Roosevelt and Churchill met at the Casablanca Conference in January 1943, the Allied offensive in North Africa had slowed to a crawl. Following the Torch landings, Hitler had reinforced the Afrika Korps across the narrow, hundred-mile-wide strait between Sicily and Tunisia, allowing the Wehrmacht to consolidate its position around the ports of Tunis and Bizerta. Allied planners had been

hoping for a quick victory in North Africa so that their plans for Continental operations might proceed. However, it was already clear that Rommel's army wouldn't be expelled from Tunisia any time soon and that plans for Bolero, the massive buildup of men and equipment in the United Kingdom, and Roundup, the cross-Channel invasion of France, would have to wait.

In general, the January 14–24 Casablanca Conference was devoted to purely military matters. The American joint chiefs met with their British counterparts to work out a mutual strategy for 1943, and Churchill and Roosevelt mostly listened. The principal difference between the two sides was whether to place more emphasis on preparing for the invasion of France or building on the gains already achieved in the Mediterranean. The British, who had important economic and political interests in the area, favored the latter; and although George Marshall bristled at further delays, the current situation in Tunisia forced him to agree that North African operations

had to be completed before any operations in France could begin.

The news that the second front in Europe would likely be delayed once again—this time until 1944— was, of course, difficult for the Soviets to bear. Stalin already doubted the loyalty of his western allies, and his mistrust was exacerbated by Churchill's apparent pursuit of narrow imperial self-interest at the expense of a great deal of Russian blood. To make the decision to postpone a bit more palatable, the president, in consultation with the prime minister, announced at the conference's closing press conference that the Allies would accept nothing less than "unconditional surrender" as the basis for peace. The intention was to reassure the Soviets that the United States and Great Britain were serious about the war and thereby keep Stalin from seeking a separate peace. The declaration, however, had little impact on Stalin (who desired no separate peace) and only served to help the Nazis argue persuasively that Germans needed to fight even harder to avoid complete Allied domination.

ROOSEVELT, CHURCHILL MAP 1943 WAR STRATEGY AT TEN-DAY CONFERENCE HELD IN CASABLANCA; GIRAUD AND DE GAULLE, PRESENT, AGREE ON AIMS

Leaders Go by Air; Aim at 'Unconditional Surrender' by Axis, President Says

By DREW MIDDLETON

CASABLANCA, French Morocco Jan. 24 (Delayed)—President Roosevelt and Prime Minister Churchill today concluded a momentous ten-day conference in which they planned Allied offensives of 1943 aimed at what the President called the "unconditional surrender" of the Axis powers.

The President flew 5,000 miles across the Atlantic with his Chiefs of Staff to confer with Mr. Churchill and British military, naval and air chieftains in a sun-splashed villa within sound of Atlantic breakers. Every phase of the global war was discussed in conferences lasting from morning until midnight. Both war leaders emphasized that the conference was wholly successful and that complete agreement had been reached on great military enterprises to be undertaken by the United Nations this year.

General Henri Honoré Giraud, High Commissioner for French North Africa, and General Charles de Gaulle, leader of Fighting France, met at the conference and found themselves in accord on the primary task of liberating France from German domination. President Roosevelt predicted that French soldiers, sailors and airmen would fight beside the Allied armies in the liberation of France.

The President and Mr. Churchill expressed regret for Premier Joseph Stalin's inability to leave the Russian offensive, which he is directing personally, but emphasized that all results of the conferences had been reported to the Soviet leader. [Generalissimo Chiang Kai-shek was similarly advised, The Associated Press reported.]

Assurance of future world peace will come only as a result of the total elimination of German and Japanese war power, the President declared. He borrowed a phrase from General Grant's famous letter to the Confederate commander at Forts Donelson and Henry—"unconditional surrender"—to describe the only terms on which the United Nations would accept the conclusion of the war.

He emphasized, however, that this did not mean the destruction of the populace of Germany, Japan and Italy, but the end of a philosophy based on the conquest and subjugation of other peoples in those countries.

Sitting side by side in the bright sunlight on the grassy lawn of the villa, the President and the Prime Minister reviewed the work of the conference, in which the Chiefs of Staff conferred two or three times a day, reporting at intervals to them.

The President saw three objectives before the United Nations in 1943.

The first of these is maintenance of the initiative won in the closing days of 1942, its extension to other theatres and an increase in those in which the Allies now hold the upper hand.

Second, the dispatch of all possible aid to the Russian offensive must be maintained with the double objective of whittling down German manpower and continuing the attrition of

Roosevelt, sitting beside Churchill on the lawn of his villa outside Casablanca, offers to reporters the text of the conference communiqué.

German munitions and material on the Russian front.

Third, Mr. Roosevelt called for assistance for the Chinese armies, now in their sixth year of war, with Japanese domination ended forever.

To gain these objectives the military and political leaders of the United Nations are determined to pool all their resources, military and economic, in 1943 to maintain the initiative wherever it is now held and to seek every opportunity to bring the enemy to battle on terms as unfavorable as those now prevailing in Tunisia.

Both leaders were extremely satisfied at the successful conclusion of the fourth meeting between them since the beginning of the war. Cooperation between the American and British Chiefs of Staff was described by Mr. Roosevelt as the closest possible, with the military leaders living together and working as personal friends more than as allies.

President Roosevelt predicted that the war would proceed according to schedule, with every indication that 1943 would be an even better year for the United Nations than 1942.

The conference, which probably made more important decisions than any other called by the United Nations, was held in a lush tropical setting in conditions of greatest secrecy. The President's villa was shaded by palm trees, with Bougainvillaea climbing on trellises around the house, and oranges nodding on trees in the yard. A swimming pool in the back yard had been turned into an air raid shelter, but no German planes approached Casablanca during the conferences, and if any had come they would have been greeted by squadrons of British and United States fighter planes flying guard over the region.

Many acres of the resort were enclosed in two lines of barbed wire, on which tin cans were hung. If any one had been foolhardy enough to approach these lines he would have been riddled by bullets from machine guns or bayoneted by some of the hundreds of American infantrymen who stood helmeted atop roofs or patrolled the shady walks around the area.

Both the President and the Prime Minister seemed confident and satisfied when they appeared at the noon press conference today. The President wore a worn gray suit and the Prime Minister was dapper in a gray pin-stripe suit topped by a somewhat battered gray Homburg hat. The sunshine winked in a jeweled "V" and an American Distinguished Service Order bar in his lapel buttonhole.

The two unmilitary-looking men, who lead half of the strongest coalition in history, were accompanied by General de Gaulle and General Giraud. For the benefit of camera men the two generals shook hands.

"A historic moment," President Roosevelt commented.

The sun beat fiercely on the group. Mr. Churchill asked the President, "Don't you want a hat?"

"I was born without a hat," Mr. Roosevelt replied.

While the President and the Prime Minister talked, guards silhouetted on near-by rooftops never relaxed their vigil and tight formations of fighters roared overhead.

Mr. Roosevelt revealed that the Allied victories in North Africa had made his fourth meeting with Mr. Churchill necessary. The situation had been reviewed in the meeting and plans made for the next steps in 1943, he said.

Both he and Mr. Churchill expressed deep regret for Premier Joseph Stalin's inability to leave the Russian offensive which he is directing personally, but emphasized that all the results of the conferences between the President, the Prime Minister and their Chiefs of Staff committees had been reported to the Soviet leader.

Mr. Churchill agreed with Mr. Roosevelt that the conference was unprecedented in history.

Describing himself again as the President's ardent lieutenant, Mr. Churchill declared they worked together as partners and friends and described their cooperation as one of the sinews of war of the Allied powers.

The Prime Minister began to speak slowly, but gradually raised his voice as he described the frustration of the enemy by the men Adolf Hitler had called incompetents and drunkards. This brought a laugh. Mr. Churchill beamed.

The events in North Africa have altered the whole strategic aspect of the war, making the Germans and Italians fight under conditions of great difficulty, he declared. He described General Field Marshal Erwin Rommel as a fugitive from Libya and Egypt now trying to pass himself off as the liberator of Tunis. But he reminded the correspondents that General Sir Bernard L. Montgomery was hot on Marshal Rommel's trail and that everywhere that Mary went the lamb was sure to go.

Design, purpose and an unconquerable will lie behind all that is being done by Britain and America, the Prime Minister said solemnly. These will be applied to enforce unconditional surrender upon the criminals who plunged the world into the war, he concluded.

Both the President and Mr. Churchill seemed hopeful on the results of the de Gaulle–Giraud meeting, in which the two French leaders found themselves in "entire agreement" on the end to be achieved, which is the liberation of France and defeat of the enemy. Yet although a joint communiqué issued by the two generals said this could be achieved only by union in war of all Frenchmen fighting side by side, it gave no clue as to how the present difficulty in the North African political situation is to be adjusted.

It is felt, however, that the conference between the generals and their talks with Mr. Churchill and Mr. Roosevelt has cleared the way for an agreement of some sort between Generals Giraud and de Gaulle on the political aspects of their crusade for the liberation of France. The mere fact that they were seen talking together and were photographed shaking hands should do much to unite the French all over North Africa and to emphasize that a union of General de Gaulle's followers with the other factions must be carried out swiftly if the French are to bulk large in the United Nations' war plans.

Mr. Roosevelt, the first President to leave the United States in wartime, became the first to inspect United States troops in the field since Abraham Lincoln when he reviewed armored and infantry units in a day snatched from the long series of arduous conferences. Riding in a jeep, the President inspected camps, talked with dozens of men and officers and ate "chow" with the soldiers.

"We had a darn good lunch," he said. "I wish the people back home could see the troops and their equipment. They have the most modern weapons we can turn out. The men are in good health and high spirits and I found the officers and men most efficient. Their morale is splendid and I know they will keep it up. Tell the folks back home that I am mighty proud of them."

The President visited Port Lyautey, scene of heavy fighting during the American landing, and placed wreaths on the graves of American and French soldiers buried there. He also directed that a wreath be placed on the grave of Edward Baudry, Canadian Broadcasting Company war correspondent, who was killed by a Spanish anti-aircraft bullet on a flight to cover the conference.

Among the happy features of his visit were talks the President had while here with two of his sons, Lieut. Col. Elliott Roosevelt, who is with the Allied Air Force, and Lieutenant Franklin D. Roosevelt Jr., who is on duty with the Navy.

Mr. Roosevelt had one other break from the conferences. This came when he dined with the Sultan of Morocco, Sidi Mohammed, at "a delightful party." According to the President, they got along extremely well and he found the Sultan deeply interested in the welfare of his people.

The President flew to Africa in two aircraft, switching from one to the other at a point on the journey. It was his first flight since his historic trip from Albany to Chicago in 1932 when he accepted the presidential nomination. He was accompanied by Mr. Hopkins on the flight, the first ever made by a President of the United States.

[The President flew by Clipper to a point in North Africa, then changed to a four-motored bomber especially fitted for comfort, The United Press reported.]

The United States Chiefs of Staff, General George C. Marshall of the Army, Admiral Ernest J. King of the Navy and Lieut. Gen. Henry H. Arnold of the Air Forces, preceded the President and already had begun conferences with their British "opposite numbers," General Sir Alan Brooke, Chief of the Imperial General Staff; Admiral Sir Dudley Pound, Chief of the Naval Staff, and Air Chief Marshal Sir Charles F. A. Portal, Chief of the Air Staff, when the rest of the party arrived. W. Averell Harriman, United States Lend-Lease Expediter, joined the conference from London.

The Chiefs of Staff were assisted by Lieut. Gen. Brehon B. Somervell, chief of the United States Services of Supply; Field Marshal Sir John Dill, chairman of the British military mission to the United States; Lord Louis Mountbatten, chief of the operational command, and Lieut. Gen. Sir Hastings Ismay, Chief of Staff to Mr. Churchill as Defense Minister.

Conferences took place two or three times daily, with constant reports going to the President and the Prime Minister.

The Prime Minister, who arrived first at the rendezvous, was accompanied by Lord Leathers, British Minister of War Transport. The President had just settled in his spacious white villa when Mr. Hopkins ushered in Mr. Churchill and the first of their many conferences began. It lasted through dinner and continued until 3 o'clock the next morning.

The Chiefs of Staff, the President and the Prime Minister conferred with Allied military and political leaders from all over the African

Roosevelt and Churchill photographed at Marrakech in French Morocco following the conclusion of the Casablanca Conference.

theatres. Lieut. Gen. Dwight D. Eisenhower, commander of Allied operations; his deputy, Lieut. Gen. Mark W. Clark, and General Sir Harold R. L. G. Alexander, Commander in Chief of the Middle East forces, represented the ground troops. Admiral of the Fleet Sir Andrew Browne Cunningham, Allied Naval Commander in Chief in North Africa, gave the naval views on what Mr. Churchill described as the great events impending, while Major Gen. Carl A. Spaatz, chief of Allied air operations; Air Marshal Sir Arthur William Tedder, vice chief of the air staff, and Lieut. Gen. Frank M. Andrews, United States Middle East commander, discussed the air situation.

Not the least interesting of these conferences were those between Mr. Churchill, Mr. Roosevelt, Harold Macmillan, British Resident Minister in North Africa, and Robert D. Murphy, civil affairs officer on General Eisenhower's staff, in which the tangled political situation was reviewed.

It is impossible to assess the value of the conference as yet, but it may be said that its close probably heralded the end of the long lull in Tunisia. Both Mr. Churchill and Mr. Roosevelt gave every indication that the Allies' watchword is "get on with the job." The Casablanca "unconditional surrender" conference was a directors' meeting of one-half of the mighty coalition now definitely on the offensive.

Two chief results of the conference appear to be, first, full admission that the Allies intend to press home the present strategic advantage during their campaigns in 1943, and, second, the fact that Generals de Gaulle and Giraud have been brought together in a meeting that, if barren of definite political agreement, at least showed France and French North Africa that they have agreed in principle and are ready to work together.

The President's use of General Grant's famous defy, "unconditional surrender," gives the key to the Allies' political strategy in the closing months of the war and indicates that, although mercy may be shown to the Axis peoples, none will be shown to their leaders.

This warning should do much to hush the German propaganda that claims that events in North Africa show that the Allies have been willing to cooperate with "Quislings" here and may be expected to do so again when the Continent is invaded.

There is no doubt that the conference was the most important of the four held by the two leaders, for this time they were not occupied by expedients to gain time or hold the enemy in check, but to fashion a crushing offensive against the Axis.

Although the meeting took place in Africa, it is unwise to believe that the Mediterranean is the only war theatre that will figure largely in the war news in the next six months. Every front was reviewed and discussed in the conferences and plans were made for new operations, and above all for maintenance of the precious initiative.

"Germany is our primary enemy."

The U.S. Joint Chiefs of Staff military strategy for 1943 and a British evaluation

The first of these documents is a December 26, 1942, memorandum drawn up by the U.S. Joint Chiefs of Staff as they prepared for the upcoming Casablanca Conference. The second—dated January 2, 1943—is the British response.

Basic Strategic Concept for 1943 (C.C.S. 135)

1. The Joint Chiefs of Staff have reviewed, in the light of current developments, references (a) to (e), inclusive, covering the evolution of United Nations strategy, for the purpose of determining what adjustments, if any, are necessary or desirable at this time, in the basic strategic concept.

CONCLUSIONS AND RECOMMENDATIONS

2. The present basic strategic concept of the United Nations, reduced to its simplest form, has been stated,

"To conduct the strategic offensive with maximum forces in the Atlantic–Western European theater at the earliest practicable date, and to maintain the strategic defensive in other theaters with appropriate forces."

In the opinion of the Joint Chiefs of Staff this concept, while basically sound, should be restated with a view to setting forth more exactly the strategic concept as regards the Pacific theater. The following statement is proposed:

"Conduct a strategic offensive in the Atlantic–Western European theater directly against Germany, employing the maximum forces consistent with maintaining the accepted strategic concept in other theaters. Continue offensive and defensive operations in the Pacific and in Burma to break the Japanese hold on positions which threaten the security of our communications and positions. Maintain the strategic defensive in other theaters.

"It is well understood that the strategic concept contained herein is based on the strategic situation as it exists and can be foreseen at this time, and that it is subject to alteration in keeping with the changing situation."

3. It is recommended that the following (see paragraph 4) be approved as the strategic objectives of the United Nations in support of the basic strategic concept as stated above. In arriving at its recommendations the Joint Chiefs of Staff have taken note:

(a) That Germany is our primary enemy;

(b) That Russia is exerting great pressure on Germany and is absorbing the major part of her war effort;

(c) That Russia's continuance as a major factor in the war is of cardinal importance;

(d) That timely and substantial support of Russia, directly by supplies and indirectly by offensive operations against Germany, must be a basic factor in our strategic policy.

(e) That until such time as major offensive operations can be undertaken against Japan, we must prevent her from consolidating and exploiting her conquests by rendering all practicable support to China and by inflicting irreplaceable losses on Japanese naval, shipping, and air resources.

(f) That a prerequisite to the successful accomplishment of the strategic concept for 1943 is an improvement in the present critical shipping situation by intensified and more effective anti-submarine warfare.

4. *Strategic objectives:*

(a) Western Hemisphere and United Kingdom.
Maintain the security, the productive capacity, and the essential communications of the Western Hemisphere and of the British Isles.

(b) Western Europe.
Insure that the primary effort of the United Nations is directed against Germany rather than against her satellite states by:

(1) Conducting from bases in United Kingdom, Northern Africa, and as practicable from the Middle East, an integrated air offensive on the largest practicable scale against German production and resources, designed to achieve a progressive deterioration of her war effort.

(2) Building up as rapidly as possible adequate balanced forces in the United Kingdom in preparation for a land offensive against Germany in 1943.

(c) North Africa.
Expel the Axis forces from North Africa, and thereafter:

(1) Consolidate and hold that area with the forces adequate for its security, including the forces necessary to maintain our lines of communication through the Straits of Gibraltar against an Axis or Spanish effort;

(2) Exploit the success of the North African operations by establishing large scale air installations in North Africa and by conducting intensive air operations against Germany and against Italy with a view to destroying Italian resources and morale, and eliminating her from the war;

(3) Transfer any excess forces from North Africa to the U.K. for employment there as part of the build-up for the invasion of Western Europe in 1943.

(d) Russia.
Support Russia to the utmost, by supplying munitions, by rendering all practicable air assistance from the Middle East, and by making the principal offensive effort of 1943 directly against Germany in Western Europe.

(e) Middle East.

(1) Maintain Turkey in a state of neutrality favorable to the United Nations until such time as she can, aided by supplies and minimum specialized forces, insure the integrity of her territory and make it available for our use.

(2) If Turkey can then be brought into the war, conduct offensive air operations from bases on her northern coast, in aid of Russia and against German controlled resources and transportation facilities in the Balkans.

(f) Pacific.

Conduct such offensive and defensive operations as are necessary to secure Alaska, Hawaii, New Zealand, Australia, and our lines of communications thereto, and to maintain the initiative in the Solomon–Bismarck–East New Guinea Area with a view to controlling that area as a base for further offensive operations and involving Japan in costly counter operations.

(g) Far East.

Conduct offensive operations in Burma with a view to reopening the supply routes to China, thereby encouraging China, and supplying her with munitions to continue her war effort and maintain, available to us, bases essential for eventual offensive operations against Japan proper.

◆   ◆   ◆

Basic Strategic Concept for 1943—The European Theater (C.C.S. 135/1)

1. We have considered the Memorandum of the Joint Chiefs of Staff and their recommendations for a Basic Strategic Concept for 1943 as set out in C.C.S. 135. We had ourselves prepared a paper on somewhat similar lines setting out our conception of what should be the American-British strategy in 1943. This is being circulated separately as C.C.S. 135/2. On most issues we are in agreement with the U. S. Chiefs of Staff. The main point of difference between us is that we advocate a policy of following up "Torch" vigorously, accompanied by as large a "Bolero" build-up as possible, while the U. S. Chiefs of Staff favor putting our main effort into "Round-Up" while adopting a holding policy in the Mediterranean, other than in the air. We therefore submit the following comments on the memorandum by the Joint Chiefs of Staff with particular reference to strategy in the European theater.

2. In support of our arguments we have divided our examination into two parts:

(a) What is the largest Anglo-American Force that can be assembled in the United Kingdom by August 1943 for re-entering France, and what would be the effect of assembling this force on operations in other theaters.

(b) What can we expect to achieve if we follow up "Torch" by offensive operations in the Mediterranean, and what forces can then be assembled in the United Kingdom for re-entering France.

Maximum "Bolero."

3. If we go for the maximum "Bolero" we calculate that the strongest land force, which we can assemble in the United Kingdom in August for an attack upon Northern France, will be—British 13 Divisions, United States 12 Divisions (at the very most).

4. Of the above, 6 divisions (4 British and 2 United States) is the maximum which could be organized as assault forces with the shipping and landing craft which can be made available, assuming that the highest priority is given to combined operational manning, training and repair requirements—possibly at the expense of the fleet.

5. The assembly of the above forces would have the following effects:—

On the Axis.

(a) We should have to accept only a small increase in the scale of bomber offensive against Germany and Italy from now onwards. This would be due to giving a higher priority to the passage of United States soldiers across the Atlantic and to the need for bringing over a larger proportion of Army cooperation type United States aircraft, i.e. fighters and light bombers.

(b) The abandonment of "Brimstone" and "Husky" and any amphibious operations in the Eastern Mediterranean.

On Turkey.

(c) There would be enough Divisions left over in the Mediterranean and Middle East area to support Turkey but these could not be used for offensive amphibious operations owing to lack of shipping and assault craft. Turkey could not fail to notice an easement of the pressure on Italy.

On China.

(d) We could not do "Anakim" in 1943 because all available landing craft would be wanted in the United Kingdom.

6. We emphasize that even if we accepted the above curtailment of our activities in other theaters, we should still be unable to stage an expedition on an adequate scale to overcome strong German resis-

Eisenhower discusses plans for the invasion of French Morocco with Lt. Comdr. Harry C. Butcher and a Major Lee in October 1942.

tance. The scale of "Round-Up" as originally planned was a total of 48 British and American Divisions. In the meanwhile the defenses on the French coast have been greatly strengthened. It is also to be noted that we cannot carry out even this reduced "Round-Up" until August. *In other words Russia would get no relief for another 7 or 8 months and the Axis would have a similar period to recuperate.*

The "Torch" Follow-Up.

7. If, on the other hand, we decide to exploit "Torch" during the spring of 1943 we consider that the effects would be as follows:—

On the Axis.

(a) We should have a good chance of knocking out Italy by a combination of amphibious operations (such as "Brimstone" and "Husky" and consequential assaults on the mainland of Italy), and an air offensive on the largest scale.

(b) We can ensure bringing the Axis air force to battle in the Mediterranean but, without surface operations, this cannot be guaranteed.

(c) We can greatly increase the number of Bombers arriving in the United Kingdom for offensive action against the Axis.

(d) German forces will be pinned in Northwest Europe by the build-up of the reduced "Bolero." (See paragraph 8 below.) Even though this build-up would be at a slower rate owing to other activities the enemy will not dare to relax their state of readiness to meet invasion.

On Turkey.

(e) We shall have some Divisions, air squadrons and aircraft to spare to help Turkey. Turkey is much more likely to come into the war on our side if she sees us putting Italy out as we should hope to do during 1943. With Turkey on our side we should be well placed for offensive operations against Crete and the Dodecanese, and possibly also the Balkans.

On China.

(f) We can probably do "Anakim" in the winter of 1943.

8. We calculate that if we adopt the above policy it would still be possible to assemble in the United Kingdom a force of some 21 British and United States Divisions by the late summer to take advantage of any opportunity which may occur for re-entering France. To do this it would be necessary to decide by the first of May at the expense of further amphibious operations.

Relief to Russia.

9. Our Intelligence Staffs have made an assessment which brings out the relief to Russia which an offensive Mediterranean policy might achieve. This shows that if we force Italy out of the war and the Germans try to maintain their line in Russia at its present length they will be some 54 divisions and 2,200 aircraft short of what they need on all fronts. This forecast is of course highly speculative but if the defection of Italy were to be followed by that of the other satellite nations the German deficiency would be still further increased.

10. Whether we adopt a maximum "Bolero" or concentrate on the "Torch" follow-up, we should be able to run a limited number of convoys to Russia.

The Axis Oil Situation.

11. The strongest argument against allowing Germany any respite in the near future is that during the next five months her oil situation will be critical. Any measures therefore that force her to go on using up her oil stocks may have a profound effect on her ability to prosecute the war.

Conclusions.

12. To sum up we consider that our policy should be—

(a) To exploit "Torch" as vigorously as possible with a view to

(1) Knocking Italy out of the war.

(2) Bringing Turkey into the war, and

(3) Giving the Axis no respite for recuperation.

(b) Increased bombing of Germany.

(c) Maintenance of supplies to Russia.

(d) The build-up of "Bolero" on the greatest scale that the above operations permit in order that we may be ready to re-enter the Continent with about 21 Divisions in August or September 1943, if the conditions are such that there is a good prospect of success. We believe that this policy will afford earlier and greater relief both direct and indirect to Russia than if we were to concentrate on "Bolero" to the exclusion of all other operations, observing that at the best we could not put a force of more than 25 Divisions on to the Continent in late summer of 1943.

14.

The Warsaw Ghetto Uprising

April–May 1943

In 1942, to carry out Hitler's "final solution" to the Jewish problem, the German government began systematically removing European Jews to occupied Poland, where they were held in walled-off urban ghettos pending their transfer to extermination camps. The ghetto in Warsaw, for example, was encircled by a brick wall ten feet high and eleven miles long. Within the ghetto, nearly half a million Jews

were crammed into housing suitable for only a small fraction of that number. Some residents lived a dozen to a room; the rest wandered the streets. Starvation and disease killed thousands daily; and then, in July 1942, the deportations began. On average, more than five thousand people a day were placed on trains bound for, they were told, labor camps in serene, rural settings. Instead, they were taken on short rides to the gas chambers at Treblinka.

Six months passed before a handful of escapees from Treblinka got word through to Warsaw that the deportations were actually death sentences. On January 18, 1943, when the Germans entered the ghetto to assemble yet another shipment, they were met with armed resistance. The street fighting lasted four days, during which about fifty German soldiers were killed and their arms seized. Afterward, the Germans halted all deportations while they assessed the situation. Finally, Reichsführer-SS Heinrich Himmler ordered the ghetto cleared. This action began on April 19, the first day of

Passover and also the day before Hitler's fifty-fourth birthday. It continued, at first intensely and then sporadically (as Jewish ammunition ran out), until May 16, when SS major general Jürgen Stroop dynamited the Great Synagogue and declared, "The Warsaw ghetto is no more."

As early as October 1941, reports had reached the West of the slaughter of Jews in Poland. In August 1942, a memorandum written by Gerard Riegner of the World Jewish Congress in Geneva provided President Roosevelt with specific details of the Holocaust, including an accurate account of the January 1942 Wannsee Conference at which the Final Solution was organized. Nevertheless, as skepticism among the Allies gave way to hesitation and indifference, the leaders of the Grand Alliance sought refuge from their guilty knowledge in a pitiless focus on purely military details. The ongoing genocide was almost never mentioned publicly, and such limited measures as bombing the railroad tracks leading to Auschwitz were rejected because the death camp wasn't a military target.

Allied prosecutors used this German April 1943 photograph of the destruction of the Warsaw Ghetto as evidence at the Nuremberg war crimes trials.

BATTLE IS REPORTED IN WARSAW'S GHETTO

Poles Say Jews Have Fought Nazis Since April 20

LONDON, May 6 (U.P.)—A battle has been raging for seventeen days in Warsaw's ghetto, where Jews have converted their homes into forts and barricaded shops and stores for defense posts, Polish sources said today.

The Jews, fighting against annihilation by the Nazis, were reported using bedsteads as bunkers and fighting with arms smuggled into the ghetto.

An underground Polish radio station several weeks ago broadcast an appeal from Warsaw for help. In a broadcast that was terminated abruptly, it reported that Warsaw's remaining Jews had been sentenced to death by the German occupation authorities and that women and children were defending themselves "with their bare arms."

Polish sources here said that when German execution squads went into the ghetto they were met by "furious resistance" and that fighting had been in progress since April 20.

Jüdische Rabiner.

Another of the German photographs introduced into evidence at Nuremberg, this one was captioned, "Jewish rabbi."

"He who has arms will fight."

An excerpt from the May 3, 1961, testimony of Tsivye Lubetkin at the trial of Adolf Eichmann in Jerusalem

This account of the Warsaw Ghetto Uprising formed part of the testimony given by Tsivye Lubetkin on May 3, 1961, at the trial of Adolf Eichmann in Jerusalem. Eichmann, the high-level SS bureaucrat who had emerged from the Wannsee Conference as the Nazis' chief executioner, had escaped after the war to Argentina, where he was later discovered by Nazi hunter Simon Wiesenthal and abducted by Israeli agents. Lubetkin was one of the few (perhaps seventy) people who managed to escape the destruction of the Warsaw Ghetto, while seven thousand of his fellow Jews were killed and fifty-six thousand sent to death and labor camps.

The 18th of April, 1943, was the day before Passover. Two days earlier the Gestapo man Brand had walked into the *Judenrat* office and said that he believed that the council did not take proper care of the Jewish children: there were not enough food and vegetables; kindergartens ought to be put up so that the Jewish children could play and laugh. He had declared for certain that those Jews who remained in Warsaw were considered productive and were therefore no longer in danger of deportation. Our experience had told us, however, that promises like this were bad omens. Besides, there had been rumors during the previous few days that the Germans were preparing to liquidate the Warsaw Ghetto before Passover. On the other hand, some had heard from one German or another the same words of encouragement: the Jews will be permitted to survive. But on the 18th a Jewish policeman, a member also of the underground organization, said that Polish policemen had told Jewish policemen that something would happen that night.

We, the members of the Jewish fighting organization in the Ghetto, declared a state of readiness. Everyone was ordered to his post. About midnight of April 18th, the policeman told us that the Ghetto was surrounded. We separated, and I went to my post, 33 Nalewki Street. The commander of that group was Zkharye Artshteyn. My comrades went to their posts. What did we say to the Jews that night? We told them: he who has arms will fight. And we did have arms, not only the fighting organization, but also some Jews who did not belong to the organization. And we said: women and children and men who have no arms will go down into the bunkers; at the first opportunity during our fighting, they were to go into the "Aryan" part of Warsaw. Thus some people would be saved.

The young men and women had been waiting for this moment for months, the moment when they would shoot back at the Germans. I was standing in an attic on 33 Nalewki Street when I saw thousands of Germans armed with machine guns surrounding the Ghetto. Suddenly, they entered, thousands, armed, and we, some twenty young men and women, had a revolver, a grenade, some bombs, home-made ones that had to be lit by matches. It must have been strange to see us twenty Jewish men and women happily standing up against the heavily armed enemy, happy because we knew that their end would come. We knew that ultimately they would conquer us, but we knew also that they would pay heavily for our lives. It is difficult to describe what happened. When the Germans approached and we threw our hand grenades and bombs and saw German blood pouring over the streets of Warsaw where so much Jewish blood had poured, we rejoiced. The future did not worry us. It was a joy for the Jewish fighters to behold the wonder of those German heroes retreating, terrified by the home-made bombs and the hand grenades of the Jews. After an hour, we saw an officer bidding his soldiers to collect their dead and wounded. But they did not collect their dead and wounded, whose arms we took later. Thus, on the first day, we few, with our poor arms, drove the Germans from the Ghetto. Of course, they came back. They had enough arms, ammunition, bread and water, which we did not have. Reinforced with tanks, they came back on the same day, and we, with our Molotov cocktails, set fire to a tank during the fight. And when we met in the evening and reported, we saw that, despite our meager arms, the number of our dead was small, two men, while hundreds of Germans had fallen, either dead or wounded.

The fighting continued at the same pace for a number of days. The Germans could not beat us; from time to time they retreated. But not all the days were like the first ones. We began to have more casualties and to kill fewer Germans. We changed our tactics; instead of fighting from our positions in the streets, we fought in small groups. We separated into many small groups which set ambush for the Germans. The Germans came no longer in large numbers, but in small groups. Our feet were wrapped in rags so that they could not hear steps; they walked in rubber-soled shoes. Each searched for the other, but, unlike the Germans, we knew the terrain, the houses, the attics and cellars.

Thus the battle was going on for several days. It is difficult to describe life in the Ghetto during that time. Jews were embracing and kissing each other during the first days. And although it was clear to each of us that we would be killed, we were satisfied to know that we had taken revenge for the death of our brothers. Fighting back made our lot easier.

From the very first day we had attempted to contact the "Aryan side," for we needed more arms. After some time Izhak Cukierman, who had been trying to get weapons there, succeeded in doing so. How would we smuggle the arms into the Ghetto? The men of the Burial Society had formerly brought in arms and taken out letters for us, but this contact had been stopped. We looked for new ways of sending some of our men outside the Ghetto.

After the main bunker of the fighters' organization at 18 Mila Street was blown up, we decided to try to cross over to the "Aryan side" through the sewers. For about forty-eight hours we wandered through the maze of sewers. Our friends of the "Aryan side" hired two trucks, allegedly to move furniture. When the trucks reached the street where we were hiding inside the sewer, our friends whipped out pistols, pointed them at the drivers, and said that if they made one sound they would be shot. They kept quiet. Our friends then opened the manhole covers and we came out. I think we numbered fifty fighters....

When Polish Warsaw revolted in August 1944, we, the remnants of the fighters of the Warsaw Ghetto, joined the Polish underground and fought together with them as a separate group.

15.

The Premiere of *Mission to Moscow*
April 1943

The wartime alliance between the United States and the Soviet Union was uneasy at best. Neither side could completely forget America's long-standing animosity toward Bolshevism, nor its attempt to reverse the course of the October Revolution by sending troops to fight alongside the Whites in the 1918–1922 civil war. The Nazi invasion of Russia in June 1941 had forced the two nations together, but the

American people still needed a great deal of sweet talk in order to accept this marriage of convenience. In the United States, this was largely provided by pro-Soviet propaganda, which portrayed the Russians as hardworking, reliable peasants and Stalin as their benevolent Uncle Joe. President Roosevelt, in particular, wanted "to show the American mothers and fathers that if their sons are killed in fighting alongside Russians in our common cause, that it was a good cause, and that the Russians are worthy allies."

Shortly after German troops began moving into Russia, Roosevelt met with his old friend Joseph E. Davies, a corporate lawyer with an interest in Russian art who had served as U.S. ambassador to the Soviet Union from 1936 until 1938. They discussed the advisability of publishing an account of Davies's experiences that would portray the Soviet government in a friendly light. The result, cobbled together by ghostwriters from Davies's diary and official state department documents, appeared in late December 1941 as *Mission to Moscow*. A huge suc-

cess for Simon & Schuster, it quickly sold seven hundred thousand copies in English and was translated into thirteen other languages. Six months later, with the backing of the president, Davies signed a contract with Warner Brothers to turn the book into a major feature film.

Written by Howard Koch and directed by Michael Curtiz (the team that had recently created *Casablanca*), the film version of *Mission to Moscow* was released on April 30, 1943. It is now considered the most outstanding example of the wartime use of entertainment to sell a political message. Explicitly appealing to "facts" known to be incorrect, the script explained away, for example, the purges of the late 1930s as misunderstood efforts to rid the Soviet leadership of Nazi fifth columnists. In a May 9 letter to *The New York Times*, philosopher John Dewey condemned the film as "the first instance in our country of totalitarian propaganda for mass consumption." Yet *Mission to Moscow* did reasonably well at the box office, became a hit overseas, and diverted millions of GIs, courtesy of the Army Motion Picture Service.

Joseph E. Davies returns to Washington in June 1943 after traveling to Moscow on behalf of President Roosevelt. In the photograph, Davies points to the seal on his briefcase, which contains Stalin's response to a letter the president had entrusted to Davies. Behind the envoy is the DC-4 on which he traveled.

MISSIONARY ZEAL

The Ecstasies in 'Mission to Moscow' Raise Doubts on Political Films

By BOSLEY CROWTHER

Now that the Warners have cut loose and turned out a feature-length film in "Mission to Moscow" which boldly puts political persuasion on the screen, it is time to start thinking about such pictures in something more than academic terms. It is time to start making an analysis of the methods by which such films invade men's minds. For finally a major Hollywood studio has done the unprecedented thing of beating the drum for a viewpoint which has controversial aspects, to say the least. Finally a big picture company, which is chiefly in the entertainment trade, has made a film which is frankly a political argument. And, although the documentary film folk have been working in this field for years, the entrance of a powerful chain producer is something to regard with careful eyes.

For there are certain essential responsibilities which go with the blessing of free speech— or with the blessing of free film production —in matters of actual fact. First is the big responsibility of telling the absolute truth as nearly as one can detect it from the available evidence at hand. And the second is one of integrity: facts should not be willfully deranged or given a biased complexion to create a misleading effect. Especially are these responsibilities encumbent upon those who have an influence upon large numbers, as the producers of motion pictures do. Yet experience has shown that dramatists—particularly dramatists for the screen—are prone to be careless of these duties when they start tossing around recorded facts. That is why we caution a careful scrutiny of Hollywood's fact films.

In the case of "Mission to Moscow" (and of all such future films, most probably), reaction will depend very largely upon the individual's point of view. The man who finds himself in thorough sympathy with the message which the film is putting across is not likely to be too critical of the manner in which the message is conveyed. He will tolerate many distortions which the unsympathetic will justly blast. And he will probably accept the rambling structure and the talk-talk sequences in which this particular film abounds. He will be satisfied that the method justifies a worthy end.

And certainly the general intentions of this picture are honorable. For they are, in broad sweep, the same ones which Joseph E. Davies had in writing his book—his report on his Ambassadorship to Russia—upon which the film (now at the Hollywood Theatre) is based: to show that the Russian nation—far from being the monstrous menace which has been charged by prejudiced propagandists—is an honest, respectable ally; to reveal that the leaders of Russia have been misrepresented and misunderstood and that they were the only strong champions for "collective security" against the Fascists in Europe; to convey that it was really the reactionaries and "appeasers" in England and France who permitted Hitler to ride roughshod by refusing to ally with Russia—and to make it clearly apparent that our own isolationists and profiteers would have gladly done business with Hitler if Pearl Harbor hadn't got in the way.

Those are respectable intentions, and they are generally realized. But the question is whether the Warners have presented the facts in the most responsible way and in a way to encourage confidence in further films of a political sort. For, in their wild endeavor to see Russia (through Mr. Davies's eyes) in a glow of benevolence and righteousness, they have committed some rather serious faults. Furthermore, they have not been entirely consistent with Mr. Davies's book.

In the first place, the film's presentation of the famous "Moscow trials" is decidedly arbitrary—even though it may accord with one's desired belief. The picture's pronouncement that the generals and other Russian leaders were "purged" in 1937 because they got caught in a Trotskyite plot to sell Russia out to Germany and Japan for political power is arguable. In fact, a lot of people who know a lot about it have been arguing it for years. The film is precise and dogmatic on the point. It covers the lengthy trials as one big gasp with a couple of measured confessions. Even Mr. Davies was not so certain in his book.

Of necessity, the picture is a digest of the original "Mission to Moscow," which would be quite forgivable if it stuck to the stuff in the original and did not go frolicking on its own. But it does not. It takes Walter Huston as Mr. Davies, Ann Harding as his wife and Eleanor Parker as Mr. Davies's daughter on a Hollywood-eye tour of Russia. It shows them taking food at a railway station from a smiling peasant just like old times. It shows that the Russian workers are just like the workers "back home"—that is, they work for wages and have a dutiful respect for the boss. It lets the American ladies know that their sisters in Russia get cosmetics from Mme. Molotoff's factory—only Mme. Molotoff is a svelte and suspiciously class-conscious dame. Her factory is decidedly Elizabeth Ardenish. And it makes a joke of the Ogpu.

Furthermore, the film is chronologically mixed up. It significantly makes it appear that Mr. Davies had a prescient conversation with Winston Churchill in 1939. Mr. Davies did report a conversation with Mr. Churchill—but in 1937, and it wasn't so apt. Such tricks have a way of imparting an omniscience to the Mr. Davies in the film, which is another form of distortion to aid the emotional impetus of the film.

Things of this sort are dangerous in pictures meant to influence men's minds. For they create false conceptions and blindly confident belief. It is fine that "Mission to Moscow" does create goodwill toward our allies, the people of Russia—a nation of humans—which is just as things should be. And it is good that it should foment reevaluation of some hidebound ideas. But it should do so with a little less ecstasy. It is just as ridiculous to pretend that Russia has been a paradise of purity as it is to say the same thing of ourselves.

"When I became commissar of the cosmetic industry...."

Scenes 100–114 of the *Mission to Moscow* screenplay

Even this short excerpt from the *Mission to Moscow* screenplay provides the reader with a broad understanding of the film's viewpoint. The production itself closely followed the script's dialogue and visual instructions.

100. [EXT. AMERICAN EMBASSY]

DAVIES: Don't stay too long. Remember, we've got a date tonight.

MRS. DAVIES: As if I'd forget my first diplomatic ball. (Half serious.) Joe, will there be all sorts of mysterious intrigues going on in alcoves and corners?

DAVIES (dryly): Oh, no doubt. Some beautiful brunette named Vera will probably offer you the plans of Yokohama, for a pair of silk stockings.

They go out, Spadebeard saluting as he opens the door.

101. MED. SHOT AT THE CAR as Freddie holds the door for Mr. and Mrs. Davies.

MRS. DAVIES: Good morning, Freddie. How did you rest?

FREDDIE: Good morning, Mrs. Davies. With one eye open.

DAVIES (laughs, then gets into the car after his wife): Freddie, drop me off at the embassy, then take Mrs. Davies to this address. (Gives him a slip of paper.) I can't pronounce it.

FREDDIE: Yes, sir—(glances at the slip) and I can't read it, sir.

DAVIES: Ask the Gay Pay Oo boys.

He nods back to the car behind theirs, which has started its motor. Mrs. Davies glances back uncomfortably.

MRS. DAVIES: I cannot get used to being followed everywhere I go.

FREDDIE (climbing into his seat): What I can't figure out, ma'am, is whether they're protecting us or watching us.

DAVIES (smiles): Probably a little bit of both.

The car pulls out of the driveway. Camera holds on the spot and we see the police car follow closely after them, with its three OGPU boys.

DISSOLVE TO:

102. CLOSE SHOT DOORWAY OF U.S. EMBASSY OFFICE with the proper inscription and insignia on the impressive double doorway.

DISSOLVE THROUGH TO:

103. FULL SHOT INT. ANTEROOM OF THE EMBASSY
People seated waiting to see the ambassador—members of the staff—secretaries walking to and fro. An air of quiet activity. An embassy undersecretary (whom we recognize as Spendler from the Kremlin scene) emerges from one door and crosses toward another. His manner indicates urgency.

104. MED. SHOT OFFICE OF THE AMBASSADOR
Davies sits at a desk in one corner of the room. Henderson is with him, going over the business of the day.

HENDERSON (as he hands Davies a stack of papers):
More applications for American passports, sir. I've written my comments on the margins.

DAVIES (looks thoughtfully at the stack):
The pile gets bigger every day. It reminds me of animals scurrying for shelter before a storm.

Spendler walks into the shot. He is an employee of the embassy, but not an American, and speaks with a slightly foreign accent. (He had a prototype in reality, but his actions here are not intended to be based upon an actual incident.) Davies and Henderson look up, noticing his air of controlled excitement.

SPENDLER: Please—forgive my interrupting, Mr. Ambassador—but something has happened that I thought you should know about at once!

DAVIES: Yes?

SPENDLER (lowers his voice confidentially): Yesterday, the workmen who are repairing the Italian embassy found dictograph wiring in the rafters. I think we should make an immediate examination. The Kremlin may be recording every word we say!

DAVIES (calmly): Maybe they had a reason with the Italians. We all know the rumors that certain embassies here in Moscow are hotbeds of foreign agents.

SPENDLER (surprised at this calm attitude): But eavesdropping, sir! It's an open affront to one's international rights.

DAVIES: Let's give them the benefit of the doubt, Spendler. Anyway, I say nothing outside the Kremlin about Russia that I wouldn't say to Stalin's face. (He pauses.) Do you?

SPENDLER (uncomfortably): Well, that's putting it a bit stiffly, sir—

DAVIES (severely): Then stop gossiping and stop listening to it. We're here in a sense as guests of the Soviet government, and I'm going to believe they trust the United States as a friend until they prove otherwise. Is that clear?

SPENDLER (flustered): Yes, sir—but if there were microphones—

DAVIES: Then let 'em hear. We'll be friends that much faster! (He glances around the room and ceiling.) And if they haven't got microphones I'm not going to insult them by ripping up the walls to find out. (He pauses and grins.) Anyway, it's much too expensive.

Henderson laughs, and even Spendler has to smile.

HENDERSON: And besides, sir—we examined these rooms thoroughly two years ago.

Davies looks at him in very amused surprise.

DISSOLVE TO:

105. STOCK SHOT MOSCOW BUSINESS THOROUGHFARE
Modern office buildings, stores, etc. Street teeming with traffic.

105A. MED. SHOT STREET
The Davies car pulls up to the curb, the Gay Pay Oo car still behind it. Freddie gets out to open the door for Mrs. Davies. In the meantime the American ambassador's car attracts the attention of people passing in the street. Urchins run up to peer through the car windows at Mrs. Davies, who smiles and waves at them. Freddie has to hoist a couple of the boys off the running board before he can open the door.

FREDDIE (good-naturedly): All right, kids, skedaddle. Please. (Timidly trying his Russian.) Pozhaluista.

The youngsters howl at Freddie's Russian accent. He now opens the door and Mrs. Davies steps out of the car.

MRS. DAVIES (to Freddie; laughing): They seem to have a healthy curiosity.

FREDDIE (grins): I guess they never heard about private property.

Mrs. Davies turns to one small youngster who still leans over the hood, eyeing the American flag with a dreamy fascination. She looks at him for a moment, then walks over, puts an arm around his shoulders, lifts one of the flags from its standard, and presents it to the child. His face registers astonishment and delight at this incredible good luck. He marches off holding his prize, with the other urchins forming an impromptu cheering parade behind him. Mrs. Davies and Freddie look after them with amused smiles, then she turns toward the door of a building which is opposite.

MRS. DAVIES: Freddie, I won't need the car until it's time to get Emlen at the rink.

FREDDIE: Yes, Mrs. Davies.

She walks toward the door of a building.

WIPE TO:

106–110. OMITTED

111. CLOSE SHOT A WINDOW with Russian lettering: USSR COSMETIC FACTORY

112. OMITTED
THE CAMERA PULLS BACK AND PANS TO:

113. CLOSE SHOT A FANCY AND VERY ATTRACTIVE DISPLAY OF COSMETICS containing lipstick, creams, soaps, perfume, and powder.

MRS. DAVIES' VOICE (OVER SCENE): What an attractive display! That might be in a Fifth Avenue window in New York.

114. MED. SHOT   MADAME MOLOTOV'S OFFICE
Simple and very modern. The two women are standing in front of the display in a corner of the room. Madame Molotov is dressed in a very simple dress.

MADAME MOLOTOV: Thank you, Mrs. Davies. When I became commissar of the cosmetic industry, I went to Paris to study their methods.

MRS. DAVIES: But I didn't realize that luxury trades were encouraged in the Soviet Union.

MADAME MOLOTOV (smiles): We discovered feminine beauty was not a luxury.

MRS. DAVIES: I guess women are no different the world over. Primarily, they want to please their men.

Crossing to the desk, Madame Molotov picks up a telephone, speaks a few words in Russian: "Please bring the tea now." She puts down the receiver.

MRS. DAVIES (taking a chair): I'm curious to know how the wife of the premier has the time to run a large industry.

MADAME MOLOTOV: Many of the commissars' wives have some work of their own. We prefer that to merely social duties.

MRS. DAVIES: So do I. For a number of years I ran my father's plant. Now I enjoy helping my husband in his work.

MADAME MOLOTOV: An American woman managing a business! (Suddenly they see the humor and both laugh.) Here we had the impression American women were ornamental and not useful, and you thought that our women were useful and not ornamental.

MRS. DAVIES: I guess we were both wrong.

MADAME MOLOTOV (with deep sincerity): I think we have much in common, Mrs. Davies.

MRS. DAVIES: That is a very nice compliment.

MADAME MOLOTOV: You must come out to our dacha and we will talk over some more of our problems.

At this moment a wholesome, intelligent-appearing young girl dressed in a white smock comes into the room, wheeling a samovar and tea service. Through the opened door we see girls with packing boxes and hear factory sounds.

MARYA: Marya, I would like you to meet Mrs. Davies, wife of the American ambassador.

MRS. DAVIES: How-do-you-do, Marya.

MARYA (forming her words very precisely): How - do - you - do . . .

MRS. DAVIES (surprised): Where did you learn to speak English?

MARYA: To night school.

MADAME MOLOTOV: At night school, Marya.

MARYA (shaking her head; smiling as she begins to pour the tea): It is so easy to forget, Mrs. Davies.

MRS. DAVIES: I think you do wonderfully. (To both of them.) How proud I'd be if I did as well with Russian!

They both laugh.

MADAME MOLOTOV: Perhaps some day we shall all speak the same language.

16.

The Detroit Race Riots

June 1943

During World War II, Detroit, the nation's fourth largest city, became the world's leading center of defense production. While the Big Three automakers converted their assembly lines to turn out tanks and jeeps, the federal government built new plants around the city to meet other pressing war needs. On what had been corn and soybean fields thirty miles west of Detroit, it built the enormous Willow Run

bomber plant for Henry Ford. To staff the plant, Ford hired tens of thousands of new workers, including many blacks who had recently emigrated from the South. Their average weekly take-home pay of $61.47 was more than most had ever earned, or ever hoped to earn, and it made their otherwise awful situation somewhat bearable.

Neither Ford nor the federal government foresaw the housing crisis that the influx of so many new workers inevitably caused—a crisis exacerbated by Detroit's strict (albeit unofficial) enforcement of residential segregation. Most blacks, therefore, had little choice but to settle in suburban shantytowns, where proper sanitation was rare, or crowd into the city's already overpopulated ghetto, known as Paradise Valley. According to a June 19, 1943, editorial in the *Detroit Free Press*, "The need for adequate housing was discussed earnestly last summer, but the parleying accomplished nothing. We came through the winter somehow and—well, here we are again with the same old problem. And it

is just as urgent, just as pressing, just as serious as it ever was, if not more so."

The next day, an unusually warm and muggy Sunday, thousands of workers brought their families to the amusement park on Belle Isle. During the afternoon, fights occasionally broke out among groups of black and white teenagers; then, later that night, as people jammed the bridge and ferry docks on their way home, the violence escalated. Fighting on the bridge spilled over onto the mainland, where a mob of five thousand whites attacked blacks coming off the bridge. From there, the rioting spread far into the city. The next morning, leaders of the black community urged Mayor Edward J. Jeffries to call in federal troops, but the mayor waited until a white mob invaded Paradise Valley late that evening before making the necessary arrangements. Six thousand soldiers eventually restored order, but it wasn't until Thursday, June 24, that the city returned to an approximation of normal. In the meantime, thirty-four people died, including twenty-five blacks, and nearly seven hundred were injured.

23 DEAD ON DETROIT RIOTING; FEDERAL TROOPS ENTER CITY ON THE ORDERS OF ROOSEVELT

Injured Reach 600; Theatres Closed, Liquor Sales Banned as U. S. Sends Armored Cars

DETROIT, June 21—Federal troops in full battle regalia, with jeeps, trucks and armored cars, moved into Detroit tonight to help city police, home guards and State troops restore order in the country's worst race riots since the East St. Louis (Ill.) disturbances in the first World War.

[After Federal troops arrived and President Roosevelt's proclamation calling for peace had been received, rioters dispersed and quiet was restored, according to The Associated Press. Mayor Edward J. Jeffries stated at midnight that the situation was much improved.]

The death toll at 10:20 P.M. had reached twenty-three, including twenty Negroes and three white persons. The injured, overflowing hospitals, numbered at least 600 and the number arrested and taken to jails and prisons exceeded that number.

With Detroit and its metropolitan-area population of about 2,500,000 persons—tens of thousands of them employed in Detroit's many war factories—under a state of emergency, Federal troops came from Fort Wayne, Ind., and Mt. Clemens, Mich., near Detroit.

They augmented two battalions of military police from Fort Custer and River Rouge Park as the shootings, beatings and pillaging continued unabated.

Late tonight local and State police pumped more than 1,000 rounds of ammunition and dozens of tear gas bombs into an apartment house to rout Negroes sniping from upper windows.

The siege had begun at 9:15 P.M., a few minutes after several Negroes were seen to run into the building with shotguns and revolvers.

The police first used the tear gas, which drove out most of the tenants on the lower floors, but the besieged group held out.

The police began to return fire with fire and the neighborhood rang with shots for more than two hours, the battle ending with the surrender of the Negroes. Two of them had been killed and a policeman, Lawrence Adams, was wounded seriously.

The Federal troops did not take part in the apartment house siege, but assisted other police in patrolling the riot areas, mostly in the downtown Negro section.

The Federal soldiers rode down Woodward Avenue, Detroit's major thoroughfare. They had orders to "clear the streets." With 1,110 assigned here, 1,200 others were held in reserve at Fort Wayne.

All persons, except those going to and from their jobs in war plants, already had been ordered to stay in their homes under the 10 P.M. to 6 A.M. curfew ordered by Gov. Harry F. Kelly when he declared that a state of emergency existed.

Brig. Gen. William E. Guthner, in charge of military police for the Army's Sixth Service Command, announced that he had been authorized by his headquarters at Chicago to "cooperate with State and city police."

General Guthner said the request for Federal troops was made by Governor Kelly after the mobs had ignored his emergency proclamation.

A Detroit mob stops a streetcar carrying blacks on June 22, 1943, two days after the race riots began.

It was learned that 2,000 additional troops would arrive in Detroit tomorrow.

Shootings, stabbings and hundreds of street fights throughout the metropolitan area had led Governor Kelly to declare the state of emergency.

Detroit's municipally owned Receiving Hospitals, whose chief surgeon, Dr. Austin Z. Howard, described the riots "as the worst calamity in Detroit's history," overflowed with injured. It was necessary to borrow blood plasma from the Red Cross to treat seriously injured victims.

Of the dead, twelve succumbed at Receiving Hospitals. Others died in ambulances en route to the hospitals, and several were found dead in the streets. One white man was found shot to death in the Negro section and a Negro was found dead in a theatre with six bullet wounds. The injured included a policeman who had been shot six times.

"We don't believe anything you niggers say."

One man's expeience of the Detroit riots

In the wake of the Detroit rioting, local civil rights activist Gloster B. Current, a notary public, collected numerous affidavits documenting the injustices to which the city's black population had been subjected. Nevertheless, the fact-finding commission appointed by Michigan governor Harry Kelly quickly determined that the blacks them- selves had been the cause of the violence.

State of Michigan
County of Wayne
No. 1353

After being duly sworn, the deponent, Alexander Robinson, who resides at 8585 Russell, states the following:

On Tuesday, June 22, about 2:30 P.M., I drove my wife to the Chevrolet plant to seek employment. The plant is located at Holbrook and St. Aubin Streets. As I started to the employment office the police came and said to me to "get over, you black bastard." I was lined against the wall of the building with a few other colored fellows and we were searched. After searching us they asked me what business I had out there. I told them that I was going to seek employment for my wife. The police then told us that we ought to be home under the bed. One officer said that he wished that he had us over in Germany, so he could line us up and shoot us down. At this point, I told the officer that my wife was waiting for me in my car. The officer said, "We don't believe anything you niggers say."

One officer put handcuffs on us. The other said, "Don't handcuff them, let them run so we can shoot them." One officer searched my car and found a butcher knife which I used for preparing and cutting vegetables from my Victory Garden.

The police patrol came and they loaded us in it. In a conversation made by the policemen they said that there have been colored people living here in Detroit for years and have never gotten into trouble because they minded their own business. He then said, "If you niggers would stay out of organizations you wouldn't get into trouble." One officer also said, "If you acted intelligent, we would treat you in an intelligent manner." At this point I asked if stand- ing minding my own business was acting intelligent. I told them that that was just what I was doing when the officers approached me. I told him as bad as I hate Hitler, I wouldn't call him the names that you called me.

I was driven to the Bethune police station. At the station one of the officers told me that he ought to take my butcher knife and run it through me. After being in the police station for a short time, I was taken, along with the other colored men, to the patrol wagon again. We had to sit in the patrol in the front of the station for about thirty minutes where we were put on exhibition. The police called pedestrians on the street as they passed. They said, "Look at the niggers we got." Some of these white persons suggested that they turn over the patrol wagon and set it afire. The officers said, "Go ahead, we'll turn our heads and pretend that we don't see it." One officer was asked by the other if he was going to get in the back of the patrol. He said, "No I wouldn't get in there because there might be bed bugs in there."

We were then transferred to the Schaefer Station where we had to sleep on the floor. From time to time, I made several requests to be allowed to communicate with my relatives. This was refused me.

I had $6.72 in my pocket in which I had to turn over to the desk at the station. This money was supposed to have been placed in my property bag. When I received my property bag I discovered that there was only $5.00 in it. I had three gas ration stamps given to me to attend to my Victory Garden. These tickets were taken from the glove compartment of my car.

I was placed on a bond of $500. I gave them $50.00 for my bond.

Signed: Alexander Robinson

Gloster B. Current,
Notary Public, Wayne County, Michigan.
My commission expires Sept. 28, 1943.

African-American workers at a Dodge plant in Detroit put together a new army truck engine in August 1942.

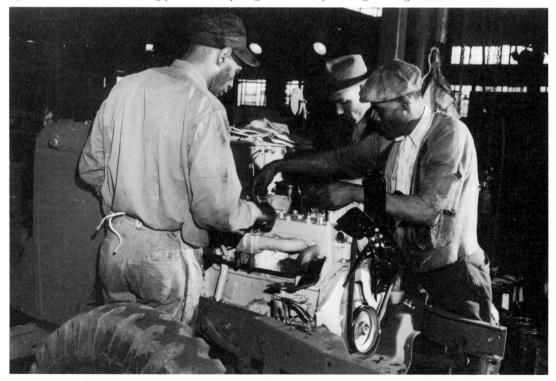

BISECTING THE AXIS

17.

The Invasion of Sicily

July 1943

The annual window for a cross-Channel invasion of France was narrow. Landings couldn't be made before the ground firmed up in the spring, nor could they take place so close to the fall that bad weather might stall a breakout from the beachheads. Therefore, once it became clear that the Tunisian campaign would likely drag on into spring, the Allied planners at the Casablanca Conference had to look

elsewhere if they were going to use their armies again in 1943. They finally chose to invade Sicily. The Combined Chiefs of Staff also decided at Casablanca that Eisenhower would be the supreme commander of the Sicilian operation, code-named Husky, with Harold Alexander serving as his principal deputy. Under Alexander would be Montgomery, commanding the British Eighth Army, and Patton, now a lieutenant general, in charge of the U.S. Seventh.

The invasion began on July 10, when Allied transports landed Montgomery's army in southeastern Sicily near the town of Syracuse. As the spearhead of the operation, the Eighth Army was ordered to drive north along the eastern coast to Messina, which guarded the narrow strait separating Sicily from the Italian mainland. Realizing that the loss of Messina would make it nearly impossible for him to evacuate his troops, Field Marshal Albert Kesselring, the German general commanding Sicily and southern Italy, concentrated his forces on the southern slopes of Mount Etna in order to block Montgomery's advance.

Meanwhile, Patton, whose army was set ashore on the island's southern coast to protect Montgomery's flank, met with little resistance. Sick of the war, the predominantly Italian defenders confronted by the Seventh Army surrendered in large numbers; and, chafing in his subordinate role, Patton soon asked Alexander for permission to take Palermo in the north. Reluctantly, Alexander agreed on July 18, and four days later Patton entered the town virtually unopposed. From there, the campaign became a race to Messina, with elements of the Seventh Army pushing rapidly ahead along Sicily's northern coast. Yet this advance, too, slowed upon encountering Kesselring's well-organized, German-manned defenses.

Another week passed before Hitler finally agreed to permit a withdrawal. While Kesselring's rear guard executed a superb delaying action, the rest of his army began crossing the Strait of Messina on August 11. By the time Patton reached the town on August 17, two hours ahead of his rival Montgomery, the Germans had already left.

Pfc. Harvey White gives a blood plasma transfusion to an American soldier wounded by shrapnel in Sicily in July 1943.

ALLIED TROOPS START INVASION OF SICILY; NAVAL ESCORTS BOMBARD SHORE DEFENSES; LANDINGS PRECEDED BY SEVERE AIR ATTACK

Several Landings; American, British and Canadian Troops Carry Out the Attack

By DREW MIDDLETON

ALLIED HEADQUARTERS IN NORTH AFRICA, Saturday, July 10—Allied infantry landed at a number of places on the rocky Sicilian coast under a canopy of naval gunfire early this morning as the long-awaited invasion began.

Gen. Dwight D. Eisenhower, Allied Commander in Chief, speaking to the people of metropolitan France, called the attack "the first page in the liberation of the European Continent," and promised "there will be others."

Allied headquarters announced the invasion in the following communiqué:

Allied forces under command of General Eisenhower began landing operations on Sicily early this morning.

The landings were preceded by Allied air attack.

Allied naval forces escorted the assault forces and bombarded the coast defenses during the assault.

[The Algiers radio, in an English-language broadcast to North America at 12:40 A.M. today, said that Allied forces had landed on the rocky western tip of Sicily, 260 miles from Rome. The broadcast was recorded by United States Government monitors.

[The broadcast said the landings were made in good weather, with German and Italian air forces providing "fierce" opposition. In anticipation of the assault, the island's Italian-German defenders blew up harbor installations, the broadcast said.]

A heavy attack was carried out by planes of the Northwest African Air Force and the Middle East Air Command for nearly two weeks, reaching blitz proportions in the last week, when a round-the-clock assault blasted Axis air bases and communication centers with hundreds of tons of bombs. This came to a furious climax yesterday and last night.

The Allied naval force that escorted the invading troops pounded the formidable defenses of Sicily with salvos of shells while infantrymen, their bayonets twinkling in the starlight, raced ashore from landing crafts. Many tanks were landed.

Sicily, largest island in the Mediterranean, has a population of just under 4,000,000 persons and has been strongly fortified, especially along the southern coast, since 1939. The coasts are heavily mined and beaches are covered by batteries of artillery that fire from hills.

General Eisenhower's announcement to the French people, which was sent by radio, asked them to remain calm and not to expose themselves to reprisals through "present rash actions."

Many of the troops involved in the invasion of Sicily are veterans of the Tunisian campaign.

Military men here expect very heavy fighting. The Germans are known to have reinforced the island comparatively recently, and despite the prolonged aerial bombardment strong fortifications remain to be overcome.

Maj. Gen. Geoffrey Keyes (left) and Lt. Gen. George S. Patton Jr. study a map of Sicily in the royal palace at Salerno on August 9, 1943.

Many military objectives were hit by American and British bombers during the two weeks' attack on the island. The main weight of the bombing at night was directed against the airfields, particularly at the one at Gerbini, which was attacked day and night.

News of the landing was given out at a press conference at Allied Force Headquarters. The aerial bombardment was most intense in the closing stages of the operation and was coordinated with a naval attack on the outer defenses of the island. This continued while Allied fleets steamed to the shores. Thousands of explosives were poured on the pillboxes that form the island's first line of defense.

"If you could see how they toil...."

Two of Ernie Pyle's dispatches from Sicily

Pulitzer Prize–winning correspondent Ernie Pyle, whose wartime reports were syndicated to three hundred newspapers in the United States, was known as "the GI's friend." Beginning with the landings in North Africa, he covered the life of the average American infantryman from Tunisia to Sicily to Italy to France. Then, as the war in Europe wound down, he transferred to the Pacific theater, where he was killed by a sniper's bullet on the island of Ie Shima, near Okinawa, in April 1945. These are two of his many dispatches from the Sicilian campaign.

The Dying Man Was Left Utterly Alone

SOMEWHERE IN SICILY—(by wireless)—It was flabbergasting to lie among a tentful of wounded soldiers recently and hear them cuss and beg to be sent right back into the fight.

Of course not all of them do. It depends on the severity of their wounds, and on their individual personalities, just as it would in peacetime. But I will say that at least a third of the moderately wounded men ask if they can't be returned to duty immediately.

When I took sick I was with the 45th Division, made up largely of men from Oklahoma and West Texas. You don't realize how different certain parts of our country are from others until you see their men set off in a frame, as it were, in some strange faraway place like this.

The men of Oklahoma are drawling and soft-spoken. They are not smart-alecks. Something of the purity of the soil seems to be in them. Even their cussing is simpler and more profound than the torrential obscenities of Eastern city men. An Oklahoman of the plains is straight and direct. He is slow to criticize and hard to anger, but once he is convinced of the wrong of something, brother, watch out.

These wounded men of Oklahoma have got madder about the war than anybody I have seen on this side of the ocean. They weren't so mad before they got into action, but now to them the Germans across the hill are all "sonsabitches."

And these quiet men of the 45th, the newest division over here, have already fought so well they have drawn the high praise of the commanding general of the corps of which the division is a part.

It was these men from the farms, ranches and small towns of Oklahoma who poured through my tent with their wounds. I lay there and listened for what each one would say first.

One fellow, seeing a friend, called out, "I think I'm gonna make her." Meaning he was going to pull through.

Another said, "Have they got beds in the hospital? Lord how I want to go to bed."

Another said, "I'm hungry, but I can't eat anything. I keep getting sick at my stomach."

Another said, as he winced from their probing for a deeply buried piece of shrapnel in his leg, "Go ahead, you're the doc. I can stand it."

Another said, "I'll have to write the old lady tonight and tell her she missed out on that $10,000 again."

Another, who was put down beside me, said, "Hi, Pop, how you getting along? I call you Pop because you're gray-headed. You don't mind, do you?"

I told him I didn't care what he called me. He was friendly, but you could tell from his forward attitude that he was not from Oklahoma. When I asked him, it turned out he was from New Jersey.

One big blond Oklahoman had slight flesh wounds in the face and the back of his neck. He had a patch on his upper lip which prevented his moving it, and made him talk in a grave, straight-faced manner that was comical. I've never seen anybody so mad in my life. He went from one doctor to another trying to get somebody to sign his card returning him to duty.

The doctors explained patiently that if he returned to the front his wounds would get infected and he would be a burden on his company instead of a help. They tried to entice him by telling him there would be nurses back in the hospital. But he said, "To hell with the nurses, I want to get back to fightin'."

Dying men were brought into our tent, men whose death rattle silenced the conversation and made all the rest of us grave.

When a man was almost gone the surgeons would put a piece of gauze over his face. He could breathe through it but we couldn't see his face well.

Twice within five minutes chaplains came running. One of these occasions haunted me for hours.

The man was still semi-conscious. The chaplain knelt down beside him and two ward boys squatted alongside. The chaplain said:

"John, I'm going to say a prayer for you."

Somehow this stark announcement hit me like a hammer. He didn't say, "I'm going to pray for you to get well," he just said he was going to say a prayer, and it was obvious he meant the final prayer. It was as though he had said, "Brother, you may not know it, but your goose is cooked."

He said a short prayer, and the weak, gasping man tried in vain to repeat the words after him. When he had finished the chaplain said, "John, you're doing fine, you're doing fine." Then he rose and dashed off on other business, and the ward boys went about their duties.

The dying man was left utterly alone, just lying there on his litter on the ground, lying in an aisle, because the tent was full. Of course it couldn't be otherwise, but the awful aloneness of that man as he went through the last few minutes of his life was what tormented me. I felt like going over and at least holding his hand while he died, but it would have been out of order and I didn't do it. I wish now I had.

A Hell of a Job

SOMEWHERE IN SICILY—(by wireless)—When the 45th Division went into reserve along the north coast of Sicily after several weeks of hard fighting, I moved on with the Third Division which took up the ax and drove the enemy on to Messina.

I am still doing engineers and it was on my very first day with the Third that we hit the most difficult and spectacular engineering job of the Sicilian campaign.

You've doubtless noticed Point Calava on your maps. It is a great stub of rock that sticks out into the sea, forming a high ridge running back into the interior. The coast highway is tunneled through this big rock, and on either side of the tunnel the road sticks out of the sheer rock wall like a shelf.

Our engineers figured the Germans would blow the tunnel entrance to seal it up. But they didn't. They had an even better idea. They picked out a spot about 50 feet beyond the tunnel mouth and blew a hole 150 feet long in the road shelf. They blew it so deeply and thoroughly that if you dropped a rock into it the rock would never stop rolling until it bounced into the sea a couple of hundred feet below.

We were beautifully bottlenecked. You couldn't by-pass around the rock, for it dropped sheer into the sea. You couldn't by-pass up over the mountain, for it would take weeks. You couldn't fill the hole, for it would keep sliding off into the water.

All you could do was bridge it, and that was a hell of a job. But bridge it they did, and in only 24 hours.

When the first engineer officers went up to inspect the tunnel, I went with them. We had to leave the jeep at a blown bridge and walk the last four miles uphill. We went with an infantry battalion that was following the retreating Germans.

When we got there we found the tunnel floor mined. But each spot where they'd dug into the hard rock floor left its telltale mark, so it was no job for the engineers to uncover and unscrew the detonators of scores of mines. Then we went on through to the vast hole beyond and the engineering officers began making their calculations.

As we did so, the regiment of infantry crawled across the chasm, one man at a time. You could just barely make it on foot by holding on to the rock juttings and practically crawling.

Another regiment went up over the ridge and took out after the evacuating enemy with only what weapons and provisions they could carry on their backs. Before another 24 hours, they'd be 20 miles ahead of us and in contact with the enemy, so getting this hole bridged and supplies and supporting guns to them was indeed a matter of life and death.

It was around 2 P.M. when we got there and in two hours the little platform of highway at the crater mouth resembled a littered street in front of a burning building. Air hoses covered the ground, serpentined over each other. Three big air compressors were parked side by side, their engines cutting off and on in that erratically deliberate manner of air compressors, and jack hammers clattered their nerve-shattering din.

Bulldozers came to clear off the stone-blocked highway at the crater edge. Trucks, with long trailers bearing railroad irons and huge timbers, came and unloaded. Steel cable was brought up. And kegs of spikes and all kinds of crowbars and sledges.

The thousands of vehicles of the division were halted some 10 miles back in order to keep the highway clear for the engineers. One platoon of men worked at a time in the hole. There was no use of throwing in the whole company, for there was room for only so many.

At suppertime, hot rations were brought up by truck. The Third Division engineers go on K ration at noon but morning and evening they get hot food up to them, regardless of the job.

If you could see how they toil, you would know how important this hot food is. By dusk the work was in full swing and half the men were stripped to the waist.

The night air of the Mediterranean was tropical. The moon came out at twilight and extended our light for a little while. The moon was new and pale, and transient high-flying night clouds brushed it and scattered shadows down on us.

Then its frail light went out, and the blinding nightlong darkness settled over the insidious abyss. But the work never slowed nor halted, throughout the night.

18.

The Overthrow of Mussolini

July 1943

During the early months of 1943, the Italian political situation deteriorated rapidly. New Allied air attacks on major Italian cities made the bad news from North Africa seem even worse. Taken together, these developments demoralized the populace and persuaded a number of influential political and military leaders that a change in government was necessary. The two central figures in this months-long conspiracy were King Victor Emmanuel III, who had previously acquiesced in Mussolini's 1925 seizure of power, and Marshal Pietro Badoglio, an aging lukewarm Fascist who had retired as chief of the Italian general staff in December 1940.

In mid-July, the poor performance of Italian troops opposing the Allied invasion of Sicily finally tipped the scales against the Duce. On the evening of July 24, the Fascist Grand Council met to oust Mussolini and return the king to power. The next day, when Mussolini visited the king to inform him of the council's action, Victor Emmanuel had the dictator arrested and imprisoned. Later that day, the king asked Badoglio to form a new, non-Fascist government.

Publicly, Badoglio assured the Germans that he intended to remain loyal to the Axis; secretly, however, he opened armistice negotiations with the British and the Americans. Although just six months had passed since their Casablanca proclamation demanding unconditional surrender, Roosevelt and Churchill immediately began to temporize, much to Stalin's displeasure. "To date," Stalin berated Roosevelt, "it has been like this: the U.S.A. and Britain reach agreement between themselves while the U.S.S.R. is informed of the agreement between the two Powers as a third party looking passively on. I must say that this situation cannot be tolerated any longer."

Nevertheless, on September 3, after weeks of frustrating foot-dragging by Badoglio, a deal was reached—albeit one far short of unconditional surrender. The Italians were to turn over their navy, merchant marine, and air force to the Allies, in exchange for which Victor Emmanuel could retain power as Italy's constitutional monarch and his nation would become a co-belligerent in the war against Germany. Yet this agreement was never implemented. Hitler, never deluded by the double-dealing Badoglio, had used the intervening weeks to send sixteen more German divisions into Italy, thereby transforming the country from an ostensible ally into an occupied territory. Soon, all the king and his general could do was flee Rome and seek safety with the Allies.

THE NEW YORK TIMES, MONDAY, JULY 26, 1943

MUSSOLINI OUSTED WITH FASCIST CABINET; BADOGLIO, HIS FOE, MADE PREMIER BY KING; SHIFT BELIEVED FIRST STEP TOWARD PEACE

Arrests Reported; Berne Hears the Fascist Leaders Are Being Held in Homes

By DANIEL T. BRIGHAM

BERNE, Switzerland, July 25—King Victor Emmanuel announced to Italy tonight that he had accepted the "resignations" of Premier Benito Mussolini and his entire Cabinet. He ordered Marshal Pietro Badoglio to form a military government "to continue the conduct of the war."

The announcement was made in a proclamation that was broadcast to the people of Italy from Rome at 11 P.M. Rome time. The Rome radio then signed off for twenty minutes, resuming its broadcast at 11:20 to carry a proclamation by Marshal Badoglio. Before giving this, however, the announcer said:

"With the fall of Mussolini and his band, Italy has taken the first step toward peace. Finished is the shame of fascism! Long live peace! Long live the King!"

Marshal Badoglio's proclamation was then read. It appealed to the nation for "calm" in this hour of trial, saying:

"Italians! On the demand of His Majesty the King-Emperor, I have assumed the military government of the country with full powers. The war will continue. Italy, bruised, her provinces invaded, and her cities ruined, will retain her faith in her given word, jealous of her ancient traditions.

"We must tighten our ranks behind the King-Emperor, the living image of the country, who stands as an example for all today. The task I have been charged with is clear and precise. It will be executed scrupulously, and whoever believes he can interrupt the normal progress of events or whoever seeks to disturb internal order will be struck down without mercy.

"Long live Italy! Long live the King! Pietro Badoglio."

For the first time in twenty-one years the Italian radio signed off a nation-wide program by playing only the royal march. "Giovinezza," the fascist anthem, like fascism, is dead.

[Field Marshal General Albert Kesselring, German Commander in Chief in Italy, and Hans-Georg Viktor von Mackensen, the German Ambassador, negotiated with Marshal Badoglio in Rome last night, according to a Rome radio bulletin picked up in Stockholm, Sweden, by Reuter.]

Following the proclamation broadcast demonstrations broke out in many parts of the country as Italians went to the streets to celebrate the end of fascism. A Milan report, received here by telephone just before telephone communications were cut at 11 o'clock, told of bloodshed there when German antiaircraft units had apparently fired on a mob. No further details were given.

With half of the Italian population fleeing in an evacuation greater than that in France and those still at home "looking for Blackshirts," the situation inside Italy is developing rapidly. Frontier reports tell of a state of "latent revolution," leaving the country still looking for a Government with which to sue for peace. Marshal Enrico Caviglia may be the spokesman, but Marshal Badoglio will be the leader—and the King will remain as long as he can.

As troubles spread in Rome, whose telephones were cut off more than an hour before the rest of Italy, fears were expressed for the safety of Signor Mussolini, Carlo Scorza, the Fascist party secretary, and the entire Cabinet, which was being detained under house arrest. They were therefore transferred to a place outside the capital, the approaches to which are being guarded by the army.

The first details received here of the origin of the Cabinet crisis—heavily censored, for the movement was still in full swing—say it began in this morning's special Cabinet session of the key Defense Ministries.

Premier Mussolini outlined "propositions" Adolf Hitler had made for the "salvation of the new European order" during their last meeting. They called for such great Italian sacrifices that the Undersecretaries of War, Air and Navy refused to accept the responsibility for their execution without consultation with the full Cabinet.

When the Cabinet met the debate was lively until it was decided to submit the entire problem to the King and his councilors, who in the last analysis would be alone responsible to the nation.

The principal "proposition" was said to be the immediate withdrawal of all possible manpower and matériel from the Sicilian front, accepting enormous losses during that operation as inevitable. The Catania front, defended by the Hermann Goering Division, was to be taken over by "sufficient Italian rear guard" to enable its withdrawal first.

Italian forces would then be called upon to fight a "retiring" rear-guard operation up the entire length of the Italian mainland from Naples, Calabria and Puglia to a line running approximately east-west through the southern limits of Tuscany, which would leave the Axis nations a

Marshal Pietro Badoglio (left) and members of his staff in a photograph taken from a 1943 Italian newsreel.

"line of elastic defense while final preparations were being completed in the Apennines."

This operation would be entirely Italian, aided only by German matériel. It was suggested the operation should be exclusively in the hands of the Italian military, while the slightly more trained Blackshirt militia formations would be reserved for "advanced line defense" in front of the Apennine positions.

Rome would be abandoned, while such matériel as could not be moved northward would be destroyed, mainly ammunition and explosives, several very big shipments of which are believed to have just arrived for the Germans.

As presented to the King, the alternative to defeat left little of his already shriveled empire and meant the abandonment of more than half of his country. His refusal was emphatic: the nation stood or fell, but it did one or the other together "despite the lacerations the nation has suffered" at the hands of the Fascist party.

The King then "accepted" the resignations of the Fascist government.

"It is simply shocking."

Mussolini's ouster from the German point of view

These excerpts from the personal diary of German propaganda minister Joseph Goebbels describe the initial Nazi reaction to the news that Hitler's junior partner Mussolini had been deposed. At first, Goebbels had little to work with. Then, in mid-September, SS commandos led by Capt. Otto Skorzeny carried out one of the most daring missions of the war. An intercepted radio transmission led Skorzeny, who had been searching for Mussolini for weeks, to the Albergo Rifugio, a remote mountaintop ski resort located high up in the Abruzzis. Normally, the hotel was reached only by funicular railway; on September 12, however, Skorzeny used gliders to crash-land his ninety-man assault force within sight of the resort. Overcoming the stunned guards without a fight, the Germans quickly recovered the imprisoned Duce and evacuated him to the Führer's headquarters at Rastenburg in East Prussia. Subsequently, Hitler returned his friend to Italy as head of a puppet regime based in Salò.

July 26, 1943

When I reached my home I was immediately called by telephone from the Fuehrer's GHQ. The news from there sounds almost unbelievable. It is to the effect that the Duce has resigned, and that Badoglio has taken over in Italy in his place. The whole situation, I was informed, was still very obscure; such news as we received had come over the radio and was given out by Reuter. At GHQ nobody can figure out just what has really happened. The Fuehrer wants me to proceed immediately to his headquarters. He wishes there to evaluate the situation with his closest collaborators....

July 27, 1943

I arrived at the Templehof airdrome early. Dr. Dietrich flew with me to GHQ. He, too, was tremendously distressed about events in Italy. He developed a series of theories that seemed somewhat far-fetched and unconvincing. As long as we have no more exact information about what actually happened in Rome than what has come through thus far, we can venture no opinion. At the moment we don't even know what the revolution was all about. In any case, following my instinct and my sound common sense, I believe we may assume that the Roman camarilla has the intention of getting out of the war in some elegant manner.

Before I could speak to the Fuehrer I had a talk at GHQ with Himmler and Bormann. They don't believe Mussolini resigned voluntarily. I, too, regard it as out of the question. I believe the crisis developed in the following manner: As a curtain raiser the radical Fascists of the type of Farinacci were sent forward to criticize the Duce. That started things rolling. Badoglio and his henchmen used this occasion to trip up Mussolini. Presumably he was then called to the Quirinal, where he was arrested *stante pede* and compelled to resign. It is simply shocking to think that in this manner a revolutionary movement that has been in power for twenty-one years could be liquidated.

With German officers in the background, Mussolini (left), Göring (center), and Hitler attend a military briefing in August 1941.

But this isn't the end yet. I believe there are still some possibilities left for directing things into a different channel. Both Himmler and Bormann indulge in the most varied theories. But these are of no real value, as they are based upon suppositions and not on facts. I look at the situation somewhat more realistically. According to the reports thus far available, I believe I can assume that the Duce actually had lost most of his authority with the Italian people. It is always true that as soon as a dictator has fallen, the man in the street is heard from. I suppose, therefore, we won't have to wait long before this happens in Italy.

At ten o'clock, together with Goering, I had my first talk with the Fuehrer. The Fuehrer impressed us with his quiet self-assurance and his sovereign superiority. Although the events in Italy made a deep impression upon him, they in nowise succeeded in throwing him off his equilibrium. On the contrary, his brain was already at work feverishly formulating and preparing new decisions. Half an hour later Ribbentrop, who had come by plane from Fuschl, joined in this decisive discussion. He had just come through an attack of pneumonia and was still in a very weakened condition.

19.

Tokyo Rose
November 1943

In November 1943, Iva Toguri began appearing regularly on *Zero Hour,* a news-and-music program that aired each night on Radio Tokyo. Like all of the other female announcers on *Zero Hour,* the twenty-seven-year-old Toguri was a native speaker of English, having been born and raised in the United States. A Nisei—that is, an American-born person of Japanese descent—she had grown up in Los

Angeles, where she received a bachelor's degree in zoology from the University of California at Los Angeles in 1941. Later that year, she sailed to Japan to care for an ailing aunt and was stranded there when the war came. Initially considered an enemy alien by the Japanese authorities, she was put to work as a typist for Radio Tokyo before being pressured, as she later claimed, into becoming one of the station's voluptuous, English-speaking on-air personalities. Although they usually referred to themselves as Orphan Anne or Orphan Annie, these women were collectively known to American servicemen as Tokyo Rose.

After the war, Toguri was arrested by U.S. occupation authorities and held for eleven months as a security risk. In August 1946, she was freed when investigators failed to turn up

any evidence to support charges of treason, but a subsequent public outcry, stoked by columnist Walter Winchell, revived her case and resulted in her extradition to the United States. Her trial, which began in July 1949, ended in September with a guilty verdict after the judge refused to accept the jurors' statement that they were deadlocked. Only the seventh American ever to be convicted of treason, Toguri was sentenced to ten years in prison and fined ten thousand dollars. Later, however, information came to light suggesting that she had indeed been coerced and that she had often risked her own safety to aid three prisoners of war assigned to Radio Tokyo. Persuaded that Toguri had been wronged, Pres. Gerald Ford pardoned her shortly before leaving office in January 1977.

American reporters interview Iva Toguri, more popularly known as Tokyo Rose, in September 1945.

'TOKYO ROSE' A HIT WITH U. S. SOLDIERS

Forces in Pacific, Immune to Propaganda, Enjoy Our Music on Japanese Radio

By GEORGE F. HORNE

ESPIRITU SANTO ATOLL, March 20 (Delayed)—If a radio popularity poll could be taken out here among American fighting forces a surprisingly large number of votes would go to "Tokyo Rose" and other of the programs beamed from the Land of the Rising Sun to the advancing American bases in the south and southwest Pacific.

Tokyo programs might even be voted first place, but unfortunately the popularity rating has little if any bearing on our morale, and as propaganda they are efficient only in the sense of being good entertainment. The consensus is that American fighting men are pretty impervious to propaganda, and that is probably a good thing, too, for otherwise they might be a victim of our own home brand of propaganda, some of which, according to officers stationed here, is pretty bad and might work in reverse.

But Tokyo is entertaining. Tokyo gives the listeners comedy and good dance music. The comedy comes when the "commercial" is plugged. Tojo, of course, is the sponsor, and the announcer, almost always speaking smooth English, puts his product over very nicely. The boys listen but they do not buy despite the fact that the oil is applied pretty lightly and sometimes there will be thirty minutes of first class American dance music without a single interruption for the commercial plug. The men say they get the best and the most music from the five Tokyo programs they hear regularly.

It will go something like this:

"Hello, our American friends. Don't you wish you were back home again, back with your wives, sweethearts, children? It's too bad you are out here, away from all that means so much to you and to enter a war in which you are not interested or concerned."

The Tokyo radio, it turns out, thinks America is a wonderful place and it understands how the boys must be longing for it. The Tokyo radio is extremely sympathetic and tries to ease the heart pain by sending over some soothing music. Then the music comes from the best American and English name bands.

There are not many programs back home that will give you thirty minutes of entertainment without breaking in every few minutes to say life cannot be complete, culturally speaking, without daily applications of heavenly rose water eyewash. That is why the programs that reach the boys down here from "Uncle Sugar," which is their way of saying the United States of America, could be a lot better and so could the movies. At least there could be a lot more of the good ones, which of course we have.

They do not want to hear a single program about how evil and dumb the enemy is or a single "back the attack" program. They are backing it already. They would like to hear more dance bands, light love stories, light musical comedies. In film form they would like newsreels, not of war but shots showing familiar streets and scenes at home, and animated cartoons and films showing the best football and baseball games of the year. They will probably continue to listen to Tokyo Rose, but no one at home need worry about that.

"Cheerio once again to all my favorite family of boneheads."

A government transcript of *Zero Hour*

This excerpt from the June 1945 Federal Communications report *Japanese Broadcasts to American Servicemen* was introduced at Toguri's trial as Exhibit XVI.

This program has provoked rumors and discussion among American servicemen and the general public because of its general identification with "Tokyo Rose." Liberal quotes will be given here from a typical program (June 7) in an attempt to convey some idea of its highly standardized presentation. The show is opened by a male announcer:

> We give you once again a 60 minute program of music as you like it, news from two fronts, a little bit of this and that, a thought for the day. (There follows music of "Strike Up The Band." Then the announcer continues) calling on the 19 and 25 meter bands, so set your dials for the Zero Hour and please stand by. (Music) The Zero Hour is on the air, and first we turn you over to the newsroom from where the Zero Hour editor brings you news from the fighting fronts.
>
> An unexpected…blackout on the American ground operations on Okinawa has stirred up quite a lot of vain speculation among American news agencies. One report said something big was in the wind…The same sort of news blackout was enforced prior to the Normandy landing, which incidentally celebrated its first anniversary yesterday, and also at the time of Marshal Rundstedt's sensational breakthrough…In the last report by Mr. Nimitz he was glad to announce that adverse weather prevented air activity on Monday and that's just about the only thing that can hamper Japanese operations. For the past few weeks, Japanese forces have been concentrating almost solely on air ramming attacks against American shipping, drawing tighter and tighter the noose around the vulnerable communication bottleneck.

There follows discussion of Japanese achievements in sinking American warships, and then the almost invariable presentation of casualty lists, in this case a barb against Anglo-American harmony:

> Supreme headquarters said that combined British and Canadian casualties from D-Day to VE-Day were 184,512, while United States casualties for the 337 days of fighting since the invasion were 514,534, or about three times the combined figure of the British and Canadian casualties. Broken down it means that the Allies have lost 1572 soldiers killed, wounded, or missing every day to the war against Germany. Concluding the gory details, Admiral Nimitz revealed today that 70 British officers and men of the British Pacific Fleet have been killed as a result of operations against the Japanese in the Ryukus.
>
> And there you have it men, fighting news for fighting men. This is the Zero Hour calling in the Pacific on the 19 and 25 meter bands, a 60 minute program of music, sweet or hot, which ever way you like it. News and what-not comes to you nightly through the facilities of the

Marines on Guadalcanal listen to a radio set left behind by the Japanese.

Zero Hour Incorporated. And now to move along, here's a bit of that pause that refreshes. It's just a little musical interlude to help a few more minutes fly by easily. Hear a delightful little serenade which is aptly entitled 'For Your Delight.' (Music)

Next comes a short skit by two radio comedians and then the popular girl announcer:

And now, gentlemen, the Zero Hour brings you Orphan Anne and her languideers. (Music, followed by a woman's voice): Cheerio once again to all my favorite family of boneheads, the fighting G.I. in the blue Pacific. This is Orphan Anne at this end of the situation hanging her shingle out for a few minutes. What for? To do business, of course…lend an ear for listening to fighting G.I.'s choice for favorite vocalist singing a well known melody, 'Two Hearts that Pass in the Night.' (Music) A trained voice is hard to beat. What say you boneheads? Oh, is that so? Well, anyway that doesn't prevent request number two from going into action. A sentimental G.I. somewhere in the Pacific asked for a number with the label, 'Apple Blossoms and Chapel Bells.' Lean back and let it penetrate. (Music, and then Orphan Anne announced Deanna Durbin in 'My Own.' This was followed by a Bob Hammond number.) I'll bet there isn't a single G.I. in the whole Pacific who can't label this one. (Music) 'Let the Rest of the World Go By'—and a most brilliant idea. Let's cooperate, boneheads…Well, the clock on the wall indicates time to quit. More tomorrow night but in the meantime this is Orphan Anne reminding you G.I.'s always to be good. (Music) Goodbye, now.

20.

The Cairo Conference
November 1943

In early 1942, President Roosevelt sent Lt. Gen. Joseph W. Stilwell to Chungking, the current capital of Chiang Kai-shek's Nationalist Chinese regime. A profane, ornery man, Vinegar Joe was chosen to command all U.S. forces in the China-Burma-India theater because of his seven years' experience as military attaché to the U.S. embassy in China and his fluency with the language. Stilwell's job was to

transform the throng that passed itself off as Chiang's army into a fighting force that could become a major factor in the war. As Stilwell learned, however, Chiang had no intention of fighting the Japanese. That struggle he would leave to the Americans. Instead, he planned to wait out the war, stockpile his Lend-Lease aid, and prepare for the coming showdown with Mao Tse-tung's Communists. Stilwell eventually became so contemptuous of the corrupt, evasive premier that he began referring to the diminutive, head-shaven Chiang as the Peanut.

In late November 1943, just prior to the Big Three summit at Teheran, Roosevelt and Churchill met with Chiang at Cairo. For nearly two years, Roosevelt had been receiving Stilwell's uncomplimentary reports about Chiang, and upon meeting him in person the president came to many of the same conclusions: Chiang was undoubtedly indecisive, scheming, and weak. Yet Roosevelt foresaw China's emergence as a major world power after the war and wanted to channel its development. To encourage Chi-

ang, Roosevelt promised him more Lend-Lease aid, greater support for the U.S. Fourteenth Air Force operating out of southeastern China, and a land offensive to reopen the Burma Road, the major overland supply route to China overrun by the Japanese in April 1942.

Roosevelt was willing to make these generous offers because he believed that a strong postwar China would act as a counter not only to a resurgent Japan but also to Soviet ambitions in the area. Churchill, on the other hand, found this analysis farcical. Like France and the Netherlands, Great Britain intended to recover the Asian colonies it had lost to Japan at the start of the war and therefore saw no purpose in strengthening China. The Americans, however, had already committed to independence for the Philippines, and Roosevelt wanted the British to follow suit in Hong Kong, Burma, Malaya, and India. As it turned out, neither man was prescient—and, despite all of Roosevelt's and Stilwell's efforts, China never became militarily relevant in the war against Japan.

CHIANG'S GAINS AT CAIRO LEAVE SOME QUESTIONS

China's Full Partnership Sealed, but a Few Vexing Problems Remain

By C. L. SULZBERGER

CAIRO, Egypt, Dec. 4—Generalissimo Chiang Kai-shek can now rest assured that China's arch-enemy, Japan, will be booted back into the late nineteenth century as far as its potential menace to Asia's peace is concerned, and that not only can China count on the recovery of all the territory she has lost, but when the accounts of this war are finally settled the Asiatic member of the United Nations should certainly find herself stronger, both actually and potentially, than at any time in her history, at least since the Middle Ages.

Moreover, vis-a-vis his Great Power Allies, America and Britain, the Generalissimo can be equally positive that at long last he is a full-fledged member of that small group of powers holding preferred stock in the United Nations enterprise after a considerable period during which it was never quite certain whether he would be admitted to such equality.

The difficulty, as far as Chiang is concerned, is that there is little question that he will at last receive dividends when the day of distribution arrives. He knows what he will be getting, but he also knows it will be a long time before, with assistance of his newly met friends, President Roosevelt and Prime Minister Churchill, he can march up the road at the end of the rainbow and collect his pot of gold.

This, in rough paraphrase, represents the results of the historic North African conference at which not only did the three chieftains of the Asiatic war personally get together for the first time with the additional expert benefit of their general staffs for five days' lengthy conversations, but in which military decisions were made to facilitate somewhat the methods by which Japan could ultimately be crushed and the crystallized status that shattered island empire will have.

The Cairo communiqué in itself represented a Pacific charter even more explicit in those terms it mentioned than the document resulting from the famous Roosevelt-Churchill meeting in mid-ocean. Pared to its volcanic core, deprived of its fabulously wealthy Manchurian industrial empire and Chinese ports, ridden of its brief hold on Malaya and countless Pacific islands bringing it the borders of the Australian continent, whether it is willing to admit it or not, the Tokyo expansionist scheme is clearly fore-doomed to failure in the face of the United Allied determination to squash it.

China obviously will be the greatest to benefit by such operations—no matter how long they take. She not only will receive back incalculably valuable pieces of land and recover vast prestige as the greatest independent power in the Orient, but, perhaps even more important, see the absolute demise for a long time to come of the most terrible enemy of all the Oriental nations.

Such developments can only be received with greatest pleasure by the Generalissimo and his brilliant wife. However, there are two factors that tend certainly to diminish to some degree their enthusiasm therein: First, as far as those territories to be handed over to China go, they have been officially demanded all along by the Chung-king Government and many a Chinese has assumed that this will be the obvious, inevitable end of the conflict; second, there is a distinctly querulous attitude on the part of the

Generalissimo and Madame Chiang Kai-shek tour the Sphinx and the pyramids during a break in the Cairo Conference.

Chinese concerning the length of time it will take to destroy the Japanese menace and foster the rebirth of a new China from its ashes.

From the viewpoint of discussion, the latter is certainly the most important point. China came to this conference for induction as a full member of the Great Power Club for the first time fully cognizant of her position at the bottom of the Allied production priority list and acutely aware that the Anglo-American program, closely collaborating with Soviet ideas, was determined to crush Germany for good and all before really putting a shoulder to the Asiatic war.

While this must obviously disappoint the Generalissimo, who can well point out that he was at war two full years before the rest of his Allies were drawn in, nevertheless there is some compensation for any such sorrow. Clearly, the Allies must have pointed out to him that the production of Western factories is increasing

and that, even though his position on the priority list has not moved up, nevertheless, his share of the production will be steadily amplified.

One of the most serious problems therein is obviously the means of access to isolated China, to which the only lines of communication at present functioning, in the order of their importance, are "over-the-hump" airways from India, the tedious Sinkiang trail from Russia, which for lack of a better name is called a road, and an almost useless explorers' track through Tibet.

Chiang can be assured that the airways will be expanded, that the Ledo Road at present under construction from Assam through Myitkina will be speeded up to carry transport equipment as well as fuel into China, that the oft-delayed Burma campaign will finally be started before the next monsoon season, that some of the maze of complications surrounding the mixed-up command areas of the Asiatic sphere will be somewhat straightened out and that Allied aerial and naval power will be gradually and increasingly concentrated in the Eastern war zone.

But many question marks remain and it would seem safe to predict that other meetings between these statesmen, who so much believe in frank face-to-face talks, will be needed before the world can again settle down to those luxurious days of peace to which it so much looks forward.

The Generalissimo, even should it discontent him that his Allies have decided, after careful judgment of the situation, that the easiest way to win the war is to defeat Germany first, then swing the weight of martial power rapidly eastward, can ultimately be absolutely confident.

However, there are many things that he presumably does not yet know. No one can predict with accuracy how easy it will be to induce the British population to carry on the Asiatic war against Japan after the defeat of Nazi Germany.

Furthermore, it would be a foolish person who would state with any certainty whether the Soviet Union, after finally crushing the Wehrmacht, largely by its own efforts, will be willing to risk further bloodshed on its distant eastern borders. Chiang must realize that the defeat of Japan largely rests on Pacific-minded America and his own presently weak, ill-equipped troops.

Furthermore, the Generalissimo is surely enough of a realist to be fully aware that, even accepting the eventual and inevitable defeat of Japan, there are many post-peace problems yet unresolved. What is the future status of Burma or Malaya is obviously a question any Chinese must ask himself. Will France secure the return of Indo-China or may it some day conceivably be handed over to the Generalissimo?

A glaring lack in the Cairo communiqué was mention of Hong Kong; will Britain insist on its retention? Does Moscow accept the pledge that China will recover all of rich Manchuria and its strategically important Chinese Eastern Railway, which links up Vladivostok with the main Trans-Siberian trunk railway? Which powers will assume control of Pacific islands such as the Carolines when Japan, as it is pledged, is finally expelled and Britain and America, in acknowledgement of their pledges, refuse territorial aggrandizement after this war?

The Soviet's position is not as yet clear. Moscow, apparently on its own initiative, has begun to move out of the huge Sinkiang Province, which for so long has been under a virtual Sino-Russian condominium. But will Russia agree to the Manchurian frontiers willingly or to the promised independence of Korea? It seems most likely, but the question is not yet fixed in the public view of the world.

On the other hand, how much can the United Nations themselves count on China's own contribution, weakened as she is, in the final stages of the war? Torn by internal dissent—it is an open secret—a chunk of China is under the hands of a Communist regime independent of the Central Government, which, while as anxious as can be to expel Japan, simultaneously is preparing for a showdown with the Generalissimo.

Now that China's Allies are fully committed to fight a war for the destruction of Japan, how much enthusiasm can be quickly inculcated in Chiang's fatigued, sick, ill-equipped conscript army, and how much can that force be counted on to afford a first-class punch in the final effort to smash Japan?

"The Chinese love a joke just as well as we do."

Excerpts from a U.S. Army guidebook for GIs serving in China

To assist U.S. servicemen being deployed to China, the War and Navy Departments provided them with *A Pocket Guide to China*. This handy booklet, excerpted here, contained sections on "Chinese Girls" and "Shopping" as well as more sober ones on "Organization of the Chinese Army" and "Chinese Strategy."

Introduction

China has been at war for years with her enemy and ours—the Japanese. She has met heavy defeats and won important victories. She has suffered more than 5,000,000 casualties in those years of war. Yet today, the free people of China are still fighting, still holding a better armed foe.

You and your outfit have been ordered to China to help this gallant ally. Your job, fighting side by side with the Chinese, is to rid that country of the Japanese. No American troops anywhere have a more important assignment.

Two problems face you right away. You don't know the language and you don't know the people. That makes it harder to be a guest in China than in a country like England or Australia.

Nobody expects you to learn a language as complex as Chinese, although the glossary at the end of this book will enable you to learn enough to get along. To understand a people is something else again. It takes a blend of curiosity, common sense, and courtesy. You might well adopt as your motto one of the many proverbs that guide the Chinese in their own conduct. They say…

"When you enter a neighborhood ask what is forbidden; when you enter a country ask what the customs are."

It is the purpose of this guide to tell you about some of these customs. It will take only about 20 minutes to read, but, by helping you to understand China and the Chinese people, it can add interest to your stay in their country and help you to do a better job for America.

Forget Your Old Notions

There are many Chinese living in America. You probably have seen some of them, and from them have formed notions about all Chinese. Perhaps those you saw were typical or perhaps they weren't. China is a big country, larger than Europe, half again as large as the United States, and with three times as many people as we have. Those you saw in America may have come from one small spot in China—the city of Canton. Judging all Chinese by those who live in one small part of the country is like judging all Americans by the residents of Hoboken, N.J.

If you think of the Chinese as a yellow-skinned people of a totally different race from us, you probably will never get to know them. What's more, you'll be playing right into the hands of Hitler and the Japs. Japan will harp on the color question first, last, and all the time. She will tell the Chinese what she has been telling them ever since Pearl Harbor—that Americans look down on nonwhite peoples and that the Chinese can never hope to be treated on terms of equality by America. "Why fight for the white man?" Japan dins into Chinese ears.

To counteract this propaganda you have to show the Chinese that Americans treat the Chinese as we treat any of our allies, and that we respect them as human beings on an equality with ourselves. Sure, there are differences. So what? There are important similarities too. If you forget the differences and think of them as neighbors, as people who eat, sleep, work, and raise families as we do, you'll be over the first hurdle.

On the matter of knowing each other, you and the Chinese start even. Millions of Chinese know little about America; millions have never seen an American. Yet, many of them know us by reputation and you can be proud of the fact that that reputation is good. Our Government has had friendly relations with China for many years. Americans who have been in China, missionaries, doctors, teachers, officials, and businessmen, have a good record. So the way to friendship is all paved for you. Added to this is the fact that we are allies—a fact in which the Chinese take pride. The first thing you should learn to say in China is "I am an American." It is the best passport you can have.

The Chinese People Are Like Americans

Of all the peoples of Asia, the Chinese are most like Americans. Those who know both peoples often remark at the likenesses. One of the reasons, perhaps, is that we both live in countries where

Chiang and his wife joke with Lt. Gen. Joseph W. Stilwell in Burma on the day after James Doolittle's April 1942 raid on Tokyo.

there is plenty of space and a great variety of climate and food. We are alike, too, because we both love independence and individual freedom.

Another likeness is that we are both humorous people. The Chinese love a joke just as well as we do, and they laugh at the same sort of thing. Their stock jokes are the same as ours—about professors, and doctors, and Irishmen—the Chinese equivalent for the Irish being people from Hunan province. They laugh about stinginess, about country hicks, and smart city people. Their conversation is full of wit, and lively humor, and they love slapstick stuff, their own and ours. Listen to a Chinese crowd laughing at Charlie Chaplin or Harold Lloyd or Laurel and Hardy and you'll think you are at home.

Then, too, we are both practical peoples. The Chinese are shrewd businessmen, generous friends, and they believe in having a good time on earth while they are alive. In the main, so do we. They are better than we are, perhaps, at human relationships. They value these above all else, and have learned to get along with people through centuries of getting along with each other. The Chinese family system keeps several generations under the same roof—grandparents and parents, sons and daughters and their families, and this has taught them the art of living together. In fact, consideration for an individual's feelings is one of the great Chinese virtues.

The Chinese loves his home and his family. He is sentimental about his children and his old parents. He loves his own bit of ground and his own roof, even if it is poor, and he never forgets his own people.

We are alike, also, because of our natural democratic tendencies. There are few class distinctions in China, no hereditary aristocracy. Anybody can get anywhere, if he can prove himself able and intelligent enough. The Chinese have their great men who were born in cabins, just as we do. Generalissimo Chiang Kai-shek himself is the son of poor parents, and Sun Yat-sen, their George Washington, was a poor boy. The rich in China behave like the rich anywhere except that they don't feel themselves permanently rich. They know that poor and rich change places quickly in the changes of democratic life. And the poor man in China is independent and energetic. He knows he has a chance to rise in the world.

What Does "Face" Mean?

The Chinese are a proud people and also a courteous one. This means that they consider it important not to hurt anyone's feelings and they will appreciate consideration of their own feelings. This is sometimes called "face," which simply means self-respect. There is about as much of it in one country as another, but the Chinese pay more attention to preserving it than we do. They do not criticize each other as frankly as we do, and there are certain rules of courtesy, particularly to the old, from the young. Old people in China are highly respected, even revered, and their advice valued. Lack of respect to the old is therefore a sign of bad manners.

Don't worry about "face" and complicated courtesy. Simply be an American, in the best sense. The Chinese don't expect you to know all their ways of polite behaviour. They will not think less of you if you break a rule or two if they are convinced you wish to respect them and to be friendly with them.

Your First Impressions

Your first impression will depend upon where you arrive. The Chinese people vary widely. In the north the people are tall and handsome. In mid-China they are of average height and in the south they are short and stocky.

During your tour of duty you will see cities, towns, and countryside. Chinese cities are of two kinds, those which have been modernized and those which remain as they have been for centuries. The largest of the modern ones are Shanghai, Tientsin, Nanking, Hongkong, Canton, Hankow, Peiping—now, temporarily, all in Japanese hands.

In the Chinese cities or towns where you are most likely to be at first, you will be impressed by three things: that the streets are narrow; that they are dirty; and that they are crowded. Chinese cities and towns are old and they were built not for automobiles but for sedan chairs and wheelbarrows and caravans of donkeys and for pedestrians.

The gutters are defective, if there are any gutters, and people often throw water and garbage out of their doors. Modern Chinese cities, of course, have wide streets and good sewers but we are speaking of the places you will probably see most often.

You may be shocked, at first, to see how desperately poor most Chinese are. Their houses and their clothing seem dirty and unkempt. There are mangy and flea-bitten dogs that you had best keep away from. You will see human strays, too, beggars of the most sorrowful sort. Do not give anything to them or you will be besieged. And nowadays there will be others—refugees and homeless poor and war-wounded. For China has suffered terribly. She was, before the war, only just beginning to have modern doctors and hospitals and nurses. War came before she could get ready and China's wounded can today be counted in the millions. What you can do to help them must be left to you. In general it is best to give money only privately, or through some reliable organization, such as the United China Relief.

After a time, however, you will discover that Chinese peasants and workmen are almost never demoralized. They keep their chins up, take what comes, help each other out, and live with amazing contentment amid the terrific struggle for the bare necessities of life.

You'll have other surprises, too. But they need not shock you if you are ready to admit that people may be the same at heart whatever their custom. Thus you will see mothers nursing their babies in public. Men and boys will relieve themselves wherever and whenever nature demands. Children will run about with nothing on at all. Take all this as a matter of course as the Chinese do, and do not offend their sense of good taste by seeming to even notice it.

Despite the strangeness and the poverty you will very soon enjoy walking along Chinese streets and seeing the rich human life going on around you, the hot-blooded quarreling, the laughter, the children, the people arguing over their buying and selling. They will enjoy you too. A crowd will very likely follow you to stare at you and discuss everything you do. They will be a friendly crowd. So accept them good humoredly and let them come along.

One thing to understand at the beginning: The Chinese think we look queer. They are accustomed to everyone having black hair and black eyes, so naturally they think it strange for people to have red or brown or blonde hair and eyes of unfamiliar colors. Also we are bigger-boned than the average Chinese, and hairier. As a matter of fact, the Chinese have an ancient belief that the hairier people are, the more uncivilized they are. Because of your appearance, you'll be a curiosity to the Chinese, and, perhaps, a source of amusement. If you take that in good part and grin back at them, they'll like you.

You'll see lots of rickshas, looking just like they did in the movies at home, and you'll soon be riding in one. The tough, lean coolies who pull them are to be treated always with respect for what they are in Chinese life and the waging of this war. They are the freight carriers, the builders of the Burma Road, the guerrilla fighters, their stomachs never filled, their bodies nothing but bone and muscle.

When you sit behind one of them in a ricksha, consider what he is and how you can help him. He will not appreciate it if you walk instead of hiring him, for he depends on his job to feed his family. But

A Chinese soldier guards American P-40 fighters painted with the shark-face emblem of the Flying Tigers at an airfield somewhere in China.

he will appreciate your sitting forward when he goes uphill, leaning back when he goes down, and at other times sitting with your weight in the middle of the vehicle.

As you walk along the street, the working man will appreciate it if you do not step over a carrying pole laid in the street for a moment's rest, or the lowered shafts of a ricksha or sedan chair, because this is supposed to bring bad luck in business for a year.

Chinese Girls

The modern Chinese girl, in her long, closely fitting gown, her bare arms and short hair, is often very pretty. Yet it is well to remember that in China the attitude toward women is different from ours in America. Chinese women in some ways are more free than they are here in America—that is, they do some things which American women don't yet do. They are in the Army, for instance, and they fight side by side with the guerrillas. But in their relations with men they haven't the same freedom as women have in America.

There are Chinese girls in cabarets and places of amusement who may be used to free and easy ways. But the average Chinese girl will be insulted if you touch her, or will take you more seriously than you probably want to be taken. A mistake in this may cause a lot of trouble.

21

The Teheran Conference

November 1943

The first face-to-face meeting among the Allied leaders known as the Big Three took place in Teheran, Iran, in November 1943. To Roosevelt, in particular, it represented an eagerly awaited opportunity to use his copious personal charm on the gruff Soviet leader. "After all," presidential aide Harry Hopkins told Lord Moran, the prime minister's personal physician, the president "has spent his life managing

men, and Stalin at bottom could not be so very different from other people." Although Roosevelt had never met Stalin before, he was well prepared by his staff. One of those briefing him was W. Averell Harriman, the U.S. ambassador to Moscow. Harriman later described Stalin as "the most inscrutable and contradictory character I have ever known." According to Harriman, Stalin was "better informed than Roosevelt, more realistic than Churchill, in some ways the most effective of the war leaders. At the same time he was, of course, a murderous tyrant."

The topics discussed at Teheran included the sensitive issue of Poland's postwar borders, the future status of a defeated Germany, the nature of a successor organization to the League of Nations, and the war in the Pacific. The focus, however, was on Overlord, the new cross-Channel invasion plan. With some prodding from Stalin, Roosevelt committed himself to a launch date of May 1, 1944, and Churchill had no choice but to go along. Stalin also wanted to know who would command the operation. The obvious choice was army chief of staff George

Marshall—whose personal prestige, it was thought, would ensure earnest British cooperation. However, Roosevelt's military advisers wanted Marshall to remain in Washington, believing that only he could resolve the various competing claims of so many services, allies, and theaters of war. Shortly after leaving Teheran, the president made his decision, giving in to the chiefs of staff and naming Eisenhower to the Overlord command.

Otherwise, FDR felt frustrated at the close of the conference. "I couldn't get any personal connection with Stalin," the president explained. "He was correct, stiff, solemn, not smiling, nothing human to get a hold of." The Soviet leader, however, left Teheran pleased. In discussing the Polish border issue with Roosevelt during a remarkably frank private session, he had learned that the president accepted as inevitable Soviet domination of Eastern Europe. Roosevelt already understood, Stalin later explained, that "whoever occupies a territory also imposes his own social system. Everyone imposes his own system as far as his army can reach."

Stalin, Roosevelt, and Churchill pose on the portico of the Soviet embassy at Teheran. Among those looking on are Gen. George C. Marshall, Adm. Ernest J. King, and Gen. H. H. Arnold (at left) and Adm. William Leahy, Marshal Klementi Voroshilov, Foreign Minister V. M. Molotov, and Anthony Eden (at right).

PERSONAL CONTACT CLOSE IN TEHERAN

Atmosphere Set for Peacetime Amity—Roosevelt Hailed Success of Parley

CAIRO, Egypt, Dec. 6—Geographically, President Roosevelt and Prime Minister Churchill met Premier Stalin considerably more than halfway when they went to Teheran. But Premier Stalin took a dramatic step that, a year ago, few would have ventured to predict—crossing his own frontiers.

The meetings were the second phase in the United Nations' campaign to accelerate victory. The conference, in the President's words, was very successful. Not only did the three leaders finally get together face to face, as the Allied world had been hoping for many months, but the atmosphere was set for the continuation of their cordiality through years of peace. Throughout the discussions Mr. Roosevelt was Premier Stalin's guest in the massive empire-style Russian Embassy.

Premier Stalin and Mr. Churchill lived within a few hundred yards. The area was closed to the public. Diplomatically, all efforts were made to avoid any competition for protocol priority, but it would seem that Mr. Roosevelt received the greatest courtesies possible because of his difficulty in moving about. Premier Stalin and Mr. Churchill called on him and the plenary sessions were held in his temporary home. The most important single meeting was held on Dec. 1, at the end of the talks. The three principals as well as Foreign Commissar Vyacheslaff M. Molotoff, Harry Hopkins, Foreign Secretary Anthony Eden and W. Averell Harriman conferred until 10:30 P.M. and agreed on a joint communiqué, including postwar problems.

From Nov. 28 through Dec. 1 the three United Nations leaders virtually lived together, maintaining a steady series of intimate conferences and eating together at least once daily. They were on good personal terms and, with all the pressure of their work, found time for many quips and jokes.

Premier Stalin arrived in Teheran on Nov. 26 after a flight from Moscow across the central Russian flatlands and the snow-topped Elburz mountain range bisecting Iran and cutting it off from Russian Azerbaijan. Messrs. Roosevelt and Churchill and their parties, including top staff officers and many diplomats, arrived by air the next day. The Americans came on five huge transport planes, which circled low over Bethlehem and the Jordan River en route to permit a glimpse of Palestine.

The formalities of the meeting had not yet begun and no one met Mr. Roosevelt except Maj. Gen. Donald Connolly, commander of the Russian Gulf Service Command, and a few protective squads of Russian soldiers, standing near several Russian fighter planes. Mr. Roosevelt, wearing a gray suit, a brown hat and a blue tie, drove off in a special car down a sycamore-lined street looking northward toward the magnificent Elburz Mountains.

Mr. Churchill and his party of seventy arrived slightly later. They were met by a few British officials, including the Minister, Sir Reader Bullard, and drove to the spacious British Legation. In contrast to the large American and British delegations, the only Russians to participate in the planning sessions were Premier Stalin, Mr. Molotoff and Marshal Klementi Voroshiloff.

Standing outside the Soviet embassy in Teheran during the Teheran Conference are (left to right) Field Marshal John Dill, chief of the British War Mission to Washington; George C. Marshall; Archibald Clark-Kerr, British ambassador to the Soviet Union; Harry Hopkins; Stalin's interpreter; Stalin himself; Anthony Eden (whose face is just visible behind Stalin); V. M. Molotov; and Klementi Voroshilov.

Early Sunday morning the first meeting between the Americans and the Russians took place outside the American Legation. The Russian attaché and two Red Army generals arrived to visit the American military party. Mr. Roosevelt conferred with his staff that morning and lunched in the legation with Mr. Churchill.

A sensational step was taken just before 3 P.M. when the President transferred his quarters to the Russian Embassy as Premier Stalin's guest. The arrangements had previously been made by Brig. Gen. Patrick Hurley and Louis G. Dreyfus, American Minister to Iran, who prepared the conference's physical details.

Mr. Churchill lived in his legation, right across the street, and both Premier Stalin and Mr. Roosevelt stayed in the Russian compound in separate buildings. Tall screens were erected to block off the entrances to the street. The Russian Embassy and British Legation gates, facing each other, were opened wide, thus joining the two compounds.

Rings of soldiers stood guard outside. Bearded Sikhs with armored cars stood behind lines of British troops in a cordon beyond the secret area. Within the gates there were Red Army men with tommy guns, and special detachments of United States military police. General Arkadieff of the NKVD was in charge of the Russian security program, and Michael Reilly, chief of the White House Secret Service, directed the American precautionary arrangements.

The large central conference room, where many of the talks were held, is situated in the center of the Embassy. It is seventy-five by forty feet and is colored light grey with an ivory frieze. South of this were the President's apartments, which, by joint agreement, were guarded by American military police and Secret Servicemen as well as Russian troops and NKVD men.

These Russian soldiers greatly impressed the Americans by their immobility. One group stood for four hours without a single movement

In a near-by building, Premier Stalin, Mr. Molotoff and Marshal Voroshiloff lived. The conferences were held in Mr. Roosevelt's residence at a perfectly round oaken table, ten feet in diameter. It was specially constructed for the talks so that none of the three statesmen would have precedence over the others by sitting at a head position.

A few minutes after Mr. Roosevelt's arrival in his new quarters his historic meeting with Premier Stalin occurred, when the latter called on his guest. Accompanied by Mr. Molotoff, a group of generals and an interpreter, as well as Mr. Roosevelt's translator, Charles Bohlen of the State Department, Premier Stalin spent one and a half hours in this conference. Then Mr. Churchill arrived, and, after another talk, the chiefs adjourned to a tea given by Mr. Molotoff.

That night Mr. Roosevelt entertained his friends at an American dinner cooked by Army chefs. The guests included, besides the three statesmen, Mr. Molotoff, Mr. Eden, Sir Archibald Clark-Kerr, Mr. Hopkins, Mr. Harriman and Admiral William Leahy.

The three leaders ate together every evening in what was described as exceedingly jovial sessions, where Premier Stalin proved himself the life of the party. There is no doubt that all got on excellently. The day after Mr. Roosevelt had moved into the Russian Embassy, Premier Stalin gave a dinner for him there with a colossal Russian menu, including plenty of caviar.

The formal staff talks commenced on Nov. 29. The general procedure followed was that whenever military questions impinged on political matters they were immediately referred to the three heads of state, who did not attend the strategic discussions but were always close at hand. Each afternoon there were plenary sessions attended by the three leaders.

The first plenary session was held from 4:30 to 7:30 P.M. on Nov. 28. This schedule was followed daily. The leaders then changed and met for dinner, which generally lasted until midnight. On Nov. 30 the heads of state lunched at the Russian Embassy and that evening they attended Mr. Churchill's sixty-ninth birthday party.

The security measures in Teheran were the strictest conceivable. The extent of the guard can best be conveyed by the fact that within one five-block area, there were seventy-two Russians armed with tommy-guns. All the Red Army men had sub-machine guns, in contrast to the British and American rifles and revolvers. All Mr. Roosevelt's servants were NKVD men. When they leaned over their brooms while sweeping up one could see their revolvers sticking out.

"Ike regards himself as a beneficiary of circumstances."

An Eisenhower aide recalls the general's promotion to command Overlord

Lt. Cmdr. Harry C. Butcher joined Eisenhower's staff as his naval aide before the Torch landings in 1942 and served with the general until after the surrender of Germany in 1945. During those three years, he kept a personal diary of his experiences with Ike; reprinted here are his entries for December 4–10, 1943.

Algiers, Saturday, December 4, 1943

This is the longest period in which I have not dictated for the diary. General Ike and party have been to Cairo, where Ike presented to the Combined Chiefs of Staff his picture of the military situation in the Mediterranean. I had the choice of going on the Cairo trip or to Naples to visit Fifth Army and attend to details of housing in connection with the establishment of our Advance CP at Caserta. I chose the latter because I had had my fill of conventions and had seen and talked with the American principals who would take part.

Ike returned to Algiers Wednesday morning, December 1, and I flew back from Naples yesterday.

He told me that Elliott Roosevelt had returned from the meeting of the President and the Prime Minister with "Uncle Joe" at Teheran and had said that the Russians insisted that we not only keep the pressure against the Germans in Italy all winter but launch the cross-Channel operation not later than May. This dictates that OVERLORD must be done. He enjoyed the trip, principally for the change of environment, but doesn't know what decisions have been taken, especially as to his own future.

The presidential party is to return to Tunis Sunday or Monday. Ike and party, including me, are to meet them. He hopes that the answers will be given to the questions which have pervaded all our thinking for three months.

While at Cairo, Ike took time to see the Pyramids, Luxor, and Jerusalem, and now displays the good effect of a change of scenery and at least momentary relaxation.

Algiers, Sunday, December 5, 1943

I have heard Ike speak of his gratitude to General Marshall, to the President, and to the country for the opportunity he has been given. He regards himself as a fortunate beneficiary of circumstances. If he hadn't told General Marshall while still in the Operations Division that he hated to serve in Washington, that he had no expectation of a promotion and didn't give a damn, perhaps G. C. M. wouldn't have pushed him into the European command in June of 1942. Since he was thoroughly informed of the variety of plans for switching from the defensive to the offensive against Germany, and the promotion of cross-Channel invasion plans, his views were sought by the British military leaders and, particularly, by the Prime Minister. When, in July, 1942, it was decided to launch the North African campaign and an American was needed to be the Allied Commander, Ike was the logical, yet "lucky," choice, as he views it.

I appraise Ike's mental attitude as akin to that of a football quarterback who has been playing an excellent game but who rebels when the coach orders him to the side lines while the game is still at fever pitch.

All will be relieved when the definite answer is forthcoming, and this is expected when the presidential party comes to Tunisia. Ike anticipates that he will have to depart for Washington quite soon because the OVERLORD operation will require immediate and personal direction of General Marshall in England.

The news from the Teheran conference with "Uncle Joe," as conveyed to Ike by Elliott Roosevelt, plainly shows that Russia is in the driver's seat. Decisions taken at Cairo by the Anglo-Americans obviously could not be effected until opinion of the Russians was obtained. Whereas the Prime Minister hoped to exploit our Mediterranean situation and, if possible, to avoid the heavy cost of life inherent in the cross-Channel attack, and the Americans were prepared to agree if Russia were willing, when the Russians firmly stated that we should continue the offensive in Italy all winter to contain German troops, and also launch OVERLORD not later than May, the die was cast. Even Churchill's persistent desire to bring Turkey into the war was blackballed by the Russians, who took the practical position that Russia, Britain, and the United States were already using all the equipment and supplies that the United States could produce, and so, reasoned the Russians, why take on another drain on supplies?

Algiers, Monday, December 6, 1943

Oddly, although we have no information and don't expect any until the General sees the President, now expected at Tunis tomorrow evening, we seem to have taken for granted that we are to go back to Washington. While we still put an "if" in our plans, Ike is considering the "round-the-world" route, including a visit to MacArthur and possibly to Lord Louis. This will give him firsthand information of conditions in their theaters, the better to prepare himself for his new job.

The battle for Mt. Comino, which I saw start last Thursday afternoon and early evening, has been generally successful, but some pockets of Germans still remain to be dealt with on the ridge above the monastery.

Apparently our air defense of Bari was not well co-ordinated. There was a failure to "lay on" the red alert when the radar detected enemy planes approaching. In any event, the enemy aircraft found the harbor lighted, the ships closely packed together, and had the good fortune to hit an ammunition ship which blew up, spreading fire to four others, one of which also was an ammunition ship, and when it blew up, a total of seventeen ships were destroyed. This loss will slow the development of Foggia and perhaps the advance of the Eighth Army.

We are preparing to fly from Maison Blanche to El Aouina, starting at 9:30 Tuesday morning, to be on hand to meet the presidential party, which is due from Cairo in the late afternoon.

Amilcar (AFHQ, Advance CP), Friday, December 10, 1943

Ike is to be Supreme Commander of the Allied Expeditionary Force in England!

We got this news direct from General Marshall, whose cable to Ike from Cairo was so vague that it indicated he assumed Ike knew he had been selected for the supreme job. We were awaiting breakfast Tuesday morning, prior to flying from Maison Blanche to meet the returning President. The phone rang, I answered, and Beetle's voice, almost trilling, asked if he still could catch the C-in-C if he came right over.

The message made clear that the Prime Minister still insists that Beetle remain in this theater because of his experience in dealing with the French and Italians.

Immediately Ike declared to Beetle that he would insist that his own Chief of Staff accompany him to his new job. Beetle thought he could easily be spared after the transition period and seemed unmindful that if he stayed in Africa as the proposed Chief of Staff to the new Allied Commander and as American Theater Commander, he would easily be entitled to his third star. General Alexander, incidentally, is to be in charge of the battle in Italy, and General "Jumbo" Wilson, of the Middle East, is to be Allied C-in-C. Why "Alex" did not get the Mediterranean command from the British, we do not know.

The President and his party arrived at El Aouina airfield in midafternoon. Ike took the President in his car to the White House and I had Harry Hopkins and Major John Boettiger with me. When opportunity permitted, Harry took me aside and told me privately that Ike was to be Supreme Commander. Hopkins said he thought the President and others thought General Marshall had come rightly to regard his job as Chief of Staff as more important to the war effort. He could devote his superior qualifications to global warfare, with which he is now intimately familiar. He could deal with Congress. The decision in Ike's favor had been made after very careful consideration of all of the factors, with important weight given to the need of General Marshall's experience in dealing with Congress in his present job and of Ike's battle-front knowledge and success in this theater. Ike's personal appearance before the Combined Chiefs of Staff at Cairo and his demonstration of his grasp of the military situation had added to the good impression already held of him.

The President, with Ike, General Spaatz, and General Smith aboard, as well as Hopkins, Admiral Leahy, Rear Admirals Ross T. McIntire and Wilson Brown, and Major General "Pa" Watson, flew to Malta Wednesday morning so the President personally could present Lord Gort an inscribed testimonial from America to brave Malta. From there they flew to an airfield in Sicily, where the President reviewed such American troops as could be assembled on the field. On Ike's recommendation, he also gave the DSC to General Clark for bravery and leadership at Salerno, the Legion of Merit to Beetle (who couldn't be found at the moment) and to a half dozen other officers from colonel to lieutenant who had distinguished themselves in action.

The plan originally was for the President and party to fly from Sicily to Marrakech to spend the night. However, when the big C-54 attempted to land at Luca Field, in Malta, Major Otis Bryan, the pilot, discovered to his dismay that the hydraulic pressure had failed and prevented opening of the wing flaps, which are useful, if not necessary, to the landing. The plane circled twenty minutes until the wing flaps could be lowered. The landing was made successfully, but two hours were required for location and repair of the broken mechanism. Consequently, the party returned to El Aouina and the President stayed overnight. The party departed at 6:30 Thursday morning for direct flight to Dakar, some 2500 miles. So far as I have heard, this is the first direct hop attempted between these points, although the mileage is well within the range of the C-54.

22

The Anzio Beachhead

January 1944

The American chiefs of staff never wanted a campaign in Italy, which they considered a waste of resources better put to use in France. However, Churchill's devotion to a Mediterranean strategy and the Italian surrender negotiations initiated a reevaluation of Allied war plans. This led, in turn, to the decision to invade the Italian mainland, albeit only with troops and equipment already available in the

theater. On September 3, 1943, the same day that Badoglio secretly signed the armistice, Montgomery's Eighth Army crossed the Strait of Messina unopposed. Six days later, however, Lt. Gen. Mark Clark's Anglo-American force encountered stiff resistance upon landing at Salerno, where mountains ringed the beachhead, providing excellent cover for the German defenders. Only an intense Allied naval bombardment prevented Kesselring's troops from pushing the Fifth Army back into the sea.

Thus began a nineteen-month war of attrition that spilled a great deal of blood for little military purpose. Kesselring's strength lay in his clever use of fortified positions built into Italy's rugged, mountainous topography. The most important of these was the Gustav line, which ran from the Adriatic to the Tyrrhenian Sea just north of Naples, its western end anchored by the formidable Apennine peak of Monte Cassino. Months of cold, rainy weather, which trapped vehicles in the mud and kept planes out of the air, resulted in such little progress against the Gustav line that Churchill finally pushed for another landing to break the

deadlock—this one up the coast at Anzio, behind the German lines and just thirty miles from Rome. American military commanders, already transferring troops and equipment to England in preparation for Overlord, resisted putting any more effort into Italy. But Churchill made a personal appeal to Roosevelt, who agreed to delay the transfer of some landing craft so that the Anzio landing could take place on January 22, 1944.

Because the operation surprised Kesselring, the initial resistance was light. Nevertheless, commanding general John P. Lucas chose to consolidate his beachhead, rather than move swiftly inland. This gave the Germans time to organize a counterattack, which (as at Salerno) nearly pushed the Allies into the surf. The unrelenting German artillery fire did, however, succeed in pinning down the Allies at Anzio, where they remained until May, when Free French troops under Alphonse Juin finally cracked the Gustav line. Juin's penetration into the Liri Valley forced the Germans to withdraw to northern Italy, where Kesselring held out successfully for the rest of the war.

Combat engineers in late February 1944 man a .30-caliber machine gun in the Anzio-Nettuno area. Their position along the Mussolini Canal overlooks a plain controlled by the Germans.

THE DOUGHBOY'S GRIM ROAD TO ROME

It is paved with mud and minefields, has rugged mountain barriers, it makes men weary. But the slogging American foot soldier won't be denied.

By C. L. SULZBERGER

WITH THE FIFTH ARMY IN ITALY—Sunny Italy, land of rich tourists and eternal bright blue sky, is to the average American doughboy an endless road of sticky mud dotted with minefields, a series of forbidding gray mountain crags filled with almost inaccessible gun pits; murky, freezing rivers rushing past shattered bridges; a collection of barren, gutted villages peopled with tattered scavengers—all set beneath a gray, cloud-filled sky dripping rain, sleet and more rain. In the vernacular he has borrowed from his British ally, the American doughboy says that so far as Italy is concerned, "I've had it."

It was a captured German general who told his interrogators that the western desert was a tactician's paradise and a quartermaster's hell. Italy is a tactician's hell and a quartermaster's purgatory. For the United States Army, from its commander to its smallest squad of infantry men, this campaign is like something out of the lower reaches of Dante's "Divine Comedy," and there is nothing either divine or comic about it. General Sherman's description of war in general, rather than Baedeker's description of Italy, is applicable in this festering, bewildered land today.

The peculiar, peak-serrated front stretching between the romantic Tyrrhenian and Adriatic Seas is a scene of heroism and disaster, of hope and gloom and suffering by a potpourri of troops representing the actuality of the United Nations in its fullest sense. Here are British, New Zealand, Indian, French, Japanese-American, Moroccan, Tunisian, Algerian, American and even a handful of Italian soldiers.

The American doughboys now in the line, determined and brave as they unquestionably are, nevertheless are a weather-beaten, weary group of men who are surviving in their dreary, tedious, costly push forward merely by the skill instilled within them by that hardest school of all—battle.

These men have fought with dogged courage equal to anything their ancestors demonstrated in their so-called harder days. They have fought with a canniness mindful of the forays by the first Continental pioneers against Indian tribesmen. And they have fought against odds and determined opposition certainly equal to those of any battle of World War I.

There are many veterans of the last war who still reminisce by their firesides in terms of the huge catastrophes of those days—the terrors of a creeping barrage and massed infantry assaults with bayonet. Certainly such features on such a scale do not prevail along the contested central belt of Italy. But artillery these days is ingeniously more accurate than ever before, thanks to new devices and new methods of observation. And artillery supported by air is devilishly powerful.

Added to artillery now are new types of mortars; swifter, stronger tanks; self-propelled guns; rocket projectiles, such as the Nebelwerfer and the bazooka.

These American men have great quantities of almost all of these weapons, but it would be most foolish to get the idea that we have the fastest planes, the best tanks, the most powerful guns in the world—because we haven't. On this

Officers of a Fifth Army tank-destroyer battalion study German positions around Anzio before beginning an assault in March 1944.

front the Germans can match almost any weapon we are using, and it is only the grim, wary, brave capability of the doughboy, tankman or pilot which enables him to surmount obstacles erected by a nation whose peacetime profession was preparation for war.

American soldiers are going into tank battles with the knowledge that the model opposing them has armor over its Achilles heel almost as thick as the best protection their own vehicle may have; that they are outgunned both in the sense of range and muzzle velocity and that it will be their own fighting skill, acuteness and daring which will have to see them through if the odds are equal.

Artillerymen pound away with huge concentrations of guns—batteries sometimes landing more than 100 projectiles simultaneously on the same target—knowing full well that when the counter-battery work begins and those 32,000-yard Nazi 170's start slowly feeling for them with shells traveling so fast that the whine is almost simultaneous with the burst, they have no single gun able to reach the enemy's batteries.

Fighter pilots often go into action with out-moded aircraft, knowing that only the greatest cunning can give them victory, but none the less they take off full of confidence.

And then the infantrymen—their job isn't, as some theorists seem to suppose, merely to march in and occupy territory evacuated under pressure from massed armor and aerial assaults. They go crawling forward toward enemy pill-boxes, tired, cold and sometimes scared, entirely aware that the German, far from being a beaten man, remains a tough, resourceful soldier—one of the best in the world.

As if to add to these difficulties there is the question of forbidden territories—those clerical monuments with which in the words of the G.I.'s

"Italy is just lousy." In the bloody battle for Cassino, it is the opinion of many an officer and private that had we started the attack by shelling the famous Abbey of Mount Cassino, which dominates the chewed-up town, and wiped it off the map at once, the tide of battle might have turned during the first week of February.

"I am a Catholic," says one lieutenant colonel, "but this thing didn't make much sense. We lost lives rather than destroy stones. If you would just let the Catholic boys in the artillery shell away at the monasteries, I think they'd do as good a job as anyone."

Why, you may ask when all these gloomy facts are pointed out, are we able to advance at all? The answer is that something which enables these Americans despite their many disadvantages to climb forward over frozen peaks, inch across mine fields and batter their way through villages, which are shambles of fallen stone.

In the first place, these men are now experienced, hard-bitten soldiers who not only have been able to utilize to the fullest that fighting mechanical capacity with which the American nation is gifted, but also have developed the instinctive scouting and sharpshooting ability of their forebears.

Secondly, they possess a vigor, health and youthfulness in its fullest and best sense that Germany no longer is able to muster among its wayward decimated menfolk drained of blood and energy by more than four years of what was meant to be a Blitzkrieg.

Thirdly, the Americans know not only that they already have definite quantitative superiority in all the necessary tools of war, but that there are more where they came from in the bomb-free factories back home.

Their quantity of weapons, their vigor, youth and fine health cared for so exactingly by medical and feeding organizations, are slowly proving the answer to what is actually a mercenary, Nazi army defensively entrenched in some of the most difficult military terrain a major engagement has ever been fought over. Mud like thick soup, mountains like barren limestone teeth, and a ravaged landscape of torn-up roads, uprooted railways, blown-up bridges—difficult as they may be, these are merely tests of the engineering ingenuity of those supply geniuses on whom the success of this or any other campaign must eventually depend.

The backbone of this American Army, as it always has been, remains the infantry. They are used to the ghastly sight of death; they are used to its strange, slightly sour, fetid smell. They know where a shell is going to burst from its sound. They know how to follow a mine tape in the darkness and cut wire on patrol.

These generally sentimental and, in its best sense, simple-minded youths have attained a somewhat remote connection with their former selves. This writer has seen them slogging silently with impassive, grimy faces past slit trenches containing the awkwardly sprawling bodies of their fellows, regarding them, if at all, as if they might be stones. Not that this unfeelingness has made them automatons, but in war it is necessary to compartmentize the mind, and softer thoughts remain very much in the innermost compartment.

In spite of the bitter cold at night and the steep terrain, topped by precipitous rock formations and coated with snow and slippery frozen mud, our infantrymen prefer to fight on these heights. Generally, such actions comprise a modern kind of American-Indian warfare, with careful probing of the enemy from behind cover until contact is established.

When the two armies meet in close-up fighting, Allied artillery generally is able to give the infantry only a modicum of support because enemy units are too closely intermixed with our own men. It then becomes a question of small arms and as many grenades as a man can pitch. Then the plodding doughboy, sweating despite the crisp wintry climate, is likely to pound the side of a friendly tank with his rifle butt and holler, "Come on over here. We've got some Kraut holed up. Dig them out, will you?" Or there will be a shout, "Don't fool with that —. Throw in a grenade."

These actions will never go down in history as battles any schoolboy ever will be expected to study, but the rate of casualties here is high, and from such pushes one gets an idea of what the ordinary, unglamorous infantryman goes through in this war. The best example of this terrible process of troops bleeding their way forward was our attempt to cross the little Rapido River. Under cover of the heaviest type of shelling and combined night and smoke screening, the infantry led the engineers to the river, where the latter put up a flimsy, railless little footbridge. Spray from the swift, swollen stream froze on the bridge.

Infantrymen staggered toward the river carrying heavy boats loaded with equipment, while other small units began crawling across the bridge, gripping its icy sides with bleeding fingers. A hail of enemy fire from fixed positions broke through the smoke. The first group lost sight of the mine tapes, and the boat and its crew blew up in a cascade of frozen earth.

Thick fire of all sorts burst about the bridge to the contrapuntal accompaniment of screaming rocket projectiles. Some units penetrated to the enemy's second line wire defenses while the Germans coolly opened up fire from their hitherto silent hidden positions. This pressure on the exposed attackers was too much, and the effort had to be given up after excessive losses.

Northward along the Tyrrhenian coast the infantrymen fighting at the Anzio-Nettuno beachhead have had better fighting weather and better terrain than those in central Italy. Here the original emphasis was laid on naval operations, supply and weather being the two big questions during the initial phase of any such battle. Clear skies afforded a much better fighter plane cover over the crowded harbors and beaches as well as improved vision for heavy bombers droning inland with their cargoes of explosives.

When the writer went into Anzio with Gen. Sir Harold R. L. Alexander the other day the usual air raid was going on under a light cloud blanket. It was rendered somewhat dramatic by the sudden plummeting to earth of a sheet of flame that was once a fighter plane, followed by the lackadaisical silver parachute of its pilot. Everyone in the harbor region was working like a beaver disregarding the invisible dogfighting above the clouds. They were unloading truck after truck of supplies from the ships, while tarpaulin-covered "ducks" were chugging in over the beaches with cases of ammunition.

Long lines of heavy guns rumbled inland past laurel groves toward the critical battlefield. Despite the marshland spreading about inshore from the beachhead, this is by far the best tank country on both Italian battlefronts. And the ugly monsters crawled steadily toward the highlands in support of the infantrymen who had already fought their way inland.

These then are Italy's two fronts. Fighting on either of them is a tough job. Before we achieve victory on either or both of them, as one general put it, "We're bound at least to get a bloody nose." As still another commander sees it, "We will have to put out plenty" before the battle is over.

But in this discussion, just as in the fighting, it is the infantrymen who have the last word. "If all roads lead to Rome," the doughboys ask, "why in hell don't the Krauts just pack up and follow them?"

"There was no place enemy shells couldn't seek you out."

Bill Mauldin's recollection of the Anzio beachhead

Pulitzer Prize–winning cartoonist Bill Mauldin's most popular characters were Willie and Joe, a pair of grimy, unshaven dogfaces who appeared regularly in the pages of the army newspaper *Stars and Stripes*. During the Italian campaign in particular, they battled, according to *Time* magazine, "tedium, wet socks, lousy K rations, and their commanding officers. GIs everywhere laughed or nodded in rueful recognition." Mauldin wrote of his experiences at Anzio in his 1945 memoir *Up Front*.

Anzio was unique.

It was the only place in Europe which held an entire corps of infantry, a British division, all kinds of artillery and special units, and maintained an immense supply and administration setup without a rear echelon. As a matter of fact, there wasn't any rear; there was no place in the entire beachhead where enemy shells couldn't seek you out.

Sometimes it was worse at the front: sometimes worse at the harbor. Quartermasters buried their dead and amphibious duck drivers went down with their craft. Infantrymen, dug into the Mussolini Canal, had the canal pushed in on top of them by armor-piercing shells, and Jerry bombers circled as they directed glider bombs into LSTs and Liberty ships. Wounded men got oak leaf clusters on their Purple Hearts when shell fragments riddled them as they lay on hospital beds. Nurses died. Planes crash-landed on the single air strip.

Planes went out to seek the "Anzio Express," that huge gun which made guys in rest areas play softball near slit trenches. The planes would report the Express destroyed and an hour later she would come in on schedule.

The krauts launched a suicidal attack which almost drove through to the sea. Evacuation was already beginning in the harbor when a single American battalion broke the point of the attack, then was engulfed and died. Bodies of fanatical young Germans piled up in front of the machine guns, and when the guns ran out of ammunition the Wehrmacht came through and was stopped only by point-blank artillery. One American artillery battalion of 155s fired 80,000 rounds of ammunition at Anzio, and there were dozens of these battalions.

You couldn't stand up in the swamps without being cut down, and you couldn't sleep if you sat down. Guys stayed in those swamps for days and weeks. Every hole had to be covered, because the "popcorn man" came over every night and shoveled hundreds of little butterfly bombs down on your head by the light of flares and exploding ack-ack. You'd wake up in the morning and find your sandbags torn open and spilled on the ground.

The krauts used little remote-control tanks filled with high explosives. You wondered how Jerry could see you and throw a shell at you every time you stuck your head up, until you climbed into the mountains after it was all over and were able to count every tree and every house in the area we had held. Tiger tanks grouped together and fired at you. Your artillery thought it was a battery and threw a concentration of shells at the tanks, and by the time your shells struck the Tigers had moved away and were firing at you from another place.

Four American tank destroyers crossed the canal and bounced armor-piercing shells off the turret of a Tiger until it turned its massive gun and disintegrated them with five shells.

German infantry rode their tanks into battle and the dogfaces shot them off like squirrels but they didn't get all of them—some came in and bayoneted our guys in their holes.

This wasn't a beachhead that was secured and enlarged until it eventually became a port for supplies coming in to supplement those being expended as the troops pushed inland. Everything was expended right here. It was a constant hellish nightmare, because when you weren't getting something you were expecting something, and it lasted for five months.

A company of infantry sat on a mountain in Italy in mud, rain, snow, and freezing cold weather. They had inadequate clothing and they didn't get relief. They sat there for weeks, and the only men who came down that mountain were dead ones, badly wounded ones, and those who had trench foot from the icy mud.

—Sgt. Bill Mauldin
"I need a couple guys what don't owe me no money for a little routine patrol."

This Bill Mauldin cartoon appeared in a January 1944 issue of Stars and Stripes. *Its caption reads, "I need a couple guys what don't owe me no money for a little routine patrol."*

During that entire period the dogfaces didn't have a hot meal. Sometimes they had little gasoline stoves and were able to heat packets of "predigested" coffee, but most often they did it with matches—hundreds of matches which barely took the chill off the brew. Soon the guys ran out of matches.

Because they were on K rations they had coffee only once a day. The dinner ration had synthetic lemonade—a mixture of carbolic acid and ersatz lemon powder. Try drinking that in a muddy foxhole in freezing weather. The supper ration had a sort of bouillon soup, which was impossible. It takes a lot of water to make it, and a lot more to drown the salty thirst it causes. Usually there wasn't even enough water for the guys to brush their teeth because there weren't enough mules to haul it up.

THE LIBERATION OF FRANCE

23.

Preparations for D-Day

April 1944

Eisenhower's chief virtue as supreme commander of Overlord was that he got along well with virtually all of his subordinates, British and American, even the prima donnas like Montgomery and Patton. In fact, Eisenhower left much of the specific invasion planning to Montgomery, who would be commanding the troops in the field, while he focused his own energies on the more pressing logistical problems of

building up the necessary forces. The final tallies included 1.5 million men, both newcomers arriving from the States and veterans transferred from the Mediterranean theater; five thousand transports to carry the GIs across the Channel; six hundred warships to protect the transports and bombard the coast; and twelve thousand fighters and bombers to guarantee air superiority. It was by far the largest amphibious invasion force ever assembled, and its target would be Normandy.

Normandy was chosen at a June 1943 interservice conference (code-named Rattle) for several reasons: First, the region had two major ports, Cherbourg and Le Havre, either of which could resupply the large number of troops to be landed on the Continent. Second, the British ports opposite Normandy were considerably larger and better equipped than those along the Pas de Calais, the other logical invasion site, two hundred miles to the northeast at the Channel's narrowest point. Third, the Cotentin Peninsula (on which Cherbourg was situated) protected the Normandy invasion beaches from the prevailing

westerly winds that often disrupted Channel shipping. Fourth, Ultra intelligence reports showed that the Germans already expected the invasion to come at the Pas de Calais.

To encourage this German misconception, the Allies engaged in elaborate efforts to persuade the German High Command that a large force under Patton, the First U.S. Army Group (FUSAG), was indeed mobilizing in southeastern England for an invasion across the Pas de Calais. Set designers from the British film industry built a dummy headquarters, fake supply depots, and even facsimile tanks for the benefit of reconnaissance aircraft, while simulated communications traffic and carefully staged appearances by Patton added credibility to the ruse, which Ultra reports showed to be working. The bulk of the German armor remained in position near Calais, and even after the first landings in Normandy, the Germans continued to believe that Overlord was itself merely a ruse to divert their Panzer divisions from the main invasion still to come in the north.

An American tank crew takes part in March 1944 pre-invasion exercises "somewhere in England."

THE NEW YORK TIMES, SUNDAY, APRIL 23, 1944

BRITISH ISLES GUARD VITAL INVASION SECRETS

Drastic Measures May Conceal Time and Place but Not Allied Purpose

By RAYMOND DANIELL

LONDON, April 22—Some day an Anglo-American Army from Britain is going to descend on the Continent, which for four years has been under German domination. That much is known to Hitler and his general staff. It has been shouted from the housetops of all Allied capitals since Teheran. Strategic surprise, therefore, is impossible, but the success or failure of the expedition might well depend upon that slight advantage which always goes to the army which enjoys tactical surprise. That is just another way of saying that while Hitler and his generals have been told what they probably had figured out for themselves, they still don't know when or where the blow will fall.

That they do not find out that vital secret of war is one of General Eisenhower's chief concerns. It isn't easy to keep such a secret these days when huge masses of supplies and equipment, such great armadas of ships must be assembled almost under the eyes of enemy observers in reconnaissance craft. But some things cannot be seen from the air and there are others which when seen may merely serve to confuse the enemy unless he has agents working for him here to interpret the meaning of the preparations and tell him such important secrets as what kind of weapons and how many of them are being gathered for use against him.

The invasion, when it comes, will be the greatest expedition of its kind in history. Upon its outcome the fate of the world for generations may well depend. Not since Wellington landed his army in Portugal has anything comparable been attempted from this island and even then the British General was assured of landing on friendly soil. This time the Anglo-American armies must batter a hole in the wall of Hitler's fortress against the greatest defensive armament ever known and they must take with them not only food and ammunition but gasoline and every other conceivable thing they may need, down to locomotives, rolling stock and track for railroads.

In his undertaking General Eisenhower will be attempting in reverse a feat which Julius Caesar and William the Conqueror managed to bring off successfully but which Napoleon and Hitler at the crucial moment found beyond their power. All the hazards and difficulties which caused these two would-be rulers of the world to hesitate—twenty miles of salt water, the fog and swell of the Channel, and the peril of landing on a hostile shore—have been considered and as far as can be told in advance, surmounted.

Even if all the statesmen who have proclaimed Allied intentions of invading Europe had held their peace, the Germans would still have known the assault was coming. It is the only way the Nazi hold on Europe can be completely and finally broken. Nor could the approximate time be kept entirely secret, for it is impossible to gather an army big enough for the job in hand without knowledge of the enemy. But while German reconnaissance pilots can probably see themselves when British harbors are glutted with ships, and huge stockpiles disclose themselves in spite of elaborate camouflage, only a mind reader can tell when those supplies have reached the point which the Commander in Chief himself regards as sufficient.

U.S. troops conduct one of the final dress rehearsals for the D-day invasion, with GIs hitting the sand after being landed from invasion craft.

Despite this fact, however, there are weather conditions, the state of the moon, the tides and the season, which any prudent military man would have to consider. The Germans know that as well as we do, and so they probably know when it is safe to relax and when it is advisable to stand on guard. But it is a large coast line that they are defending and unless they are told they cannot tell just where we will strike.

In a general way, of course, they know that a large port, or ports, must be taken if the invasion is to be a success. But there are ports all the way from Narvik to Marseilles, all of which are threatened. No matter how observant they are nor how skillful their general staff may be in deductive reasoning, there are vital links in the chain of evidence they need for defense which they can get only from observers of this base with access either to secret radio or reasonably fast mail.

The British Government has made an elaborate effort involving drastic and unprecedented action to insure that no leak from here imperils the safety of the expedition. These precautions begin at supreme headquarters and affect every individual on this island. Only a handful of men close to General Eisenhower know just what is being planned. Everyone in the services has been impressed with the necessity for keeping his lips buttoned up and not even making guesses aloud for the sake of his own safety.

The garrulous soul who might be tempted to so much as mention anything to do with military matters in a public place is restrained by the knowledge that he is likely to have an anonymous note passed to him by the bartender, waiter or tram conductor, reading something like this: "Do go on with your story. We're all listening. So is Hitler."

Not to emphasize the seamy side of life but for the sake of the record it is true that among those ladies of the evening with whom soldiers, sailors and airmen sometimes spend their leisure there are many who came to this country from the Continent with other refugees some years ago. Scotland Yard has not overlooked them and those whose loyalty, regardless of virtue, is doubted have been placed beyond temptation. There has been a general checking up all over the country until officials now are reasonably sure that all those who might want to help the enemy are either under surveillance or where they cannot do any damage.

Much that has happened on this island in the past few weeks must be regarded as part of the general campaign to make this country spy-proof. The recent round-up of labor agitators was not undertaken solely in the interest of industrial peace and harmony but was partly dictated by security considerations. Of course, at the time when the crucial battle begins, strikes and other stoppages cannot be tolerated and the Government has taken strong action to discourage them. But a good deal of the fanfare about agitators was designed to make the public even more security-minded than they were.

Many of the things that have been done were of the nature that Germany in the past has left to the last moment before attacking some unsuspecting neighbor. But for the British to adopt the same policy and wait for zero hour would be a sure way of notifying the enemy that now at last the hour had struck. So, in accordance with Prime Minister Churchill's policy of keeping the enemy guessing with many feints and false alarms, the necessary steps have been taken one by one and nobody on either side of the Channel knows from day to day whether the event that the whole world is waiting for so anxiously is near or far away.

In this category falls the ban on travel to coastal areas by any but those who have good reason for being there. So, too, does the warning to the public that if they embark on long rail journeys they may find themselves cut off from the rest of the country for days and weeks. The repeated warnings to the people of the Continent to prepare for invasion helps keep the Germans guessing.

The recent American note to Eire calling on that country to close German and Japanese legations provided the British with a good excuse for tightening restrictions on travel and communication with that neighboring neutral member of the British Commonwealth of Nations after President de Valera had rejected this demand. Now it is almost impossible for anyone to travel between the two countries; telephonic communication is cut off and the mails are slow. It is true the border between northern and southern Ireland is open but it is about as well controlled as it would be if it were closed.

The most drastic action this country has taken to insure against leakage of military secrets was the order restricting movements of foreign diplomats, making diplomatic bags subject to censorship, and directing that all cables and messages to their Governments be sent in plain English or in British code. Only those dominions fighting at Britain's side and the United States and Russia are exempt from the order abrogating the privileges diplomats have enjoyed since earliest times. Not even those other foreign Governments which are members of the United Nations were exempt from the order which is designed to prevent secret information from reaching Germany by accident or design. It will cause some inconvenience to many neutral and Allied Governments but where so much is at stake the British are confident their action will be understood and accepted with protests.

These measures together with normal censorship are counted on to prevent leaks from here. The British are pretty confident that in the four and a half years they have been at war they have isolated and identified most if not all of the enemy's effective secret agents. The diplomatic corps was regarded as the last remaining danger to our plans.

What is going on here and has been going on for some time is material of major interest to military and naval attachés of every neutral country. Even those innocent of any desire or design to help the enemy could hardly be blamed if they reported in detail to their Governments what they had observed. The new British order is designed to prevent distillates of such reports reaching the enemy.

That secrecy can be maintained until the information is too late to help the enemy was believed to have been demonstrated by the North African expedition of November, 1942. Huge armadas sailed from the United States and Britain for Morocco and Algeria.

As it happened, Malta was in dire straits and they appear to have jumped to the conclusion that it was intended for the relief of that sorely beset island stronghold. Maybe they thought it was aimed at Spain's Balearic Islands, for it swerved toward them. Then under cover of night the ships changed course for Oran and Algiers and the Germans were caught flat-footed. General Eisenhower with the help of Anglo-American diplomacy and police work hopes to duplicate that feat.

"You are not all going to die."

George S. Patton's address to his troops before D-day

Patton was available for the FUSAG deception (and not leading troops in Italy) because he had been stripped of his command following the capture of Sicily. During his drive on Messina, Patton had twice slapped patients at field hospitals whom he considered cowards because their battle fatigue was largely mental. After knocking the helmet off one man's head (and into the next tent), the general shouted at the receiving officer, "Don't admit this yellow bastard; there's nothing the matter with him. I won't have the hospitals cluttered up with these sons of bitches who haven't got the guts to fight." Then, reaching for his pistol, he turned back to the patient and yelled, "In fact, I ought to shoot you myself, you goddamned whimpering coward." Several reporters who witnessed these incidents decided among themselves to suppress them, yet the story leaked anyway after medical staff filed reports critical of the general. Ike ordered Patton to apologize publicly and removed him from command, but later he relented and gave Gorgeous Georgie another chance. While Patton masqueraded as head of FUSAG, Eisenhower quietly named him to lead the newly created Third Army, whose task it would be to break out from the Normandy beachhead. Believing (like Rommel) that a general needed to be seen as often as possible by his troops, Patton toured his new command during the weeks preceding the invasion, delivering this speech in several slightly different versions.

Be seated.

Men, this stuff we hear about America wanting to stay out of the war, not wanting to fight, is a lot of bullshit. Americans love to fight—traditionally. All real Americans love the sting and clash of battle. When you were kids, you all admired the champion marble player; the fastest runner; the big league ball players; the toughest boxers. Americans love a winner and will not tolerate a loser. Americans despise cowards. Americans play to win—all the time. I wouldn't give a hoot in hell for a man who lost and laughed. That's why Americans have never lost, not ever will lose a war, for the very thought of losing is hateful to an American.

You are not all going to die. Only two percent of you here today would die in a major battle. Death must not be feared. Every man is frightened at first in battle. If he says he isn't, he's a goddamn liar. Some men are cowards, yes! But they fight just the same, or get the hell shamed out of them watching men who do fight who are just as scared. The real hero is the man who fights even though he is scared. Some get over their fright in a minute under fire, some take an hour. For some it takes days. But the real man never lets fear of death overpower his honor, his sense of duty to this country and his innate manhood.

All through your army career you men have bitched about "This chickenshit drilling." That is all for a purpose. Drilling and discipline must be maintained in any army if for only one reason—*instant obedience to orders and to create constant alertness.* I don't give a damn for a man who is not always on his toes. You men are veterans or you wouldn't be here. You are ready. A man to continue breathing must be alert at all times. If not, sometime a German son-of-a-bitch will sneak up behind him and beat him to death with a sock full of shit.

There are 400 neatly marked graves somewhere in Sicily all because one man went to sleep on his job—but they were German graves for we caught the bastard asleep before his officers did. An Army is a team. Lives, sleeps, eats, fights as a team. This individual heroic stuff is a lot of crap. The bilious bastards who wrote that kind of stuff for the *Saturday Evening Post* don't know any more about real fighting, under fire, than they do about fucking. We have the best food, the finest equipment, the best spirit and the best fighting men in the world. Why, by God, I actually pity these poor sons-of-bitches we are going up against. By God, I do!

My men don't surrender. I don't want to hear of any soldier under my command being captured unless he is hit. Even if you are hit, you can still fight. That's not just bullshit, either. The kind of man I want under me is like the lieutenant in Libya, who, with a Lugar against his chest, jerked off his helmet, swept the gun aside with one hand and busted hell out of the Boche with the helmet. Then he jumped on the gun and went out and killed another German: All this with a bullet through his lung. That's a man for you.

All real heroes are not storybook combat fighters either. Every man in the army plays a vital part. Every little job is essential. Don't ever let down, thinking your role is unimportant. Every man has a job to do. Every man is a link in the great chain. What if every truck driver decided that he didn't like the whine of the shells overhead, turned yellow and jumped headlong into the ditch? He could say to himself, "They won't miss me—just one in thousands." What if every man said that? Where in hell would we be now? No, thank God, Americans don't say that! Every man does his job; every man serves

Patton Jr. inspects troops of his new, undisclosed Third Army command in late April 1944.

the whole. Every department, every unit, is important to the vast scheme of things. The Ordnance men are needed to supply the guns, the Quartermaster to bring up the food and clothes to us—for where we're going there isn't a hell of a lot to steal. Every last man in the mess hall, even the one who heats the water to keep us from getting the GI shits has a job to do. Even the chaplain is important, for if we get killed and if he is not there to bury us we'd all go to hell.

Each man must not only think of himself, but of his buddy fighting beside him. We don't want yellow cowards in this army. They should all be killed off like flies. If not they will go back home after the war and breed more cowards. The brave men will breed brave men. Kill off the goddamn cowards and we'll have a nation of brave men.

One of the bravest men I ever saw in the African campaign was the fellow I saw on top of a telegraph pole in the midst of furious fire while we were plowing toward Tunis. I stopped and asked what the hell he was doing up there at that time. He answered, "Fixing the wire, sir." "Isn't it a little unhealthy right now?," I asked. "Yes sir, but this goddamn wire's got to be fixed." There was a real soldier. There was a man who devoted all he had to his duty, no matter how great the odds, no matter how seemingly insignificant his duty might appear at the time.

You should have seen those trucks on the road to Gabes. The drivers were magnificent. All day and all night they rolled over those son-of-a-bitching roads, never stopping, never faltering from their course, with shells bursting around them all the time. We got through on good old American guts. Many of these men drove over forty consecutive hours. These weren't combat men. But they were soldiers with a job to do. They did it—and in a whale of a way they did it. They were part of a team. Without them the fight would have been lost. All the links in the chain pulled together and that chain became unbreakable.

Don't forget, you don't know I'm here. No word of the fact is to be mentioned in any letters. The world is not supposed to know what the hell became of me. I'm not supposed to be commanding this Army. I'm not even supposed to be in England. Let the first bastards to find out be the goddamn Germans. Someday I want them to raise up on their hind legs and howl, "Jesus Christ, it's the goddamn Third Army and that son-of-a-bitch Patton again."

We want to get the hell over there. We want to get over there and clear the goddamn thing up. You can't win a war lying down. The quicker we clean up this goddamn mess, the quicker we can take a jaunt against the purple pissing Japs and clean their nest out too, before the Marines get all the goddamn credit.

Sure, we all want to be home. We want this thing over with. The quickest way to get it over is to get the bastards. The quicker they are whipped, the quicker we go home. The shortest way home is through Berlin. When a man is lying in a shell hole, if he just stays there all day, a Boche will get him eventually, and the hell with that idea. The hell with taking it. My men don't dig foxholes. I don't want them to. Foxholes only slow up an offensive. Keep moving. And don't give the enemy time to dig one. We'll win this war but we'll win it only by fighting and by showing the Germans we've got more guts than they have.

There is one great thing you men will all be able to say when you go home. You may thank God for it. Thank God, that at least, thirty years from now, when you are sitting around the fireside with your grandson on your knees, and he asks you what you did in the great war, you won't have to cough and say, "I shoveled shit in Louisiana."

24

Segregation in the Army
April 1944

It was A. Philip Randolph's view that the best way to advance the cause of civil rights was to organize black workers. In 1925, he founded the Brotherhood of Sleeping Car Porters to represent the predominantly black men who tended the nation's Pullman cars—workers then excluded from all other railway unions. In early 1941, with defense production gearing up, he began making plans for a huge march on

Washington to protest segregation in the defense industries. President Roosevelt opposed the idea, fearing that it would prove divisive, especially if the demonstration turned violent. He sent his wife, Eleanor, and New York mayor Fiorello La Guardia—both of whom Randolph knew and trusted—to persuade the union leader to call off the July 1 march. Randolph was warned that such an effort would most likely bring about reprisals from bigoted whites and do more harm than good. Yet Randolph refused to back down until one week before the march, when the president issued Executive Order 8802, prohibiting racial discrimination in defense hiring and establishing a Fair Employment Practice Committee to enforce the order.

Randolph's victory, however, didn't apply to the nation's armed forces, which remained segregated throughout World War II. Although African Americans made up more than 15 percent of the available national manpower, the few inducted into the army were generally restricted to supply and service duty. Despite the pressing need for more combat troops, only three

"colored" combat divisions were formed, and only one of these saw extensive action. Inserted along the Gustav line in southern Italy, the Ninety-second Division made little progress and suffered heavy losses, apparently confirming the myth that blacks couldn't fight. Subsequent investigations, however, showed that the division's white leadership had been woeful. Maj. Gen. Edward M. Almond, the division commander, was an unabashed racist who believed that training blacks was a waste of time, so he didn't. His subordinates, following suit, also ignored many of their leadership responsibilities.

There were, however, several segregated combat battalions that performed heroically, the most famous of these being the 761st Tank Battalion. Assigned to Patton's Third Army—over the general's strong objection, because he didn't believe blacks could "think fast enough to fight in armor"—the 761st nevertheless won Patton over. "I have nothing but the best in my army," the general declared in late 1944. "I don't care what color you are as long as you go up there and kill those Kraut sons-of-bitches."

NEGROES' COURAGE UPHELD IN INQUIRY

Gibson Lays the Difficulties of 92d Division in Italy to Its High Illiteracy

By MILTON BRACKER

ROME, March 14—The circumstances surrounding the American Ninety-second Division and its combat record present "a rather dismal picture," but one that may contribute greatly to working out the difficult Army race problem in the future, it was asserted here today by Truman K. Gibson Jr., civilian aide to Secretary of War Henry L. Stimson.

All the enlisted men in the Ninety-second Division are Negroes. The division's accomplishments so far in the Tyrrhenian sector of the Italian front have been limited in terms of the map and highly controversial in terms of general discussion throughout the Mediterranean theatre.

Largely because of this controversy, which spread to the general and Negro press at home, Mr. Gibson came here at the end of February. He has visited most Negro units, as well as high Army officers. His appraisal must be taken most seriously because he is the official representative of the War Department and is a Negro. He also is the first Government official to make a candid publishable appraisal of the situation.

To understand the situation it must be realized that the generalization that "Negro troops can't fight" has been depressingly prevalent on and behind the Italian front virtually since the Ninety-second Division arrived. As usual it has been picked up by the worst elements in the Army, but too often it has been repeated by high officers of unquestioned integrity, although often they are men whose knowledge of the Ninety-second Division is not first hand.

Mr. Gibson denied this generalization on the basis of his inspection.

"If the division proves anything," he said, "it does not prove that Negroes can't fight. There is no question in my mind about the courage of Negro officers or soldiers and any generalization on the basis of race is entirely unfounded."

Mr. Gibson then frankly went into the touchiest aspect of all. He conceded that certain units of the Ninety-second Division had engaged in "more or less panicky retreats, particularly at night when the attitude of some individual soldiers seemed to be 'I'm up here all alone; why in hell should I stay up here?'"

But, he added, "not all the straggling and running has happened in the Ninety-second Division."

In other divisions, he said, it seemed to be that it was more often the case of some individuals falling back in every unit while with the Ninety-second "the disintegration was likely to be the behavior pattern of some patrols or platoons as units."

In the relatively high percentage of illiteracy of the division Mr. Gibson felt lay the key to the trouble and certainly a reason for making unfair any comparison of it with veteran white outfits like the Thirty-fourth Division. Ninety-two per cent of the Negro Division were in Class 4 or Class 5 in Army literacy tests.

Class 5 is the worst. Seventy-five per cent of the Ninety-second's men were in Class 4, semi-literacy.

Black and white soldiers eat separately in the enlisted men's mess aboard the SS Uruguay *en route to North Africa in November 1944.*

"You can't apply the same training schedules where that many men are illiterate as where only 3 per cent are," Mr. Gibson commented.

He said that normally all Class 5 men would have had a special period of "basic education" but that the men in the Ninety-second were not because the division was being activated at the time they were called up and they were sent to it immediately.

General Army figures show 46.4 per cent of Negroes are in Class 5 and 35 per cent are in Class 4, against 4 per cent of whites in Class 5 and 16 per cent in Class 4.

"What is the Negro soldier fighting for?"

Letters to the editor of *Yank*

Black soldiers' hard feelings about racial segregation finally surfaced in the pages of the army weekly *Yank* in April 1944, when Cpl. Rupert Trimmingham wrote a letter from Fort Huachuca, Arizona, complaining of the substandard treatment African Americans in the army received. Other letters followed.

April 28, 1944

Dear YANK:

Here is a question that each Negro soldier is asking. What is the Negro soldier fighting for? On whose team are we playing? Myself and eight other soldiers were on our way from Camp Claiborne, La., to the hospital here at Fort Huachuca. We had to lay over until the next day for our train. On the next day we could not purchase a cup of coffee at any of the lunchrooms around there. As you know, Old Man Jim Crow rules. The only place where we could be served was at the lunchroom at the railroad station but, of course, we had to go into the kitchen. But that's not all; 11:30 A.M. about two dozen German prisoners of war, with two American guards, came to the station. They entered the lunchroom, sat at the tables, had their meals served, talked, smoked, in fact had quite a swell time. I stood on the outside looking on, and I could not help but ask myself these questions: Are these men sworn enemies of this country? Are they not taught to hate and destroy…all democratic governments? Are we not American soldiers, sworn to fight for and die if need be for this our country? Then why are they treated better than we are? Why are we pushed around like cattle? If we are fighting for the same thing, if we are to die for our country, then why does the Government allow such things to go on? Some of the boys are saying that you will not print this letter. I'm saying that you will….

Cpl. Rupert Trimmingham
Fort Huachuca, Ariz.

June 9, 1944

Dear YANK:

I am writing to you in regard to the incident told in a letter to you by Cpl. Trimmingham (Negro) describing the way he was forced to eat in the kitchen of a station restaurant while a group of German prisoners were fed with the rest of the white civilians in the restaurant. Gentlemen, I am a Southern rebel, but this incident makes me none the more proud of my Southern heritage! Frankly, I think that this incident is a disgrace to a democratic nation such as ours is supposed to be. Are we fighting for such a thing as this? Certainly not. If this incident is democracy, I don't want any part of it!…I wonder what the "Aryan supermen" think when they get a firsthand glimpse of our racial discrimination. Are we not waging a war, in part, for this fundamental of democracy? In closing, let me say that a lot of us, especially in the South, should cast the beam out of our own eyes before we try to do so in others, across the seas.

Cpl. Henry S. Wootton Jr.
S/Sgt. A. S. Tepper
Pfc. Jose Rosenzweig

June 9, 1944

Dear YANK:

You are to be complimented on having the courage to print Cpl. Trimmingham's letter in an April issue of YANK. It simply proves that your policy is maturing editorially. He probes an old wound when he exposes the problem of our colored soldiers throughout the South. It seems incredible that German prisoners of war should be afforded the amenities while our own men—in uniform and changing stations—are denied similar attention because of color and the vicious attitude of certain portions of our country. What sort of a deal is this? It is, I think, high time that this festering sore was cut out by intelligent social surgeons once and for all. I can well understand and sympathize with the corporal's implied but unwritten question: why, then, are we in uniform. Has it occurred to anyone that those Boche prisoners of war must be still laughing at us?

S/Sgt. Arthur J. Kaplan

June 9, 1944

Dear YANK:

…I'm not a Negro, but I've been around and know what the score is. I want to thank the YANK…and congratulate Cpl. Rupert Trimmingham.

Pvt. Gustave Santiago

July 28, 1944

Dear YANK:

Just read Cpl. Rupert Trimmingham's letter titled "Democracy?" in a May edition of YANK. We are white soldiers in the Burma jungles, and there are many Negro outfits working with us. They are doing more than their part to win this war. We are proud of the colored men here. When we are away from camp working in the jungles, we can go to any colored camp and be treated like one of their own. I think it is a disgrace that, while we are away from home doing our part to help win the war, some people back home are knocking down everything that we are fighting for.

We are among many Allied Nations' soldiers that are fighting here, and they marvel at how the American Army, which is composed of so many nationalities and different races, gets along so well. We are ashamed to read that the German soldier, who is the sworn enemy of our country, is treated better than the soldier of our country, because of race.

Cpl. Trimmingham asked: What is a Negro fighting for? If this sort of thing continues, we the white soldiers will begin to wonder: What are we fighting for?

> Pvt. Joseph Poscucci (Italian)
> Cpl. Edward A. Kreutler (French)
> Pfc. Maurice E. Wenson (Swedish)
> Pvt. James F. Malloy (Irish)

July 28, 1944

Dear YANK:

Allow me to thank you for publishing my letter. Although there was some doubt about its being published, yet some how I felt that YANK was too great a paper not to.... Each day brings three, four or five letters to me in answer to my letter. I just returned from my furlough and found 25 letters awaiting me. To date I've received 287 letters, and, strange as it may seem, 183 are from white men and women in the armed service. Another strange feature about these letters is that the most of these people are from the Deep South. They are all proud of the fact that they are of the South but ashamed to learn that there are so many of their own people who by their actions and manner toward the Negro are playing Hitler's game. Nevertheless, it gives me new hope to realize that there are doubtless thousands of whites who are willing to fight this Frankenstein that so many white people are keeping alive. All that the Negro is asking for is to be given half a chance and he will soon demonstrate his worth to his country. Should these white people who realize that the Negro is a man who is loyal—one who would gladly give his life for this our wonderful country—would stand up, join with us and help us to prove to their white friends that we are worthy, I'm sure that we would bury race hate and unfair treatment. Thanks again.

> Cpl. Rupert Trimmingham

Since YANK printed Cpl. Trimmingham's letter we have received a great number of comments from GIs, almost all of whom were outraged by the treatment given the corporal. His letter has been taken from YANK and widely quoted. The incident has been dramatized on the air and was the basis for a moving short story published recently in the New Yorker *magazine.*

25.

The Plight of Women Defense Workers

May 1944

World War II transformed the American woman's place in the workforce more thoroughly than any other event in the twentieth century. A decade earlier, during the Great Depression, the federal government had warned women not to take jobs that might otherwise go to unemployed men. After 1941, however, with so many male workers leaving their jobs for the armed forces and defense industries creating more

and more new openings, the federal government reversed itself and began encouraging women to work. Long-standing bans on the employment of older (that is, over thirty-five) and married women were relaxed, and approximately six million wives, mothers, and daughters responded. By 1945, their influx had driven up the proportion of women in the American workforce from 25 to 36 percent. One million of them took jobs with the federal government, pushing war-related paper; twice as many, however, found employment in heavy industry, hardly traditional female work.

A government inspection of seven aircraft factories in 1941 revealed a total of 143 women employed there. Eighteen months later, that number had shot up to sixty-five thousand. Finally, in 1944, at the height of the country's war production, women workers made up an astonishing 40 percent of the aircraft industry's workforce. The comparable figure for shipyards was a still-impressive 12 percent. As with other defense workers, African Americans benefited the most. Before the war, three out of four working black

women were domestics; nearly all of the rest were farmhands. By war's end, however, almost 20 percent had found factory jobs paying at least double their previous earnings and often much more. In fact, nearly all women workers earned much better money during the war than at any time previous—yet their take-home pay was still less than what men earned in comparable jobs. The federal government had endorsed the concept of equal pay for equal work, but most employers either ignored the policy or got around it by reclassifying jobs.

In the meantime, more and more women discovered that they wanted to keep working. At the start of the war, 95 percent of married workers said they intended to quit their new jobs once their husbands returned home; by the end of the war, most had changed their minds, and more than 80 percent reported wanting to keep their jobs, typically because they liked the additional income. Nevertheless, once the war ended, women workers were fired en masse to make room for the returning servicemen.

NATION CONCENTRATING ON RAISING WAR OUTPUT

Labor Shortage Is Chief Bottleneck in Attaining Our Production Goals

By JOHN MACCORMAC

WASHINGTON, Oct. 2—How to push war production from the new high it reached in August to the stratospheric levels to which it must soar next year if war goals are to be attained continued to be the chief preoccupation of the President and his advisers this week.

The President took a step toward this end when he created an Army-Navy Production Survey Committee to see that only what is needed at the front to meet the changing conditions of combat is produced. Robert P. Patterson, Under-Secretary of War, pleaded with 200 industrial, labor and newspaper leaders to drive home the necessity of an even greater production effort. Mrs. Roosevelt explained to a press conference how the fighting men whom she had met in the Pacific could not understand why output should lag at home. Finally, the country's warplane manufacturers met in a two-day conference with interested Government agencies to thresh over the manpower problems which continue to be the biggest obstacle to pushing an admittedly magnificent productive performance to still greater heights.

Meanwhile the man most directly concerned with the supervision of war production, Donald Nelson of the War Production Board, was in England telling our Allies what we had accomplished and seeking from them answers to some of the problems which they had faced before and we were facing now.

Mr. Nelson was able to assure them that American war output this year would be at least one and a half times as great as that of the whole Axis and next year should be twice as great, that the United States had produced 110,000 military planes since Pearl Harbor and soon would be completing one every five minutes of the day. He was asking them what expedients would enable women to work in factories without worrying too much about the welfare of their children and the state of their homes, how to cope with absenteeism and cut down on labor turnover.

These, according to the aircraft manufacturers who met in Washington this week, are the chief difficulties which stand in the way of their achieving the 50 per cent increase in dollar production of warplanes demanded of them next year. This means a plane output of something like 10,000 a month in 1944, although, with the concentration of construction on ever heavier aircraft, weight rather than number is becoming a better index of output as time goes on.

It was announced this week by Robert A. Lovett, Assistant Secretary of War for Air, that more than 50 per cent of 1944 Army production must be airplanes. It was obvious from what the airplane makers said that the supply and flow of materials was no longer the hard core of the production problem. Aircraft output, they reported, still suffered from some shortages in materials, sub-assemblies, parts and fittings. But many of these material shortages, they said, were traceable not to actual lack of raw materials, but to lack of workers in the fabricating and processing industries, indicating that manpower was a problem which must be considered all down the line.

It is certainly one they themselves have to consider every minute of the day, since not only

This photograph shows female welders at the Ingalls Shipbuilding Corporation in Pascagoula, Mississippi, in February 1943.

are workers hard to find, and must be trained when found, but after training they have a distressing habit of taking their newly acquired skills to other markets. As a result some 70 per cent of the working force they hire one year is gone the next. Many of the men go to other occupations, such as shipbuilding, which are allowed a higher wage scale. Many of the women go home.

The plane makers reserved judgment on the "referral hiring plan" which succeeded with heavy industry in the Buffalo area and is now being tried on the West Coast for the benefit of aircraft manufacture. Most of them favored and some said they were already experimenting with incentive-payment schemes, but they were not unanimous in recommending adoption of such plans.

Although they wanted help from the Government in fields where neither industry-wide nor community effort was adequate, the plane makers thought that the manpower problem would

have to be licked mainly by management effort in individual plants and by cooperation with other industries in communities and areas. As for the form that management effort should take, the consensus seemed to be that it would boil down to a case of "cherchez la femme."

Use of women in airplane plants has long since passed the 50 per cent mark, and one manufacturer thought it might eventually exceed 75 per cent.

Perhaps the problem could better be stated, not as one of finding the woman, since she has been found, but of keeping her. "Female absenteeism," according to a report of the East Coast Air Council, is far higher than male absenteeism and therefore as the numbers of women workers increase so will the absenteeism ratio.

How can women be induced to stay on the job? Philip Johnson, president of Boeing, which builds the Flying Fortresses, thought that in-plant feeding, shopping centers, branch banks and transportation committees to arrange for ride-sharing might be part of the answer. The trouble is the old saw that "man's work is from sun to sun but woman's work is never done" still holds true of Swing-Shift Susie, who not only has a home to go to after she has finished her work but housework to be done there, children to be cared for and household shopping to do.

Doubt that there will be a national service draft in an election year is expressed in Washington. It seems likely, therefore, that the employment of more and more women will be the answer to the manpower problem and that women's psychology and women's needs will be a subject of flattering study in Washington by public figures who never had to delve into such matters before.

There are, of course, other aspects of the labor question which must be considered. The War Production Board took action to deal with one of them some days ago when it decreed that war contracts cannot be let in areas with extreme labor shortage, and it may deal with another by ordering that civilian orders be filled in other than war production centers.

A third measure advocated in some quarters is further "concentration and standardization" of civilian production to free labor for war output. Another step which is almost certain to be taken is the transfer of war work from large critical manpower areas to surplus areas by subcontracting or—as Boeing is doing on the West Coast— by opening small branch factories.

Another suggestion in connection with the failure of war production to maintain a sufficiently sharp climb was that offered this week by the newspaper editors and publishers, who constitute the Office of War Information's Newspaper Advisory Committee: that the American public was not getting enough information about the war from the higher command of the Army and Navy. It was that, rather than a lack of patriotism, which should be blamed for any let-up in the war effort, in the opinion of the committee.

"Your request for lockers is ridiculous."

Susan B. Anthony II's decription of women's work at a navy yard

Susan B. Anthony II, the grandniece of the eminent suffragist, worked as a reporter for the *Washington Star* from 1942 until 1943, when she published *Out of the Kitchen—Into the War: Women's Winning Role in the Nation's Drama.* She wrote this article for the May 1, 1944, issue of the *New Republic.*

Working at the Navy Yard

My first night on the midnight shift at the Washington Navy Yard, I met Esther, a fellow ordnance worker, who ran the machine next to mine. Dreading the changeover from swing shift to "graveyard," I asked Esther's advice on the best hours for eating and sleeping after 8 A.M. "When do you go to bed?" I asked.

"Bed!" exclaimed Esther, a swarthy woman of about 35. "I haven't slept in a bed for five months."

Esther, the mother of five children, then told me the seemingly unbelievable schedule she has followed for the five months she has been working on ordnance to pad her husband's daily wage of $4.83, made as a trucker on the railroad.

"I have to run out of here to catch my bus at 8:10 in the morning so I can get home right after he leaves for work," said Esther. "I see that the three older kids are dressed OK for school and have had something to eat. Then I feed the little ones. Tommy is four and Mary is almost three. I feed myself and wash the dishes, straighten up the house, wash if I have to and take the kids out with me to buy groceries. Then I give the little ones lunch and make some sandwiches for the kids that go to school.

"After lunch I try to get some sleep—not in bed though—I just sit in a big chair in the living room and prop my feet up. Have you ever tried getting to sleep and staying asleep while watching two little kids tear the house apart?"

I could only look at Esther's tired face and wonder how many more months she could continue on such a regime. Next month, Tommy will go to half-day kindergarten. There are no nursery schools in the neighborhood for Mary, however, and the only one near the navy yard has a waiting list of 40 children.

Two nights after my talk with Esther, I came in at midnight and found her the center of a buzzing, indignant group of women workers.

"Esther's house almost caught fire this morning," explained Louise excitedly. "The new ruling that we have to take our coats all the way down to the ladies' room at the far end of the shop instead of hanging them in here, made Esther lose her bus. When she got home the kids were fooling with the gas stove and a towel had already caught fire."

The master mechanic, head of the shop, had decreed that we must take a ten-minute round-trip walk to hang up our coats. This meant that women workers had to get to work ten minutes earlier and were delayed ten minutes afterwards.

"Why can't we have lockers right up here near the elevator, like most of the men?" protested one of women.

This led to a petition asking for conveniently located lockers which we planned to get all the women in the shop to sign and then present to the master mechanic. Only four of us had a chance to sign it, however, before a personnel man on his daily check-up rounds, picked it up and turned it over to the master mechanic. We four were called on the carpet.

"Your request for lockers is ridiculous and will never be granted," he said. "Don't ever let me hear another word of this."

Two of the women who had signed were immediately transferred from our room. I was threatened with disciplinary action and was asked to explain my conduct in writing. I did explain. I protested the women's lack of representation on any grievance body. For our locker gripe was the least of our grievances. Working at the navy yard is like working in a completely open shop, since women are not members of the main union at the plant—the International Association of Machinists, AFL. We therefore had no shop steward, no grievance committee, no representation on union bodies and, least of all, no benefits of equal pay, promotion policies or other standards that a union contract would ensure.

Take our wages, for example. Though research for my book had shown stories of high pay for women workers to be an utter myth, I had no idea, until I became a war worker myself, how **LOW** wages actually were. When my skimpy little paycheck of $23 a week came to me, I wondered how on earth I could ever live on that in wartime Washington if I were forced to pay my own room, board, transportation, doctors' bills and other necessities out of it. Then I would look around the shop and wonder how the married women and mothers—the majority there—could support their children and parents as well as themselves on these wages.

Navy-yard women start at $4.65 a day, which, with time and one-half for the sixth day, is $29.64 a week. Deduct the 20-percent withholding tax, and you find that we luxuriate on $23 a week. The highest-paid woman on production in our shop receives $6.95 a day, a peak she has attained after two years at the yard. Men get as high as $22 a day. The same low wages for beginning women workers prevail at most of the other eight navy yards in the country. Welders, however, and others who get preemployment training are better paid. Welders at one yard receive $1.14 an hour. The wages of mechanics-learners, which is the classification we came under at the Washington yard and in which many women start at other yards, begin at 57 or 58 cents an hour.

Not only do the women start at a low wage—they stay at it. At the Washington yard and at the other navy yards in the East and West, there are no automatic raises. Miriam, who had been in the yard for eighteen months, said to me:

"At this place, it ain't what you know—it's who you know."

Raises were accorded on some indeterminate basis. Promotions to supervisory jobs seem to be unknown not only at Washington but elsewhere in navy yards. I could discover no women foremen, no women job instructors, or "snappers"—the lowest rank in the supervisory hierarchy. Up to last fall, I had heard of only three women "snappers" working at all navy yards. Others may have been promoted since then, but the going is slow.

Equal pay and promotions for women are one of the government standards of employment supported in writing by the Navy Department and seven other federal agencies. The navy yards themselves seem to be unaware of the fact; nor do they observe other standards adhered to on paper by the Department.

Production aides Ruby Reed and Merle Judd working for the Grumman Aircraft Engineering Corporation in 1944.

A few minutes before my first lunch on the day shift, I saw a woman, crouching almost double, come over to a bucket of dirty water used for cooling tools. She glanced furtively through the glass partitions separating our room from the rest of the shop and then stooped quickly and washed her hands in the filthy water.

"We aren't allowed to go out to the ladies' room and wash our hands before lunch—so this is the only water in the room and at least I can get some of the grease off my hands before I eat. If one of the bosses catches you washing you get docked and suspended," she explained, while keeping an eye out for the bosses.

Following most of the women workers, I quickly adapted myself to eating sandwiches held between grimy hands. I also had to learn to gulp down lunch in 15 minutes. The yard gave us 20 minutes for lunch, but at least five minutes were gone by the time you had raced and waited at the understaffed canteen for cold, watery chocolate milk or cola drinks (no coffee except on the midnight shift). The government standard of 30-minute lunch periods, hot lunches and a decent place to eat them is ignored by the Washington yard, which is nearer being the rule than the exception. Four out of seven yards in the nation give workers lunch periods of less than 30 minutes—5 in one yard, 20 in two and 25 in a fourth. In the other three yards, the lunch period, which is on the workers' own time, is 30, 40 and 45 minutes, respectively. Some of these other yards have hot lunches served from mobile or stationary canteens. We had to choose between cold sandwiches bought from the yard and cold sandwiches which we brought with us.

Another standard neglected by yard officials was the 15-minute rest period, morning and afternoon, advocated for women workers. I don't think many of us at the Washington yard missed these breathing spells, however. The fact was that although the work in our room was physically hard and required standing almost eight hours at a stretch in some cases (such as mine), there was such a slowdown, stemming from the top, that no one hurried. When I first caught on to my particular job, I began working at my normal speed, which is fast. The woman next to me said to me in a blasé tone:

"Don't break your neck working so fast—no one else does and the bosses won't like you any better for it."

Later a boss actually warned me:

"Take it easy; there's no rush. If you finish that there won't be anything else for you to do for a while."

On day shift we were kept fairly busy. The swing shift, from four to midnight, was the slowest. Workers stood around obviously idle for want of work, and would look alert only when a naval officer came by. The workers accepted the slowdown along with the bosses. When I asked one man the cause of it, he replied:

"Oh, it's red tape. The stuff we need in this shop is laying around in another shop and the orders to send it over here are tied up somewhere else."

I do not know whether workers at the other navy yards need rest periods more than those at Washington. Only two out of seven yards reporting have said that their women get formal rest periods, and in one of these, rests were given in the machine shop alone. In the other, women in the sail loft were given a rest period of 10 minutes every two hours. Rest periods for women, just like convenient lunch facilities for all workers, seem to be considered luxuries by yard officials.

At the Washington yard the lack of formal rest periods could not be attributed to the rush of work. Nor could one attribute it to a shortage of workers or overvaluation of the workers' time. I had mistakenly thought before going to work at the yard that minutes were precious in production. Once on the job, personnel officers and posters proclaimed the need for punctuality and perfect attendance.

I was naturally surprised to learn after one day's work that the main method of disciplining these "precious" workers was to lay them off for as much as a week at a time.

Bertha, who took two or three days without permission to be with her sailor husband who was shipping out for a long time, was laid off for an entire week as a penalty. If you were one minute late in the morning, you were made to stand idle for one hour and be docked accordingly. If you forgot to tag in upon arrival at work or at lunch time, after three offenses you were laid off for a day.

There were other penalties besides being laid off, I learned when I was on the midnight shift. I saw Miriam, who had held the day shift for months, standing at a machine one night and asked her why she had changed from day work.

"You can bet your life I didn't change because I wanted to. The boss told me today at the end of my shift that I had to come in tonight."

Miriam had just married a soldier. She had accumulated one week's annual leave so she could take her honeymoon when her husband got his furlough. Before her vacation began, however, she took a day's sick leave. When she put in a slip for her vacation, the personnel officer, who had previously promised her the week off, told her:

"You don't get that week's leave now. Taking that day off when you were sick means that you can't take the week."

Miriam decided she would go ahead and take her honeymoon as planned. The result was that her first day back on the job she was forced to work 16 hours, 8 on the day shift and 8 on midnight. She was being punished by assignment to midnight for two weeks.

"Why do you stand for it?" I asked.

"I need the money, that's why," she replied simply.

That was the attitude of most of the women whom I met at the yard. They would stand for practically anything—five months without sleeping in a bed, a solid year on the graveyard shift so as to be home with the kids during the day, the double job, indigestible lunches, long hours and no promise of a future after the war—all for miserably low wages. The longer I worked side by side with them, the more I admired their endurance—but the more I seethed to see them organized in a union that would help solve their problems. And the more I saw the necessity for really planned production, planned community service, labor-utilization inspectors, labor-management committees that function and are recognized, and a program to educate the workers about the issues of the war abroad and at home. I admired the patience of the women who stuck by their jobs, day after day, though it was obvious that their usefulness to the war effort was cut in half by the very working conditions which they endured.

26

D-Day

Montgomery's plan for the invasion of France called for an initial amphibious landing of six divisions—three American, two British, and one Canadian. The U.S. troops—commanded by Lt. Gen. Omar N. Bradley, Eisenhower's West Point classmate and a respected tactician—would include the nucleus of the Fifth Army. Its task would be to force its way ashore at two beaches, code-named Omaha and Utah,

at the base of the Cotentin Peninsula and, from there, to drive on Cherbourg. Meanwhile, advance elements of the Anglo-Canadian Second Army under Lt. Gen. Miles Dempsey, a Montgomery protégé, would land farther east near the mouth of the Orne River at beaches code-named Sword, Juno, and Gold. Dempsey's job would be to capture the important crossroads at Caen, ten miles inland. In addition, beginning just after midnight (British time) on D-day, Allied aircraft would begin dropping three airborne divisions, two American and one British, to provide cover on the armies' flanks.

Field Marshal Gerd von Rundstedt was the German general with overall responsibility for the western front. In 1942, the capricious Hitler had removed Rundstedt from his command in the east, only to rehabilitate him several months later with an even more prestigious command in the west. Under Rundstedt, Hitler placed Rommel, whom he transferred from Tunisia shortly before that country's fall. Rommel was given field command of Army Group B, whose territory included the southern Nether-

lands, Belgium, and northern France. His task was to prepare France for the invasion that everyone knew was coming. Certainly his strengthening of the coastal defenses in Normandy made the Allied landings there much more difficult and costly than they otherwise would have been. Yet the timing of the invasion took both Rommel and his colleagues by surprise. On the morning of D-day, for instance, Rommel was in Germany, attending his wife's birthday celebration.

At half past six on D-day morning, the first Allied soldiers plunged from their landing craft into the cold, waist-deep waters of the Channel and began wading ashore. Aboard one of those landing craft was novelist-turned-war-correspondent Ernest Hemingway. "As we moved in toward the land in the gray early light," Hemingway later wrote, "the 36-foot coffin-shaped steel boat took solid green sheets of water that fell on the helmeted heads of the troops packed shoulder to shoulder in the stiff, awkward, uncomfortable, lonely companionship of men going to battle."

Coast Guard troops wade ashore from their landing craft onto Omaha Beach during the D-day invasion.

ALLIED ARMIES LAND IN FRANCE IN THE HAVRE-CHERBOURG AREA; GREAT INVASION IS UNDER WAY

Eisenhower Acts; U. S., British, Canadian Troops Backed by Sea, Air Forces

By RAYMOND DANIELL

SUPREME HEADQUARTERS ALLIED EXPEDITIONARY FORCES, Tuesday, June 6—The invasion of Europe from the west has begun.

In the gray light of a summer dawn Gen. Dwight D. Eisenhower threw his great Anglo-American force into action today for the liberation of the Continent. The spearhead of attack was an Army group commanded by Gen. Sir Bernard L. Montgomery and comprising troops of the United States, Britain and Canada.

General Eisenhower's first communiqué was terse and calculated to give little information to the enemy. It said merely that "Allied naval forces supported by strong air forces began landing Allied armies this morning on the northern coast of France."

After the first communiqué was released it was announced that the Allied landing was in Normandy.

German broadcasts, beginning at 6:30 A.M., London time, [12:30 A.M. Eastern war time] gave first word of the assault. [The Associated Press said General Eisenhower, for the sake of surprise, deliberately let the Germans have the "first word."]

The German DNB agency said the Allied invasion operations began with the landing of airborne troops in the area of the mouth of the Seine River.

[Berlin said the "center of gravity" of the fierce fighting was at Caen, thirty miles southwest of Havre and sixty-five miles southeast of Cherbourg, The Associated Press reported. Caen is ten miles inland from the sea, at the base of the seventy-five-mile-wide Normandy Peninsula, and fighting there might indicate the Allies' seizing of a beachhead.

[DNB said in a broadcast just before 10 A.M. (4 A.M. Eastern war time) that the Anglo-American troops had been reinforced at dawn at the mouth of the Seine River in the Havre area.]

[An Allied correspondent broadcasting from Supreme Headquarters, according to the Columbia Broadcasting System, said this morning that "German tanks are moving up the roads toward the beachhead" in France.]

The German accounts told of Nazi shock troops thrown in to meet Allied airborne units and parachutists. The first attacks ranged from Cherbourg to Havre, the Germans said.

[United States battleships and planes took part in the bombardment of the French coast, Allied Headquarters announced, according to Reuter.]

The weather was not particularly favorable for the Allies. There was a heavy chop in the Channel and the skies were overcast. Whether the enemy was taken by surprise was not known yet.

Not until the attack began was it made known officially that General Montgomery was in command of the Army group, including American troops. The hero of El Alamein hitherto had been referred to as the senior British Field Commander.

Transports and landing craft disgorge reinforcements and supplies onto Omaha Beach on the day after D-day.

In his order of the day, made public at the same time as the first communiqué, General Eisenhower told his forces that they were about to embark on a "great crusade."

The eyes of the world are upon you, he said, and the "hopes and prayers of liberty-loving people everywhere march with you." The order, which reflected a full appreciation of the mighty task ahead and yet reflected the calm, sober confidence that permeates these headquarters, was distributed to assault elements after their embarkation. It was read by the commanders to all other troops in the Allied Expeditionary Force.

The news that has been so long and so eagerly awaited broke as war-weary Londoners were going to work. Hardly any of them knew what was happening, for there had been no disclosure of the news that the invasion had started in the British Broadcasting Corporation's 7 o'clock broadcast.

Even the masses of planes roaring overhead did not give the secret away, for the people of this country have grown accustomed to seeing huge armadas of aircraft flying out in their almost daily attacks against German-held Europe.

Details of how the assault developed are still lacking. It is known that the huge armada of Allied landing craft that crept to the French coast in darkness was preceded by mine sweepers whose task was to sweep the Channel of German mine fields and submarine obstructions.

Big Allied warships closed in and engaged the enemy's shore batteries.

Airborne troops landed simultaneously behind the Nazis' coast defenses.

Not only were the troops of the United States, Canada and Britain united in a single fighting team, but their huge land, sea and air forces operated as a perfectly integrated machine.

Today provided the first example in northwest Europe of "triphibious strategy" in which Navy and Air Forces first help the Army gain a foothold on enemy territory as the Army goes about the grim business of seizing airports and harbors for development of the attack.

Soon after his first communiqué and order of the day were published General Eisenhower broadcast a message to the underground movement of Europe, warning its members to stand fast and continue passive resistance but not to endanger lives "until I give you the signal to rise and strike the enemy."

In the coastal area where the Allies have landed little help is expected at the outset from French patriots because the Germans have been at pains to remove from there all but old men, women and children.

However, there was indication in General Eisenhower's broadcast that the Army of France would fight under the United Nations banner, for he said:

"Citizens of France, I am proud to have again under my command the armed forces of France."

Announcement of the great "triphibious" attack was undramatic in its setting. Correspondents assigned to the Supreme Allied Headquarters were summoned by telephone just as the official German news agency, DNB, was broadcasting the fact that the invasion had begun. To maintain the initiative in battle it was necessary to surrender the initiative in the war of words.

In a room, the walls of which were plastered with maps, the correspondents gathered at pine tables and listened to officers lay down the law on censorship and fill in the background of the manner in which the soldiers of Britain and America and all fighting services of the countries had been welded into one fighting unit.

German broadcasts at 9 o'clock, London time, said:

"Combined landing operations of the Anglo-Americans, which were launched both from sea and air against the European west coast early today, extended over the whole coastal sector between Havre and Cherbourg.

"The main centers of air landing attacks are in the whole of Normandy as well as at the most important river mouths in the Seine Bight. Amphibious operations on a large scale were simultaneously begun between the Seine estuary and the mouth of Vire River, thirty miles south of Cherbourg.

"In addition to the numerous landing craft of various types, light naval craft of the Allies are being employed in considerable numbers," the Germans went on.

"Off the Seine estuary six heavy naval units and twenty destroyers were made out.

"German coastal batteries engaged (Allied) naval craft off shore.

"Considerable parts of the parachute formations that had to carry out the initial attack on western Europe against massed defense at the the river mouth and near most important airfields on Normandy Peninsula already have been wiped out.

"According to preliminary reports the First British Parachute Division may already be considered badly mauled."

"That was a bomb hit. Another one!"

A reporter's D-day broadcast from a warship in the Channel

George Hicks, London bureau chief for the Blue Network (later the American Broadcasting Company), broadcast this pool report from the deck of an Allied warship crossing the Channel to Normandy on the night of June 6–7.

We have yet to see a German plane over the amphibious convoy, which doesn't necessarily mean that we shan't see them before the attack is over. Our air support has been fine…and the loudspeakers call…almost constantly. Spitfires on the port are overhead, our B-17's passing on the starboard side. As far as I know, no report has come in of attack by Nazi sea craft on to the convoys. Now it's almost blacked out and you see the ships lying in all directions just like black shadows on the water…some signaling out to sea, sheltered on the inside from the German eyes.…signaling with red lights blinking, code.…There are four fires on the shore, looking like pin points winking, suppressed by smoke. Our planes are going overhead. (*roar of low airplane motor*)

The baby was plenty low. We just made the statement that no German planes have been seen.…This was the first one seen so far. It came very low, just cleared our stack and as he passed he let go a stream of tracers that did no harm, and just as that happened there was a burst of fire on the coast just off five miles. German planes have been in the sky now. The darkness is on us and the tracers have been flying up. They seem to have been withdrawn for the moment, but the plane that just had come over our ship was the first Nazi we've seen so far. He took a pass at us and nothing in particular happened. (*screeching siren*)

Our own ship is just sounding the warning whistles and now flak is coming up in the sky, with streamers from the warships behind us. The sparks just seem to float up in the sky and we're too far away to hear their explosions. Heavy firing now, just behind us, and anti-aircraft bursts in the sky and bombs bursting on the shore and along in the convoy of the German planes that are beginning their first attack on the night of June 6. Now the darkness has come on us. These planes you hear overhead now are the motors of the Nazis coming and going in the cloudy sky. (*the reverberation of bombs*) Every once in a while you see a burst of fire of a bigger caliber on the warships (*deep boom*) flying up. That was a bomb hit. Another one! The tracer lines keep arching up into the darkness. Very heavy fire now at the stern. More ships in that area. Fire bursts and the flak (*loud crash of ack-ack*) and streamers going out in a diagonal slant…right over our head…right over our head from a ship…(*continuing ack-ack which slowly dies down*) right over our head we can't see the plane—nothing but the flak bursts as they ack-ack in the dark sky. Here come the planes. More anti-aircraft fire. Inward toward the shore—and the Germans must be attacking low with their planes off our stern because the stream of fire, the tracer, is almost parallel with the water. Our tracer lines are coming up almost all around us off the stern and off the side toward the French coast. Flares are coming down now. You can hear the machine gunning. The whole sea side is covered with tracer fire, going up meeting the bombs, machine gunning, the planes come over closer…low thick smoke, firing down low toward the French coast a couple of miles. I don't know whether it's on the coast or whether the ship's on fire. Here's heavy ack-ack now. *(very loud noise of firing; muffled shouts of crew)* Well, that's the first time we've shot our guns.…Still coming down. *(drone of a plane)* Burst right over our heads…the way of the outboard side. Flares are going up in almost every direction as we pick up the German bomber overhead.…Heavy fire from a naval warship as well as 20 millimeter and 40 millimeter tracers were the sounds you just heard…and perhaps the burst or two of the bombs…Quiet for a moment now. There is nothing but black cloud tufts from the explosions in the sky and the distant.…*(roar of plane motor)* They're working toward our aft again. Down there near some of the British convoys.

You'll excuse me, I'll just take a deep breath for a moment and stop speaking.

Now the air attack seems to have died down except for the British convoy off a couple of miles beyond us and for that one fire burning near the shore, the French shore, which is beginning to die down somewhat.

Can't report that there were any hits because there seem to have been none on any of the ships around us at all. I see nothing in the night, no fires, or anything of that kind. *(loud firing of guns)* Here we go again! Another plane has come over. *(roar of plane motors)* Right over our port side. It's right over our bow now…before they burst. Tracers still going up and now the plane is probably gone beyond. It looks like we're going to have a night tonight. Here we go boys. Another one coming over. The cruiser right alongside of us is pouring up. Streams of tracer, hot fire coming out of all the small ships and the barge as well. Something burning is falling down through the sky and circling down. It may be a hit plane. *(machine guns fire for many seconds)* Here we go. They got one—they got one. *For a moment Hicks turned away from microphone to speak to a gunnery officer.*

VOICE OF SOME OF CREW: We got it. *(loud cheers by crew)*

HICKS: They got one.

CREW VOICE: We got that one with the gun right here.

HICKS: That big one?

VOICE: Yeah.

HICKS: Great block and fire…came down and is now just off our port side in the sea, an oozing mass of smoke and flame.

CREW VOICES: We got one—you said it! We made it look like polka dots.

HICKS: We've had a few minutes' pause. The lights of that burning Nazi plane are just twinkling now in the sea and going out. When the tracer starts up again, and there's warning of another plane coming in. It's now 10 past 12 and the German attack seems to have died out.

To recapitulate, the first plane that was over that we described at the beginning of the broadcast was a low-flying German, probably JU-88 that was leading the flight and came on the convoy, in surprise we believe, because he drew up and only fired as he passed by and perhaps he was as surprised as we were to see each other, and there seems to be no damage to the amphibious force that we can discover. One bomb fell astern of this warship, 150 yards away. A string of rockets was fired at a cruiser

Soldiers of the Sixteenth Infantry Regiment, wounded while storming Omaha Beach, wait on D-day for evacuation to a field hospital.

beside us on the port side. No damage was done and gun number 42 at our port just beside the microphone shot down a plane that fell into the sea off to the port side.

It was Ensign William Shriner, of Houston, Texas, who's the gunnery control officer, and Seaman Thomas Squirer, of Baltimore, Md., handled the direction finder. It was the first kill for this gun. The boys were all pretty excited about it. It's a twin-barreled 40 millimeter anti-aircraft piece. They are already thinking now of painting a big star on their turret. They'll be at that the first thing tomorrow morning when it's daylight.

Meantime now, the French coast has quieted down. There seems to be no more shelling into it and all around it is darkness and no light or no firing. Now it's 10 past 12, the beginning of June 7, 1944.

This is George Hicks speaking.

27.

V-Weapons

June 1944

In November 1939, an unusual document arrived on the windowsill of the British legation in Oslo. (An attached note identified its author merely as "a German scientist who wishes you well.") The ten-page memorandum, known as the Oslo Report, provided specific technical data concerning a number of secret German weapons projects. Accompanying the document, and bolstering its credibility, was a

prototype proximity fuse. The report's most important revelation, however, was that the Nazis were developing long-range rockets at a secret installation near Peenemünde on the Baltic coast. During the next four years, the British tracked this program closely with significant help from the American Office of Strategic Services, the predecessor of the Central Intelligence Agency, which Col. William J. Donovan organized at Roosevelt's request in 1942.

Future CIA director Allen Dulles, the OSS chief in Switzerland, provided especially useful reports that led to the decision to bomb Peenemünde in August 1943. The 597-plane raid didn't destroy the research center, but it did persuade the Nazis to shift their production lines from Peenemünde to an underground facility near Nordhausen in the Harz Mountains. The resulting delay of about three months proved to be enormously significant. Hitler called the weapons he was developing at Peenemünde *Vergeltungswaffen*, or "reprisal weapons," because he intended to use them to punish the British for their area bombing of Germany

(which he had repeatedly promised the Germans would never happen). Because of the Peenemünde raid, the first V-weapons weren't ready until June 13, 1944, a week after D-day. Had they debuted much earlier, the terror they caused might well have forced a postponement of Operation Overlord.

The V-1 "flying bomb," also called a "buzz bomb," was actually a small pilotless plane propelled by a primitive ramjet engine. It was twenty-five feet long (not including its tailpipe), had a wingspan of eighteen feet, carried a thousand-pound warhead, and reminded both sides that the war wasn't yet over. Because the V-1 wasn't very accurate, it was virtually useless against specific military targets; however, its substantial destructive punch made it an excellent weapon of terror. Hitler initially planned to launch five hundred V-1s a day against England, but a combination of German production problems, Royal Air Force (RAF) raids on V-1 launch sites, and improved fighter and antiaircraft defenses soon brought the threat under control.

A V-1 rocket in flight over London.

NEW ROBOT SPEEDS 600 MILES AN HOUR

Spitfires Fade Like Gliders in Pursuit of Latest German Missile Passing Over Ship

By GENE CURRIVAN

ABOARD THE JOHN E. WARD, off England, June 19—Adolf Hitler's newest terrifying weapon, a jet-propelled bomb larger and faster than anything heretofore revealed, passed over this ship last night among twenty-seven similar but smaller pilotless planes that streaked through the skies toward the English coast. Its speed is such as to make pursuing Spitfires appear as gliders.

It was the first of a procession of robot planes that started at 6:30 P.M. and continued until 4 o'clock this morning. The last, which appeared as a ball of fire directly over this ship, was less than 1,000 feet over the stack.

[The flying torpedoes hurtled over England early Tuesday for the sixth consecutive day, The United Press reported. It was disclosed that a United States anti-aircraft battery shot down the first enemy projectile the night of June 15.]

The "super-robot" came in at 1,000 to 2,000 feet. It shot on a straight line, apparently from the Calais area toward a port on the southeast coast not far from our position. At a distance the robot bomb's sound is like that of an approaching E-boat or motor torpedo boat.

The missile suddenly appeared off the ship's bow, cutting in front of four Spitfires headed for France. As it shot by them, slightly below their line of flight, the pilots realized it was an enemy craft, and one by one they peeled off and darted after it. As it passed our ship a roar of 40 millimeter gunfire was heard and a trail of flames belched from its stovepipe-like tail.

Royal Air Force observers aboard estimated its speed at more than 600 miles an hour. [The Air Ministry, describing what was presumably another robot-plane type, fixed the speed at 300 to 350 miles an hour.] The Spits, traveling at a conservative 400, were hopelessly left behind, although they disappeared after it into a haze, firing as they went. A few moments later a great explosion was heard.

Whether the Spits or shore batteries shot down the robot or it crashed was undisclosed. Its sudden appearance and extraordinary speed so took all gunners by surprise that not a single shell was fired at it from this ship.

The robot resembled nothing that experienced observers had ever seen. It was black, with no marking, and its length was probably forty feet, with a wingspread of not more than twenty-five feet. Its blunt wings were set about midway in the fuselage, which seemed barrel-shaped and tapered toward the tail. The fiery exhaust came through the stovepipe arrangement protruding just below a small, horizontal stabilizer. The plane's nose was propellorless and blunt. There was no cockpit, hood or undercarriage.

A second plane appeared off our bow three and a half hours later. As it passed, our guns fired without effect. Red tracers could be seen missing the swift-moving mark by wide margins. As darkness set in the orders were that the guns were not to be used except in case of a direct attack because tracers would give our position to the enemy. Throughout the night and far into the morning the "aircraft approaching" alarm was given. Each time a tiny, flickering light could be seen for several miles heading toward us. As it

A U.S. congressional delegation investigating German atrocities inspects an unfinished V-2 rocket in an underground factory at Nordhausen.

approached within a few miles a roar was heard and the tiny light became a large red ball with white flames shooting to the rear.

On several occasions gunners with "itchy fingers" could not resist the impulse to fire at this new man-made monster of the air and about half the guns opened up.

On one such occasion the gunners threw up a fierce barrage as a robot came within range and sparks peppered from the forward part of the fuselage as it flew directly through this wall of fire. Gradually it lost altitude and within a few moments headed for the sea, where it exploded with a great blast.

The rest of the night only the shore batteries fired. Meanwhile searchlight batteries picked up the robots in a cone of light and marked them for the fighter planes, which by that time were hovering about, waiting for the flying torpedoes to appear. Several fighters were right on the tails of the missiles, firing with all they had, but the results were not visible.

Six rockets were brought down. It could not be determined from this ship which guns had delivered the deathblows.

It seemed that the robots that were pursued successfully by fighters were of a small and slower type.

None of the missiles that passed near enough to this ship to be seen distinctly was of the faster type except the first. All the others appeared smaller and flew no faster than a fighter. It appeared as if their line of flight had been predetermined and could not be altered en route. The first robot flew directly under the noses of the Spitfires and over the guns of this ship.

"Source stressed that rocket bomb should be taken seriously."

Intelligence reports on the development of Hitler's V-weapons

Reprinted here are OSS dispatches sent by Allen Dulles from his office in Bern. The later ones concern Hitler's second secret weapon, the V-2, which became operational on September 6, 1944. Developed by a team led by Wernher von Braun, the V-2 was a true rocket, powered by a liquid-oxygen-fueled engine. It was the first rocket to surpass the speed of sound and proved to be a forerunner of the ICBMs that Braun later developed for the United States. The forty-seven-foot-long V-2 carried a one-ton payload to an altitude of sixty miles, then plunged back down to earth at a velocity reaching thirty-six hundred miles per hour. Moving so quickly, no fighter plane or ack-ack fire could possibly catch it; and, because it outran its own sound waves, there was never any warning before it struck. Altogether 1,115 V-2s fell on England between September 8 and March 27, killing 2,754 people and injuring about 6,500. Even more fell on Antwerp, which became during the winter of 1944–1945 the main supply port for the Allied push into Germany. Because the V-2s could be launched from trucks parked on any level spot, the only effective defense against them was to destroy them while they were still on the ground.

Telegram 44–45, February 5, 1943

From German sources he considers reliable, 490 reports that the Germans are producing a secret weapon whose exact nature was not disclosed to him with the exception that [it] is a flying contraption perhaps in the form of an aerial torpedo. He believes that one of his factories in Germany is making one small part of the machine. It is believed that the tests have not been completed to the satisfaction of the Germans....

Telegram 338–42, June 24, 1943

I have received further details regarding the rocket weapon mentioned in my #186. This additional information is from a well placed but non-technical source.

The rocket is approximately 60 cm in diameter and 3 meters in length. It is said to weigh 2,000 kilos. The driving turbine and propelling material etc. occupy four fifths of the volume, and about one fifth is devoted to the projectile. I understand that the explosions which drive the turbine are produced by a saltpeter solution (possibly meaning Nitrate) and gas-oil under a pressure of 50 atmospheres. The assembly plant and the testing grounds are in Pomerania at Tpeonemuende between Greifswald and Swinemuende. The tube is manufactured by the Deutscher Oehrenwerke Muehlheim Ruhr and certain other parts are reported to be made by Witkowitz. Experimental tests are made in the general direction of Gdynia and the range is stated to be over 200 kilometers with a deviation of less than a half of one percent. Manufacture is now at a point where quantity production is expected for use in September, October. Our informant understands that a much larger model is in the experimental stage.

In a recent report the source of my #186 says that he contacted a person who was actually present at the tests and this person gives the same general characteristics regarding the weapon itself and the testing place, but he has nothing further to offer in the way of important technical data. Sulukas also received practically the same information from my first mentioned source above. Particularly in view of the fact that information regarding secret reprisal weapons is being allowed to leak out to strengthen German morale, neither of us are convinced as to how much of the above is a plant either innocent or otherwise. Nevertheless I feel it is my duty to report with reserve on this matter since I possess no technical knowledge of my own to form an independent opinion. I certainly feel that there is some evidence here which would indicate that the Germans are trying to develop such a rocket weapon. The first mentioned source above has also reported that long range cannon barrels, 60 cm calibre and 140 (received OMEFORTY) meters long, are being manufactured at the same Muehlheim factory.

Telegram 703–5, September 9, 1943

A report from 643 states that *Das Reich* and *Adolf Hitler* panzer divisions are in the area of North Italy, most likely in the vicinity of Villach. These divisions were recently transferred from the front at Kharkov. According to this source which, although non-technical, is exceptionally well-informed, there are 15 German divisions in Italy. Source stressed the point that rocket bomb should be taken very seriously. It is his conviction that, at the present time, the weapon is sufficiently perfect to allow the effective bombing of cities; further, that the margin of error has been cut to 1000 yards. A delay of 1 to 2 months in assemblage work was caused as a result of the bombardment of Peenemuende; however, there is still much there to be destroyed. It appears that some assembly plants on the island are located underground; however, there are important surface objectives which have not yet been demolished.

Telegram 1257–61, December 9, 1943

The following is from source Sanders, our 321, by way of 493.
1. Rocket projectiles.
They weigh 40 tons and have a speed of 800 kilometers per hour for 25 minutes and a range of 333 kilometers. This is told to us by an electrical expert who was employed to measure their speed and course. They are launched by catapults and each one contains 6 mechanical and 22 electrical ignitions for explosive charge. Accuracy within 2 seconds is called for in specifications. It is said that a rocket projectile fired from Peenemünde landed in Sweden, and that trees within a thousand meter radius were destroyed. They are still being assembled at Peenemünde, and this expert says that only the drafting room there was destroyed. Both the Air Force and the Army are working on projectiles, but it was impossible to meet Hitler's deadline of November 30. The general in charge of the matter does not want to begin using the projectile until he has 1,000 catapults ready. Professor Braun is the scientist behind it. According to the expert, the final difficulty lies in finding the right moment for ignition—whatever that means.

Telegram 2674–75, March 31, 1944

The following information is from source 284-F and deals with rocket torpedo installations on the Cotentin peninsula. It is dated March 30th. Underground batteries, composed of galleries sloping at a constant angle, launch these projectiles. An electric gun system, in which the gallery plays the part of a gun tube, projects the torpedo. It is not until the projectile reaches a particular initial velocity that it is ignited. The galleries are built of cement and are completely without metal, because of the fact that the propulsion is electric and in order to eliminate magnetic interferences. By projecting the rocket torpedo together with a chariot, which drops off while the rocket is moving through space, the initial problem of separating the chariot from the projectile was solved. The newest model of rocket torpedo is equipped with a device which allows it to be guided by "telecommande" employing Hertzian waves. Only German laborers participated in the construction of the underground batteries on the Cotentin peninsula. These batteries are alleged to be bomb-proof and are successfully camouflaged. It is recommended by the source that the sole means of demolishing them would be by employing French Commandos who have a good knowledge of that area or by partisan activity.

Telegram 770–72 to London, June 27, 1944

Although the reports are not all in, Swiss correspondents in Berlin have gained the general impression that the low morale in Germany had gone up quite a lot as a result of the initial German propaganda reports about the secret weapon. Over a period of some months the latter had been given an extremely powerful build-up. A large part of the population feels that only a miracle can save the country, and the propaganda led some of them to believe that at last the miracle might have happened. No permanent

A B-17 Flying Fortress assigned to the Eighth U.S. Army Air Force attacks the "robot bomb" fuel plant at Peenemünde in August 1944.

effect will be produced by this shot of adrenaline. As a matter of fact, if this secret weapon does not lead to any positive results, such as delaying the 3-front offensive, or decreasing the air raids, it is likely that German morale will fall to a new low. It is evident that the Nazi chiefs are afraid of having gone too far, as the newspapers have tended lately to advise the people against too cheerful an outlook so far as regards immediate concrete results from the use of the secret weapon.

328's German friends report that the appearance of the new weapon has caused a few people to think that there is now a chance for Germany. This may mirror the view held in labor and leftist circles. Most people, however, are still holding to the belief that in a few months the Allies will have developed countermeasures which will bring about an even greater deterioration in the situation. Many say they would rather have had the invasion keep on according to schedule, as in that case the war might come to a close sooner, but that the secret weapon will only lengthen it. In view of the foregoing reasons, 328 reports, there is no indication of much jubilation in those circles. Undoubtedly, one of the reasons for the paling of the first flush of enthusiasm is the fear of countermeasures by the Allies.

Telegram 3918–20, June 28, 1944

The report which follows is a brief summary of the information given to us by 3 separate sources including Breakers: V-2, a large rocket, is the 2nd secret weapon of the Nazis. It is charged with a new and more potent explosive which very likely is liquid air and it is fired into the stratosphere from underground chambers in practically a vertical direction. During the tests made with unfilled rockets, a high degree of accuracy was shown, although charged rockets at a high altitude almost always went to pieces. According to one of our sources, this rocket is being manufactured at Freifssberg in the vicinity of Stettin (this may be Greiffenberg or Greifenberg). A 2nd source indicates that it is being produced in lower Silesia at Marklissa and will be used on London very soon, according to Nazi plans. One source describes it as weighing between 12 and 14 tons with a maximum range of 400 kilometers and a speed of 1000 kilometers per hour.

As nearly as we can determine from these reports, the torpedo receives its first impetus in the same way that rockets are propelled and when it reaches the stratosphere, it travels on its way by virtue of its imparted momentum. It proceeds at very great altitudes until its momentum is lost, and then it falls to earth. In the past, we had many reports of the explosion of such rockets while being tested, since the problem of stratosphere operation has evidently not been solved by the Nazi experts. Realize that this information is extremely indefinite, but it may offer you some leads.

We have more information from a Nazi deserter indicating that recent raids on Kluftern in the vicinity of Friedrichshafen have evidently had little effect, since production is still going forward on a secret weapon there.

28.

The Plot to Kill Hitler

July 1944

Hitler never placed much trust in the personal loyalty of the Wehrmacht's officer corps—and with good reason. Many of these men, especially those who belonged to the aristocratic Junker class of German society, were intensely patriotic yet disdainful of the Nazis, whom they considered thugs and boors. Beginning in 1938, groups of these officers repeatedly conspired to assassinate the Führer in order to

block policies that they considered disastrous for the Fatherland—Hitler's Sudeten demands and the 1940 invasion of the Low Countries being two prominent examples. The Allied landings in Normandy, of course, produced the worst crisis yet. Although most German officers knew already that they would lose the war, with D-day they came to understand how complete that loss would be if they kept following Hitler.

On July 20, 1944, Claus von Stauffenberg flew to Rastenburg to attend a conference with the Führer. The thirty-seven-year-old colonel, who had lost an arm and an eye with the Afrika Korps, told his pilot to remain at the ready. Then he traveled by staff car to Hitler's underground bunker. When he arrived, he learned that the meeting had been shifted to a wooden hut because the bunker was being strengthened. Inside the hut, Stauffenberg found Hitler leaning on a large oaken table, studying maps with about two dozen other officers. Entering the room, Stauffenberg placed his briefcase, which contained a bomb, under the table, about six feet

from the Führer. Reaching down, he crushed a tiny vial of acid and then excused himself to make a telephone call. Ten minutes later, at 12:42 P.M., the acid ate through a wire holding back the firing pin, and the bomb detonated. Four people were killed—none of them Hitler, who was saved by the heavy oak table and the hut's flimsy construction. (The concrete walls of the bunker would certainly have magnified the effect of the blast.)

After witnessing the explosion, Stauffenberg activated Valkyrie, the conspirators' plan to topple the Nazi regime and install a new government willing to seek peace with the western Allies. Hitler's survival, however, made Valkyrie impossible. Later that day, the purges began when Stauffenberg and his immediate circle were arrested at the War Ministry in Berlin and summarily executed. Still later, other conspirators were hanged with piano wire, their gruesome deaths filmed so that Hitler might watch and enjoy their suffering. In all, five thousand people were executed before the Führer was satisfied.

Hitler with (left to right) Mussolini, Martin Bormann, an unknown man, Karl Dönitz, Göring, SS-Gruppenführer Hermann Fegelein, and Col. Gen. Bruno Lörzer in an unidentified location five days after the failure of the Bomb Plot. On Hitler's left hand is the wound he received in the assassination attempt.

NAZIS BLOCK PLOT TO SEIZE GOVERNMENT

Hitler Hunts Foes; Thousands of Officers Reported Arrested in Purge of Army

By RAYMOND DANIELL

LONDON, Saturday, July 22—Although reports from Berlin insist that the plot of army officers to overthrow the Nazi regime and seize power themselves has been suppressed and its instigators liquidated, the isolation of the Reich from the rest of the world continues and it is apparent that counter-measures are being pressed.

[A Swiss report to The United Press said it was understood that German naval units had revolted at Kiel and Stettin. Stockholm dispatches said 5,500 German officers had been arrested throughout Germany and that there had been disorders in eastern Germany and East Prussia.]

Everything suggests that the plot that had its climax in the attempt to assassinate Adolf Hitler was deep and well laid, with far-reaching ramifications. On evidence supplied by the highest Nazi authorities it is known that the plotters, who included Col. Gen. Ludwig Beck, who was dismissed as Chief of Staff by Hitler in November, 1938, attempted to kill Hitler and bring off a coup d'état.

The scheme apparently succeeded to the point where the conspirators were able to issue orders in conflict with the plans of Hitler and other Nazi leaders.

The extent of the disaffection seemingly caused such consternation in the Nazi camp that Hitler, Reichmarshal Hermann Goering and Grand Admiral Karl Doenitz felt impelled in the small hours yesterday morning to try to set things straight by urgent appeals, even though their action involved disclosure to a hostile world that a rift had developed between some high army officers and the Nazi party on the best way to save Germany from destruction.

There is no evidence to show that the challenge to Hitler's leadership and domination of the Nazi party has spread to the civilian population but Transocean, German news agency, revealed that certain "precautionary measures" had been taken in the center of Berlin.

Alfred Rosenberg, Nazi party "philosopher," writing in a special edition of the Voelkischer Beobachter yesterday morning, called the attempt on Hitler's life the opening of hostilities on a "fifth front."

Some additional light on what happened in the Reich in those crucial hours preceding Hitler's broadcast was provided last night from Berlin. According to the official story, provided for soldiers in the field, a clique that was connected with "an enemy power" had obtained control of "certain means of communications" through a subordinate officer.

Through these channels, it was said, orders were sent to Major Remer, commandant of a battalion of the Berlin guard, telling him Hitler was dead, that disorders had been reported in the Reich and that the Wehrmacht had taken over the government. Major Remer was directed to occupy with his force the administrative headquarters at Berlin, which he did.

But then, according to this account, Major Remer immediately communicated with Propaganda Minister Joseph Goebbels, head of the Berlin municipal administration, who convinced him that he had been obeying faked orders. The fact that "traitors" had laid hands on certain

The wreckage at Hitler's headquarters caused by the bomb planted by Stauffenberg.

communications systems brought about yesterday morning's unexpected radio performance by Hitler, Goering and Doenitz, according to the German news agency.

Messages of loyalty to Hitler came, according to German sources, from Field Marshal Baron Maximilian von Weichs in the Balkans, Col. Gen. Nikolas Falkenhorst in Norway and Gen. Friedrich C. Christianson in the Netherlands.

Field Marshal Gen. Guenther von Kluge in Normandy issued an order of the day calling on his troops for loyalty to Hitler and assuring them that all was quiet on the home front despite the machinations of a small clique of officers.

"For us," said the remarkable order, "there will be no repetition of the year 1918 or of the example set by Italy."

External evidence indicates that Germany is still in a state of siege, notwithstanding Nazi claims to have suppressed the revolt completely.

Telephone communication with Sweden, restored temporarily while the Nazi leaders were broadcasting, was interrupted again immediately afterward and has not been restored.

The usual plane from Berlin to Stockholm arrived at the Swedish capital ten hours late yesterday and it was reported that all contact between the Reich and Switzerland and Spain was broken for considerable time. Train service between Germany and Basle was interrupted for the first time since the war began.

All this might be accounted for by the Nazis' desire for privacy while Heinrich Himmler, Hitler-appointed dictator of the home front, carries out repressive measures. Reports from German sources indicated that the execution of traitors and suspects was proceeding ruthlessly. Another interpretation of Germany's Nazi-imposed isolation was that the Nazis had not yet stamped out all the elements that threatened them.

"Hitler's despotism has been broken."

The broadcast that the conspirators never made

This proclamation was to have been broadcast after Hitler's assassination but, of course, was never aired. Instead, the Führer himself took to the airwaves soon after midnight on July 21.

Germans!

In recent years terrible things have taken place before our very eyes. Against the advice of experts Hitler has ruthlessly sacrificed whole armies for *his* passion for glory, *his* megalomania, *his* blasphemous delusion that he was the chosen and favoured instrument of 'Providence.'

Not called to power by the German people, but becoming the Head of the Government by intrigues of the worst kind, he has spread confusion by his devilish arts and lies and by tremendous extravagance which on the surface seemed to bring prosperity to all, but which in reality plunged the German people into terrible debt. In order to remain in power, he added to this an unbridled reign of terror, destroyed law, outlawed decency, scorned the divine commands of pure humanity and destroyed the happiness of millions of human beings.

His insane disregard for all mankind could not fail to bring our nation to misfortune with deadly certainty; his self-imagined supremacy could not but bring ruin to our brave sons, fathers, husbands and brothers, and his bloody terror against the defenceless could not but bring shame to the German name. He enthroned lawlessness, oppression of conscience, crime and corruption in our Fatherland which had always been proud of its integrity and honesty. Truthfulness and veracity, virtues which even the simplest people think it their duty to inculcate in their children, are punished and persecuted. Thus public activity and private life are threatened by a deadly poison.

This must not be, this cannot go on. The lives and deaths of our men, women and children must no longer be abused for this purpose. We would not be worthy of our fathers, we would be despised by our children if we had not the courage to do everything, I repeat everything, to ward off this danger from ourselves and to achieve self-respect again.

It is for this purpose that, after searching our conscience before God, we have taken over power. Our brave Wehrmacht is a pledge of security and order. The police will do their duty.

Each civil servant shall carry out his duties according to his technical knowledge, following only the law and his own conscience. Let each of you help by discipline and confidence. Carry out your daily work with new hope. Help one another! Your tortured souls shall again find peace and comfort.

Far from all hatred we will strive for inward reconciliation and with dignity for outward reconciliation. Our first task will be to cleanse the war from its degeneration and end the devastating destruction of human life, of cultural and economic values behind the fronts. We all know that we are not masters of peace and war. Firmly relying on our incomparable Wehrmacht and in confident

Lt. Col. Robert Bernardis, who accompanied Stauffenberg to Rastenburg, learns of his death sentence on August 8, 1944.

belief in the tasks assigned to man by God we will sacrifice everything to defend the Fatherland and to restore a lawful solemn state of order, to live once more for honour and peace with respect for the divine commandments, in purity and truth!

Germans!

Hitler's despotism has been broken.

29

The Allied Breakout in France

July 1944

On June 17, 1944, when Hitler met with Rundstedt and Rommel at Soissons, he still believed that Operation Overlord was a ruse and that the main landings were still to come at Calais. Therefore, he refused to release the Fifteenth Army, deployed east of the Seine, to fight with the Seventh Army in Normandy. "You must stay where you are," Hitler ordered his generals, condemning the Seventh Army to a futile battle of attrition.

Meanwhile, Overlord was proceeding slowly through its three stages. The first, "break-in," covered the June 6 landings and the consolidation of the beachhead. The second, "buildup," included the expansion of the beachhead and the accumulation of forces. The third, "breakout," referred to the punching of a hole through the German lines so that Allied armor might advance swiftly in the direction of Paris and the Rhine. The first stage went more or less according to schedule, but the second bogged down. By the time Montgomery's troops took Caen (a D-day objective) on July 10, they were more than a month behind schedule, and the spirited German resistance in the area made it seem unlikely that the British and Canadians would break out any time soon. Therefore, Eisenhower ordered Montgomery's Twenty-first Army Group to hold the German Panzers at Caen while Bradley's Twelfth Army Group attempted a breakout at St. Lô.

Composed of the First Army under Courtney Hodges and the Third under a rehabilitated George Patton, the Twelfth Army Group prepared to attack on a narrow front south of St. Lô on July 25. The night before, a powerful armada of Allied bombers pummeled the enemy lines, destroying half of the German defenses—and, along with them, more than a few American positions. (GIs unintentionally hit by these short bomb drops nicknamed the pilots involved "the American Luftwaffe.")

Bradley's first major objective was Avranches at the western end of the Cotentin Peninsula—which units of the First Army reached on July 30. Meanwhile, Patton sent his Third Army scurrying through the breach in the German lines into territory virtually devoid of German troops, all of whom had been massed on the front lines. Not until mid-August did Hitler authorize the transfer of the Fifteenth Army to stabilize a front that, in reality, no longer existed. On August 19, a pincer movement trapped sixty thousand Germans in the "Falaise pocket," which Eisenhower termed "a killing ground." The fifty thousand Germans who survived all surrendered.

An American gunner pulls the lanyard on a howitzer while shelling Germans at the base of the Cotentin Peninsula on July 11, 1944. The Germans were retreating from Carentan, which had been liberated on June 12 during the initial U.S. drive on Cherbourg.

FOE REELS BEFORE BLITZKRIEG MIGHTIER THAN HIS IN 1940

By HAROLD DENNY

WITH THE AMERICAN FORCES in Normandy, July 27—The American break-through west of St. Lô widened and deepened today into a torrent that swept swiftly south and west toward the sea. Tonight the battle had become a race. Our forces, both armored and infantry, with aircraft giving spectacular aid, were boldly driving a wedge through the rear of the German forces. Already they threaten to cut off several enemy divisions, and the Germans have begun withdrawing in an attempt to save themselves.

Late this afternoon our troops had conquered high ground within five miles of the important town of Coutances, which governs the corridor through which the Germans must retreat. That town, with its railroad and its nexus of vital highways, thus has been brought within range of our artillery. And the sea lies only six miles farther westward from Coutances.

To add to the danger and discomfort of the Germans our aircraft have knocked out two bridges over the Sienne River west of Coutances. This should force the retreating Germans to evacuate by the crowded and perilous route of Coutances itself.

In the first steps toward attempting to save this threatened army corps the Germans withdrew before dawn this morning from their strong positions behind the flooded River Ay at Lessay and for some distance to the east from Lessay. They left only a rear guard from which the Americans already have captured prisoners. These revealed their orders were to make a stand each night, then retire each day six kilometers [three and a half miles] farther back.

It was not all a walkaway today. In many places our men encountered stiff resistance, but the enemy defense in general was described by one senior American officer tonight as "sporadic, disorganized and chaotic." Our men have at last blasted the Germans loose from their strong line and are continuing to smash them so hard and swiftly that they do not have time to catch their breath and make a coordinated stand anywhere.

These past twenty-four hours have seen not only a fine victory on the part of our troops. They have seen the best piece of coordinated, high-power fighting our men have done since D-day. There have been other days as filled with gallantry but none in which so much skill has been revealed. The men in the forward units are rejoicing tonight in their newly found power.

And today almost as much as D-day marks the beginning of the end, for today has brought a visible reversal of history. A little over four years ago this writer as a correspondent with the British Army was seeing another battle in France. German armored columns were slashing through us and into our rear, while German aircraft cleared a path ahead and German infantry poured in to consolidate the gains. The British were in a desperate retreat to save their armies.

Today again I saw armored columns slashing forward in harmony with infantry, while aircraft blasted a way ahead of them. But this time the tanks and infantry and airplanes were ours, and the forces trying to escape from the trap were Germans. Four years ago we could not but admire the precision and power of the Germans' combined armored, infantry and air attack.

Today our own men put on a similar attack but with better weapons, better tactics and more power than the Germans had in 1940.

And today's assault was only a sample of what the Americans and British can hurl at the enemy.

The fighting of the past twenty-four hours was still through hedgerow country, but it was into larger fields and on to higher ground, so that for the first time since Cherbourg one could get some adequate view of the battle.

And our forces advanced with such speed that the fighting never had a chance to bog down into the hedgerow crawling of which our men have become so weary. By contrast, today's fighting was more spectacular than is often seen in land warfare. An armored assault, with an air attack thrown in, is a clamorous affair and hard on the nerves even when it is going well and there is little danger.

I caught up with the armored units as they were moving southward this morning from St. Gilles, which our forces captured yesterday. The first part of the trip was over the three miles broad area that our air forces had bombed for two succeeding days before the jump-off Tuesday morning. Trees were blasted and the ground was churned into a cratered waste strewn with broken German tanks and trucks and occasional German dead. That stretch of ground was a greater obstacle to our advance today than the Germans. Our tanks and armored cars and supply trucks rocked over it through storms of yellow dust in which one sometimes could not see ten yards ahead.

St. Gilles was smashed flat by bombs and shells as though a giant had turned his heel on it.

Our column ground on two miles farther to Canisy, which our men took at 9 o'clock last night. Here we began to get into the fringes of today's battle.

In yesterday's swift thrust into the enemy's vitals our forces had disdained to get until their flanks were cleared and there was a tough pocket of resistance on a wooded hill just west of Canisy.

An American officer fights alongside a French partisan during a street battle in an unidentified French city.

There the Germans had artillery and six Tiger tanks, together with infantry.

Our air force—fighter and medium bombers—were on call for quick, hard missions and apparently anxious to make up for the accidents of the two preceding days, when some of their bombs fell among our own troops. They low-level bombed, dive-bombed and machine-gunned enemy positions all day with fruitful results.

As we went through Canisy this morning fighter bombers were diving down on that hill-top German fortress just outside the town, releasing bombs on the first attack and then coming down again and machine gunning.

Meanwhile the enemy knew that our armor, always a tasty target on the road, was pouring through Canisy and the Germans were laying down harassing artillery fire.

Canisy also had been terribly wrecked and also was veiled in smoke and was uncomfortably hot from buildings still burning briskly. On the sidewalk alongside a shop on Canisy's little town square an American soldier was crouched on one knee, rifle in hand, though he was dead. He had given his life in a brisk twenty-minute fire fight, which it took to capture Canisy last night.

Our armored forces were going full tilt, "their tails up," as their commanders put it in horse language, when they charged on south from St. Gilles last evening and roared into Canisy. The infantry were riding on the outside of tanks. Whenever serious resistance was encountered— machine guns or mortars or anti-tank guns—the tanks stopped and the infantry hopped down and went into action. If the position was a machine gun or other small-arms fire, our infantry took cover while the tank machine-gunned and shelled that opposition to silence.

If it was an anti-tank gun our tanks withdrew to safety, and the infantry crept up with rifles, bazookas and grenades and put the gun out of business. Then the infantry jumped up onto the tanks again and clattered on until they struck the next hard spot, when they repeated the process. That is the way it went yesterday and today, with the air force coming in when really formidable opposition appeared.

The scene going through Canisy today was a Hollywood conception of a battle. Our tanks were making an unholy racket on the macadam streets of this dusty and smoke-wreathed town. Everywhere were smashed-up and burned-out German tanks, armored cars and trucks. German equipment—hand grenades, family photographs, messkits, blankets and pillows—were strewn everywhere in the haste of the beaten enemy. As we passed that dead American soldier still on guard, shells were falling uncomfortably near.

It was good to get out of that town, even though it was safely in our hands. We continued southward in the thinning traffic, which finally dwindled to an occasional jeep or reconnaissance car, as we got to Le Mesnil-Herman. Our armor and supporting infantry had just taken this hamlet and were defending it with machine guns, mortars and tank cannon against the despairing gesture of a German counter-attack.

The bodies of Americans who had been killed a few minutes before by mortar fire lay where we stopped to escape machine-gun fire, so we withdrew farther to sit out the repulse of the German attack on a wooded hill that gave us a fair view for miles.

Our planes were circling, peeling off and diving down so close we feared they were strafing our own troops. We checked later and found they were not. They were going after a knot of German resistance alongside the Vire River which we had bypassed.

While we were watching this we were unexpectedly machine-gunned from the air. Then we saw approaching four fighter aircraft, which we first mistook for American but a moment later recognized as German. One enemy pilot dropped a bomb that exploded harmlessly in the muddy earth. He instantly swerved away but just then an American fighter plane pounced and shot him down. His chute opened just before he reached the ground.

Whether the other three of those German planes got away we did not learn.

"I feel myself in duty bound to speak plainly."

Erwin Rommel's report to Hitler on the untenable situation in Normandy

No one knows exactly what part Erwin Rommel played in the conspiracy to overthrow Hitler because he destroyed whatever evidence was in his possession. (He opposed murder for political reasons and therefore was probably *not* told of the assassination plot.) There is no doubt, however, that Rommel believed Hitler had to be removed for Germany to survive. Five days before the planting of the bomb at the Führer's headquarters, Rommel sent Hitler this report outlining conditions on the western front, which he believed necessitated the opening of peace talks with the western Allies. The report's purpose, according to Rommel's son Manfred, "was to state his case clearly and in all urgency, so that it could never be said that he had stabbed anyone in the back." Two days later (and three days before the assassination attempt), Rommel was severely wounded when British fighter-bombers attacked his staff car near Livarot. He sustained serious cranial injuries requiring his immediate hospitalization in Germany, followed by a long convalescence at home. In October, when Hitler learned of Rommel's association with the conspiracy, he gave the Desert Fox two choices: public court-martial or suicide. Rommel chose the latter, after which Hitler announced that he had died of his battle injuries.

C.-IN-C. ARMY GROUP B
H.Q. 15 July

The situation on the Normandy front is growing worse every day and is now approaching a grave crisis.

Due to the severity of the fighting, the enemy's enormous use of material—above all, artillery and tanks—and the effect of his unrestricted command of the air over the battle area, our casualties are so high that the fighting power of our divisions is rapidly diminishing. Replacements from home are few in number and, with the difficult transport situation, take weeks to get to the front. As against 97,000 casualties (including 2,360 officers)—i.e. an average of 2,500 to 3,000 a day—replacements to date number 10,000, of whom about 6,000 have actually arrived at the front.

Material losses are also huge and have so far been replaced on a very small scale; in tanks, for example, only 17 replacements have arrived to date as compared with 225 losses.

The newly arrived infantry divisions are raw and, with their small establishment of artillery, anti-tank guns and close-combat anti-tank weapons, are in no state to make a lengthy stand against major enemy attacks coming after hours of drum-fire and heavy bombing. The fighting has shown that with this use of material by the enemy, even the bravest army will be smashed piece by piece, losing men, arms and territory in the process.

Due to the destruction of the railway system and the threat of the enemy air force to roads and tracks up to 90 miles behind the front, supply conditions are so bad that only the barest essentials can be brought to the front. It is consequently now necessary to exercise the greatest economy in all fields, and especially in artillery and mortar ammunition. These conditions are unlikely to improve, as enemy

Rommel tours the western front shortly after Hitler put him in charge of German defenses there in late November 1943.

action is steadily reducing the transport capacity available. Moreover, this activity in the air is likely to become even more effective as the numerous air-strips in the bridgehead are taken into use.

No new forces of any consequence can be brought up to the Normandy front except by weakening Fifteenth Army's front on the Channel, or the Mediterranean front in southern France. Yet Seventh Army's front, taken over all, urgently requires two fresh divisions, as the troops in Normandy are exhausted.

On the enemy's side, fresh forces and great quantities of war material are flowing into his front every day. His supplies are undisturbed by our air force. Enemy pressure is growing steadily stronger.

In these circumstances we must expect that in the foreseeable future the enemy will succeed in breaking through our thin front, above all, Seventh Army's, and thrusting deep into France. Apart from the Panzer Group's sector reserves, which are at present tied down by the fighting on their own front and—due to the enemy's command of the air—can only move by night, we dispose of no mobile reserve for defence against such a break-through. Action by our air force will, as in the past, have little effect.

The troops are everywhere fighting heroically, but the unequal struggle is approaching its end. It is urgently necessary for the proper conclusion to be drawn from this situation. As C.-in-C. of the Army Group I feel myself in duty bound to speak plainly on this point.

Rommel

30.

The Liberation of Paris

August 1944

It was originally Eisenhower's intention to bypass Paris. He worried that street fighting might damage historic buildings in the French capital, and he didn't want to assume the burden of provisioning two million Parisians any sooner than necessary. He preferred to let the Germans withdraw on their own, which he was sure they would do once Allied troops crossed the Seine.

The French Forces of the Interior, however, forced Ike's hand. The FFI was a well-organized band of partisans, which had emerged out of the more loosely structured French Resistance in early 1944 after expansion of the German forced-labor program swelled the ranks of the active opposition. Untrained and poorly armed, yet with a numerical strength equivalent to about fifteen divisions, the FFI had liberated much of lightly defended central France in the weeks after the D-day invasion. Now, in mid-August, as Bradley's Twelfth Army Group approached Paris, FFI cells in the capital staged an uprising against the German garrison there.

Although ostensibly aligned with Charles de Gaulle's Free French movement, the FFI was, in fact, a diverse group with numerous Communists in positions of authority, especially among the Paris leadership. Therefore, when word of the uprising there reached de Gaulle, the French leader-in-exile demanded on August 20 that Eisenhower send Allied troops into Paris to preempt what he considered a Communist grab for power. When Ike demurred, de Gaulle ordered (with questionable legitimacy) the French Second Armored Division under Maj. Gen. Jacques Leclerc to leave Bradley's Twelfth Army Group and advance on its own toward Paris. Presented with a fait accompli, Eisenhower had no choice but to go along and order Bradley to reinforce Leclerc with the U.S. Fourth Infantry Division late on August 22. These troops liberated Paris on August 25. The next day, de Gaulle personally led a victory parade down the Champs-Elysées, never flinching at the crack of the occasional rifle shot taken at him by German snipers still holed up in the city.

Yet, as Eisenhower had expected, the liberation of Paris contributed significantly to the Allies' growing logistical problems. The push out of Normandy had been so swift that the transportation system couldn't keep up. In late August, the Americans reached the banks of the Meuse, while the British entered the valley of the Somme—and in these familiar World War I battlegrounds, the advance paused for lack of supplies, especially fuel.

PARIS IS FREED; GERMAN FLIGHT NEARS A ROUT

Parisians Rout Foe; 50,000 FFI Troops With Civilians' Aid Battle Germans 4 Days

By RAYMOND DANIELL

LONDON, Aug. 23—Paris is free again and, because of that, the rest of the world can breathe a little more freely. In a manner befitting a capital with the history and tradition of Paris, its own citizens rose and threw off the tyrant's yoke as soon as their own troops and the Allies' armies of liberation had given them the opportunity to challenge their conquerors on equal terms.

In leaving it to the French themselves to announce that the swastika had been lowered and the Tricolor had been raised over their own gracious and lovely capital, the Allies were following a policy that was both strategically and politically sound.

Gen. Dwight D. Eisenhower's columns were able to continue their eastward sweep unimpeded by the need for pausing to mop up, and France, which was knocked out of the war more than four years ago, was able to stand before the world on her own feet again.

The French Second Armored Division, which fought its way across the African desert under Maj. Gen. Jacques LeClerc, seems to have been the first Allied force to enter Paris. It went in after the local leader of the FFI had concluded an armistice with the Germans, it was said here.

But before many more hours have passed, the Arc de Triomphe at the head of Champs-Elysées will be the scene of yet another pageant in the panoply of history, when the tread of victorious armies will mark the close of more than four years in which the City of Light had been the outpost of the jack-booted forces of darkness.

Paris, which began to weep but not to cringe on June 14, 1940, when the German heel first

echoed in the boulevards, will laugh and sing again to welcome an army of repatriates and of aliens who come not to conquer but to insure the newly won freedom.

Maj. Gen. Joseph Pierre Koenig, commander of the French Forces of the Interior, informed the world that the French people had at last chased the Germans out of their beloved capital. He gave some of the details. But the full story of what happened in Paris between Aug. 19 and today is a saga that will have to be written by many men over a long period before the whole story is told.

Tonight, however—seventy-seven days after D-day—the world can rejoice without asking the whys and wherefores, for Paris is free again. "The Marseillaise" again is sung there, the Tricolor flies there again and the German tide is on the ebb in western Europe.

Until the newspaper correspondents now in Paris or waiting on the outskirts to get there can write their stories and transmit them, General Koenig's terse official statement will have to suffice.

A general insurrection, he said, began four days ago, when, in response to the orders of the underground leaders and the self-styled Provisional Government of France for a general uprising against the Germans, 50,000 members of the FFI, armed and supported by "several hundred thousand unarmed patriots," went into action against the Germans.

The Paris police, according to General Koenig's announcement, were already on strike. They took possession of the headquarters and

U.S. infantrymen march through the Arc de Triomphe in the August 29 victory parade that followed the liberation of Paris.

turned the Ile de la Cité into a fortress, he said. After four days' fighting, the enemy was driven out of all the public buildings and all the Vichy representatives who had not fled were arrested. General Koenig's communiqué concluded:

"Thus the people of Paris have taken a prominent part in the liberation of the capital."

The first news of the liberation of Paris reached the world through the Algiers radio. General Koenig's statement came later.

The fighting behind the barricades in Paris began last Friday, according to French sources here. Shots were fired by both sides in the Boulevard Bonnes-Nouvelles in the heart of the city. It was along this avenue that workers' protest meetings, beginning at the Place de la République, which has been mentioned in reports of unrest in Paris, used to take their way before the Germans' advent halted all that sort of thing.

In those historic four days there was fighting in the Rue de Rivoli, where the Germans used small field guns against the rifles and pistols of the French. The casualties among the people of Paris, it is understood, were fairly heavy.

They paid their share of the cost of freedom. But, with Paris free again, the liberation of a large part of France is assured. Gen. Charles de Gaulle, who is now on his own soil, is expected to go there at once and establish the capital of his "Provisional Government" there. This is not only the liberation of an old country temporarily in thrall; it is the birth of a new France, still dedicated to the old ideals that made her great.

"Herr General, how lucky we are to have *you* in Paris."

Two of Hitler's commanders discuss the Führer's order to destroy the French capital

On August 22, Maj. Gen. Dietrich von Choltitz, commander of the German garrison in Paris, received by radio these orders drawn up personally by Hitler: "Paris will be transformed into a heap of rubble. The General Commanding in Chief will defend the city to the last man and, if necessary, will be buried beneath it." Placing the text of the signal in his pocket, Choltitz next called Army Group B headquarters near Cambrai to speak with Lt. Gen. Hans Speidel (who, as Rommel's chief of staff, had been deeply involved in the Generals' Plot against Hitler). The transcript of their conversation shows how Choltitz used barbaric suggestions to probe his superior's state of mind and determine whether Speidel would protect him if he disobeyed Hitler's orders. Speidel's ambiguous final statement could hardly have been criticized by SS agents eavesdropping on their conversation, yet it was enough to persuade Choltitz that they had reached an understanding. Repeatedly during the last days of August, Hitler demanded of his staff, "Is Paris burning?" The answer was always no.

CHOLTITZ: I am telephoning you to thank you for the splendid order you have transmitted to me.

SPEIDEL: What order, Herr General?

CHOLTITZ: The order to reduce Paris to a heap of rubble, of course. Would you care to hear the dispositions I have made? Three tons of explosives have been placed in the Cathedral of Notre-Dame, two tons under the dome of the Invalides, one ton in the Chamber of Deputies. I am preparing to blow up the Arc de Triomphe to clear the field of fire.

SPEIDEL sighs into the telephone.

CHOLTITZ: Well, my dear Speidel, I take it you agree?

SPEIDEL (stammering): Yes…all right, yes…Herr General.

CHOLTITZ: But surely you ordered me to do this?

SPEIDEL: No, no, we haven't ordered anything of the kind; the order came from the Führer.

CHOLTITZ: Forgive me, you transmitted the order. And it is you who will bear the responsibility for it in the face of history.

SPEIDEL makes no reply.

Dietrich von Choltitz (left) leads the surrender of his staff and ten thousand troops during the final liberation of Paris.

CHOLTITZ (continuing): I can tell you other dispositions I have made. We shall blow up the Madeleine and the Opéra at one go.

SPEIDEL still makes no reply.

CHOLTITZ (continuing): I shall blow up the Eiffel Tower and its iron girders will deny access to the bridges which will have been previously demolished.

SPEIDEL: Herr General, how lucky we are to have *you* in Paris.

TOWARD A POSTWAR WORLD

31

The Dumbarton Oaks Conference
August–October 1944

During World War II, for propaganda purposes, the Allies generally referred to themselves as the United Nations when describing their formal alliance against Germany, Italy, and Japan. In January 1942, for example, twenty-six nations signed the Declaration of the United Nations (based on the August 1941 Atlantic Charter), which set forth the major Allied war aims. Later, discussions began regarding a successor

organization to the failed League of Nations—one that could more effectively guarantee the political goals for which the Allies were fighting. Paragraph Four of the October 1943 Moscow Declaration recognized the need to establish such an organization "at the earliest practicable date." On August 21, 1944, the Big Four nations (the United States, Great Britain, the Soviet Union, and China) met at the Dumbarton Oaks mansion in Washington to develop specific proposals.

The task with which the Dumbarton Oaks conferees were charged was the creation of a detailed framework for an international security organization that could oppose future aggression and ensure the maintenance of world peace after the war. The process took about six weeks; when it was over, the basic structure of the new United Nations Organization had emerged. This included the now-familiar General Assembly, to which "all peace-loving states" could belong, and an eleven-member Security Council, of which the Big Four plus France would be permanent members.

One major point, however, was not resolved at Dumbarton Oaks. It was the matter of whether the five permanent members of the Security Council should possess vetoes, especially when voting on questions concerning their own aggressive behavior. The dispute wasn't settled until the following February, when Roosevelt, Churchill, and Stalin, meeting at Yalta, agreed on Security Council voting rules. On questions concerning UN operating procedure, there would be no permanent-member veto, and a vote of any seven Security Council members would be sufficient. On other matters, however, no resolution could pass the Security Council unless those seven members also included the entire Big Five. The one exception was that no state (including one of the Big Five) could vote on a question recommending a *peaceful* solution to a security problem in which it was involved. Yet a permanent member could still veto the imposition of economic (or military) sanctions against itself because these were not considered "peaceful."

The U.S., British, and Soviet delegations to the Conference on Security Organization for Peace in the Postwar World pose outside the Dumbarton Oaks mansion in early August 1944. Secretary of State Cordell Hull can be seen standing in the front row, eighth from the left.

FOUR POWERS AGREE ON A NEW LEAGUE CHARTER

To Maintain Peace; Council of World Body Would Have France as Permanent Member

By JAMES B. RESTON

WASHINGTON, Oct. 8—The United States, Great Britain, Soviet Russia and China are expected to announce tomorrow the decision of the delegates at the Dumbarton Oaks conference to recommend creation of an international organization "to promote the establishment and maintenance of international peace and security with the least diversion of the world's human and economic resources for armaments."

In their first report to the world on the results of "the Washington Conversations on International Organization," held for seven weeks at the Dumbarton Oaks mansion in Georgetown, the four governments will make public a long document outlining proposals for the creation of "a general assembly," "a security council," "an international court of justice," "a secretariat," "a military staff committee" and "a social economic council."

It can be stated on reliable authority that the proposed charter for the new League of Nations, drafted at Dumbarton Oaks, will contain the following essential points:

1. The central purpose of the organization, the four-power agreement says, is "to maintain international peace and security" and to that end to "take collective measures for the preservation and removal of threats to the peace, and the suppression of acts of aggression, or other breaches of the peace, to bring about peaceful means of adjustment or settlement of international disputes which may lead to a breach of the peace."

2. The agreement emphasizes that, while this should be an association of sovereign States with equal rights, the principal authority for maintaining peace, security and "order" should rest with what is called a "security council" of eleven nations, four of these, the United States, Britain, Russia and China, to be "permanent members," with France to be added "in due course," and six other non-permanent nations to be elected by the general assembly for two-year terms.

3. The agreement confirms that no agreement has yet been reached among "the big four" on the procedure of voting in the council in the event of a charge of aggression against one of the "permanent members" of the council.

It does state that in the general assembly each nation should have one vote and that decisions should be taken by "a two-thirds majority of those present and voting," but it also states specifically that "the question of voting procedure in the 'security council' is still under consideration."

4. The agreement proposes the creation of a military staff committee to advise the security council on the use of force to repel aggression and to draft plans for the creation of a system to regulate and limit the manufacture of weapons of war. The agreement makes clear, however, that as soon as the organization is created, the member states should negotiate another agreement outlining the number and type of forces they are willing to place at the disposal of the executive council.

5. The wording of the text outlining the functions of assembly emphasizes the fact that, unlike the original League of Nations, which gave all nations in its assembly the right to veto action against an aggressor, the joint proposals for the new league limit the assembly to an

Dr. V. K. Wellington Koo, chief of the Chinese delegation at Dumbarton Oaks, confers with Undersecretary of State Edward R. Stettinius Jr. (center), chairman of the U.S. delegation, and Alexander Cadogan (right), chairman of the British delegation.

advisory function and even limit its powers of recommendation.

The general assembly, the agreement is understood to state, would have "the right to consider the general principles of cooperation in the maintenance of international peace and security, including principles governing disarmament and the regulation of armaments." But, it adds, the assembly should not "on its own initiative, make recommendations on any matter relating to the maintenance of international peace and security which is being dealt with by the security council."

6. The agreement does not attempt in any way to stipulate how each government should instruct its delegate on the security council to vote. Indeed, while it is known that the delegates all agreed that all "permanent members" of the council should have the right to veto any proposal to use force against any aggressor who was not a "permanent member," no mention of

this agreement is made and the whole question of voting in the council is understood to have been referred to the meeting of the heads of state, which is expected to take place some time before the end of the year.

It is clear that the security council of the eleven nations is the heart of the proposed new organization and that this council would concentrate, first of all, on establishing the principle of constant consultation among the Big Five with a view to preventing aggression before war actually breaks out.

Consequently, there is no attempt in this draft agreement to rely on agreed definitions of aggression as a basis for action. On the contrary, the language used in defining the purpose of the organization is in broad terms, with the objective of assuring that the security council could deal with any act that might endanger the peace of the world.

The agreement suggests that the council should "function continuously" with "permanent representatives" at the headquarters of the new organization and should be empowered to set up such agencies as it may deem necessary for the performance of its functions.

It is further proposed that the council should not only have a military staff committee working with it but might also wish to create regional military subcommittees to deal with problems arising in any part of the world.

While the four-power agreement is being described as "ruthlessly realistic" in its determination to repel future aggression, it emphasizes settling disputes by pacific means and doing whatever can be done safely to relieve the peoples of the world from the crushing financial and economic burden of maintaining vast armies.

"In order to promote the establishment and maintenance of international peace and security with the least diversion of the world's human and economic resources for armaments," the agreement states, "the security council, with the assistance of the military staff committee, should have the responsibility for formulating plans for the establishment of a system of regulation of armaments for submission to the members of the organization."

Reflecting an aim to bring the force of collective action to bear on any danger spot early rather than late, the agreement emphasized that the security council "should be empowered to investigate any dispute likely to endanger peace."

The parties to the dispute would have every opportunity to choose whatever means of pacific settlement they like, but the intent is generally recognized that they should do so with full knowledge that any attempt to abandon peaceful means of settlement would be met quickly and effectively by those forces and facilities of the member states which the Dumbarton Oaks charter hopes will be put at the disposal of the security council.

This agreement does not undertake to indicate what kind of forces or facilities the various member nations should put at the disposal of the security council. The delegates are understood to intend that these matters should be negotiated separately after the heads of state iron out the points on which no full agreement was reached at Dumbarton Oaks and after the United Nations security organization is called to discuss the recommendations of the conferees.

Nor is there any suggestion in the draft that the security council should have authority to order our troops into action against any future aggressor without the approval of the United States.

Although this point is not made clear in the draft because of the failure to reach an understanding on the procedure of voting in the event of a charge of aggression against one of the permanent members of the council, it is known that the delegates of all four powers agreed that each of the "permanent members," including the United States, should have the right to veto any proposed action by the league.

The delegates are known to have agreed that action could not be taken against a nation not a permanent member of the security council before a majority of the eleven members of the council, including the United States, Soviet Russia, Britain, China and France, voted to do so.

While the terms of the agreement specifically propose that the security council should be able to deal with "any situation" which might lead to international friction, it is apparent from the proposed structure that the council would not, except in very special cases, deal with the economic and social causes of war.

The Russian delegation, especially, argued that the security council should deal primarily with security. The Chinese delegation proposed that several commissions, to deal with economic, social, cultural and colonial problems, be established under the council to deal with the causes of war, but it is significant that while all these problems were recognized at Dumbarton Oaks as bearing directly on the problem of security, the draft agreement established a social and economic council and stated specifically that responsibility for the discharge of the duties of this council should be vested in the general assembly.

As to the membership of the organization as a whole, the delegates at Dumbarton Oaks contemplate that the organization should begin first with the United Nations, but that generally its base should be broadened to include all peace-loving States.

The regulations proposed for the General Assembly are outlined in the Dumbarton Oaks agreement as follows:

Each nation to have a single vote, and a two-third majority of those present and voting to govern action. The Assembly could consider the general principles of cooperation in the maintenance of peace and security, including the general question of disarmament, but it should not, on its own initiative, make recommendations on security questions under consideration in the council.

Furthermore, the agreement adds, the General Assembly should "be empowered to suspend from exercise of any rights or privileges any member of the organization against which preventive or enforcement action shall have been taken by the Security Council." It is also suggested, however, that this suspension could be restored by a decision of the council.

In addition to these rights, the Assembly would, under the Dumbarton Oaks agreement, be authorized to elect the non-permanent members of the council. These, the agreement states, would serve for two years, with three of the six non-permanent members retiring each year and not being eligible for immediate re-election.

Those who have seen the four-power agreement note several omissions from this proposed league which they consider to be significant. It does not, for example, contain what were generally regarded as the three most controversial articles of the League of Nations covenant. Those were Article Five, giving to all member nations in the Assembly the right to veto any proposed action against an aggressor; Article Ten, obligating each member State to guarantee the territorial integrity and political independence of all other member States; and Article Sixteen, obligating all member States to sever automatically all trade and financial relations with any State which resorted to war against the regulations of the League covenant.

Although the four-power agreement does not say so specifically, it is known that the Dumbarton Oaks delegates specifically rejected the "unanimity rule," the "general guarantee" and the "automatic sanctions" clause, and adopted, instead, the general principle that it was more practical, if less idealistic, to leave these questions to the judgment of the Security Council, in the light of the facts pertaining at the time of the dispute.

Officials here stress, of course, that the agreement reached at Dumbarton Oaks does not in any way commit the governments whose officials have worked out the draft outlined above. It is true that every clause in the agreement was gone over carefully, not only by the delegates but also by the highest officials of the four governments, to whom all points were referred before the "ninety per cent agreement" was approved.

"...to make not merely a peace but a peace that will last."

Franklin Roosevelt's charge to the Dumbarton Oaks delegates

On August 23, 1944, the president delivered these remarks before the assembled delegates to the Dumbarton Oaks Conference, more formally known as the Conference on Security Organization for Peace in the Postwar World.

Gentlemen, this is an informal occasion. I have not prepared any speech. This is merely a feeling on my part that I would like to shake hands with you. I should like to be able to go out to Dumbarton Oaks, to take a part in your discussions.

A conference of this kind always reminds me of an old saying of a gentleman called Alfred E. Smith, who used to be Governor of New York. He was very, very successful in settling any problem between capital and labor, or anything that had to do with the State Government in which there was a controversy.

He said if you can get the parties into one room with a big table and make them take their coats off and put their feet up on the table, and give each one of them a good cigar, you can always make them agree. Well, there was something in the idea.

You have a great responsibility. In a way, it is a preliminary responsibility. But, after all, we learn from experience, and what I hope is that in planning for the peace that is to come we will arrive at the same good cooperation and unity of action as we have in the carrying on of the war. It is a very remarkable fact, that we have carried on this war with such great unanimity.

I think that often it comes down to personalities. When, back in 1941, at the time of the Atlantic Charter, just for example, I did not know Mr. Churchill at all well. I had met him once or twice very informally during the first World War. I did not know Mr. Eden. But up there in the North Atlantic—three or four days together, with our two ships lying close together—we got awfully fond of each other. I got to know him, and he got to know me. In other words, we met, and you cannot hate a man that you know well.

Later on, Mr. Molotov came here and we had a grand time together. Then, during the following year, at Teheran, the Marshal and I got to know each other. We got on beautifully. We cracked the ice, if there ever was any ice; and since then there has been no ice. And that's the spirit in which I know you are going about your work.

I was just talking with the Secretary of War, Mr. Stimson. He was saying that one of the tasks we face is making this conference of ours—and the successor conferences—something that will last, last a long time. He said that unfortunately in Germany the young people, the young Nazis, favor an idea which will be dangerous to the peace of the world just as long as they have anything to say about it.

The prisoners of 17, 18, 20 that we are capturing now—both on the French front and the Soviet front—these German prisoners of that age are even worse in their Nazism than the prisoners of 40 or 45. And, therefore, as long as these young men have anything to say about it, the peril of Nazism will always be before us.

Members of the U.S., British, and Soviet delegations leave the White House on August 23, 1944, after calling on President Roosevelt.

And we have got to make not merely a peace but a peace that will last, and a peace in which the larger Nations will work absolutely in unison in preventing war by force. But the four of us have to be friends, conferring all the time—the basis of getting to know each other—"putting their feet up on the table."

And so I am very hopeful that it can be done because of the spirit that has been shown in the past in getting together for the winning of the war. But that is the spirit that we have learned so well in the last few years. It is something new, this close relationship between the British Empire and the United States. This great friendship between the Russian people and the American people—that is new. Let's hang on to both friendships, and by spreading that spirit around the world, we may have a peaceful period for our grandchildren to grow up in.

All I can do is to wish you every possible success in this great task that you have undertaken. It will not be a final task, but at least it gives us something to build on, so that we can accomplish the one thing that humanity has been looking forward to for a great many hundreds of years.

It is good to see you. Good luck.

32

The Batle of Leyte Gulf

October 1944

During 1943 and 1944, the American forces in the Pacific pursued two separate campaigns, one led by the navy (and Chester Nimitz) in the Central Pacific and the other managed by the army (and Douglas MacArthur) in the Southwest Pacific. Admiral Nimitz's plan called for an island-hopping march through the Gilbert, Marshall, Caroline, and Mariana Islands in that order. Meanwhile, MacArthur's forces would

hop among fewer, bigger islands, from Bougainville in the northern Solomons to New Georgia in the Choiseuls to New Britain in the Bismarck Archipelago. MacArthur's eventual objective, of course, was a return to the Philippines.

Between the Philippine Islands and the Marianas (some thirteen hundred miles to the east) lay the Philippine Sea. When American troops began the invasion of Saipan in the Northern Marianas on June 15, 1944, Adm. Toyoda Soemu, the current commander in chief of the Japanese navy, sent the First Mobile Fleet under Vice Adm. Ozawa Jisaburo from its anchorage at Tawitawi in the Philippines into the Philippine Sea for a showdown with Adm. Raymond A. Spruance's Fifth Fleet protecting the Saipan transports. Learning of Ozawa's approach, Spruance ordered Vice Adm. Marc Mitscher's Task Force 58 of seven heavy and eight light carriers (plus numerous supporting warships) to respond. The result was a spanking of the Japanese, who had only half the number of warships and aircraft.

Meanwhile, the Joint Chiefs of Staff set October 20 as the invasion date for the Philip-

pines. The first landings were to take place on the central island of Leyte. To support this invasion, the navy assigned both the Third Fleet under Adm. William F. "Bull" Halsey and the Seventh Fleet under Vice Adm. Thomas C. Kinkaid. The Seventh Fleet was given the specific task of transporting and protecting the invasion troops (Lt. Gen. Walter Krueger's Sixth Army), while the Third Fleet, complete with Mitscher's powerful Task Force 58, provided cover.

Despite the rout of Ozawa in the first battle of the Philippine Sea, Toyoda decided to gamble again, ordering almost everything he had to converge on the Philippines, with the main attack coming in the Leyte Gulf. Following Toyoda's plan, the remnants of Ozawa's fleet, now in Japanese waters, sailed south to act as a decoy, luring Halsey and Mitscher away from Leyte. At the same time, two other Japanese task forces raced north from Singapore to attack the Leyte transports and Kinkaid's supporting warships. The result was the greatest naval battle of the war and perhaps of all time.

A Japanese plane, tentatively identified as a "Jill," passes over the radar tower of the USS Essex a few seconds before crashing into the carrier's flight deck on November 25, 1944, during operations off the Philippines.

NIMITZ PUTS JAPAN'S LOSS AT 58 OF 60 SHIPS; 24 SUNK, 13 OTHERS HIT MAY HAVE GONE DOWN

4 Carriers Sunk; Third Fleet Destroyed Them at Loss of Only Ten U. S. Planes

By GEORGE HORNE

PEARL HARBOR, Oct. 29—Admiral Chester W. Nimitz made his report to America today on the second battle of the Philippine Sea and the action will stand as one of the outstanding naval events of history.

The United States forces sank or damaged fifty-eight Japanese warships. They sent to the bottom twenty-four warships, aggregating nearly 200,000 displacement tons and including four carriers and two battleships, a crucial loss for the enemy's already depleted and battered fleet.

Of the fifty-nine or sixty Japanese warships engaged, possibly one or two escaped damage.

Goaded from hiding at last by the implacable advance of American forces into the very doorways of the empire, the enemy ships came out and were, the admiral said, "decisively defeated and routed."

Planes and warships of Admiral William F. Halsey's Third Fleet and Vice Admiral Thomas C. Kinkaid's Seventh Fleet, with submarines joining in to play major roles and some land-based air power arriving from fields of the Southwest Pacific Command, bombed, strafed, shelled and torpedoed the enemy for six days.

They saw ships explode and go down at sea, they harried the damaged ones mercilessly back along the green fringes of the many islands where they thought to escape.

Our forces detected the enemy's two western fleet groups long before they were within striking distance. We swept from his northern force the element of surprise when he planned to engage us near the central islands and then tear into our flanks with his carriers and supporting warships.

The Third Fleet sent all four of his carriers to the bottom with a loss of only ten of our aircraft. Eight pilots and ten crewmen of enlisted rank gave their lives in this battle that probably left the enemy with only a weakling naval force.

Some of their planes came out from land to join the carriers, but the carriers were gone and our combat patrol shot down twenty-one planes and chased off the rest.

Enemy warships sunk were two battleships of the Yamasiro class; one 20,000-ton carrier of the Zuikaku class; one carrier of the Zuiho class; two carriers of the Chitose class; six heavy cruisers, three light cruisers, three small cruisers or large destroyers, and six destroyers.

The following ships were severely damaged and may have gone down: one battleship, three heavy cruisers, two light cruisers and seven destroyers.

The Admiral listed six battleships, four heavy cruisers, a light cruiser and ten destroyers that escaped in a damaged condition.

For three and a half days Fleet Headquarters issued no details on the battle supplementing the announcement of Wednesday midnight. In that time reports and photographs have been carefully studied and the data gathered and offered in today's communiqué are the result. It includes everything definitely known about the battle to date.

For the first time, it is believed here, the names of victorious American ships engaged in a major sea action are listed, not all of them, but eight of them—ships with names of special significance to the Japanese. There were five battleships seriously damaged at Pearl Harbor when the enemy thought he had broken American naval power beyond repair: the West Virginia, the Maryland, the Tennessee, the California and the Pennsylvania.

They were in the battle but the parts they played cannot yet be told.

The other ships named were three new carriers, the Lexington, the Wasp and the Hornet, names which also mean something to the enemy.

Admiral Nimitz said that in all the actions American submarines played a highly important part and are credited with sinking and damaging several enemy warships both before and after the air and sea battle.

Submarines, in fact, opened the action when they sighted Japanese Singapore on Oct. 21 and 22 and sank two heavy cruisers and damaged a third, and although the communiqué gives no details, probably they were on hand to track down and deliver the coup de grace to those unable to complete their escape. There yet may be additional reports on stragglers.

This is by far the most comprehensive official report ever issued by Admiral Nimitz on a naval engagement. He conservatively calls it one of the major sea battles of World War II, ranking it with the Battles of the Coral Sea, Midway, Guadalcanal and the First Battle of the Philippine Sea last June. But by all standards of measurement it exceeds any of these.

The enemy lost far more than in the Coral Sea, where five ships were sunk and four damaged; at Midway, where he lost six and had seven damaged, or Guadalcanal, in which eighteen are listed as sunk and eight damaged. Twelve of those sunk at that time were auxiliaries, either freighters or transports.

In the Battle of the Philippine Sea in June he lost five ships and probably seven, eleven were damaged.

Gen. Douglas MacArthur (right) poses with reporters aboard the ship carrying him back to the Philippines.

Actually then the Second Battle of the Philippine Sea is the greatest naval action of the war, and it is no indulgence of enthusiasm to rank it with Jutland, when seventy-five ships were sunk or damaged. More warships were involved in the Second Battle of the Philippine Sea than in Jutland, although more were put out of action in that decisive action of the first World War. [The British lost fourteen ships at Jutland and the Germans eleven, The Associated Press recalled.]

In a sense it is idle to make the Philippine-Jutland comparison, for fire power, which is the prime measurement, was incomparably higher in the latest Pacific action.

The Admiral's fine presentation of the data gathered by experts through the battle—of course, it is still not as complete as it will be, since the battle descriptions are missing—makes a few corrections on earlier reports. There were, for example, nine battleships instead of ten, two of which were ships of the Ise class, old battleships with small flight decks aft, but definitely classed at battleships. The middle force, which came through the Sibuyan Sea and San

Bernardino Strait, had five battleships instead of four.

Moreover, the northern force discovered off Luzon was somewhat smaller than at first believed.

An outstanding feature of the engagement, one that regrettably forced the Third Fleet to break off the attack when it might have finished off the entire seventeen ships instead of seven, was the urgent call from the American forces off Surigao Strait at the entrance to Leyte. The Third Fleet could undoubtedly have finished off the ships that escaped in damaged condition, but it had to speed southward, where a furious battle was raging between elements of the Seventh Fleet and the powerful Sibuyan force that had penetrated through San Bernardino to engage the screening force off Surigao and Samar Island.

It was here that some of the greatest damage was done to the enemy. It was here also undoubtedly that American forces suffered their greatest damage. Admiral Nimitz confirms earlier reports of our losses—two escort carriers, two destroyers, one destroyer-escort and "a few lesser craft." These were in addition to the Princeton, the light carrier announced earlier.

Admiral Nimitz reported the diversion of the Third Fleet group in these words: "Before all the damaged enemy ships could be tracked down and destroyed the engagement was broken off to proceed to the assistance of Seventh Fleet carrier escort groups, then under attack off Samar Island."

The Admiral does not say where the two enemy battleships were sunk. This damage was done in a battle or battles under the MacArthur command, and official reporting on such actions is left to Gen. Douglas MacArthur.

The Admiral's over-all figure includes all enemy ships sunk and damaged and presumably any earlier duplication has now been eliminated.

From the time the submarine scouts sighted the enemy force on Oct. 21, which was a week ago Saturday, to the 27th when our sea based and land based planes pursued the tattered Rising Sun back through Sibuyan Sea there was action stretching across hundreds of miles.

The submarines straight off sank two Atago class cruisers and seriously damaged a third. That was the enemy's first taste of the strength he had finally come out to test.

The report was speeded to Admiral Halsey, and he moved ships of the Third Fleet into position along the eastern side of the archipelago, in three groups, one off Surigao Strait, one off San Bernardino Strait and one off the Polill Island.

Photographs taken by carrier planes show that the Sibuyan force had battleships believed to be the Yamato, the Musashi, the Nagato, the Kongo and the Haruna, the latter the battlewagon that once we thought had gone down in the Philippines but never claimed by the Navy. [The Yamato and Musashi are new and probably are 45,000-ton 30-knot ships, according to The Associated Press.] It had eight cruisers, two of the Mogami class, two Tone class, two Nachi class, one Atago and one Noshiro. In addition there were thirteen destroyers—twenty-six ships in all.

The Sulu Sea force, moving eastward, consisted of two battleships of the Yamasiro class (one of these was definitely sunk), two heavy cruisers, two light cruisers and seven or eight destroyers—a total of thirteen or fourteen ships.

On Oct. 23, which was Monday, Hellcat fighters, Avenger torpedo planes and Helldiver bombers from the Third Fleet carriers attacked them, severely damaging and setting afire one battleship and one cruiser. They may have sunk, the Admiral said. Three other battleships got bombs and torpedoes as did three heavy cruisers. One light cruiser was torpedoed and it capsized and went down.

In the Sulu Sea bomb bits were made on both battleships and our planes strafed the cruisers and destroyers with rockets and machine guns.

While this was going on enemy land-based aircraft were attacking our carriers in the large-scale strike in which the Princeton was lost. We shot down at least 150 enemy planes, and our own losses, on which figures are not yet available, were light.

On this same afternoon—Monday—a land-based naval search plane discovered the enemy carrier force to the north about 200 miles off Cape Engano on northern Luzon. It was a seventeen-ship force with four carriers, one of the large Zuikaku class, three light carriers of the Chitose and Zuiho classes, the two Ise class battleships and a heavy cruiser of the Mogami class, a light cruiser of the Noshiro class, three Kiso class cruisers and six destroyers accompanying them.

Admiral Halsey started his fleet speeding northward at high speed during the night for a dawn attack.

For some reason the enemy must have believed our force was too occupied to get him such quick attention.

Whatever the reasons our planes plunged out of the sky the next morning and the enemy was definitely off balance.

In this single action, which lasted many hours, Admiral Nimitz listed the following damaged: ships definitely sunk, the four carriers, three by carrier aircraft and one damaged by planes and later sunk by cruiser and destroyer gunfire; one light cruiser or large destroyer sunk by gunfire; one destroyer by gunfire and a cruiser severely damaged by carriers, later to be sent down during the night of Tuesday by a submarine.

Not one of our ships was hit.

Then the Third Fleet force—just how much of it is not made clear—sped southward off Samar, there to wade into the melee going on between the Seventh Fleet screen and the enemy's Sibuyan force, which had slipped through during the night.

Here one cruiser of the Mogami class was seen to sink and a destroyer was left dead in the water. The enemy force ran northwest—presumably late in the day after a battle lasting some hours—and about 2 A.M. on Wednesday morning gunfire accounted for a straggler cruiser as it limped into San Bernardino.

Meanwhile, the southern enemy force had crossed the Sulu Sea, the Mindanao Sea and was moving still strong but considerably damaged toward Leyte. It was met during that same night, Tuesday, and decisively defeated by the Seventh Fleet.

The final concerted action took place the next day, the 25th, when the retiring Sibuyan force, hopelessly defeated, was again attacked by air forces of both the Third and Seventh Fleet, which sank one Mogami cruiser off Mindoro Island, far into the Philippine Islands.

Another Noshiro class cruiser was sunk south of Mindoro and one battleship was possibly sunk and three other battleships and three other cruisers were damaged.

That was the end of action and details. Admiral Nimitz said the total figure of twenty-four ships sunk, thirteen that may have been sunk and twenty-one definitely damaged included all reported action through Oct. 27. If submarines or other United States vessels caught more of the damaged craft they have not yet reported on it.

Admiral Nimitz's unprecedented communiqué, which represents his first departure from the traditional terseness, says simply: "Much of the credit for the destruction inflicted on the Japanese Fleet goes to the naval airmen who gallantly and relentlessly pressed their attack home with telling effect."

There can be no doubt about that. Most of these same airmen and to a large extent the same ships have been spreading over the entire Western Pacific since early September. That sentence of the Admiral's is most modest.

"Everything I do today will be for the last time."

The final entry from a kamikaze's diary

The battle of Leyte Gulf was also notable for the introduction of a new Japanese weapon: the kamikaze. The kamikaze's name, which means "divine wind," referred to the thirteenth-century typhoon that scattered the invasion fleet of Mongol emperor Kublai Khan, thus saving medieval Japan from subjugation. The latter-day kamikazes were suicide pilots who deliberately crashed their bomb-laden planes into American ships. The first kamikaze attack took place on October 21, badly damaging an Australian cruiser. The main assault at Leyte, however, didn't come until four days later, when kamikazes sank the *St. Lô* and damaged four other escort carriers. The volunteer pilots prepared for their missions with elaborate ceremonies, including ritual prayer and the composition of "farewell poems." This diary excerpt was written by a twenty-three-year-old kamikaze on the day that he died off Okinawa in April 1945.

This morning I got up at six and I breathed the pure mountain air. It is the last time that I shall breathe the fresh air of the morning. Everything I do today will be for the last time.

The pilots are to parade at 2 P.M. We will take off at three.

It is extraordinary. I have the impression that I want to write many things, but when I try I can find nothing to say.

I have not got the feeling that I am going towards my death. I am relaxed and light-hearted as though I were leaving on a journey. I look at myself in the mirror; my face does not seem to be that of a man about to die.

Father...please do not worry about your rheumatism. If you lead a quiet life everything will be all right. I would like to have a last cup of saké with you, but that is no longer possible. We will never pray together at the Buddhist altar again.

Mother, you weigh eight stone, three pounds, a little less than I. That is as it should be, but you must not lose weight because of my death. Since I joined the navy I have always hoped that you would remain in good health. The prosperity of the family depends on that. I know that you have a tendency to weep easily, but you must not weep, for I shall die with a smile on my lips. My father often used to say: "The others are laughing, so we must laugh too." I shall smile, so you, Mother, must also smile.

Junko and Sazuko, my dear sisters, take good care of your health. You must not allow your sorrow to make you ill.

The cherry blossom will soon be falling from the trees in Tokyo. Fall, fall, cherry blossom. Why should you continue to flower when my life is being cut off?

33.

The Presidential Election of 1944

November 1944

In 1944, unlike 1940, Roosevelt made no secret of his intention to seek another term as president. The only question was, Who would be his running mate? Vice Pres. Henry A. Wallace, an unapologetic (and somewhat overenthusiastic) liberal, had so infuriated the conservative wing of the Democratic party that party bosses were desperate to be rid of him. Office of War Mobilization chief James F. Byrnes

wanted the job and had some backing, but he was as unacceptable to the liberals as Wallace was to the conservatives. Finally, at a private White House dinner on July 11, just one week before the start of the Democrats' national convention in Chicago, the president agreed to the nomination of Missouri senator Harry Truman, who had recently won respect for his capable investigations into profiteering and mismanagement in the defense industries.

Most of those within the president's inner circle knew that the choice of vice president was crucial because few of Roosevelt's intimates expected him to live out his fourth term. His failing health had become particularly noticeable to his staff after the Teheran Conference, and in March 1944 an extensive examination by cardiologist Howard G. Bruenn revealed that the president was suffering from severe hypertension and heart failure. Roosevelt was immediately placed on a regimen of digitalis, diet, and rest, but his symptoms remained a cause of concern until his death the next year. (The president, meanwhile,

chose to ignore his heart condition and believed for a time that he was suffering from walking pneumonia.) "I had no idea he was in such a feeble condition," Truman told his administrative assistant after lunching with the president on August 18 (his only personal contact with Roosevelt during the campaign). "In pouring cream into his tea, he got more cream in the saucer than he did in the cup. His hands are shaking, and he talks with considerable difficulty....It doesn't seem to be any mental lapse of any kind, but physically he's just going to pieces."

Although New York governor Thomas E. Dewey, the Republican nominee, tried to make an issue out of Roosevelt's health (and the alleged influence of Communists in the president's administration), voters were reluctant to jettison a commander in chief who was winning the war. Dewey made the race closer than Wendell Willkie had in 1940 but still lost by 3.6 million popular votes and much more decisively in the electoral college, 432–99, failing even to hold New York.

ROOSEVELT WINS FOURTH TERM; RECORD POPULAR VOTE IS CLOSE

Dewey Concedes; His Action Comes as Roosevelt Leads in 33 States

By ARTHUR KROCK

Franklin Delano Roosevelt, who broke more than a century-old tradition in 1940 when he was elected to a third term as President, made another political record yesterday when he was chosen for a fourth term by a heavy electoral but much narrower popular majority over Thomas E. Dewey, Governor of New York.

At 3:15 A.M. Governor Dewey conceded Mr. Roosevelt's re-election, sending his best wishes by radio, to which the President quickly responded with an appreciative telegram.

Early this morning Mr. Roosevelt was leading in mounting returns in thirty-three States with a total of 391 electoral votes and in half a dozen more a trend was developing that could increase this figure to more than 400. Governor Dewey was ahead in fifteen States with 140 electoral votes, but some were see-sawing away from him and back again. Typical of these were Wisconsin, where he overtook the President's lead about 2 A.M.; Nevada, where Mr. Roosevelt passed him at about the same time, and Missouri.

In the contests for seats in Congress, the Democrats had shown gains of 11 to 20 in the House of Representatives, assuring that party's continued control of this branch. In the Senate the net of losses and gains appeared to be an addition of one Republican to the Senate, which would give that party twenty-eight members—far short of the forty-nine necessary to a majority. A surprise was the indicated defeat of the veteran Pennsylvania Republican, Senator James J. Davis.

The Congressional races were featured by a mass Democratic attempt, in which the Presi-

dent and Vice President Henry A. Wallace personally participated, to unseat Representative Clare Boothe Luce of Connecticut. But shortly after 3 A.M., following a night in which the lead had swung back and forth, her election was conceded by her opponent, Miss Margaret Connors. Some hours before, to his neighbors at Hyde Park, the President had expressed rejoicing over Mrs. Luce's "defeat." Her success is the vitriol in the Democratic honey.

Despite the great general victories by the Democrats, the popular vote will evidently show a huge minority protest against a fourth term for the President. Tabulations by the press associations indicated that the disparity between the ballots cast for the two candidates will be so small that a change of several hundred thousand votes in the key States, distributed in a certain way, would have reversed the electoral majority. At 4:40 A.M. The Associated Press reported 16,387,999 for Mr. Roosevelt and 14,235,051 for Mr. Dewey from more than one-third of the country's election districts. This ratio, if carried through, would leave only about 3,000,000 votes between the candidates.

One or the most interesting struggles for the Presidency was that in Wisconsin, where Mr. Dewey took an early lead, lost it and regained it again. Wisconsin is the State where the late Wendell L. Willkie made his stand for renomination, posing the issue of "isolationism" versus "internationalism." He ran last in the Presidential primary and expressed the belief,

Roosevelt tours Washington on November 21, 1944, with Harry Truman (center) and outgoing vice president Henry Wallace (right).

in then withdrawing from the race, that isolationism controlled the thinking of Wisconsin Republicans.

The close race between the President and Mr. Dewey, however, supported the view of others that Mr. Willkie was defeated by a combination between the followers of Mr. Dewey and Harold E. Stassen and that his contrary interpretation was not sound.

Pennsylvania was another scene of an intense struggle. Mr. Roosevelt got a much reduced majority in Philadelphia, but Allegheny County (Pittsburgh) exceeded expectations, and at 4 A.M. the State's thirty-five electors seemed moving toward Mr. Roosevelt's list.

In Ohio Mr. Dewey's early lead was being cut sharply by the President early this morning. New York's forty-seven electoral votes are certain for Mr. Roosevelt, and, with Illinois, Minnesota, Massachusetts, Connecticut and the 127

electors of the old Confederacy plus Tennessee in his column, the President was far beyond the 266 electors who constitute a majority.

The States in which Mr. Roosevelt was leading at 4 A.M. were:

Alabama, 11; Arizona, 4; Arkansas, 9; California, 25; Connecticut, 8; Delaware, 3; Florida, 8; Georgia, 12; Idaho, 4; Illinois, 28; Kentucky, 11; Louisiana, 10; Mississippi, 9; Maryland, 8; Missouri, 15; Montana, 4; Massachusetts, 16; Minnesota, 11; New Hampshire, 4; New Mexico, 4; New York, 47; Nevada, 3; North Carolina, 14; Oklahoma, 10; Pennsylvania, 35; Rhode Island, 4; South Carolina, 8; Tennessee, 12; Texas, 23; Virginia, 11; West Virginia, 8; Washington, 8, and Utah, 4—a total of 391.

The States with margins for Mr. Dewey were:

Colorado, 6; Indiana, 13; Iowa, 10; Kansas, 8; Maine, 5; Michigan, 19; Nebraska, 6; New Jersey, 16; North Dakota, 4; Ohio, 25; Oregon, 6;

South Dakota, 4; Vermont, 3; Wisconsin, 12; Wyoming, 3—a total of 140.

To win Mr. Dewey was obliged to effect a combination of Massachusetts (or Connecticut), New York (or Pennsylvania), the Border States, the Midwestern States and Oregon on the Pacific Coast. This is because the President, despite the midsummer "revolts" in Texas, South Carolina, Mississippi and Louisiana, was sure to start with 127 certain electors—the old South, plus Tennessee. Mr. Dewey failed to come within spyglass distance of this feat.

The popular vote ran so close until after 11 o'clock that even the most optimistic supporters of the President were cautious in their claims. But Mr. Wallace was not so timorous. He established a national record as a forecasting statistician by announcing at 9:30 P.M. that the President had been re-elected by a large electoral majority, that he had been given a Democratic House with a "mandate" to carry out his war and post-war program and that "bipartisan isolationism has been destroyed."

When Mr. Wallace issued this statement few were ready to accept his conclusion. But an hour later he had become a major prophet.

Early in the day, throughout the United States, it became evident that the heavy registration was the true portent of a larger vote than was anticipated when the campaign began. Soon after the national conventions were held the predictions in both political camps were for a vote well below that of 1940, under 45,000,000 and perhaps little more than 40,000,000.

Faced with this prospect, Democratic spokesmen openly conceded that so light a vote meant the re-election odds would be against the President and that only with a tally of 45,000,000 or more could his true strength be registered—in which event they were confident of success.

But within a few weeks after the nominations, the Political Action Committee of the Congress of Industrial Organizations, under the chairmanship of Sidney Hillman, began its effort to bring out the vote. Pamphlets urging citizens to go to the polls, and making arguments for Mr. Roosevelt's re-election, were distributed in great numbers in all parts of the country, but particularly in the large cities and even more intensively in those areas where war industry had sprung up and the normal population was much enlarged.

When the registration periods arrived it was demonstrated that these activities of Mr. Hillman's group were very effective. By the end of this period a vote that may exceed 50,000,000 (including ballots from the armed services) was indicated, and Democratic hopes rose accordingly. Reports from the sections where CIO-PAC had been busiest accentuated the view that, in bringing out votes which otherwise might not have been registered, Mr. Hillman's committee had been more vigilant and more successful than the regular Democratic organizations.

One interesting phase of this new note in national political campaigns was that the Hillman group did not neglect the Solid South, where Democratic nomination is equivalent to election and the November vote accordingly is light. To make sure that the President's popular vote would represent his real November strength, and to avert any possibility of an electoral victory without a popular majority—or a popular vote far below the electoral vote of the Democratic national ticket in percentage—the CIO-PAC besought Southern Democrats, especially the war industrial workers, to go to the polls and swell Mr. Roosevelt's general totals.

Not until the returns are all in will it be possible to make an estimate of the degree to which this innovation materialized. But there was no doubt in the minds of the professional politicians, after registration, that in the areas of normally close party division the CIO-PAC has done notable work in preventing a light poll this year.

The proof of this in every large industrial city was received with mixed feelings by the regular Democratic organizations, which hitherto have had all the credit for the votes registered and cast for their ticket. They were obliged to accept a competitor which, they were certain, would not be hesitant in pointing to its contribution in the event of the President's election to a fourth term which, on analysis, would prove to have been achieved by the voters in the large industrial areas where the CIO-PAC is strong and has been very active. This would presage a rivalry for influence and reward in the next administration to which dispute Mr. Hillman and his group could bring impressive support of their claims.

For a space in the campaign, when the Republican orators and organizers concentrated their fire on Mr. Hillman, and he was put down as a liability, the Democratic National Committee subordinated the role of his group as best it could and declined to certify its members as official spokesmen of the President's re-election.

But as the voters turned out yesterday in unusual and unexpected numbers, the dispute was suspended in the mutual wish to win, to be resumed in the event of Mr. Roosevelt's re-election by citizens in PAC territory and demonstrably responsive to its influence. Before the campaign ended Robert E. Hannegan, chairman of the Democratic National Committee, was vigorously defending Mr. Hillman from the Republican attacks and making the PAC cause his own in so far as he could.

"Dr. Odel was obviously disturbed and uneasy."

An FBI report on rumors of the president's poor health

The state of Roosevelt's health, especially the extent of his paralysis, had always been kept a well-guarded secret. His heart condition was treated likewise. However, as the 1944 election approached, White House press secretary Stephen Early learned of some politically disquieting rumors. At the time of the Democratic convention, FDR had been in San Diego, preparing to embark for Hawaii to discuss the Pacific war with Nimitz and MacArthur. Accompanying him was Dr. Bruenn, who happened to be standing behind the president when a photographer from *Life* took some pictures. When Bruenn's colleagues recognized the cardiologist, they naturally began speculating as to why the president might require his services. Early had the FBI investigate, and agents produced the report reprinted here. "Boiled down," FBI director J. Edgar Hoover wrote in his cover letter to Early, "the sum and substance of the whole situation seems to be that by reason of the fact that a Doctor Bruenn, a heart specialist, was in the group picture taken of the President at San Diego, it was assumed that the President was suffering from some heart ailment. There seems to have been a great deal of gossip and conversation at the Bethesda Hospital upon the part of doctors attached there, and the story seems to have originated there and then to have been carried to the Mayo Clinic, where again there seems to have been a lot of loose conversation and talk."

October 29, 1944

Memorandum Re: Circulation of story alleging the President has a serious heart affliction

Investigation of this matter is predicated upon telephonic request of Mr. Steve Early, who arranged through Mr. Breckinridge Long for a copy of the following letter to be made available by Mr. Breckinridge Long:

October 26, 1944

Dear Steve:
The name of that Colonel is B. R. Kirklin, Medical Corps. He is the X-ray specialist at Mayo Clinic and holds a commission in the Army with the rank of Colonel. He is relieved from his military duties from time to time to return to his work at the Mayo Clinic.

The statement was made to a closed group in the Clinic. It was in response to a question as to whether he knew anything of the President's condition. His answer, as quoted to me, was that "It is common knowledge at Bethesda and in the Surgeon General's office in Washington, etc." He then said, "I have this direct from Bethesda."

To the statement was also appended the remark that "in spite of his illness he is going ahead anyhow and doing his regular job."

Shortly previous to the time of the statement in Rochester, Minnesota, the Colonel had attended a medical meeting in Chicago. It was a civilian medical meeting but it is understood that certain persons holding commissions in the Army and Navy were in attendance at this meeting. However, it was not indicated that he obtained his information at that meeting.

Very sincerely,
Breckinridge Long

At Rochester, Minnesota, Colonel Byrl Raymond Kirklin was interviewed. Colonel Kirklin is a member of the U.S. Army Reserve presently on active duty, attached to the Surgeon General's office and is in charge of X-ray work for the United States Army. A large part of his time is devoted to instructing Medical Corps men in the Army who are attending school at the Mayo Clinic in Rochester, Minnesota. Colonel Kirklin stated that on October 21, 1944, he was at luncheon at the Kahler Hotel in Rochester, Minnesota, with a number of persons from the Mayo Clinic. Also present were Mr. Harwick, General Manager and President of the Clinic, and Dr. A. R. Barnes, head of the Diagnostic Section of the Mayo Clinic. Dr. Barnes had but recently returned from Bethesda, Maryland, where he had attended a meeting of heart specialists. During the luncheon Dr. Barnes stated that the President had a serious heart ailment. Colonel Kirklin heard Dr. Barnes make this comment but stated that Dr. Barnes did not make any further comment and there was no additional discussion of the subject at that time.

Later, on October 21st, according to Colonel Kirklin, he participated in a poker game at Rochester, Minnesota, and among those present were Mr. Harwick, Roy Watson, President of the Kahler Corpora-

The White House released this photograph of Roosevelt with Churchill at Yalta in April 1957 after FDR aide Jonathan Daniels revealed that numerous Yalta photos had been withheld to conceal the obviously poor state of the president's health.

tion, a Dr. Gardy, a Dr. Harrington, a Dr. Hollenbeck and a Dr. Dixon. During the course of the poker game Colonel Kirklin quoted Dr. Barnes' previous statement made at the luncheon that the President had a serious heart ailment. No further discussion or comment was made by him or anyone else at this time.

Collaterally, Colonel Kirklin stated that he had previously heard some discussion of the President's health on the occasion of a meeting of the Board of Examiners of Radiology, held in Room 1650 of the Palmer House, Chicago, Illinois, about September 23, 1944. According to Colonel Kirklin, several members of the Radiology Association, including himself, had just heard or were going to hear a speech made by either Mr. Dewey or Mr. Roosevelt, when Dr. Ross Golden, a radiologist assigned to the Presbyterian Hospital in New York City, referred to a photograph of the President giving his acceptance speech in San Diego, and stated—"Did you notice the unidentified profile in the picture to the right of the President. That man is Dr. ____, a cardiologist at the Presbyterian Hospital in New York City." No further discussion of the matter occurred at the time and Colonel Kirklin stated that he did not recall the name of the man referred to by Dr. Golden. Dr. Golden, according to Colonel Kirklin, is a civilian having no connection with the Military forces and is a heart specialist attached to the Presbyterian Hospital in New York City. Colonel Kirklin further furnished the information that on one occasion his wife had heard a similar story about the President's health from some source with which he is not acquainted.

Dr. A. R. Barnes, a civilian, head of the Diagnostic Section at the Mayo Clinic, upon interview admitted making the statement attributed to him by Colonel Kirklin on the occasion of an informal luncheon attended, according to Dr. Barnes' recollection, by three or four other Mayo Clinic associates at the Kahler Hotel. Dr. Barnes does not recall exactly the day upon which he made this statement or the persons present.

When questioned concerning the source of his information, Dr. Barnes stated that he visited with Dr. Howard Odel, a Navy Lieutenant at the Naval Hospital in Bethesda at 11:00 A.M. Thursday, October 19th. Dr. Odel is a close, personal friend of Dr. Barnes and a former protege of his at the Mayo Clinic. After Dr. Odel showed Dr. Barnes through the wards of the hospital, the two doctors walked about the grounds and at approximately 11:30 A.M. they began discussing Minnesota politics, at which time Dr. Odel made the statement—"The President is a very sick man—heart disease." Dr. Barnes stated that he asked no questions but that Dr. Odel made the statement as a fact and with no reference to the source of his information. Dr. Barnes stated he had never heard this information from any other source.

It was ascertained that Dr. Howard Odel is a Lieutenant in the Navy assigned to the Bethesda Naval Medical Center and residing at 3971 Langley Court, McLean Gardens, Washington, D.C. When interviewed on the evening of October 27th relative to any statements which he had made concerning the state of the President's health, Dr. Odel denied making any statements of this kind, but stated that the President's health had been the subject of a general discussion at a luncheon recently held at the Naval Hospital in Bethesda. When asked to name specifically the persons who had attended this luncheon, Dr. Odel declined to do so and stated that the discussions were only general in nature and no specific statement was made concerning the president's health. Dr. Odel stated that the reason the president's health had been discussed at the hospital was because members of the hospital staff recognized the picture of one of the Navy Hospital doctors, Dr. H. G. Bruenn, on the President's train at the time the President was making his acceptance speech. Dr. Odel stated that he had not discussed the subject of the President's health with Dr. Bruenn.

Dr. Odel was obviously disturbed and uneasy during this interview.

On October 28th Dr. Odel was again interviewed and after some questioning, in which no information was obtained, he was confronted with the fact that Dr. Barnes specifically attributed the statement heretofore set out to Dr. Odel. Dr. Odel stated that there was some divergence between Dr. Barnes' statement and what actually transpired. Dr. Odel stated that on the occasion of Dr. Barnes' visit to Bethesda, he had been showing Dr. Barnes through the Bethesda Naval Center and upon reaching the seventeenth "deck" of the hospital, he, Dr. Odel, explained that this floor was reserved for high ranking Government officials. Dr. Barnes asked whether this was where the President stayed and Dr. Odel stated that the President had not stayed there but had been at the hospital on two or three occasions for examination. Dr. Odel stated to Dr. Barnes that there had been rumors circulating about the President's health and. he, Dr. Odel, wondered if the President had heart disease or hypertension. Dr. Odel stated to Dr. Barnes that the President had been at the Bethesda Hospital on two or three occasions for examination and for that reason Dr. Odel had wondered if something was wrong with the President's heart. Dr. Odel advised on interview that while he had no definite recollection as to any further statement made by him to Dr. Barnes, he may have added something to the effect that "I suspect there may be something to it." Dr. Odel stated that he was positive that he had not made a flat statement that the President is a very sick man. He stated he was certain he had not used the words "very sick man."

Dr. Odel stated he realized his statement to Dr. Barnes had been very imprudent but that he had worked for Dr. Barnes for a period of twelve years and knew of his interest in heart disease because Dr. Barnes is an eminent heart specialist. Dr. Odel explained that his discussion with Dr. Barnes had been so casual that it had not recurred to him on the occasion of his previous interview. Dr. Odel volunteered the information that a Dr. Feldman of Rochester, Minnesota, had recently been at Bethesda and had asked him, Dr. Odel, if he knew anything of the President's health, at which time Dr. Odel stated that he did not. He explained that he took this position because he did not feel that he knew Dr. Feldman well enough to talk to him.

Dr. Odel, when asked as to the identity of other Naval Medical Corps doctors who have discussed the President's health, stated that this discussion has occurred on four or five occasions at luncheon when he, Dr. Odel, was in attendance, but Dr. Odel claimed inability to recall the identity of any other doctors participating in this discussion. Dr. Odel claimed that he has had lunch on various occasions with more than one-half of the doctors in the hospital and that consequently he could not recall specifically anyone participating in these discussions. He stated that these discussions grew out of the fact that Dr. Howard G. Bruenn, who had been photographed with the President, is known as a heart specialist. This discussion was recently revived when someone at the hospital received a newspaper clipping from a midwestern newspaper which commented upon the fact that Dr. Howard G. Bruenn, prominent heart specialist, had been photographed with the President, the newspaper article inquiring whether there was any significance to this fact. Dr. Odel stated that discussions among the doctors at Bethesda about the President's health have undoubtedly occurred on other occasions when he was not present. He said he believed that a number of the doctors at the hospital have expressed opinions to the effect that the President might be sick but Dr. Odel was careful to reiterate the statement that this was all in the way of personal opinion and that no one had purported to express any official or authoritative opinion. According to Dr. Odel, at least half of the doctors at the Naval Hospital have been engaged in discussions of this sort.

34.

The Battle of the Bulge

December 1944

The Allies' remarkable advance through France in August 1944 produced, as one might expect, many hopeful predictions of an early end to the war. George Marshall, who was already planning the transfer of troops from Europe to the Pacific, estimated that the capitulation of Germany would likely come in September or October. Eisenhower was much more cautious, especially in light of growing Allied supply

problems. Ike's planners hadn't expected their troops to reach the German border until a year after D day and hadn't made contingency plans for provisioning an army so far out in the field. In September 1944, therefore, it became clear to Eisenhower that no further advances could be made until the logistical problems were solved. All the Allies could do until then was chip away at the fortified West Wall along the German border and wait for the supply famine to end.

Meanwhile, Hitler was already planning a desperate—or glorious, as he thought—counterattack. Its goal was the Belgian port of Antwerp. Montgomery had already captured the city on September 4, but the Germans still held the Scheldt River estuary and thus blocked access to the port. Hitler believed that recapturing Antwerp would ensure continuing Allied supply problems, allow him to concentrate his V-2 campaign on England, and thereby force a negotiated peace with the western Allies. This would, in turn, he thought, free up the Wehrmacht in the west for duty in the east. The

German High Command was skeptical, to say the least, but in the aftermath of the Bomb Plot purges, none of the Führer's generals was prepared to question his judgment, publicly or privately. Survival had also strengthened Hitler's own sense of his personal invincibility, and he wouldn't have listened anyway.

The attack began at 5:30 A.M. on December 16, when ten Panzer divisions, illuminating their way with searchlights, burst out of the Ardennes Forest along the Belgian-German border and headed west for the Meuse. The location that Hitler had chosen was a weak point in the Allied lines between groupings of British troops in the north and Americans in the south. Eisenhower had deployed only four divisions of Lt. Gen. Courtney Hodges's First Army opposite the Ardennes because he didn't think the Germans could strike through such thick woodland successfully (even though Hitler had done exactly that in 1940). With ease the Germans tore through Hodges's men—producing panic, confusion, and surrender.

Soldiers of the 289th Infantry Regiment march in January 1945 to cut off the St. Vith–Houffalize road in Belgium during the Battle of the Bulge.

GERMANS SWEEP WEST THROUGH LUXEMBOURG; REPORT PATTON ATTACKING ON SOUTH FLANK; EISENHOWER URGES GREATEST ALLIED EFFORT

Rail Hub Isolated; Panzers Smash 15 Miles Past Bastogne—Enemy Slowed on Flanks

By DREW MIDDLETON

SUPREME HEADQUARTERS, Allied Expeditionary Force, Dec. 22—The great German winter offensive smashed westward through Belgium unchecked today for the seventh consecutive day.

Although American infantry and tanks have managed to hold positions along the sides of the flood tide of enemy soldiery, the advance in the center shows no signs of slowing down.

By late Wednesday panzer units had swept through the duchy of Luxembourg, isolated the great railroad communications center of Bastogne in Belgium and then pushed on thirteen and a half miles northwest to the vicinity of La Roche.

Front-line reports said that another German column advancing from Bastogne had rolled fifteen miles west through a pine forest and snow-covered fields to reach the vicinity of St. Hubert. The German communiqué reported today that the enemy had crossed the Ourthe River, probably in the La Roche area.

American counter-measures on the flanks had by Wednesday night retaken Malmedy as well as Stavelot in the north, and in the south had checked the German onslaught in the vicinity of Echternach and at Diekweiler, Osweiler and Berdorf, small villages two and a half miles south southwest of Echternach. Moreover, the German push through Consdorf toward the city of Luxembourg, twelve miles away, had by that time been checked.

These reports are forty-eight hours old, however. When they were made the Germans were concentrating armor in the Stavelot-Malmedy-St. Vith triangle and it is probable that they planned a resumption of the drive, which on Tuesday had sent armored reconnaissance elements into Habiemont, thirty miles west of the German frontier.

[An Associated Press field dispatch reported that the fighting had spread far south through Belgium to the area of Arlon, ten miles from the French border and forty miles due east of historic Sedan.]

For the fourth consecutive day low clouds kept the Ninth Air Force's bombers and fighter-bombers pinned to their airfields. The weather cleared a bit in the north, however, and the British Second Tactical Air Force sent 300 bombers and fighters down to give what aid was possible to the hard-pressed doughboys.

Mitchells bombed a German supply dump supporting Field Marshal Gen. Karl von Rundstedt's columns, but a thick overcast prevented observation of results. Spitfires flew armed reconnaissance in the area but reported the Luftwaffe inactive.

The recapture of both Malmedy and Stavelot increased the enemy's supply difficulties at Habiemont if, as it is assumed here, the Germans moved directly westward along the Butgenbach-Malmedy-Stavelot road.

Weary infantrymen rest in Bastogne, Belgium, on December 19, 1944, following German breakthroughs in that area.

The German communiqué today reported heavy fighting around Stavelot with American armored forces brought down from the Aachen sector.

The thrust to La Roche marks the deepest enemy gain, for it is thirty-five miles from Vianden [the frontier point whence this drive was launched] to La Roche through Bastogne.

With the enemy widening his offensive, which approached its second week, Gen. Dwight D. Eisenhower called on all American forces to turn the German's gamble "into his worst defeat."

Although on Wednesday night the doughboys were still clinging gamely to their positions around St. Vith, today's German communiqué claimed that the town was taken yesterday after an encircling movement and that the garrison was taken prisoner. If this is true, the enemy appreciably opened up the northern

flank of the offensive, for St. Vith is a road center whose possession should give Marshal von Rundstedt greater freedom of movement in the north.

North of St. Vith, however, the First Army position had been restored with the reoccupation of both Stavelot and Malmedy and our position was much better Wednesday night. What happened when the German armor that was concentrating there reopened the attack, censorship has not yet revealed.

The fighting around Monschau has subsided appreciably. On Wednesday the Germans put on several local attacks near Hoven, two miles southeast of Monschau, where they gained some small ground. Here, too, however, the Germans have concentrated a considerable number of troops and the position is by no means permanently stabilized.

The danger area is still the center, where German and panzer grenadier forces are maintaining the pace of the offensive against opposition that has not yet showed signs of stiffening.

Two German columns that on Tuesday had reached Wiltz and Clervaux joined, and after sharp action in which, front-line reports said, fifty-five German tanks were knocked out, smashed westward out of Luxembourg toward Bastogne. Wiltz, thirteen miles west of Vianden, was encircled and German forces were in the town itself.

Crossing the frontier into Belgium, German tanks spilled out around Bastogne, cutting roads to the north, south and east of the town, including the Bastogne-Arlon road, formerly an important lateral communication behind the American front.

One armored column by-passed Bastogne, which is twenty-two miles west of Vianden and four miles inside Belgium, and struck northwest toward La Roche, reaching the area of the town, which is on the Ourthe River and a junction of five main highways.

The positions in Wiltz and Bastogne are somewhat similar for the Americans, although the Germans have in both cases fought their way into built-up areas.

There is great activity throughout this area, where counter-measures initiated by Supreme Headquarters early this week apparently have not yet taken effect. The Germans report that the Americans are suffering heavily from surprise blows in this area and it is evident that the enemy is doing everything possible to create confusion among Allied soldiers and civilians throughout the area.

A German radio station is broadcasting news reports purporting to come from the British Broadcasting Corporation and these are picked up and retransmitted by the Swiss radio and featured by French newspapers. Today they reported a German penetration of fifty miles and the occupation of three-quarters of Luxembourg by the enemy.

This correspondent believes that the next German move will be an attempt to break out in the north, probably in the Monschau area. Pressure there is a likely method of pinning down American troops who might be diverted elsewhere to try to stem the enemy spearhead biting into eastern Belgium. Heavy fighting continued in this area Wednesday afternoon. This would probably not be the case if the Germans were content with a stabilized flank there.

The German communiqué made much of the offensive's success in forcing Allied Supreme Headquarters to withdraw "substantial" forces from areas where they had been attacking. The enemy reported that Lieut. Gen. George S. Patton Jr. had been forced to evacuate bridgeheads over the Saar in the vicinity of Dillingen and Ensdorf, near Saarlautern, where the Third Army was fighting in the Siegfried Line. There has been no news here today from this sector. The enemy also reported a lessening of the Seventh Army's attacks around Bitche.

There is a general view expressed here that the situation is somewhat easier. This must be based more on knowledge of what is planned as counter-measures than on what has actually been accomplished on the field of battle.

The enemy in one week has dislocated the entire center of the Allied front, apparently caused the cessation of large-scale attacks both on the Cologne plain and in the Saar and smashed a number of good American formations. In addition, considerable supplies of stores have been destroyed or captured.

Under these circumstances, this correspondent believes that it is unwise to assume that the situation is in hand except in the sense that the machinery for halting and, if possible, destroying the German force has been put in motion. Nor is it advisable to pin faith on familiar allusions to the length of the enemy's supply line or on the difficulties of his tanks in snow and mud.

A mood of sober confidence has replaced the confusion and uncertainty of the early part of this week and the bouncing confidence of two weeks.

United States Army and French authorities tightened security restrictions today, but official sources have denied that German paratroopers landed near Paris.

North of the break-through there was little activity. The United States Ninth Army had no changes to report on its front in Germany. Only a shelling of a bridge over the Maas [Meuse] at Grave, south of Nijmegen, by German long-range guns broke the quiet on the front of the British Second Army.

To the south there were patrolling and artillery fire on the Third Army's front while farther east Lieut. Gen. Alexander M. Patch's American Seventh Army has been confined to local attacks and patrolling.

The French First Army continued to hammer out small gains in the Vosges, occupying the town of La Chappelle, three miles south of La Pouterie. In a sector three miles to the southwest of that town the ground lost to German counter-attacks last week in the vicinity of Noirmont has been regained.

The Germans counter-attacked at Mittelwihr, northwest of Colmar, but the attack was broken up. Elsewhere on the Alsace plain there was only small local action.

Thunderbolts of the American First Tactical Air Force operating in this area flew eighty-six sorties, destroying six of twelve German planes encountered in the area of Marvarch, twenty miles east of Freiburg. In addition, more than fifty tons of bombs were dropped and two locomotives were destroyed and twelve damaged and seventy-three railroad cars were destroyed and 101 damaged.

"NUTS!"

An exchange between the German and American commanders at Bastogne

The German counteroffensive created a "bulge" in the Allied lines forty-five miles wide and sixty-five miles deep. Near the center of the bulge was Bastogne, an important crossroads being held by the 101st Airborne Division under Brig. Gen. Anthony C. McAuliffe. On December 22, the commander of the German forces surrounding Bastogne demanded McAuliffe's surrender. The general's memorable reply has since become part of the war's folklore. Meanwhile, Patton accomplished what many thought impossible—pivoting three of his eastward-facing divisions, hurrying them north a hundred miles, and attacking the German flank within forty-eight hours. His Third Army relieved Bastogne on December 26. Montgomery followed with a coordinated attack from the north, and together they halted the German advance several miles short of the Meuse before forcing the Wehrmacht into a costly retreat.

To the USA Commander of the encircled town of Bastogne:
The fortune of war is changing. This time the USA forces in and near Bastogne have been encircled by strong German armored units. More German armored units have crossed the river Our near Ortheuville, have taken Marche and reached St Hubert by passing through Homeres-Sibret-Tillet. Librimont is in German hands.

There is only one possibility to save the encircled USA troops from total annihilation: that is the honorable surrender of the encircled town. In order to think it over, a term of two hours will be granted beginning with the presentation of this note.

If this proposal should be rejected, one German Arty Corps and six heavy AA Battalions are ready to annihilate the USA Troops in and near Bastogne. The order of firing will be given immediately after this two hour's term.

All the serious civilian losses caused by this artillery fire would not correspond with the well-known American humanity.

The German Commander

◆　◆　◆

To the German Commander:
NUTS!

The American Commander

35.

The Yalta Conference

February 1945

Franklin Roosevelt's failing health during the last year of his life made it difficult for him to resist the demands of his more aggressive allies. For example, in October 1944, he allowed Chiang to dictate the removal of Stilwell, whose continuing pressure on the Nationalists to fight the Japanese had become intolerable to Chiang. Similarly, the president agreed to allow France to reclaim Indochina, ignoring

both his own principle of self-determination and the pleas of Ho Chi Minh and other Vietnamese nationalists. Of course, the example of Roosevelt's decline cited most often has been his performance at the Crimea Conference, held in Yalta on the Black Sea during early February 1945.

Four issues dominated the second wartime meeting of the Big Three: the creation of a new United Nations Organization, the future of liberated Eastern Europe (especially Poland), the status of a defeated Germany, and Soviet entry into the Pacific war. Concerning each of these, Stalin knew both his own mind and his strength. With regard to the United Nations, he pushed for two additions to the framework developed at the fall 1944 Dumbarton Oaks Conference: veto power for permanent members of the Security Council and (much less reasonably) additional General Assembly votes for Ukraine and Belorussia (White Russia). With respect to Poland, he demanded recognition of the Communist-directed Lublin government over the British- and American-supported London government-in-exile. From a defeated Germany, he

wanted ten billion dollars' worth of industrial equipment as war reparations. And, in exchange for a secret Soviet promise to declare war on Japan "two or three months" after the German surrender, he arranged for his country's annexation of the Kuril Islands and the return of all territory lost to Japan during the 1904–1905 Russo-Japanese War.

Roosevelt conceded nearly everything, and so did Churchill—but for reasons having little to do with either's health. Whatever shape the American president was in, Stalin held all the best cards in early 1945, and he knew it. The Red Army's hard-won gains placed the Soviet Union in a commanding military position. Its troops had already overrun Rumania, Bulgaria, Hungary, and Poland—and were, at the time of the Crimea Conference, within mere miles of Berlin. On the other hand, the British and Americans had yet to cross the Rhine. Given this situation, there was little Roosevelt or Churchill could have done to prevent Stalin from transforming his impressive military advantage into lasting political gains.

CONGRESS SPLITS ON CRIMEA PARLEY

Wheeler Sees Russia Ruling Europe—Several Attack Polish Settlement

By LANSING WARREN

WASHINGTON, Feb. 13—Considered Congressional opinion on the Crimea Conference, while showing a large preponderance of support, revealed divergences over the results today.

The two views were expressed in their most extreme forms by Senator Claude Pepper, Democrat of Florida, who considered the Crimea accords as the "greatest step toward lasting peace that has ever been taken," and Senator Burton K. Wheeler, Democrat, of Montana, who called them "a great victory for Stalin and for Russian imperialism."

Between these positions, Representative Helen Gahagan Douglas, Democrat, of California, said that the results "were better than the most optimistic expectations." Representative Alvin E. O'Konski, Republican, of Wisconsin, called the settlement over Poland a success for Propaganda Minister Joseph Goebbels "second only to that of Munich."

Representative George H. Mahon, Democrat, of Texas, saying that the United Nations' security conference in San Francisco was only ten weeks off, urged a nationwide campaign for public study and discussion of the Dumbarton Oaks proposals. He said that he felt that, if the American people wished to make such a study, they would not be able to find the necessary documents. For this reason he read into the Congressional Record the texts of the Dumbarton Oaks charter, the Fulbright and Connally resolution on world peace, the Atlantic Charter and President Roosevelt's declaration on the Four Freedoms. He said that there were no better texts for study than these documents themselves.

Senator Pepper said that the Crimea Conference was an achievement of untold importance because for the first time it had established the principle of consultation among the three great powers that would now direct the organization of world peace. It meant, he said, that in the settlement there would be no unilateral decisions, but each of the three powers would have a voice in determining any action in a way that would have avoided the regrettable incidents in Greece. All three nations, though different in their governmental structures, have now pledged themselves to a common effort in war and in peace, he said, and will determine together what shall be done in countries as they are liberated.

He said that most nations that reached the position of power now held by Russia had in the past set out on a course of domination, but the Crimea accords were an indication that this would not be the case. The "tripod" established among these powers, he said, could and should be made the foundation for world organization.

Senator Pepper said that he was glad that the world conference had been set for an early date in San Francisco. He predicted that the Dumbarton Oaks plan would be adopted there and ratified by the Senate at the present term.

Senator Wheeler had no such confidence in the Russian plans. "Russia," he said, "is going to dominate Europe, and there will be no question of anything else. The Crimea conference is a great victory for Stalin and for Russian imperialism."

Senator Wheeler said that the clauses in the announcement referring to free elections and consultation were merely words and would be so as long as Russia controlled the Baltic and Balkan States to be reorganized. It means, he said, that we shall return to spheres of influence, under which all the smaller states of Europe will be under the domination of one of their great neighbors and we shall go back to the system of frontier barriers and economic warfare. The conference report, he said, gives no hope for a lasting peace, which can be reached only by a federated system of a United States of Europe. "I am ready," he said, "for the United States to help, but not if we are to return to the old system."

Representative Jerry Voorhis, Democrat of California, approved the conference, saying: "The most important provision is that in all liberated nations new governments shall be formed by the process of open elections by secret ballot, supervised by all three powers."

Protesting the Polish border settlement on the Curzon Line, Representative O'Konski said: "The selling out of Poland is a stab in the back to freedom and a stab in the back to the freedom-loving country that has done most to crush Nazism." Later, Representative O'Konski, remarking that his mother and father were born in Poland, cried out:

"The Polish people have been killing Nazis for five years or more. I hope nobody will call me Nazi because I disagree with the outcome of the Black Sea conference.

"This sixth partition of Poland is a denunciation of the Atlantic Charter. What Pole was ever consulted before the Big Three met? No European was at the conference. Stalin is not a European; Churchill is not a European; our own President is not a European. The Atlantic Charter has been torn up and thrown into the Black Sea."

Representative Mahon said that he did not believe that 100,000 people in the United States

The Big Three pose in the garden of the Livadia Palace in Yalta during the Crimea Conference.

had read the Dumbarton Oaks proposals. He said that the State Department had published 75,000 copies of the document with explanations and 75,000 more had been ordered. The public printer, he said, has issued 20,000 for sale at 5 cents a copy and the Senate has printed 1,500 copies and more are on order.

"It is quite evident," he said, "that the American people have not had the opportunity to read or study the document."

Representative Clare Boothe Luce, Republican, of Connecticut, expressed disappointment at the decisions. She asked whether Germany was to be made the "fountain-head of post-war reconstruction" under the reparations plan outlined.

The basic settlement as revealed, she said, "does not correspond in my mind with what I thought President Roosevelt and Prime Minister Churchill had in theirs when they promulgated the Atlantic Charter."

"The right of all peoples to choose...."
The Protocol of the Proceedings of the Crimea Conference

The official text produced at Yalta was full of empty words. When presidential chief of staff Adm. William D. Leahy first saw the Declaration on Liberated Europe, he exclaimed, "Mr. President, this is so elastic that the Russians can stretch it all the way from Yalta to Washington without ever technically breaking it." "I know, Bill—I know it," the president replied. "But it's the best I can do for Poland at this time." In reality, the declaration's meaningless assertions about "democratic means" and "self-government" merely provided political cover for Roosevelt, who justifiably feared the anger of millions of embittered Polish Americans.

The Crimea Conference of the Heads of the Governments of the United States of America, the United Kingdom, and the Union of Soviet Socialist Republics which took place from February 4th to 11th came to the following conclusions.

I. WORLD ORGANISATION

It was decided:

(1) that a United Nations Conference on the proposed world organisation should be summoned for Wednesday, 25th April, 1945, and should be held in the United States of America.

(2) the Nations to be invited to this Conference should be:

(a) the United Nations as they existed on the 8th February, 1945, and

(b) such of the Associated Nations as have declared war on the common enemy by 1st March, 1945. (For this purpose by the term "Associated Nation" was meant the eight Associated Nations and Turkey.) When the Conference on World Organization is held, the delegates of the United Kingdom and United States of America will support a proposal to admit to original membership two Soviet Socialist Republics, i.e. the Ukraine and White Russia.

(3) that the United States Government on behalf of the Three Powers should consult the Government of China and the French Provisional Government in regard to the decisions taken at the present Conference concerning the proposed World Organisation.

(4) that the text of the invitation to be issued to all the nations which would take part in the United Nations Conference should be as follows:

INVITATION

"The Government of the United States of America, on behalf of itself and of the Governments of the United Kingdom, the Union of Soviet Socialist Republics, and the Republic of China and of the Provisional Government of the French Republic, invite the Government of _____ to send representatives to a Conference of the United Nations to be held on 25th April, 1945, or soon thereafter, at San Francisco in the United States of America to prepare a Charter for a General International Organisation for the maintenance of international peace and security.

"The above named governments suggest that the Conference consider as affording a basis for such a Charter the Proposals for the Establishment of a General International Organisation, which were made public last October as a result of the Dumbarton Oaks Conference, and which have now been supplemented by the following provisions for Section C of Chapter VI:

" 'C. Voting

'1. Each member of the Security Council should have one vote.

'2. Decisions of the Security Council on procedural matters should be made by an affirmative vote of seven members.

'3. Decisions of the Security Council on all other matters should be made by an affirmative vote of seven members including the concurring votes of the permanent members; provided that, in decisions under Chapter VIII, Section A, and under the second sentence of paragraph 1 of Chapter VIII, Section C, a party to a dispute should abstain from voting.'

"Further information as to arrangements will be transmitted subsequently.

"In the event that the Government of _____ desires in advance of the Conference to present views or comments concerning the proposals, the Government of the United States of America will be pleased to transmit such views and comments to the other participating Governments."

Seated at a Yalta conference table, Roosevelt and Churchill exchange a few private words.

It was agreed that the five Nations which will have permanent seats on the Security Council should consult each other prior to the United Nations Conference on the question of territorial trusteeship.

The acceptance of this recommendation is subject to its being made clear that territorial trusteeship will only apply to (a) existing mandates of the League of Nations; (b) territories detached from the enemy as a result of the present war; (c) any other territory which might voluntarily be placed under trusteeship; and (d) no discussion of actual territories is contemplated at the forthcoming United Nations Conference or in the preliminary consultations, and it will be a matter for subsequent agreement which territories within the above categories will be placed under trusteeship.

II. DECLARATION ON LIBERATED EUROPE
The following declaration has been approved:

"The Premier of the Union of Soviet Socialist Republics, the Prime Minister of the United Kingdom and the President of the United States of America have consulted with each other in the common interests of the peoples of their countries and those of liberated Europe. They jointly declare their mutual agreement to concert during the temporary period of instability in liberated Europe the policies of their three governments in assisting the peoples liberated from the domination of Nazi Germany and the peoples of the former Axis satellite states of Europe to solve by democratic means their pressing political and economic problems.

"The establishment of order in Europe and the re-building of national economic life must be achieved by processes which will enable the liberated peoples to destroy the last vestiges of Nazism and Fascism and to create democratic institutions of their own choice. This is a principle of the Atlantic Charter—the right of all peoples to choose the form of government under which they will live—the restoration of sovereign rights and self-government to those peoples who have been forcibly deprived of them by the aggressor nations.

"To foster the conditions in which the liberated peoples may exercise these rights, the three governments will jointly assist the people in any European liberated state or former Axis satellite state in Europe where in their judgment conditions require (a) to establish conditions of internal peace; (b) to carry out emergency measures for the relief of distressed peoples; (c) to form interim governmental authorities broadly representative of all democratic elements in the population and pledged to the earliest possible establishment through free elections of governments responsive to the will of the people; and (d) to facilitate where necessary the holding of such elections.

"The three governments will consult the other United Nations and provisional authorities or other governments in Europe when matters of direct interest to them are under consideration.

"When, in the opinion of the three governments, conditions in any European liberated state or any former Axis satellite state in Europe make such action necessary, they will immediately consult together on the measures necessary to discharge the joint responsibilities set forth in this declaration.

"By this declaration we reaffirm our faith in the principles of the Atlantic Charter, our pledge in the Declaration by the United Nations, and our determination to build in co-operation with other peace-loving nations world order under law, dedicated to peace, security, freedom and general well-being of all mankind.

"In issuing this declaration, the Three Powers express the hope that the Provisional Government of the French Republic may be associated with them in the procedure suggested."

III. Dismemberment of Germany

It was agreed that Article 12 (a) of the Surrender Terms for Germany should be amended to read as follows:

"The United Kingdom, the United States of America and the Union of Soviet Socialist Republics shall possess supreme authority with respect to Germany. In the exercise of such authority they will take such steps, including the complete disarmament, demilitarisation and the dismemberment of Germany, as they deem requisite for future peace and security."

The study of the procedure for the dismemberment of Germany was referred to a Committee, consisting of Mr. Eden (Chairman), Mr. Winant and Mr. Gousev. This body would consider the desirability of associating with it a French representative.

IV. Zone of Occupation for the French and Control Council for Germany

It was agreed that a zone in Germany, to be occupied by the French Forces, should be allocated to France. This zone would be formed out of the British and American zones and its extent would be settled by the British and Americans in consultation with the French Provisional Government.

It was also agreed that the French Provisional Government should be invited to become a member of the Allied Control Council for Germany.

V. Reparation

The following protocol has been approved:

(1) Germany must pay in kind for the losses caused by her to the Allied nations in the course of the war. Reparations are to be received in the first instance by those countries which have borne the main burden of the war, have suffered the heaviest losses and have organised victory over the enemy.

(2) Reparation in kind is to be exacted from Germany in three following forms:

(a) Removals within 2 years from the surrender of Germany or the cessation of organised resistance from the national wealth of Germany located on the territory of Germany herself as well as outside her territory (equipment, machine-tools, ships, rolling stock, German investments abroad, shares of industrial, transport and other enterprises in Germany etc.), these removals to be carried out chiefly for purpose of destroying the war potential of Germany.

(b) Annual deliveries of goods from current production for a period to be fixed.

(c) Use of German labour.

(3) For the working out on the above principles of a detailed plan for exaction of reparation from Germany an Allied Reparation Commission will be set up in Moscow. It will consist of three representatives—one from the Union of Soviet Socialist Republics, one from the United Kingdom and one from the United States of America.

(4) With regard to the fixing of the total sum of the reparation as well as the distribution of it among the countries which suffered from the German aggression the Soviet and American delegations agreed as follows:

Alger Hiss (right) at Yalta with a group including Andrei Vishinsky (second from left), Averell Harriman (fourth from left), Molotov (fifth from left), Anthony Eden (sixth from left), Edward R. Stettinius Jr. (seventh from left), and Alexander Cadogan (eighth from left).

"The Moscow Reparation Commission should take in its initial studies as a basis for discussion the suggestion of the Soviet Government that the total sum of the reparation in accordance with the points (a) and (b) of the paragraph 2 should be 20 billion dollars and that 50% of it should go to the Union of Soviet Socialist Republics."

The British delegation was of the opinion that pending consideration of the reparation question by the Moscow Reparation Commission no figures of reparation should be mentioned.

The above Soviet-American proposal has been passed to the Moscow Reparation Commission as one of the proposals to be considered by the Commission.

VI. Major War Criminals

The Conference agreed that the question of the major war criminals should be the subject of enquiry by the three Foreign Secretaries for report in due course after the close of the Conference.

VII. Poland

The following Declaration on Poland was agreed by the Conference:

"A new situation has been created in Poland as a result of her complete liberation by the Red Army. This calls for the establishment of a Polish Provisional Government which can be more broadly based than was possible before the recent liberation of the Western part of Poland. The Provisional Government which is now functioning in Poland should therefore be reorganised on a broader democratic basis with the inclusion of democratic leaders from Poland itself and from Poles abroad. This new Government should then be called the Polish Provisional Government of National Unity.

"M. Molotov, Mr. Harriman and Sir A. Clark Kerr are authorised as a commission to consult in the first instance in Moscow with members of the present Provisional Government and with other Polish democratic leaders from within Poland and from abroad, with a view to the reorganisation of the present Government along the above lines. This Polish Provisional Government of National Unity shall be pledged to the holding of free and unfettered elections as soon as possible on the basis of universal suffrage and secret ballot. In these elections all democratic and anti-Nazi parties shall have the right to take part and to put forward candidates.

"When a Polish Provisional Government of National Unity has been properly formed in conformity with the above, the Government of the U.S.S.R., which now maintains diplomatic relations with the present Provisional Government of Poland, and the Government of the United Kingdom and the Government of the U.S.A. will establish diplomatic relations with the new Polish Provisional Government of National Unity, and will exchange Ambassadors by whose reports the respective Governments will be kept informed about the situation in Poland.

"The three Heads of Government consider that the Eastern frontier of Poland should follow the Curzon Line with digressions from it in some regions of five to eight kilometres in favour of Poland. They recognise that Poland must receive substantial accessions of territory in the North and West. They feel that the opinion of the new Polish Provisional Government of National Unity should be sought in due course on the extent of these accessions and that the final delimitation of the Western frontier of Poland should thereafter await the Peace Conference."

VIII. YUGOSLAVIA

It was agreed to recommend to Marshal Tito and to Dr. Subasic:

(1) that the Tito-Subasic Agreement should immediately be put into effect and a new Government formed on the basis of the Agreement.

(2) that as soon as the new Government has been formed it should declare:

(a) that the Anti-Fascist Assembly of National Liberation (AUNOJ) will be extended to include members of the last Yugoslav Skupstina who have not compromised themselves by collaboration with the enemy, thus forming a body to be known as a temporary Parliament, and

(b) that legislative acts passed by the Anti-Fascist Assemb[l]y of National Liberation (AUNOJ) will be subject to subsequent ratification by a Constituent Assembly;

and that this statement should be published in the communique of the Conference.

IX. ITALO-YUGOSLAV FRONTIER
ITALO-AUSTRIA FRONTIER

Notes on these subjects were put in by the British delegation and the American and Soviet delegations agreed to consider them and give their views later.

X. Yugoslav-Bulgarian Relations

There was an exchange of views between the Foreign Secretaries on the question of the desirability of a Yugoslav-Bulgarian pact of alliance. The question at issue was whether a state still under an armistice regime could be allowed to enter into a treaty with another state. Mr. Eden suggested that the Bulgarian and Yugoslav Governments should be informed that this could not be approved. Mr. Stettinius suggested that the British and American Ambassadors should discuss the matter further with M. Molotov in Moscow. M. Molotov agreed with the proposal of Mr. Stettinius.

XI. South Eastern Europe

The British Delegation put in notes for the consideration of their colleagues on the following subjects:

(1) the Control Commission in Bulgaria.

(2) Greek claims upon Bulgaria, more particularly with reference to reparations.

(3) oil equipment in Roumania.

XII. Iran

Mr. Eden, Mr. Stettinius and M. Molotov exchanged views on the situation in Iran. It was agreed that this matter should be pursued through the diplomatic channel.

XIII. Meetings of the Three Foreign Secretaries

The Conference agreed that permanent machinery should be set up for consultation between the three Foreign Secretaries; they should meet as often as necessary, probably about every three or four months.

These meetings will be held in rotation in the three capitals, the first meeting being held in London.

XIV. The Montreux Convention and the Straits

It was agreed that at the next meeting of the three Foreign Secretaries to be held in London, they should consider proposals which it was understood the Soviet Government would put forward in relation to the Montreux Convention and report to their Governments. The Turkish Government should be informed at the appropriate moment.

The foregoing Protocol was approved and signed by the three Foreign Secretaries at the Crimean Conference, February 11, 1945.

E. R. Stettinius, Jr.
V. Molotov
Anthony Eden

Protocol on the Talks Between the Heads of the Three Governments at the Crimean Conference on the Question of the German Reparation in Kind

The Heads of the three governments agreed as follows:

(1) Germany must pay in kind for the losses caused by her to the Allied nations in the course of the war. Reparation are to be received in the first instance by those countries which have borne the main burden of the war, have suffered the heaviest losses and have organised victory over the enemy.

(2) Reparation in kind are to be exacted from Germany in three following forms:

(a) Removals within 2 years from the surrender of Germany or the cessation of organised resistance from the national wealth of Germany located on the territory of Germany herself as well as outside her territory (equipment, machine-tools, ships, rolling stock, German investments abroad, shares of industrial, transport and other enterprises in Germany etc.), these removals to be carried out chiefly for purpose of destroying the war potential of Germany.

(b) Annual deliveries of goods from current production for a period to be fixed.

(c) Use of German labour.

(3) For the working out on the above principles of a detailed plan for exaction of reparation from Germany an Allied Reparation Commission will be set up in Moscow. It will consist of three representatives—one from the Union of Soviet Socialist Republics, one from the United Kingdom and one from the United States of America.

(4) With regard to the fixing of the total sum of the reparation as well as the distribution of it among the countries which suffered from the German aggression the Soviet and American delegations agreed as follows:

"The Moscow Reparation Commission should take in its initial studies as a basis for discussion the suggestion of the Soviet Government that the total sum of the reparation in accordance with the points (a) and (b) of the paragraph 2 should be 20 billion dollars and that 50% of it should go to the Union of Soviet Socialist Republics."

The British delegation was of the opinion that pending consideration of the reparation question by the Moscow Reparation Commission no figures of reparation should be mentioned.

The above Soviet-American proposal has been passed to the Moscow Reparation Commission as one of the proposals to be considered by the Commission.

Winston S. Churchill
Franklin D. Roosevelt
J. Stalin
February 11, 1945.

Agreement Regarding Entry of the Soviet Union Into the War Against Japan

The leaders of the three Great Powers—the Soviet Union, the United States of America and Great Britain—have agreed that in two or three months after Germany has surrendered and the war in Europe has terminated the Soviet Union shall enter into the war against Japan on the side of the Allies on condition that:

(1) The *status quo* in Outer-Mongolia (The Mongolian People's Republic) shall be preserved;

(2) The former rights of Russia violated by the treacherous attack of Japan in 1904 shall be restored, viz:

(a) the southern part of Sakhalin as well as all the islands adjacent to it shall be returned to the Soviet Union,

(b) the commercial port of Dairen shall be internationalized, the preeminent interests of the Soviet Union in this port being safeguarded and the lease of Port Arthur as a naval base of the USSR restored,

(c) the Chinese-Eastern Railroad and the South-Manchurian Railroad which provides an outlet to Dairen shall be jointly operated by the establishment of a joint Soviet-Chinese Company it being understood that the preeminent interests of the Soviet Union shall be safeguarded and that China shall retain full sovereignty in Manchuria;

(3) The Kuril islands shall be handed over to the Soviet Union.

It is understood, that the agreement concerning Outer-Mongolia and the ports and railroads referred to above will require concurrence of Generalissimo Chiang Kai-Shek. The President will take measures in order to obtain this concurrence on advice from Marshal Stalin.

The Heads of the three Great Powers have agreed that these claims of the Soviet Union shall be unquestionably fulfilled after Japan has been defeated.

For its part the Soviet Union expresses its readiness to conclude with the National Government of China a pact of friendship and alliance between the USSR and China in order to render assistance to China with its armed forces for the purpose of liberating China from the Japanese yoke.

J. Stalin
Franklin D. Roosevelt
Winston S. Churchill
February 11, 1945.

36.

The Firebombing of Dresden
February 1945

In July 1942, just two months after the RAF's triumphant thousand-plane raid on Cologne, Lt. Gen. Carl Spaatz arrived in London to take over command of the U.S. Eighth Air Force, which had been tasked with supporting the RAF's strategic air war against Germany. From the start, Spaatz's advocacy of daylight precision bombing brought him into conflict with Air Chief Marshal Arthur "Bomber" Harris, whose

Bomber Command had embraced the nighttime area-bombing tactics that Harris had personally developed and employed over Cologne. During the next two years, while Spaatz managed the aerial components of the Torch and Overlord landings, the Eighth Air Force somewhat sanctimoniously kept its distance from Harris's attacks on civilian targets. Yet, once the Allies secured the Normandy beachhead and their planes returned to the strategic bombing of Germany, the upper echelons of the U.S. command staff began to reconsider their previous aversion to what one senior officer called British "baby-killing schemes."

According to historian David M. Kennedy, "Beneath the economy-strangling logic of 'strategic' aerial warfare, another idea about the role of bombing had long slumbered in the minds of some American air strategists. In the war's final weeks it stirred uneasily to life: that bombardment might not only inflict physical damage but could break the enemy's spirit as well, by so terrorizing civilian populations that they would compel their governments to beg for peace."

When the British proposed during the late summer of 1944 a plan, dubbed Operation Thunderclap, to devastate Berlin—casualties for the campaign were estimated at 275,000— Spaatz predictably advised Eisenhower to turn it down. But Ike, who had consistently supported precision bombing in the past, now disagreed. "I am always prepared to take part in anything that gives real promise to ending the war quickly," he told Spaatz. As a result, on February 3, 1945, the British and Americans staged a joint attack on Berlin that killed twenty-five thousand people. Ten days later, a similar raid targeted the medieval city of Dresden, world famous for its beauty.

Twelve hundred planes took part in this two-day, three-wave attack, dropping incendiary bombs that created a firestorm. Estimates of the number of civilian dead range from thirty-five thousand to more than one hundred thousand, rivaling Hiroshima. Yet, because so many of the million people living in Dresden at the time were refugees from other cities, no death count can ever be certain.

DRESDEN, ONCE REICH PRIDE, ERASED BY BOMBS, GERMAN RADIO ASSERTS

LONDON, March 4—Dresden, one of the Reich's most ancient and cherished cities, has ceased to exist, the German radio asserted tonight. Whether for propaganda effect or in a burst of unaccustomed frankness, the capital of Saxony was described as a great city that had been "wiped from the map of Europe."

Referring to the massive air blows of Feb. 14 and 15, Rudolf Sparing, German Transocean news agency correspondent, said that not one building remained in Dresden and that tens of thousands of the city's inhabitants lay buried under the rubble created by the Allies' bombs. His broadcast purported to give a description of the havoc caused by the Royal Air Force and United States Eighth Air Force.

This is the version of Dresden's plight recited by Sparing:

"The Allied air raids on Dresden on Feb. 14 and 15 caused the greatest destruction a big urban area has ever suffered.

"The Dresden catastrophe is without precedent. Not a single detached building remains intact or even capable of reconstruction. The town area is devoid of human life. A great city has been wiped from the map of Europe.

"Tens of thousands who lived and worked in the city are now buried under its ruins. Even an attempt at identification of the victims is hopeless.

"What happened on that evening of Feb. 15? There were 1,000,000 people in Dresden at the time, including 600,000 bombed-out evacuees and refugees from the east.

"The raging fires that spread rapidly in the narrow streets killed a great many from sheer lack of oxygen.

"Tens of thousands who succeeded in getting out—no one knows how—fled to the green belt surrounding the city. Then, at midnight, another British bomber fleet appered on the blood-red horizon and caused further destruction among them with fragmentation bombs and machine guns.

"Twelve hours later—the siren system had long since ceased to function—a third wave spread further devastation.

"Today we can only speak of what once was Dresden in the past tense."

Allied communiqués reported no air attack on Dresden the night of Feb. 14 or 15.

A British Air Ministry communiqué issued Feb. 14 said that the RAF Bomber Command on the night of Feb. 13–14 "made two very heavy attacks on Dresden, an important center of communication and a base for the defense of eastern Germany."

The United States Strategic Air Forces in Europe announced on Feb. 14 a heavy bomber attack by the Eighth Air Force on "industrial and transportation targets at Dresden." On Feb. 15 a Strategic Air Forces communiqué reported another daylight attack by Eighth Air Force bombers on "transportation targets in Dresden."

"The smell of burning filled the cellar."

A survivor's account of the Dresden firebombing

Erika Dienel, the author of this account, was a fifteen-year-old Dresden schoolgirl in 1939, when Germany invaded Poland. Five years passed, however, before the brutality of the war finally came to Dienel's hometown. In October 1944, the first Allied bombing mission leveled two factories on the outskirts of the city—where French and Belgian prisoners of war had been forced to work. "Then," Dienel remembered, "came the fateful night of 13 February."

I was working as a typist in the training school for the air-raid warning system. Our small staff had a little afternoon party with homemade doughnuts—rather grey-looking, but by that time our flour was no longer white. Our boss was away; with a small ration of red wine, we brewed a hot punch and talked about where we would go should the Russians overrun us. But the Americans were also not too far away, and we only hoped they would come first. Some of our staff came from the Saarland and the western part of Germany. They had already lost contact with their relatives: The post had stopped because the Americans had occupied their home towns. We decided that whoever had a home left would take the others in.

Going home that night, I paid a visit to a friend in one of the Red Cross hospitals for wounded soldiers. His arm had been amputated and shell splinters extracted from his throat. He could hardly speak. I left very depressed and crossed the Elbe by the Carol bridge on that still night, bringing me into Steinstrasse, the street where we lived. Little did I know that it was the last time I would cross this bridge.

My mother was packing some very large rucksacks, which she had made. Our Breslau evacuees advised us to have them ready in case we had to go at once (they had left their home with very little). I wanted to go to bed early, and had started getting ready when the air-raid warning sounded. We heard on the local radio that many aircraft were heading for Dresden. We were just going down to our cellar when we saw the whole town become floodlit with what we called "Christmas trees"—flares, ready for the arrival of the bombers.

At 10:15 P.M. the first bombs came down on us. One detonation after another shook the house. It was a strong four-story building, and in our air-raid cellar were about 15 people. The all-clear came after about half an hour—thanking God for being spared, we all went upstairs and started to clear up. All the electric lights were gone and the windows blown out, glass was shattered everywhere from the blast, but our house was not on fire. Nearby, people emerged from burning houses, many in great distress, and started to rescue the remnants of their belongings, bringing what they could carry to the riverbanks.

My mother went across the street to see if some neighbours were all right. She soon returned and told me that their house was in darkness and unusually quiet. We did not know then that they had all died in their basement cellars. Our terraced houses were joined to those in the next streets, in L-shapes; our terrace was joined to Marschallstrasse on one side and Terrassenufer, facing the Elbe. Some houses had caught fire, and it was astonishing how quickly the blaze moved from one to another. We were told by the air-raid warden to put a fire watcher in our attic, in case the fire should spread to our roof. As the youngest member of our household, I had this job. I will never forget looking across the rooftops of Dresden's burning houses. Those greedy flames seemed to eat up large houses in no time, coming nearer and nearer to us. It was the first time in my life I had felt really afraid.

I decided to warn the other occupants of our house to bring their most valuable belongings to the embankment for security. My mother and I started packing a great wicker basket—but in the middle of doing it we heard another very faint siren far away, and our hearts nearly stopped beating. Surely one attack would be enough? We went back down to the cellar. It was about 1:30 A.M. when we heard the bombs falling. More and more people rushed into our cellar—many came from the embankments, where they had escaped after the first raid. Children began to cry as, minute by minute, the detonations grew more violent. Each time the whistling noise of a heavy bomb came nearer, we expected that it would hit us. Some began to pray; others were numb with fear. It seemed endless. We died a thousand times. Hell could not be worse.

Then, all of a sudden, a tremendous bang shook us and the sizzling noise of fire could be heard. The smell of burning filled the cellar. It was one of those dreadful petrol-filled firebombs, and it had set our house on fire. Now the panic began, as the smoke filled the cellar. Between all the terraced houses, wall-breaches had been made in the cellars, so that it would be possible to break through the walls easily and get trapped people out. In the terrible panic which developed in our cellar, where more than 80 people were now crammed together, one man—an air-raid warden—halted the panic and saved us all from nearly certain death. He promised to find us a way out.

We didn't know how long we had been down in the cellar; we didn't even know if the bombardment outside was still going on, because time bombs were exploding, too. Above us, the stairways were burning fiercely, blocking that exit. Very soon the warden returned and told us that if we would follow him calmly through five more wall breaches, we could all be saved. He led the way, and we followed what was for the older people a difficult route, since many breaches were cut too high or too narrow. At the end of the journey through the cellars the warden stood at the top of another staircase, beneath a burning ceiling, directing people out through the windows of a ground-floor flat. How many lives he saved we will never know; without him, we would all have suffocated.

But our nightmare was not over. As soon as we jumped into the street, we saw the inferno outside. Like the flakes in a snowstorm, fire showered down on us. My mother looked at it all, panicked, and started running towards the city. Thinking of water, I quickly managed to get her to run with me to the end of our road, to the embankment of the Elbe. We were just in time: Soon after we passed, the houses on both sides of the street collapsed and blocked the end of the road. And had it not been such a short distance, the heat of the firestorm would have set our hair and our clothes alight, turned us into human candles.

Dresden was to burn for seven nights and days. The heat reached over 1,000 degrees Fahrenheit. In the centre, there was no escape. The town was a mass of flames. People, burning like torches, jumped into the Elbe on this cold February night. Screams and cries for help were heard everywhere. The embankment was covered with bodies or pieces of flesh. Many who had gone there after the first raid had not heard the second warnings and met their deaths there in the open, as the bombs fell.

We started to walk towards the outskirts of the town, to our relatives along the embankment. It was a march I will never forget. Every house we passed stood in flames; under our feet there were bodies, nothing but bodies. Across the Elbe, the hospital in which I had visited my soldier friend earlier was now also in flames. There had been a red cross on the hospital rooftop. I thought, has nothing been spared this horror? We walked and walked, but each house where we hoped to find shelter was burning, so all our friends and relatives—if they were still alive—must have gone through an experience similar to ours.

37.

Raising the Flag on Iwo Jima
February 1945

On the day in July 1944 that Saipan fell, Tojo Hideki, recognizing the strategic importance of the defeat, resigned as premier of Japan. Tojo understood that because the Northern Marianas lay within twelve hundred miles of Tokyo, B-29 Superfortresses based there could reach the Japanese home islands at will. Four months later, in fact, B-29s flying out of Saipan, Guam, and Tinian began targeting Japanese cities.

After the Marianas, the next stop on Nimitz's Central Pacific campaign was Iwo Jima, an island belonging to the Bonin group, located about halfway between Saipan and Tokyo. Nimitz prized the island's two airfields, from which Japanese fighters currently threatened B-29s en route to Japan. Alternatively, under American control, these airfields could be used to provide fighter support for the B-29s or possibly as advance bases for the bombers themselves. All this provided substantial motivation for the Japanese defending the island, yet they had a strong emotional incentive as well. Japan had formally annexed the Bonins in 1876, and the islands were thus considered part of the Tokyo prefecture and sacred imperial soil, requiring their defense to the last man.

Topographically, Iwo Jima was a volcanic island five and a half miles long and two and a half miles wide at its broadest point. Bubbling sulfur pits gave the place, which looked like "hell with the fire out," a pervasively acrid smell. Even more ominous were the Japanese fortifications there.

Combat engineers had used concrete and steel to reinforce caves, which they interlinked with tunnels to create nearly impregnable bunkers. Neither three months of aerial bombardment nor three days of close-range naval shelling had been able to dent them. Therefore, when the Fifth Marine Amphibious Corps landed on February 19, 1945, it faced murderous fire—which it returned with equally deadly flamethrowers, the island-hopper's weapon of choice.

The carnage lasted more than a month. Marine casualties numbered twenty-three thousand, or nearly one in three, including six thousand dead. On the Japanese side, however, the figures were beyond what most Americans could imagine. There were virtually no Japanese survivors. Only a few hundred had allowed themselves to be captured, and most of these were too badly wounded to resist. The rest of the twenty-one-thousand-man Japanese garrison either died in the fighting or sacrificed themselves in hopeless suicide charges that preceded the final pacification of the island in late March.

OUR VAST LIFELINE ACROSS THE PACIFIC

Along it flows guns, ammunition and food for the men and ships closing in on Japan.

By SIDNEY SHALETT

WASHINGTON—A powerful weapon is working on the side of our men who are pounding at Japan's inner citadel and at Tokyo itself. Without it the Marines could not have stormed ashore on Iwo Jima. Admiral Chester W. Nimitz, boss of the Pacific Fleet, likes to call it "one of the Navy's greatest secret weapons." Admiral Ernest J. King, boss of the whole Navy, says the way the weapon has worked is "nothing short of colossal." Navy Secretary James Forrestal says we couldn't win the Pacific war without it.

That weapon is: Logistics.

The leatherneck at Iwo Jima doesn't have much time for philosophizing. He doesn't ponder about the vastness of the Pacific. The rifle in his hand is a thing to shoot back with; he doesn't stop to wonder at the fact that it was manufactured somewhere in the United States, maybe 10,000 miles away, and brought to him through an incredible supply chain.

Yet the marine taking the stepping-stones to Japan, his bluejacket brother who handles the landing craft, the muddy, sweaty doughfoot on Luzon and Corregidor, and Admiral Mitscher's flattop fliers who joined the Army Superfortress pilots in hammering Tokyo, all have that weapon behind them—working, in our hands, better than any military power ever has used it under similar circumstances.

Logistics is a big order. When your admirals and your generals sit down and figure out what they're going to need two years hence, and set the wheels in motion to have it ready at the right time, that's logistics. When the ships come and move the hundreds of thousands of men and the mountains of supplies—the guns, the bullets, the beans and coffee and shoe polish and underwear, the tanks and planes and rockets and flame-throwers, the refrigerators and meat and beer, the wool socks and cigarettes—that's logistics, too.

Logistics is so important that when the strategy-planners in Washington sit down to plan the next move in the Pacific, six months or a year hence, they have the supply experts at their right hand. Admiral King and his strategic plans section tell Admiral Frederick J. Horne and his logistics-planners what they are to do. Then Logistics Plans goes to work with all the bureaus—ordnance, ships, supplies and accounts and all the rest—and tells Strategic Plans whether it can fill the bill. Sometimes strategy actually has to be altered or delayed if logistics says no.

Supplying the Atlantic war is a tremendous thing, because of the volume of the fighting involved, but the Pacific war, because of the great distances with which we had to contend and the remote and inadequate bases, captures the imagination as the Logistics War. England and now France are worthy bases and 3,000 miles do not seem insuperable. After visiting the United Kingdom it is necessary only to fly the Pacific, as this writer did recently, to appreciate the differences between the two theatres.

Instead of England, we had dots such as Espiritu Santo and Funafuti in the beginning; then Guadalcanal, the Russells, New Guinea, Saipan, Guam and incredible Manus in the Admiralties. Instead of 3,000 miles and then a hop across the Channel, we had 2,400 miles between lonesome bases—7,000 miles from San Francisco to Manila, and then it's still 1,800 miles to Tokyo.

Fly over Ulithi and see the unbelievable sight of a great fleet anchored around a crescent strip of coral; watch the Liberty ships unloading at Saipan and the trucks hauling the goods at breakneck speed over the roads hazy with coral dust; fly over a plodding convoy, bobbing in the blue-green sea between New Guinea and the Philippines; step ashore on Manus and see the Yankee-made piers, the huge, floating sectional drydocks, the cavernous warehouses bursting with supplies for an invasion-bound fleet; then you'll know what logistics means.

Nowhere on this side of the ocean, in the places where the flow of supplies has its beginning, can you forget that word—logistics. You feel it on the foggy, dank piers of the West Coast, where the cranes move nets of cargo, where stevedores bend their backs to load the ships that slip out of harbor like gray ghosts, bound for the regions where our men fight in the sun against a fanatical enemy. You feel it in Washington, where page after page of figures, where almost unending conferences are all bent toward keeping the supply chain moving—from factory to beachhead. You feel it in the vast industrial centers of the country, where the machine-gun bullets which will stop the death-throe banzai charges of the enemy on a dozen desolate islands, or the flame-throwers which will burn them out of coral caves, are made.

Observers in Europe earlier in the war, and even those who remember the darkness of the East Coast at an earlier period, think of war and blackout as synonymous. Not so in the Pacific—logistics there couldn't stand the handicap of a blackout. At the primitive ports of the Pacific—a prominent admiral once declared that we're doing the job in some places out there under conditions as rudimentary as Robinson Crusoe had to face—they keep the lights on all night, for the

Marines on Iwo Jima unload supplies from Coast Guard and navy landing craft.

docks are few and the ships have to be unloaded. Let a Japanese plane sneak through our aircraft defenses and attempt a raid and then they'll flick the switch. Otherwise the labor—much of it by hand—goes on, often through the night hours.

Travel to Pearl Harbor, Australia or New Zealand and you'll feel that the supply problem can't be so bad, for the facilities there are impressive. But then track the convoys out in the forward areas, watch them skirting the coral reefs to put in at an atoll better suited to receive a canoe than a Liberty ship, and again you appreciate the magnitude of the job. Or visit a recently invaded island, where landing craft and amphibious ducks still crawl up to the beachhead from the hundreds of ships anchored out at sea, and where multigeared vehicles struggle through the sand and mud and sweating men form a human chain to pass the equivalent of many war bonds from the surf to supply dumps, whence it flows to the fronts, where the thunder of cannon and the crackle of machine guns never stop their din—then you take off your hat to the men who know how to keep this gigantic thing moving.

That's logistics—colossal rather than mysterious; a combination of shrewd planning in advance ("crystal ball gazing," the admirals sometimes call it), big business methods, and plain courage and sweat.

Little things sometimes tell the story better than all the impressive statistics in the world. You can read page after page about how the Navy, in two years, has increased its general storage space from 31,000,000 to 65,310,000 square feet and plans to go to 86,000,000 by the end of the year; how the West Coast port of Oakland handled 233,511 inbound tons and 252,710 outbound tons in August alone; how the Navy's transportation bill is more than $45,000,000 a month; how it plans to use 470,000,000 barrels of petroleum and 2,700,000 tons of coal in 1945; how the Navy last year ate (just to mention a few of more than 100 food items) 320,000,000 pounds of fresh beef, 57,000,000 pounds of ham, 350,000,000 pounds of wheat flour, 68,000,000 pounds of butter and 750,000,000 pounds of potatoes.

Yet this writer, at least, was more impressed by seeing a huge pile of truck tires on Los Negros, an island of which most of us never had heard two years ago; by flying over a long line of vehicles, waiting to be taken off a Central Pacific island we had fought for but now were abandoning as too far in the rear; by seeing the gallant, life-bringing convoys in Leyte harbor at a time when the Japanese special attack corps planes still were coming over, and by dozens of other small but significant bits of evidence.

Approximately 25 per cent of the industrial output of the United States now is being moved out to the Pacific. War's appetite is insatiable. To land a force of 250,000 men (and it has been estimated that at least that number of troops are committed to the Philippines operation, though not that many were landed initially either in Leyte or Luzon), it requires 1,557,000 tons of supplies, with 332,000 additional tons for thirty days' maintenance. To land this number of men and their equipment requires some 5,000 separate

beachings by assorted landing craft, and thirty to thirty-five Liberty ships, plus fifteen tankers, would keep busy supplying them for thirty days. To supply 100,000 men and build up a base on Saipan, Admiral Horne has pointed out, 2,000,000 tons of freight, entirely exclusive of supplies for warships, were shipped in within sixty days.

There are more than 5,000,000 separate items, "from corn flakes to floating drydocks," as Admiral Horne puts it, on the Navy's Pacific-bound list. To accomplish a smooth, efficient flow of the corn flakes and floating drydocks—to say nothing of the gun mounts, binoculars, prayer books, radio stations, spare propellers, new hulls, first-aid kits, 16-inch battleship ammunition, coffee cups, aerial torpedoes, gold stripes for new admirals, depth charges for old destroyers and the rest of the 5,000,000 items—the Navy has worked out a catalogue system that makes the big mail order houses look almost like corner drug stores.

It was obvious, of course, that the Navy's area commanders could not run ashore with the 5,000,000 items in their head (or even on paper) every time we invaded a new island. So the Navy decided to "package" its items into what it efficiently but unromantically called "functional components." It divided up its various units, after long and painstaking study of the needs of the Pacific war, into some 214 "functional components"—including everything from administrative set-ups to PT repair shops, seaplane bases, cobbler and bake shops, post offices, medical dispensaries, recuperation camps and shore patrol and ship salvage rescue outfits—and gave each of them a code letter.

It also set up three major types of units. The smallest unit, an "Acorn," for instance, is an advanced base for either land or seaplanes. An "Acorn" would consist of sixty-six officers and 1,600 men, equipped with material to lay down two 6,000-foot runways and to do everything necessary in operating an airfield. An "Acorn" packed for shipment weighs 13,979 long tons and its cube is 22,374 tons.

Then the Navy put all these functional components into a slim pound-and-a-quarter book. When the area commander goes ashore, he takes the "order book" with him, and, if he wants any of the units, he simply cables the Navy one word, such as "Acorn" or "Z-32," and the units, the personnel of which may have been training together for as long as two years, already in waiting at some forward base, come in as speedily as transportation can bring them.

There also is a bigger book (weight: 2 1/2 pounds) which tells the area commander how he may "beef up" his basic units with additional men or matériel. Then, for final, awesome, master reference (and obviously the commander cannot carry these around with him in his landing barge) comes the Bureau of Supplies and Accounts' detailed list of the whole works on the Navy's shelves; this runs to 479 volumes, weighs 250 pounds and makes a pile some five feet high.

In Capt. Terry B. Thompson's necessarily large office in the Logistics Plans Division of Naval Operations in Washington, huge charts line the walls. Hundreds of variously colored cards, marked with code letters, are attached to the charts. Each of the cards represents a "functional unit" in varying stages of readiness, and Captain Thompson, who deprecatingly calls himself manager of the "nuts and bolts department," can supply the strategy-planners almost instantly with the information they need as to how many "Acorns" and their brothers are ready to move into any spot the Navy may pinpoint for future action.

Every conceivable factor, however minute, fits into the logistics mosaic. A strike in Detroit, crippling, say, the production of one small part that goes into a cylinder head of an airplane engine, could upset estimates on "ready" aircraft and delay the sailing of a carrier. Lack of housing or a shortage of eating places for stevedores in a California port could disrupt the loading of ships.

The factor which Navy men call "turnaround"—the time required for a ship to be loaded, delivered, reassembled in a convoy and returned for a new cargo—is a major item of strategical planning. Three round trips a year for a ship in the Pacific service—less than half the average of Atlantic cargo-carriers—is considered an excellent record. Slow speed, poor port facilities and time lost in mechanical overhauling sometimes keep a Pacific freighter's yearly average down to two or two and one-quarter trips.

Although the United States has built 4,319 cargo ships between Jan. 1, 1942, and Dec. 31, 1944, thus adding 43,671,000 tons to the shipping with which it started the war, shipping still is a critical item. This has been particularly true since there was some tendency, toward mid-1944, to estimate future shipping availability on the assumption that the European war would be cleaned up before the end of the year.

Now the men who plan our operations in Washington have issued strict orders to the commanders in the field—and they haven't minced words about it—not to order more matériel than can can be unloaded readily. The planners here, with the world picture at their fingertips, know the importance to the soldier in the Philippines and to the sailor at sea of having every implement of war in the right place at the right time; they are determined that, whatever the obstacles, the Battle of Logistics shall not be lost.

"The Marines watching from below raised the cry."

A description of the first Iwo Jima flag-raising

Wounded early in the invasion, marine corporal Richard Wheeler was being treated aboard a hospital ship when his platoon reached the summit of Iwo Jima's Mount Suribachi on the morning of February 23. Wheeler's account of his comrades' activities fails to mention the famous flag-raising photograph taken by Joe Rosenthal of the Associated Press because Rosenthal's image actually captured the *second* flag-raising that took place atop Suribachi three hours later.

The two-day assault on the fortifications was accompanied by a sustained din. Only our flame throwers wrought their slaughter quietly. They went into action with a metallic click and a long whoosh. But these were no doubt the most terrifying sounds the Japanese heard.

Hand-to-hand fighting sometimes resulted when enemy soldiers would suddenly dart from cover to attack or to make a break for the safety of more remote defenses. There were a number of bayonetings and knife killings. One Marine, attacked by a saber-swinging Japanese officer, caught the blade with his bare hands, wrested it from the man and hacked him to death with it. I saw this Marine later when he was brought aboard the hospital ship I occupied a mile or two offshore. He stopped by my bunk and told me his story. Both his hands were badly gashed and were swathed in bandages—but he still had the Japanese sword.

Several organized counterattacks were launched, but each was soon broken up. It isn't likely that the Japanese expected to accomplish much with these measures, but charging the advancing Marines was a way of death that many doubtless preferred to being exterminated in their failing defenses.

At one time during the bloody activities a Marine officer who could speak Japanese took a loudspeaker into the front lines and called upon Suribachi's surviving defenders to lay down their arms and surrender. But the appeal was ignored.

Attacking on the extreme left, the 3rd Platoon and the other units of Easy Company reached the volcano's base on the afternoon of the first day. They next sliced around its left flank. Once they had reached the area where the defenses thinned, they were ordered by Colonel Johnson to dig in and hold.

A similar attack was made by the 1st Battalion on the right. But in the center, where the 3rd Battalion was operating, going was tougher. An extra day was required for these units to batter their way to the base.

By the end of D-plus-3 the fight was largely won. There were still substantial numbers of the enemy in caves and other places of concealment, but hundreds had been slain and the pernicious power of the fortress had been broken.

It was time for the regiment to start climbing. But the craggy 550-foot dome was so steep that a cooperative move could not be made. It was discovered that the only route to the crater lay in the 2nd Battalion zone, so the job of planning the climb fell to Colonel Johnson. And he soon decided to send one of his rifle platoons up as an assault patrol.

A marine stands guard during the raising of the first (and smaller) flag atop Mount Suribachi.

The twenty-five men of the 3rd Platoon were by this time very dirty and very tired. They no longer looked nor felt like crack combat troops. Although they'd just had a relatively free day their rest had been marred by a chilling rain. They hardly yearned for the distinction of being the first Marines to tackle the volcano. But the colonel didn't bother to ask them how they felt about it.

By this time our unit had more than proved its combat capability. It almost seemed as though our high-spirited lieutenant had been granted the fifty men he'd wished for in training—the fifty who weren't afraid to die and could take any position.

About 8:00 o'clock on the morning of D-plus-4 Lieutenant Harold Schrier, our company executive officer, assembled the platoon. After its thin ranks had been bolstered by replacements from other Easy Company units, he led it back around the volcano to 2nd Battalion headquarters near the northeast base.

The men found our dynamic battalion commander standing outside an improvised pup tent sipping from a cup of steaming coffee. He was wearing his fatigue cap with its visor bent upward, and this gave him a jaunty appearance that belied his stern nature. He was smiling this morning, however, so he must have been pleased with the way things were going.

While Johnson and Harold Schrier consulted, the men were issued an abundant replenishment of cartridges, hand grenades, demolitions and flame thrower fuel. They were also provided large water cans from which they filled their canteens. During these preparations they were joined by a radioman, two teams of stretcher bearers and a photographer, Staff Sergeant Louis R. Lowery of *Leatherneck* magazine.

As the forty-man patrol loaded up to move out, the colonel handed Schrier a folded American flag that had been brought ashore by our battalion adjutant, 1st Lieutenant George G. Wells. He had been carrying it in his map case. The flag had been obtained from the *Missoula*, the transport that had borne our battalion to Saipan, our staging area.

Johnson's orders were simple. The patrol was to climb to the summit, secure the crater and raise the flag. Though our men hoped fervently that their mission would prove as uncomplicated as the colonel made it sound, most had serious misgivings.

Harold Keller said later: "When I looked at the two stretchers that were being sent along, I thought to myself, 'We'll probably need a hell of a lot more than that.'"

However, Johnson had earlier sent two small patrols up the dome on reconnoitering missions, and both had reached the rim of the crater and had then withdrawn without running into any trouble.

Falling into an irregular column, our men headed directly for the volcano's base. They moved briskly at first, soon passing a Marine howitzer that had taken a direct hit from an enemy gun in the north. There were two dead men lying by the weapon. A little farther on they passed several enemy corpses, one of which was wearing bright orange shoes.

When the route turned steep and going became difficult, the lieutenant sent out flankers to guard the vulnerable column against surprise attack. Heavily laden with weapons and ammunition, the men climbed slowly and were forced to stop from time to time to catch their breath. Some areas were so steep they had to be negotiated on hands and knees. Though several cave entrances were sighted, no resistance developed.

Far below, the Marines located about the northeast base watched the patrol's laborious ascent. Also observing, some through binoculars, were many men of the fleet.

Within a half hour after leaving battalion headquarters the patrol reached the crater's rim. Schrier called a halt here while he took stock of the situation. He could see two or three battered gun emplacements and some cave entrances, but there were no Japanese in evidence. So he gave the signal for the men to start filing over.

My bold friend Howard Snyder went over first. Had I remained unwounded I probably would have been second—whether I wanted to be or not. As it was, Harold Keller occupied this spot. Chick Robeson was third. Then came Harold Schrier, his radioman and Leo Rozek. Robert Leader was seventh, and, fully expecting to be fired at, he hoped that number seven was really the lucky number it was supposed to be.

As the men entered the crater they fanned out and took up positions just inside the rim. They were tensed for action, but the rim caves and the yawning reaches below them remained silent. Finally one of the men stood up and urinated down the crater's slope. But even this insulting gesture didn't bring the Japanese to life.

While half the patrol stayed at the rim, the other half now began to press into the crater to probe for resistance and to look for something that could be used as a flagpole.

Harold Keller, moving in the lead, made the first contact with the enemy. He says of this: "The Jap started to climb out of a deep hole, his back toward me. I fired three times from the hip, and he dropped out of sight."

Several caves now began to disgorge hand grenades. The Marines in the hot spots took cover and replied with grenades of their own. Some of these came flying back out of the dark entrances before exploding.

Even while this action waxed, Robert Leader and Leo Rozek discovered a long piece of pipe, seemingly a remnant of a raincatching system, and passed it to the summit. Waiting with the flag were Harold Schrier, Ernest Thomas, Hank Hansen and Chuck Lindberg. They promptly began fixing it to the pole.

It was about 10:30 A.M. when the pole was planted and the Stars and Stripes, seized by the wind, began to whip proudly over the volcano. The date February 23, 1945, had suddenly become historically significant. Mount Suribachi was the first piece of Japanese-owned territory—not counting mandates like Saipan—to be captured by American forces during World War II.

The Marines watching from below raised the cry. "There goes the flag!" And the electrifying word quickly spread to all the units about the volcano's base and to the regiments fighting the main battle to the north. Our combat-weary troops felt a great swell of pride and exultation. They felt a certain relief too. A part of the "impregnable" island had fallen. Victory seemed a little nearer now. Some men cheered, and some wiped at brimming eyes.

The cry was also taken up by the fleet. Ship whistles tooted a spirited salute. Aboard my hospital ship I thrilled to the news as it came over the public address system—though I wasn't aware at the time that it was my own platoon that had raised the flag.

38

The Firebombing of Tokyo
March 1945

Serving with the U.S. Eighth Air Force in England between 1942 and mid-1944, Maj. Gen. Curtis E. LeMay won recognition for his innovative flight tactics, especially his development of the "combat box" bomber formation. However, like British air marshal Arthur "Bomber" Harris, what LeMay most wanted to prove was that strategic air power could win a war. After a brief stint in the China-Burma-India

theater, LeMay finally got his chance in January 1945, when he was assigned to lead the new Twenty-first Bomber Command in the Northern Marianas.

Before LeMay's arrival, the damage done by the Twenty-first's 350 B-29s hardly merited notice. The command's daylight raids, begun in November 1944, were supposed to be "precision" runs, yet the bombers flew at such high altitudes (about thirty thousand feet) that cloud cover and bomb drift badly affected their accuracy. As a result, only 5 percent of the bombs they dropped landed within a thousand feet of their targets, mostly aircraft-engine plants. Such ineffectiveness came as no surprise to LeMay, who had already learned over Europe the weaknesses of precision bombing and come instead to favor terror attacks on the civilian population—a lesson he felt was underscored by the savage firebombing of Dresden in mid-February 1945. "I'll tell you what war is about," LeMay once declared. "You've got to kill people, and when you've killed enough, they stop fighting."

As commander of the Twenty-first, LeMay completely revamped its strategy. He shifted to nighttime missions to take advantage of Japanese deficiencies in antiaircraft defenses and night fighters. This, in turn, allowed his planes to fly at much lower altitudes, dramatically improving both their accuracy and their fuel efficiency. With more fuel, the planes could carry heavier bomb loads, and LeMay changed their munitions as well, switching from high explosives to incendiaries.

LeMay debuted this new configuration on the night of March 9–10, when 279 of his B-29s dropped 1,667 tons of incendiaries on Tokyo from altitudes ranging between five thousand and ten thousand feet. Within thirty minutes, the blazes were out of control. Some residents died from the heat, the hot gases burning their lungs; others were killed by suffocation, as the flames sucked all the oxygen from the atmosphere. Still others, who sought refuge in canals, died when the water in those canals boiled. In all, the raid killed eighty-three thousand people and injured another forty thousand, destroying 267,000 buildings and leaving a million people homeless.

A P-51 nicknamed My Girl *takes off from Iwo Jima in March 1945 to join a fighter escort for B-29s flying from the Northern Marianas on a bombing mission to Japan.*

CENTER OF TOKYO DEVASTATED BY FIRE BOMBS

City's Heart Gone; Not a Building Is Left Intact in 15 Square Miles, Photos Show

By WARREN MOSCOW

GUAM, Sunday, March 11—The heart of Tokyo is gone. Ashes and still flaming ruins cover the ground where large industry, small industry and homes stood only twenty-four hours ago in fifteen square miles of the center of Japan's capital.

Imagine Manhattan from Washington Square northward to Sixtieth Street plus the Borough Hall, Bay Ridge, Greenpoint, Williamsburg and Fulton Street sections of Brooklyn, add Long Island City and Astoria and Staten Island burned out so not a roof top is visible and the picture becomes clearer of the area laid waste by the American bombers yesterday morning.

Tokyo is a great sprawling city covering 365 square miles. The fleet of more than 300 B-29's that hit the target yesterday concentrated on an area of ten square miles. Their bombs and fires spread out over fifteen square miles, 9,700 acres. Eight identifiable industrial targets lie in ruins along with hundreds of other industrial plants.

The original target lay in equal parts on either side of the Sumida River but the additional area hit put the great bulk of the ravaged area east of the Sumida almost over the Naka River. The Emperor's palace, outside the target area, remained unhit.

[A fleet of India-based Superfortresses battered the Malayan railway center of Kuala Lumpur Saturday, soon after the Marianas B-29 attack on Tokyo.]

At B-29 headquarters here the commanders could not believe pilot reports in entirety till reconnaisance photos were available late last night. Then they were completely convinced that the job intended was done. The pictures brought to press headquarters were startling enough to convince sleepy correspondents routed out at 4 A.M.

They showed Toyko's vaunted fire-break system didn't work this time. The attack was too big, the incendiaries too effective. Fires just skipped the bare spots, spreading so rapidly that the entire area was aflame in the space of an hour and a half. Seven large fires on the border of the target area where something was still left to burn were burning at 3 o'clock in the afternoon, twelve hours after the match was set to Japan's tinderbox capital.

Setting the torch to an area of fifteen square miles in Tokyo makes homeless a population comparable to that of the Bronx or Queens, posing a refugee problem for the Japanese Government. How many perished in the holocaust cannot be estimated.

Maj. Gen. Curtis E. Lemay, commander of the B-29's of the entire Marianas area, declared that if the war is shortened by a single day the attack will have served its purpose.

General Lemay, speaking of his officers and men, said:

"They will pursue that purpose stubbornly. They are fighting for a quicker end to this war and will continue to fight for a quicker end to it with all the brains and strength they have."

General Lemay's statement was issued with a release of pictures. It summarized the B-29 damage and B-29 attitude, as follows:

The B-29's from bases on Saipan, Tinian and Guam attacked with incendiary bombs in

A Japanese man stoops to drink from a broken water pipe amid the rubble of Tokyo after its firebombing on the night of March 9–10.

the early hours of Saturday, March 10, an urban industrial area of Tokyo consisting of ten square miles, centered about 10,000 feet east northeast of the Emperor's Palace. The Palace itself was not a target.

The area attacked is now entirely burned out and an area of five square miles surrounding it is similarly gutted by fire. This fire left nothing but twisted, tumbled-down rubble in its path. These facts are incontrovertibly established by reconnaissance photographs taken on the afternoon of the strike.

The area totally destroyed by this incendiary strike, clearly identifiable in these photographs, covers a total of 422,500 square feet, which is approximately 9,700 acres, or fifteen square miles.

Other identifiable industrial and urban targets lie in ruins within the destroyed area, including the previously damaged Ueno rail-

road station, the Rising Sun Petroleum Terminal, the Ogura Oil Company, the Nisshin Spinning Mill, the Japan Machine Industry, the Marunouchi telephone exchange, Kanda Market and Hattori Company. Hundreds of small business establishments directly concerned with the war industry, many important administrative buildings and other thousands of home industries were also in the area wiped out.

So much for the facts of accomplishments, the statistics of devastation. As the commander of the air crew members who flew and fought this mission and as the commander of the other officers and men who by their work on the ground at our bases here in the Marianas made this mission possible, I have something else to say at this time. What I want to say is not easy to say. I shall try to say it as if I were saying it to the people at home who belong to my officers and men and to whom my officers and men belong.

I believe that all those under my command on these island bases have by their participation in this single operation shortened this war. To what extent they have shortened it no one can tell, but I believe that if there has been cut from its duration only one day or one hour my officers and men have served a high purpose. They will pursue that purpose stubbornly. They are fighting for a quicker end to this war, and all will continue to fight for a quicker end to it with all the brains and strength they have.

Yesterday morning's attack was the first one reported from the B-29 base in Guam though headquarters moved here from Saipain some months ago. Three main islands in the Marianas are now serving as bases from which the big planes will be taking off in increasing numbers and intensity.

Big bombers are coming in daily to join the family group headed by Tokyo Rose, which made the first Tokyo visit as photo ship last Thanksgiving Day. How much the Japanese war industry effort was impaired, how many millions of dollars in damage has been done by the B-29's cannot be figured now. How many American planes were lost on this trip is not certain but the losses apparently were small. One or two Superfortresses were regarded as probably lost but a number landed on the new hard-won stopping place, little Iwo Island, half way home from Tokyo. The exact number is not known, so the losses cannot be announced yet.

"They could not help as much as they wished to."

The Tokyo fire chief's assesssment of his department's response to the raid

The firebombing of Tokyo, described in this report by the city's chief firefighter, was the first of five raids in ten days targeting Japan's four largest cities. In all, LeMay's bombers flew 1,595 sorties, delivering 9,373 tons of incendiaries against Nagoya, Osaka, and Kobe, as well as Tokyo. Thirty-one square miles were destroyed at the cost of twenty-two airplanes. Although operations in Europe had already demonstrated the devastating possibilities of such incendiary raids, the results in Japan were far superior because, as LeMay correctly reasoned, the wood-and-paper construction of most Japanese dwellings proved much more vulnerable to fire than the primarily masonry construction of German buildings.

Chief N. Shinoda's Report on Damages Resulting from 10 March 1945 Air Raid

On March 10 air raid, 1 special fire-fighting unit, 41 fire stations (1 of them a marine fire-fighting station), were waiting and at 1:15 A.M. the air-raid warnings were sounded. Immediately after the alarms were sounded, B-29's came in singly, then in groups of 2 and 3; formations came in small groups, and 100-odd planes came to Tokyo's sky and dropped fire bombs at different places.

At this time a north wind was blowing, velocity of 20 to 30 meters per second (approximately 45 miles per hour), and the fire became very intense, especially in the region of Asakusa, flames came close to Sumida, and this fire, together with the fires that had been burning at Honjo Ku, Fukagawa Ku, Joto Ku, Edogawa Ku, was ravaging.

At different fire stations, fire engines were stationed at their designated and planned places and they fought and continued to fight losing battles. At this time, 200 fire engines came to the rescue from various fire stations, and on top of that fire engines totaling 100 in number came from Kanagawa Ken and Shiba Ken. The fire engines that came for assistance from Kanagawa Ken were stationed at Nihonbashi, Kyobashi, and Shiba. Fire engines that came from Shiba Ken were directed to Joto, Edogawa, and Honjo, and fire engines that came for assistance from Saitama Ken were directed to Shitaya, Aasakusa, and Kanda, and these units that were stationed there continued to fight very bravely, but, due to the strong wind plus insufficient water to cope with the situation, their actions were very much hindered and they could not help as much as they wished to. So, as a result, the damages amounted to as shown in the following table. The fire began to abate at around 5:15 A.M. next morning.

Total buildings burned in damaged area, 276,791.

Total area damaged, 4,237,342 tsubo (5.4 square miles).

VICTORY IN EUROPE

39.

The Crossing of the Rhine

March 1945

The Anglo-American goal for early 1945 was to reach and cross the wide, swift-flowing Rhine, the greatest natural barrier in western Germany. The push was originally scheduled for January, but Hitler's counterattack in the Ardennes forced a postponement until early February. Eisenhower's master plan called for simultaneous attacks along three fronts. In the north, Montgomery's Twenty-first Army Group

would make the primary thrust, aiming for a crossing point opposite the town of Wesel. Meanwhile, in the center, Bradley's Twelfth Army Group was assigned a stretch of river between Cologne and Koblenz. In the south, Ike ordered Lt. Gen. Jacob Devers's Sixth Army Group to clear the Saarland before reaching the Rhine at Mannheim.

Because the Battle of the Bulge had cost Hitler the last of his reserves, there was little the Führer could do to oppose the advance. The German general staff recommended that he withdraw what was left of the battered Wehrmacht to the east bank of the Rhine, but Hitler refused this strategy, insisting that every last inch of the Fatherland be defended. As a result, the Allies were able to capture nearly three hundred thousand Germans during their drive to the Rhine.

The first crossing came almost by accident at the small town of Remagen, south of Bonn. Hitler had ordered all of the bridges across the Rhine destroyed, but when troops of Hodges's First Army reached the bank opposite Remagen on March 7, they found the railroad bridge there still intact. Two explosions had caused some structural damage, but the German engineers hadn't yet been able to detonate the main charge. Immediately, a platoon of the Ninth Armored Division charged across the bridge and, despite heavy enemy machine-gun fire, secured a position on the other side. Within twenty-four hours, eight thousand more GIs were across.

At first, the capture of the bridge unsettled Allied planners. "Sure, you've got a bridge, Brad," one headquarters officer told the Twelfth Group commander, "but it's in the wrong place." The countryside around Remagen was particularly rugged, making expansion of the bridgehead difficult. But Eisenhower saw the same opportunity that Bradley did and sent reinforcements, if only to divert German strength from other sectors. Not wanting to be upstaged, Patton took advantage of this with a surprise crossing of his own at Oppenheim on the night of March 22–23. By the time that the methodical Montgomery took Wesel on the following night, Patton had already stolen the headlines.

American soldiers in an assault boat cross the Rhine under enemy fire near St. Goar.

PATTON CROSSES RHINE IN A DARING DRIVE WITHOUT BARRAGE, EXPANDS BRIDGEHEAD

3d Wins Firm Hold; Spans the River at Night Above Ludwigshafen, Catches Foe Asleep

By DREW MIDDLETON

PARIS, March 23—Troops of Lieut. Gen. George S. Patton's United States Third Army have established a bridgehead over the Rhine in a bold, skillful assault.

The river was crossed at 10:25 o'clock Thursday night. The bridgehead established at that time has been steadily expanded since. [Press services said the crossing was virtually unopposed for two hours.]

The Twelfth Army Group, whose announcement was released here tonight, did not locate the bridgehead, but the German radio said that it was east of Frankenthal, four and a half miles north of the northern outskirts of Ludwigshafen.

[Earlier German broadcasts said that Third Army troops had crossed the Rhine at Oppenheim, ten miles south of Mainz, and that other American troops had attempted crossings at Duesseldorf and six miles south of Cologne, The Associated Press reported. The Germans said the crossings at Duesseldorf and in the Cologne area had been repulsed.]

At his headquarters, Lieut. Gen. Omar N. Bradley, Twelfth Army Group Commander, said that the Allies were in a position to cross the Rhine virtually "anywhere at any time."

The Third Army's crossing of the Rhine was an operation as daring as the character of its commander. General Patton hurled his troops across the river without preparation by artillery or air force in a surprise move that evidently caught the enemy asleep.

Since that time his troops have been striking out from the bridgehead and expanding it.

A great east-west highway runs through Frankenthal. There was a bridge under construction there in May, 1944. No recent information concerning the bridge is available here.

Frankenthal, where the Germans said the crossing was made, is six miles northwest of Mannheim on the east bank of the Rhine opposite Ludwigshafen. If the crossing was made in this area, as the enemy claimed, then General Patton has placed his troops in a fine position to attack Mannheim from the north or east. Frankenthal also is twenty-five miles southwest of the industrial city of Darmstadt.

Meanwhile Gen. Dwight D. Eisenhower's order to destroy the German Armies west of the Rhine is almost fulfilled.

Tanks of General Patton's Third Army rumbled into Speyer, one of the last German strongholds west of the Rhine, today, while a series of savage blows by armored and infantry divisions of the Third Army and Lieut. Gen. Alexander M. Patch's Seventh Army hammered down the enemy bridgehead in the Palatinate to a rough triangle fifteen miles from east to west with a base of less than twenty miles along the west bank of the Rhine.

The tremendous aerial assault on the German Army's defense depots and communications in the area north of the Ruhr and west of the Rhine opposite the front of Field Marshal Sir Bernard L. Montgomery's Twenty-first Army Group was maintained from early morning today.

Nothing more than routine patrolling was reported by the Allies' ground forces in this sec-

U.S. soldiers employ mortars to establish a beachhead on the far bank of the Rhine.

tor today. [The United Press said Allied Head-quarters confirmed reports that some patrols were across the Rhine.]

The Third and Seventh Armies are squeezing the enemy pocket with concerted advances north and south in the Rhine valley between the river and the Pfalzerwald.

The unidentified armored division of the Third Army, which captured Speyer, immediately swung a column southward onto the plain, while another column, this one from the Tenth Armored Division, smashed southeastward six miles to reach Hochstadt, ten miles southwest of Speyer on the plain west of the river. A light counter-attack by German infantry was reported in this area.

Meanwhile, General Patch's troops hammered their way northward on the southern flank of the pocket. The 103d Infantry Division broke through Slitz into the outskirts of Klingenmuenster on the western end of the pocket five miles southwest of Landau, which was captured yesterday by the Third Army. This advance narrowed the front at the western end of the pocket to about five miles.

East of the 103d Division two American and two French divisions of the Seventh Army bit deep into the enemy's Siegfried Line positions.

Doughboys of the Thirty-sixth Infantry Division stormed Bergzabern on the edge of the plain six miles north of Wissembourg, after having taken the high ground that commands the town. Tanks and armored infantry of the Fourteenth Armored Division, fighting on the right of the Thirty-sixth, have cleared all of Steinfeld, four miles east of Wissembourg save for a few houses on the northern edge of the town.

The French Fifth Armored Division and the Algerian Third Infantry Division were making slow but steady progress in the Bienwald, where they have been reinforced by some

Goumiers, Moroccan native troops, who excel in forest fighting.

With the capture of Pirmasens yesterday, German resistance west of the Rhenish plain all but collapsed, and in the west pocket other troops of both armies were mopping up stray German units.

Northwest of the bridgehead armored and infantry columns are clearing up German positions. Tanks of the division that took Speyer smashed into the German positions at Iggelheim, five and a half miles northwest of Speyer, while the Tenth Armored Division, which took Landau, sent a column west of the town to clear the area south of the Pirmasens-Landau road. Another column established itself on a northern lateral road from Kaiserslautern to Ludwigshafen, clearing a seven-mile stretch of road west of Bad Durkheim.

The Ninety-fourth Infantry Division, plus some elements of the Fourth Armored Division, were mopping up the west bank of the Rhine and Ludwigshafen. Doughboys cleared Rheingonnheim, southern suburb of Ludwigshafen, and are fighting their way through the town, which should soon be cleared.

Farther north they cleared a pocket a mile and a half north of Worms, thus completing the clearing of the Rhine from Speyer north to Mains.

Small groups of bedraggled Germans were trying to cross the Rhine, but they were being rounded up. The Americans can see other German troops digging intrenchments and laying mines on the east bank of the river.

The Fourth Armored Division cleared a pocket on the Rhine eight miles north of Worms while the Ninetieth Infantry Division finished the clearing of Mainz, where 3,000 prisoners were taken. [The Associated Press said 10,000 Germans were surrounded in this area.]

Seventh Army divisions are clearing the area west of the pocket. Hundreds of Germans, most of them heartily sick of the war, have been rounded up by the Third Infantry Division, which captured Rodalben, north of Pirmasens.

Doughboys of the 100th Infantry Division continued the job of policing the area around Pirmasens. The Seventy-first Infantry Division captured Erlenbrunn, south of the city in the Pfalzerwald, while the Forty-second Infantry Division smashed a German concentration eight miles south of Pirmasens at Budenthal after a sharp fight. Earlier the Forty-second took Dahn and Busenberg, ten miles southeast of Pirmasens, while the 103d Infantry Division advanced through slackening resistance into Vord and Wiedenthal northwest of Wissembourg.

The Seventy-first Infantry Division continued to push northward through the Hardt Mountains, after having broken through the Siegfried Line, and reached Reipertsweiler, three miles east of Pirmasens.

Meanwhile the Sixth Armored Division reached the Rhine at points between Worms and Ludwigshafen, thus becoming the first Seventh Army armored division to reach the Rhine north of Karlsruhe.

This expansion of the Remagen bridgehead proceeded at a rapid pace today along the southern end of the front, which is now thirty-one miles long and ten miles in depth at the deepest point.

Lieut. Gen. Courtney H. Hodges' troops have passed over the Wied River to the southeast, meeting light resistance save for some artillery fire at Breitscheid, due north of Neuwied.

Troops of the Ninth Infantry Division are now up to the Autobahn just east of Rahms, ten miles east of the Rhine. Another advance of 500 yards took the troops to Niederbieber, just east of the Wied, two miles north of Neuwied on the Rhine.

During the advance across the Wied, the Ninety-ninth Infantry Division captured Rossbach, Hochscheid, Waldbreitbach, Wuescheid, Niederbreitbach and Datzeroth.

General Hodges' troops took 1,153 prisoners yesterday and since the bridgehead was established through March 22 counted 25,328 captives. A greater proportion of these were taken in the bridgehead, although some were captured in policing operations along the west bank of the Rhine.

"This place been looted yet?"

An excerpt from the memoirs of one of the first GIs across the Rhine

Drafted at age thirty-five, Lester Atwell served with Company G of the 345th Infantry Regiment in a front-line medical aid station. The 345th was part of the Eighty-seventh Infantry Division, which fought with Patton's Third Army. A contributor of short stories to the *Saturday Evening Post* before the war, Atwell took extensive notes on his experiences in Europe and used them later to create the 1957 "nonfiction novel" *Private*. The excerpt reprinted here describes events that took place shortly after his unit crossed the Rhine.

The Germans, letting go the Rhine, fell back in retreat, leaving road blocks and detachments of men to engage us in delaying actions. Sometimes during the following week, the enemy dug in to make a desperate stand only to have large numbers of its men throw down their arms and stream toward us in surrender. After a disorganized rout, collapse and retreat, more road blocks were thrown up and the wounded German Army fell back still farther.

One of the delaying actions made by the Germans, though of short duration and of obvious uselessness, stands out as one of the more ghastly episodes of the war. We were advancing down a road in convoy when a German tank drove out of a grove of trees, fired point-blank, killed two of our men, and then retreated from sight again. The convoy halted and two of our rifle companies went forward and surrounded the little grove that contained, they discovered, a platoon of German soldiers in deep foxholes. The German tank kept swiveling and firing, and after a while four of our own tanks came up. Each from a different direction sprayed the tiny stretch of woods with long streams of flaming gasoline. Within a few seconds the place became an inferno, and the shrieks and screams of the Germans could be heard through the high curtains of fire. A few, in flames, tried to crawl through, but they were mowed down by our machine guns. Within a half hour we went on, and all that was left of the little woods was a deep bed of glowing golden coals, hideous to see and to think about in the spring sunlight.

The countryside grew extremely hilly and wooded; small towns, flying surrender flags, lay hidden in hollows. In the swiftness of pursuit one company by mistake often seized another company's town and had to double back to take its own objective. The convoy of trucks rushed into the towns; the infantrymen hopped down, cleared out the snipers, rounded up the prisoners, jumped into the trucks again and set out for the next town. Some days, in this fashion, as many as thirty miles were covered.

We had been traveling since early morning in the ambulance, jouncing and rolling along in second gear on the heels of the last rifle company—Phil, Warren Troy, Preacher and I. All during the winter the captain had ridden everywhere in the heated ambulance, but now he had transferred to the jeep. The litter bearers were out riding with the companies and we did not see them until the entire convoy pulled up in a higgledy-piggledy village with small, low cottages and a few round, turreted medieval buildings that seemed to have no windows. The place looked like a page from a Mother Goose watercolor book. It was full noon; the dusty road and white cottages, the bed sheets and tablecloths gave back a white glare. When the trucks stopped, the men jumped down and then there were khaki uniforms swarming everywhere over the bleached whiteness of the little street, opening gates, going into back yards searching for eggs, forcing open front doors to loot and hunt for liquor.

Not knowing how long we were to stay, we sat in the kitchen of one of the little houses, having our lunch. The old woman who lived there had just been dispossessed. The litter bearers had come in and Jimmy McDonough gave me a tea bag from a package his wife had sent him. When the tea had drawn I poured a little lemon powder into it. A canteen cup made a good long drink of tea. With it I was eating a K ration of cheese and the oblong hard crackers. The kitchen was crowded with men walking about, eating and talking; Silly Willie was frying a can of C-ration hash and causing a stench. As I ate, I took out a few letters I had not had time to read. Friends at home were asking if I had stopped off at the Monopole-Metropole Hotel? Had I visited Cologne? Had I taken a launch down the Rhine? If I stopped at such and such a hotel I mustn't fail to try a whole peach in champagne; and the next time I was in Paris, would I please send some Chanel No. 5? I had no idea of the privations at home! The things one went through at the butcher shops! Even toilet paper was awfully hard to get.

At the moment, two line-company boys smashed down the flimsy back door of the house with their rifles and came in, asking, "This place been looted yet?" The old woman who lived in the house had returned and there was a commotion behind me in the room. Either someone had burned the bottom out of her only good pot or she had seen someone going out of the house with her only good pot. At any rate, she set up a loud keening about it and taxed Phil, who had promised her that nothing would be disturbed. "Hey, get her the hell outta here," someone was saying. "What's she bitchin' about anyway?

Infantrymen of the Third Army rest in a courtyard in Geinsheim, two miles east of the Rhine, on March 23 or 24.

Go on, ya old bastard, git out! Git outta here!" She took herself off on her sore feet, whimpering and crying, followed by a few oaths and careless laughter. Sipping my tea, looking out the window at the sunlit back yard, the thought suddenly came to me, "I'm tired of this, tired of war, of human beings, of everything." From the front door someone shouted in, "Snap s—— in there. We're moving!"

At night the rolling convoy stopped; we unloaded and carried our equipment into a large stone community farmhouse on a bare hill enclosed by a corral fence. The litter bearers joined us instead of sleeping in foxholes, and while the aid station occupied the ground floor with Battalion Headquarters, we were given two rooms upstairs. These we did not see thoroughly till morning when we awoke and found ourselves in a separate apartment: there was a stove and sink in a corner of the living room. It was a bright, cold spring day. Intermittent sunlight flashed and dimmed on a worn rug with reds and blues in it; the windows rattled with the wind; the fire was kept stoked up. Word drifted down that we were to remain here for a while. No one knew why, but it was a relief after entire days of jouncing along on the hard seat of the ambulance. We heated water after a K-ration breakfast, shaved, took sponge baths, and sat at the kitchen table writing letters. There was no sound but the bluster of wind pressing against the windowpanes, the scratch of pens, the crackle of the fire. We looked as though we were taking a final examination.

My usual desire to investigate the place we were in had vanished; I did not even look at the other rooms on our floor. Polish slave labor had been used on the farm and work had now come to a complete standstill. Many of the laborers had bolted for freedom the night before when we first arrived, but the eight or ten who hung on after their years of servitude did not seem especially jubilant. Rather they appeared mentally tired and without plans for the future. On the way to the latrine I saw three of them sitting in a little shed; they had a bottle of liquor, which they hid as I passed. On my way back, one was lying in the hay; the other two were smoking cigarettes, staring dully out at the hard dirt of the farm yard. Near the house other slave laborers were saying to some uninterested American troops, "Me Polski! Me Polski!" in the expectation of American cigarettes, but by now the men were accustomed to hearing "Me Polski," and everyone seemed played out. It was difficult to summon up any but the most distant feeling.

And yet, only a few days before, on Good Friday, during the attack a half mile ahead on the town of Eisenach, I had seen the high wire gates of a slave-labor camp being swung open by men of our battalion, and the inmates, with a rush and a tremendous roar, had come pouring out onto the street. For me, it was one of the most thrilling moments of the war. They surrounded the handful of us who were there—I had come down the street with Phil to watch—and they crowded about to shake our hands, to thank us individually, laughing and crying and in their jubilation addressing us in their native tongues. There were no interpreters; we could only smile and smile and continue shaking hands. I offered my cigarettes around until they were gone and kept asking, "Polski? Russki?" In time I could feel my smile growing stretched, but there was nothing to do but go on smiling and smiling and shaking hands. A few of the slave laborers, their meager possessions slung over their shoulder, giving us a wave and a cheer as they came out, pointed to a direction—to the east, probably—and struck off without a backward glance. Then two slave laborers ran up the street, each with a bottle of liquor, and at that they all scattered and began to burst into the nearby houses in search of liquor to celebrate their freedom. The American troops were a half step ahead of them in the search, and a fast-paced looting contest started up.

40.

The Liberation of Buchenwald

April 1945

On April 4, 1945, soldiers of the Fourth Armored Division attached to Patton's Third Army were searching south of the town of Gotha for a secret Nazi communications center when they found instead the Ohrdruf-Nord forced-labor camp, a subsidiary of the much larger Buchenwald concentration camp twenty-five miles away. Ohrdruf-Nord was the first "horror camp," to use Eisenhower's term, discovered

by the western Allies as they drove across Germany. Soviet forces had already overrun several Nazi death camps in Poland, but British and American troops hadn't really believed that the reports coming out of Majdanek (liberated in July 1944) and Auschwitz (January 1945) were true. Consequently, they were unprepared for what they found at Ohrdruf-Nord and, a week later, at Buchenwald itself.

A delegation of American generals led by Eisenhower, Bradley, and Patton visited Ohrdruf-Nord on April 12. Little had been done for the prisoners, and the stench of the rotting corpses had grown so foul that even "Old Blood and Guts" Patton vomited his lunch behind one of the barracks. In an April 15 letter to Chief of Staff Marshall, Eisenhower wrote, "I made the visit deliberately, in order to be in a position to give firsthand evidence of these things if ever, in the future, there develops a tendency to charge these allegations merely to 'propaganda.' "

It was, of course, too late by then to save the millions already slaughtered by the Nazis. During 1943 and 1944, as the prospects for a German victory decreased, the killings had accelerated so that at least the Final Solution might be achieved before the war ended. Meanwhile, the few opportunities that existed to save European Jews were mostly ignored because of British opposition to more Jews in Palestine, the likely destination for any rescued refugees. For example, in late 1943, Rumania, then a German satellite, floated a proposal for the ransoming of seventy thousand Rumanian Jews, which the State Department quietly buried for fear of disgruntling the British. When Treasury Department officials learned what had happened, they wrote a January 1944 report for Secretary Henry Morgenthau Jr., the only Jew in the cabinet, entitled "Report to the Secretary on the Acquiescence of the Government in the Murder of the Jews." Two weeks later, at Morgenthau's insistence, Roosevelt created the War Refugee Board, but, as journalist I. F. Stone described it, the president's gesture was "a kind of token payment to decency."

This photograph of inmates at Buchenwald was taken by a soldier of the Eightieth U.S. Army Division, which liberated the camp. Prisoners at Buchenwald were forced to sleep five to a bunk in a horse stable, which once held eighty horses but was converted to hold twelve hundred men.

NAZI DEATH FACTORY SHOCKS GERMANS ON A FORCED TOUR

By GENE CURRIVAN

BUCHENWALD, Germany, April 16 (Delayed)— German civilians—1,200 of them—were brought from the neighboring city of Weimar today to see for themselves the horror, brutality and human indecency perpetrated against their "neighbors" at the infamous Buchenwald concentration camp. They saw sights that brought tears to their eyes, and scores of them, including German nurses, just fainted away.

They saw more than 20,000 nondescript prisoners, many of them barely living, who were all that remained of the normal complement of 80,000. The Germans were able to evacuate the others before we overran the place on April 10.

There were 32,705 that the "visiting" Germans didn't see, although they saw some of their bodies. It was this number that had been murdered since the camp was established in July, 1937. There was a time when the population reached more than 110,000, but the average was always below that. It included doctors, professors, scientists, statesmen, army officers, diplomats and an assortment of peasants and merchants from all over Europe and Asia.

There was a group of British officers among those left behind and one of seven French generals, but this was obviously an oversight in the great confusion that followed the news of our approach.

Five generals died and one escaped. This Government-controlled camp was considered second only to that at Dachau, near Munich, as the world's worst atrocity center.

It had its gallows, torture rooms, dissection rooms, modern crematoria, laboratories where fiendish experiments were made on living human beings and its sections where people were systematically starved to death.

This correspondent made a tour of the camp today and saw everything herein described. The statistics and an account of the events that happened before our troops liberated the camp were obtained from a special committee of prisoners, some of whom had been in the camp since its inception and others who had been German prisoners for twelve years. Their information was documented and in most cases confirmed by the records.

This story has already been told in part, but not until today has the full import of the atrocities been completely felt.

One of the first things that the German civilian visitors saw as they passed through the gates and into the interior of the camp was a display of "parchment." This consisted of large pieces of human flesh on which were elaborate tattooed markings. These strips had been collected by a German doctor who was writing a treatise on tattooes, and also by the 28-year-old wife of the Standartenfuehrer or commanding officer. This woman, according to prisoners, was an energetic sportswoman who, back in Brandenburg, used to ride to hounds. She had a mania for unusual tattooes, and whenever a prisoner arrived who had a rare marking on his body, she would indicate that that trophy would make a valuable addition to her collection.

Third Army soldiers on April 25, 1945, force local German civilians to view a truckload of emaciated corpses at Buchenwald.

In addition to the "parchments" were two large table lamps, with parchment shades also made of human flesh.

The German people saw all this today, and they wept. Those who didn't weep were ashamed. They said they didn't know about it, and maybe they didn't, because the camp was restricted to Army personnel, but there it was right at their back doors for eight years.

The visitors stood in lines, one group at a time passing by the table on which the exhibits were displayed. A German-speaking American sergeant explained from an adjacent jeep what they were witnessing, while all around them were thousands of liberated "slaves" just looking on. Even the barracks roof was crowded with them. They watched silently. Some of them looked as if they were about to die, but this assemblage of "slaves" constituted the more healthy elements of the camp.

In barracks farther down the line were 3,000 sick who could not move and 4,800 aged who were unable to leave their squalid quarters. In addition, there were untold hundreds just roaming around, not knowing where they were or what was going on.

There were human skeletons who had lost all likeness to anything human. Most of them had become idiots, but they still had the power of locomotion. Those in the sick bay were beyond all help. They were packed into three-tier bunks, which ran to the roof of the barnlike barracks. They were dying there and no one could do anything about it.

The German visitors were to see them, too— and much more—but at the moment they were merely seeing "Exhibit A" and fainting.

Some Germans were skeptical at first as if this show had been staged for their benefit, but they were soon convinced. Even as they had milled along from one place to another, their own countrymen, who had been prisoners there, told them the story. Men went white and women turned away. It was too much for them.

These persons, who had been fed on Nazi propaganda since 1933, were beginning to see the light. They were seeing with their own eyes what no quantity of American propaganda could convince them of. Here was what their own Government had perpetrated.

But they hadn't seen anything yet. In a barracks building in front of them was a scientific laboratory where captured scientists worked with material supplied by their overlords. There were shelves of bottles filled with various organs of the human body. In one was half a human head. It had been cut longitudinally to show all its component parts. This head once belonged to a prisoner, as did all the other human parts so displayed. In another room were a dozen death masks, skulls and shrunken human heads. A Czechoslovak scientist and surgeon who worked in the laboratory told us the history of each part, each head, each mask—because he had known the human beings to which they belonged. Some had been his own countrymen.

The German visitors saw this, too.

And then they were taken to another laboratory, where victims had been injected with typhus so that Germany could have typhus serum. There were still a score of "patients" who were still alive although the Polish doctor left behind, who had been forced to give these injections even to his own people, said the death rate had been 98 per cent.

This sight was too much for many German housewives, especially a little farther on, where only the children were kept. One 9-year-old boy, who had had only the first few injections, seemed quite chipper. He was Andor Gutman, a Hungarian Jew of Budapest. He had been in the camp three years. When asked where his parents were, he replied, without any emotion: "My father was killed and my mother was burned to death."

As one watched the Germans filing out of this building there was hardly a dry eye, although some tried to maintain their composure. There was real horror ahead, but some of them just couldn't go on.

From there they were taken to the living quarters. The stench, filth and misery here defied description. Those human wrecks standing in the corridor were beyond the stage where any amount of hospitalization could restore them to normal, while others peering helplessly from their bunks would be fortunate when they died.

There was a still lower grade in another barracks, where the prisoners were alive but could not rouse themselves. They were living skeletons. This was Barracks 58, and it was from here that they were taken to the crematory. This was the end of the road, and for them it was probably a godsend. The Germans saw this, too—and there was more to come.

The next exhibit was the most ghastly of all, although it was merely the disposal of the dead.

In a little one-story red brick building, with a red tile roof, was a crematory with the most modern ovens that science can provide. But before you enter, you see a trailer stacked high with withered, starved, naked bodies. A few moments ago you saw the same thing, but those still had life in them. On top of the pile was a big robust body, fully clothed. This one had been murdered brutally.

Next to him was the body of an SS guard who had hanged himself on the day of our arrival. Former prisoners who had felt the lash of his whip cheerfully pointed out his body, and it was easy to identify because it had one stump leg.

In the crematory itself were two batteries of three ovens, each prominently marked with the makers' name—J. A. Topf & Sohne, Erfurt. This concern customarily manufactured baking ovens. These ovens were of extremely modern design and heated by coke. Narrow-gauge trucks were built into the concrete floor, and over these traveled steel contrivances resembling stretchers. Each oven had the remains of at least two bodies that had not yet been sifted into the chamber below. On a table near by were urns for the ashes. They looked like flower pots and were packed within metal containers, which, in turn, were packed in cardboard boxes for shipment to relatives. The names on the boxes, however, indicated that only Germans' remains were shipped.

Diminishing columns of German civilians also saw this. Then they were taken to the rear of the building where there was a gallows equipped for hanging five persons at a time. Just beyond was a pile of ashes from the furnaces.

The basement of the building was a torture chamber, where victims were forced to stand on low chairs, place a rope through a ring high on the wall and fasten the noose around their necks. The next victim got the job of kicking the chair from under them.

The next exhibit was the dissection room, adjacent to the crematory. This was a small, well-equipped cubicle with a white tile operating table and cabinets filled with surgical instruments. On hooks were several rubber aprons, and on the floor piles of prisoners' clothing. This was the room where the original owners of the "parchments" had been stripped of their skin.

The first prisoners to arrive at this camp were from Sachsenburg and Lichtenburg. In May and June of 1938, during the Gestapo wave of terror, the death rate was 10 per cent. After von Rath was shot in Paris, 12,500 Jews were transported to Buchenwald.

In September, 1939, arrivals at the camp included 2,500 Jews from old people's homes in Vienna. The following month 2,900 more arrived.

After the attempted assassination of Hitler twenty-one Jews were selected arbitrarily and shot to death. All other Jews were kept in darkness for three days without food, and several days later the entire camp was deprived of food for five days.

Before Buchenwald obtained its elaborate crematories prisoners who no longer could work were sent to Auschwitz to die or be killed in gas chambers. Auschwitz also had great furnaces. Reliable statements claim that 5,000 were disposed of there in three days. It was also at Auschwitz that Jewish women among the 30,000 once here at Buchenwald were sent to be exterminated after they had become pregnant. "Aryan" women in this group who were in similar physical condition were sent to Ravensbruck to have their children.

Buchenwald was bombed from the air on August 24 of last year because it was the site of a V-2 plant, which was just outside the main gates of the camp. It was here that many prisoners worked. The Nazis claimed that this bombing was the excuse for the murder of the German Communist party leader Ernst Thaelmann, but records show that Thaelmann was never in the camp.

The camp was liberated April 10 by the Eightieth Division. Two days later President Roosevelt died, and the liberated prisoners unfurled a large black flag over the building at the entrance way. It still flies as a memorial to his death and to the dead within the camp. Those still living realize what he tried to do, and they doff their caps every time they see an American uniform.

As the sun went down tonight, and its last glow gave a softer touch to this distorted scene, which, paradoxically, is in a magnificent setting on a hilltop overlooking a valley, the German visitors were taken back to their homes. If they still think that Hitler and what he stands for is supreme, then we have lost the war. But observations made by this correspondent indicate that they are chastened people who have suffered today, but who will benefit by reflection in the long run.

"What seems so pointless is the elaboration of horror."

A Patton aide recalls Buchenwald as he found it

"Ohrdruf was the first, and all of us prayed the last, concentration camp any of us would ever see," Col. Charles R. Codman, Patton's aide-de-camp, wrote in his 1957 memoir *Drive*. Three days later, however, Patton ordered Codman to visit Buchenwald and bring back a full report. Codman's account of the visit is excerpted here.

While not large, the crematory is, as I remember it, the only solidly constructed building in the camp. In a smaller yard, enclosed by a wooden fence, a large wagon like a farmer's cart had just been brought in. Over it the flies buzzed lazily. Its contents, the Military Government officer explained, were part of the day's toll—thirty or forty bodies, naked, crisscrossed like matches, and about as substantial. The crematory itself is not unlike the standard variety, with certain additional features. It seems that the routine was as follows: Prisoners who died from "natural causes" were simply carted into the ground floor of the crematory proper and tossed into six coke ovens, in which are still to be seen the charred remains of the last overhasty and incomplete job that the arrival of our troops interrupted.

The unusual feature is the basement. Here, according to eye witnesses whom I have no reason to disbelieve, were brought prisoners condemned of capital crimes—for example, attempting to escape, insubordination, stealing a potato, smiling in ranks—usually in groups of twenty or so at a time. They were lined up against the walls, each one under a hook fixed at a height of about eight feet from the floor. (The hooks are no longer there. They were hastily removed the day we came in, but the emplacements are clearly visible.) A short slip-noose was placed about the neck of the condemned, who was then raised by the guards the distance necessary to affix the end of the noose to the hook.

If the ensuing strangulation took too long a time to suit the mood of the guards, they beat out the brains of the condemned with a long-handled club resembling a potato masher. (Specimens of the nooses and "potato mashers" are on view in the basement.) The remains were then placed on an elevator which lifted them directly to the crematory proper, the final run being made on a miniature railway of metal litters leading from the elevator platform to the furnace doors. Efficient.

Having seen and photographed the end products, we proceeded to the place whence they came—the infamous Barrack 61. Exteriorly, Barrack 61 is like the other barracks, roughly 150 feet long by 30 feet wide. Inside, four tiers of wooden shelves incline slightly towards the central corridor. In the rush season this single barrack housed twenty-three hundred prisoners jammed together on those shelves, twenty-three hundred "nonworkers" that tuberculosis, dysentery, pneumonia, and plain starvation had rendered incapable of the daily twelve-hour stretch at the armament factory or nearby quarries. There were fewer when I was there. I did not count them, but the shelves were still well filled. Some of them were living human beings, but the majority were almost indistinguishable from the corpses we saw in the death cart.

On one shelf barer than the rest, three shadowy figures huddled together for warmth. Cold comfort for the outside two, since the middle one had been dead for several hours. Under the old regime he would eventually have been stripped and thrown out onto the flagstones to await the next tour of the wagon. Farther on, an emaciated specter of a man who had managed to get to the latrine and back was attempting to crawl up onto the first shelf. It was only three feet from the floor, but he could not make it. As he collapsed, his shirt—he had no other clothing on—fell open. A living—barely living—skeleton, with a long prison serial number tattooed on the inside of the thigh. Two of the inmates who accompanied us picked him up by the shoulders and ankles and placed him on the shelf.

So much for Barrack 61. Barrack 47 was like it, but frankly, I hadn't the stomach.

Any redeeming features? Yes. A number of individuals who through sheer will power and incredible fortitude managed to preserve their sanity and their self-respect, such as Professor Richet of the Académie de Médecine. An inmate of the camp for over a year, he had been allowed to organize his own clinic within the prison. With means so slender as to be negligible from the German point of view, he nevertheless brought some relief to those who could find room in the meager space allotted him—meantime amassing a wealth of informative data. From Barrack 61 we went there.

"What seems so pointless," I said, "is the elaboration of horror. If extermination is the object, why haven't they just wiped you all out once and for all?"

"Ah, my friend, there are certain considerations to be taken into account," he said.

"Such as?"

"Applied slave labor, turnover, example, and even public opinion."

"What public opinion?"

"German public opinion."

"The system is not pointless," he continued. "It is carefully thought out. In this camp are twenty-five thousand Russians, Poles, Czechs, French, Belgians, and others who are in disagreement with the tenets of the Reich. True, they must disappear, but before they go they must contribute their bit. On arriving here they are put to work, twelve hours a day at the factory or in the quarries or elsewhere. A workingman requires a diet of two thousand or twenty-five hundred calories per day. Here he is put on a diet of eight hundred calories per day—a diet calculated to produce death by starvation in a certain period of time. That period may be lengthened or shortened in accordance with available replacements. If the replacements are ample, the quotas of nonworkers sent to what are frankly known as extermination camps, such as Ohrdruf, are increased. There the principle is the same, but the tempo is accelerated."

"Why not exterminate them here?"

"They do. During the months of January, February, and March of this year there were fourteen thousand deaths. With the milder weather the rate has dropped slightly. Around three thousand a month."

"From what cause?"

"Overcrowding, disease, beating, hanging, starvation—chiefly starvation."

"Then why bother with extermination camps?"

"A certain amount of distribution spreads the number of 'deaths from natural causes' over a wider area. Public opinion, you see. Also, among the workers the threat of being sent to an extermination camp has its uses."

41.

The Death of Roosevelt

April 1945

Although President Roosevelt's health had little effect on the outcome of the Crimea Conference, there was no question at Yalta that he was already quite ill. British foreign minister Anthony Eden found him "vague and loose and ineffective," and Churchill's personal physician, Lord Moran, wrote in his diary that he thought the president had only a few months to live.

At his last White House press conference on March 20, Roosevelt appeared mentally alert; but during the following week, he more than once repeated lengthy anecdotes to guests who had already heard the same story from Roosevelt earlier in their visit. His cardiologist, Dr. Bruenn, prescribed total rest, and on March 29, the president boarded the *Ferdinand Magellan*, his specially equipped armor-plated Pullman car, for a trip to his Warm Springs, Georgia, retreat.

On April 12, the president awoke with a headache but went to work regardless. Shortly after one o'clock, he reached his hand to his forehead and then slumped forward, never regaining consciousness. At 3:35 P.M., Bruenn pronounced him dead of a cerebral hemorrhage. With the president at his death—newspaper reports to the contrary—was Lucy Mercer, who had worked as Eleanor Roosevelt's private secretary from 1913 until 1918, when Eleanor discovered that Franklin and Lucy had been having an affair. At Eleanor's insistence, Franklin ended the relationship; nevertheless, some years later—

with the complicity of Franklin and Eleanor's daughter, Anna—contact between the two was secretly reestablished.

Although Roosevelt's death had little discernible effect on the nation's prosecution of the war, the passing of the man who had so dominated national events for more than a decade had an acute psychological impact on the country. So many years had passed since another man had occupied the White House that few Americans could imagine someone else in Roosevelt's place—and certainly not the little-known former senator from Missouri who had only recently been elected vice president. It was a problem to which Roosevelt himself greatly contributed by failing to make any preparations for Harry Truman's succession. Unwilling to contemplate his own mortality, Roosevelt had kept Truman out of the loop, rarely inviting him to the White House and never briefing him on the most important military, diplomatic, and administrative matters. He never told Truman, for instance, of the existence of the atomic bomb.

These men were but two of the thousands of mourners who lined the streets of Washington to view the funeral cortege of Franklin Roosevelt as it passed on April 14, 1945.

PRESIDENT ROOSEVELT IS DEAD; TRUMAN TO CONTINUE POLICIES

End Comes Suddenly at Warm Springs

By ARTHUR KROCK

WASHINGTON, April 12—Franklin Delano Roosevelt, War President of the United States and the only Chief Executive in history who was chosen for more than two terms, died suddenly and unexpectedly at 4:35 P.M. today at Warm Springs, Ga., and the White House announced his death at 5:48 o'clock. He was 63.

The President, stricken by a cerebral hemorrhage, passed from unconsciousness to death on the eighty-third day of his fourth term and in an hour of high triumph. The armies and fleets under his direction as Commander in Chief were at the gates of Berlin and the shores of Japan's home islands as Mr. Roosevelt died, and the cause he represented and led was nearing the conclusive phase of success.

Less than two hours after the official announcement, Harry S. Truman of Missouri, the Vice President, took the oath as the thirty-second President. The oath was administered by the Chief Justice of the United States, Harlan F. Stone, in a one-minute ceremony at the White House. Mr. Truman immediately let it be known that Mr. Roosevelt's Cabinet is remaining in office at his request, and that he had authorized Secretary of State Edward R. Stettinius Jr. to proceed with plans for the United Nations Conference on international organization at San Francisco, scheduled to begin April 25. A report was circulated that he leans somewhat to the idea of a coalition Cabinet, but this is unsubstantiated.

It was disclosed by the White House that funeral services for Mr. Roosevelt would take place at 4 P.M. (E.W.T.) Saturday in the East Room of the Executive Mansion. The Rev. Angus Dun, Episcopal Bishop of Washington; the Rev. Howard S. Wilkinson of St. Thomas's Church in Washington and the Rev. John G. McGee of St. John's in Washington will conduct the services.

The body will be interred at Hyde Park, N. Y., Sunday, with the Rev. George W. Anthony of St. James Church officiating. The time has not yet been fixed.

Jonathan Daniels, White House secretary, said Mr. Roosevelt's body would not lie in state. He added that, in view of the limited size of the East Room, which holds only about 200 persons, the list of those attending the funeral services would be limited to high Government officials, representatives of the membership of both houses of Congress, heads of foreign missions, and friends of the family.

President Truman, in his first official pronouncement, pledged prosecution of the war to a successful conclusion. His statement, issued for him at the White House by press secretary Jonathan Daniels, said:

"The world may be sure that we will prosecute the war on both fronts, East and West, with all the vigor we possess to a successful conclusion."

The impact of the news of the of the President's death on the capital was tremendous. Although rumor and a marked change in Mr. Roosevelt's appearance and manner had brought anxiety to many regarding his health, and there had been increasing speculation as to the effects his death would have on the national and world

A crowd gathers in front of the White House on April 12, waiting for further news after the announcement of the president's death.

situation, the fact stunned the Government and the citizens of the capital.

It was not long, however, before the wheels of Government began once more to turn. Mr. Stettinius, the first of the late President's Ministers to arrive at the White House, summoned the Cabinet to meet at once. Mr. Truman, his face gray and drawn, responded to the first summons given to any outside Mr. Roosevelt's family and official intimates by rushing from the Capitol.

Mrs. Roosevelt had immediately given voice to the spirit that animated the entire Government, once the first shock of the news had passed. She cabled to her four sons, all on active service:

"He did his job to the end as he would want you to do. Bless you all and all our love. Mother."

Those who have served with the late President in peace and in war accepted that as their obligation. The comment of members of Congress unanimously reflected this spirit. Those who supported or opposed Mr. Roosevelt during his long and controversial years as President did not deviate in this. And all hailed him as the greatest leader of his time.

No President of the United States has died in circumstances so triumphant and yet so grave. The War of the States had been won by the Union when Abraham Lincoln was assassinated, and though the shadow of post-war problems hung heavy and dark, the nation's troubles were internal. World War II, which the United States entered in Mr. Roosevelt's third term, still was being waged at the time of his death, and in the Far East the enemy's resistance was still formidable. The United States and its chief allies, as victory nears, were struggling to resolve differences of international policy on political and economic issues that have arisen and will arise. And the late President's great objective—a league of nations that will be formed and be able to keep the peace—was meeting obstacles on its way to attainment.

Mr. Roosevelt died also in a position unique insofar as the history of American statesmen reveals. He was regarded by millions as indispensable to winning the war and making a just and lasting peace. On the basis of this opinion, they elected him to a fourth term in 1944. He was regarded by those same millions as the one American qualified to deal successfully and effectively with the leaders of other nations—particularly Prime Minister Winston Churchill and Marshal Joseph Stalin—and this was another reason for his re-election.

Yet the constitutional transition to the Presidency of Mr. Truman was accomplished without a visible sign of anxiety or fear on the part of any of those responsible for waging war and negotiating peace under the Chief Executive. Though the democratic process has never had a greater shock, the human and official machines withstood it, once the first wave of grief had passed for a leader who was crushed by the burdens of war.

President Truman entered upon the duties imposed by destiny with a modest and calm, and yet a resolute, manner. Those who were with him through the late afternoon and evening were deeply impressed with his approach to the task.

"He is conscious of limitations greater than he has," said one. "But for the time being that is not a bad thing for the country."

How unexpected was President Roosevelt's death despite the obvious physical decline of the last few months is attested by the circumstance that no member of his family was with him at Warm Springs, no high-ranking associate or long-time intimate, and that his personal physician, Rear Admiral Ross McIntyre, was in Washington, totally unprepared for the news.

The Admiral, in answer to questions from the press today, said "this came out of a clear sky," that no operations had been performed recently on Mr. Roosevelt and that there had never been the slightest indication of cerebral hemorrhage. His optimistic reports of the late President's health, he declared, had been completely justified by the known tests.

This ease of mind is borne out by the fact that Mrs. Roosevelt was attending a meeting of the Thrift Club near Dupont Circle when Stephen Early, the President's secretary, telephoned her to come to the White House as soon as possible. Mrs. John Boettiger, the only daughter of the family, was visiting her slightly ailing son at the Naval Hospital at Bethesda, Md., some miles away.

While these simple offices were being performed by those nearest and dearest, the President lay in the faint from which he never roused. A lesser human being would have been prostrated by the sudden and calamitous tidings, but Mrs. Roosevelt entered at once upon her responsibilities, sent off her message to her sons and told Mr. Early and Admiral McIntire, "I am more sorry for the people of the country and the world than I am for us." When Mr. Truman arrived and asked what he could do for her, Mrs. Roosevelt rejoined calmly, "Tell us what we can do. Is there any way we can help you?"

As soon as the news became a certainty the White House flag was lowered to half-staff—the first time marking the death of an occupant since Warren G. Harding died at the Palace Hotel in San Francisco, Aug. 2, 1923, following a heart attack that succeeded pneumonia. The flag over the Capitol was lowered at 6:30 P.M. Between these two manifestations of the blow that had befallen the nation and the world, the news had spread throughout the city and respectful crowds gathered on the Lafayette Square pavement across from the executive mansion. They made no demonstration. But the men's hats were off, and the tears that were shed were not to be seen only on the cheeks of women. Some Presidents have been held in lukewarm esteem here, and some have been disliked by the local population, but Mr. Roosevelt held a high place in the rare affections of the capital.

The spoken tributes paid by members of Congress, a body with which the late President had many encounters, also testified to the extraordinary impression Mr. Roosevelt made on his times and the unparalleled position in the world he had attained. The comment of Senator Robert A. Taft of Ohio, a constant adversary on policy, was typical. "The greatest figure of our time," he called him, who had been removed "at the very climax of his career," who died "a hero of the war, for he literally worked himself to death in the service of the American people." And Senator Arthur H. Vandenberg of Michigan, another Republican and frequent critic, said that the late President has "left an imperishable imprint on the history of America and of the world."

These were not mere words, uttered in conformity to the rule of "nil nisi bonum." Mr. Roosevelt's political opponents did what they could to retire him to private life, and their concern over his long tenure was real and grew as the tenure increased. But ever since his fourth-term victory in 1944 they have felt sincerely that it would be best for the country if he were spared to finish the great enterprises of war and peace which the country had commissioned him to carry through. And when they called his death a national and international tragedy they meant it.

But this tribute paid, this anxiety expressed, they and the late President's political supporters and official aides turned their hearts and minds again to the tasks before the nation. No one said "On to Berlin and Tokyo!" For Americans do not speak dramatically. But that is what every one meant, and it was the gist of what President Truman said and did after the homely ceremony that made him the head of the State.

When the dignitaries were assembled with Mr. Truman for this solemn purpose, there was a slight delay until his wife and daughter should arrive. Then the Chief Justice, using a Bible borrowed from Mr. Roosevelt's office and speaking from memory, read the oath and the new President repeated it after him. Then he and Mrs. Truman called on Mrs. Roosevelt and, as the President said, went "home to bed."

He wore a gray suit, a white shirt and a polka-dot tie. His face was grave but his lips were firm and his voice was strong. He said through Mr. Early that his effort will be "to carry on as he believed the President would have done." And he arranged to meet with the Army and Navy chiefs tomorrow, to assure them as tonight he did the people that his purpose is to continue the conduct of the war with the utmost vigor and to the earliest possible and successful conclusion.

While these simple but dignified processes of democracy were in motion, preparations were being made to render fit respect to the memory of the dead President. It was decided that Mrs. Roosevelt, their daughter and other members of the family should fly to Warm Springs to accompany the remains to Washington, arriving Saturday.

Meanwhile, it was announced that the nation-wide series of Jefferson Day dinners have been canceled, and similar honors of observance will be paid at the Capitol, throughout the United States and at many places in the world that looked to Mr. Roosevelt as its leader from darkness to the light.

"Modern civilization might be completely destroyed."

The new president learns about the atomic bomb

The first of these documents is a transcript of a telephone conversation between then-Senator Truman and Secretary of War Henry L. Stimson—recorded on June 17, 1943—in which Truman nearly stumbled on the secret of the atomic bomb. Two years later, at the first cabinet meeting following Roosevelt's death, Stimson took the new president aside and told him vaguely of "an immense project that was under way—a project looking to the development of a new explosive of almost unbelievable destructive power," according to Truman's memoirs. A week later, Stimson requested a formal meeting with the president to discuss "a highly secret matter." The second document reprinted here memorializes the briefing that Stimson (along with Maj. Gen. Leslie R. Groves, military commander of the atom-bomb project) finally gave Truman on April 25.

STIMSON: The other matter is a very different matter. It's connected with—I think I've had a letter from Mr. Hally, I think, who is an assistant of Mr. Fulton of your office.

TRUMAN: That's right.

STIMSON: In connection with the plant at Pasco, Washington.

TRUMAN: That's right.

STIMSON: Now that's a matter which I know all about personally, and I am one of the group of two or three men in the whole world who know about it.

TRUMAN: I see.

STIMSON: It's part of a very important secret development.

TRUMAN: Well, all right then—

STIMSON: And I—

TRUMAN: I herewith see the situation, Mr. Secretary, and you won't have to say another word to me. Whenever you say that to me, that's all I want to hear.

STIMSON: All right.

Secretary of War Henry L. Stimson arriving at the White House for a cabinet meeting on August 10, 1945.

TRUMAN: Here is what caused that letter. There is a plant in Minneapolis that was constructed for a similar purpose and it had not been used, and we had been informed that they were taking the machinery out of that plant and using it at this other one for the same purpose, and we just couldn't understand that and that's the reason for the letter.

STIMSON: No, no, something—

TRUMAN: You assure that this is for a specific purpose and you think it's all right; that's all I need to know.

STIMSON: Not only for a specific purpose, but a unique purpose.

TRUMAN: All right, then.

STIMSON: Thank you very much.

TRUMAN: You don't need to tell me anything else.

STIMSON: Well, I'm very much obliged.

TRUMAN: Thank you very much.

STIMSON: Goodby.

TRUMAN: Goodby.

◆ ◆ ◆

Memorandum discussed with the President
April 25, 1945

1. Within four months we shall in all probability have completed the most terrible weapon ever known in human history, one bomb of which could destroy a whole city.

2. Although we have shared its development with the UK, physically the US is at present in the position of controlling the resources with which to construct and use it and no other nation could reach this position for some years.

3. Nevertheless it is practically certain that we could not remain in this position indefinitely.

   a. Various segments of its discovery and production are widely known among many scientists in many countries, although few scientists are now acquainted with the whole process which we have developed.

b. Although its construction under present methods requires great scientific and industrial effort and raw materials, which are temporarily mainly within the possession and knowledge of US and UK, it is extremely probable that much easier and cheaper methods of production will be discovered by scientists in the future, together with the use of materials of much wider distribution. As a result, it is extremely probable that the future will make it possible to be constructed by smaller nations or even groups, or at least by a large nation in a much shorter time.

4. As a result, it is indicated that the future may see a time when such a weapon may be constructed in secret and used suddenly and effectively with devastating power by a willful nation or group against an unsuspecting nation or group of much greater size and material power. With its aid even a very powerful unsuspecting nation might be conquered within a very few days by a very much smaller one, although probably the only nation which could enter into production within the next few years is Russia.

5. The world in its present state of moral advancement compared with its technical development would be eventually at the mercy of such a weapon. In other words, modern civilization might be completely destroyed.

6. To approach any world peace organization [the United Nations] of any pattern now likely to be considered, without an appreciation by the leaders of our country of the power of this new weapon, would seem to be unrealistic. No system of control heretofore considered would be adequate to control this menace. Both inside any particular country and between the nations of the world, the control of this weapon will undoubtedly be a matter of the greatest difficulty and would involve such thorough-going rights of inspection and internal controls as we have never heretofore contemplated.

7. Furthermore, in the light of our present position with reference to this weapon, the question of sharing it with other nations and, if so shared, upon what terms, becomes a primary question of our foreign relations. Also our leadership in the war and in the development of this weapon has placed a certain moral responsibility upon us which we cannot shirk without very serious responsibility for any disaster to civilization which it would further.

8. On the other hand, if the problem of the proper use of this weapon can be solved, we would have the opportunity to bring the world into a pattern in which the peace of the world and our civilization can be saved.

9. As stated in General Groves' report, steps are under way looking towards the establishment of a select committee of particular qualifications for recommending action to the Executive and legislative branches of our government when secrecy is no longer in full effect. The committee would also recommend the actions to be taken by the War Department prior to that time in anticipation of the postwar problems. All recommendations would of course be first submitted to the President. [Truman agreed to the formation of this committee, which would be called the Interim Committee.]

42.

The San Francisco Conference

April–June 1945

Even after the Big Three worked out the Security Council voting procedures at Yalta, there was still a great deal to be decided at the United Nations Conference on International Organization, scheduled to begin in San Francisco on April 25, 1945. The UN's basic framework had been established seven months earlier at Dumbarton Oaks, but a certain amount of mistrust had developed among the various

delegations, particularly among those of the United States and Great Britain on one side and the Soviet Union on the other. These would have to be overcome before any final settlements could be reached, and at first prospects for cooperation seemed doubtful.

The attendees at the San Francisco Conference included delegations from the twenty-six countries that had signed the 1942 Declaration of the United Nations, plus twenty other nations that had declared war on the Axis between January 1942 and March 1945. Controversy arose, however, when five additional "nations" were proposed for membership: Ukraine, Belorussia, Argentina, Denmark, and the Lublin government of Poland. Although the first four of these states were admitted promptly, membership for the Lublin government (which none of the western Allies recognized) was withheld until after the San Francisco Conference had adjourned.

The other notable source of controversy was Soviet foreign minister Molotov's insistence that the veto power already granted to the five permanent members of the Security Council (the Big Four plus France) be extended beyond the actions of the council to include its agenda as well. (In other words, the Soviets wanted to be able to prevent public discussions of issues that they deemed unsuitable.) This impasse was resolved only after President Truman sent Harry Hopkins to Moscow, where Hopkins managed to persuade Stalin to drop the demand.

Meanwhile, the conference's secretariat provided the delegates with interpreters and translators, who made possible the daily distribution of documents and speeches in each of the conference's five official languages: English, French, Spanish, Russian, and Chinese. Two months later, the conferees concluded their work with the formal signing of the United Nations Charter on June 26.

President Truman addresses the closing session of the United Nations Conference on International Organization in San Francisco on June 26, 1945.

TRUMAN OPENS WORLD SECURITY PARLEY

Justice Put First; We Will Bow Only to That 'Power,' the President Tells Delegates

By JAMES B. RESTON

SAN FRANCISCO, April 25—The United Nations Conference on International Organization opened here today in a mood of solemn deliberation. There was no great excitement, no ritual, and very little celebration.

The alliance started making peace as it has made war, with efficient determination but with full admission that difficulties lie ahead.

President Harry S. Truman set the tone of the meeting. In a short address by telephone from the White House to the delegates in the Opera House here, which was rebroadcast to the world, he appealed to the world representatives to "rise above personal interests" and create a world security organization which would enforce justice and redeem the terrible sacrifices of the war.

The President charged the diplomats from forty-six United Nations with the task of creating an international organization that would make another world war impossible.

Emphasizing repeatedly that justice must be the criterion of the new organization the delegates had gathered here to establish, President Truman said that all states, large and small, must obligate themselves to use force only in defense of the law.

"Justice remains the greatest power on earth," he said. "To that tremendous power alone will we submit."

The President's remarks to the delegates were followed by speeches of welcome by Edward R. Stettinius Jr., Secretary of State and president of the conference; Gov. Earl Warren of California and Mayor Roger D. Lapham of San Francisco.

These formal addresses were the only official business of the day, but the Foreign Secretaries of the United States, Russia, Britain and China met for more than an hour this morning in order to discuss some of the problems facing the conference.

First among these problems were the questions of seating the representatives of Poland and Argentina, but although these questions were understood to have been discussed privately among the Foreign Ministers of the four countries sponsoring the conference, no announcement was made about them and officials said privately that no formula had been found for solving either question.

So far, the conference preliminaries have been conducted behind the scenes by the Foreign Secretaries of the sponsor powers, the United States, Britain, Russia and China. Tomorrow morning, for the first time, the other countries will have an opportunity to speak when the heads of delegations meet in executive session.

At that time it is expected that each delegation will be permitted to raise any question of procedure, and there were indications tonight that several delegations would raise the question of permitting Poland, Argentina, White Russia and the Ukraine to be represented at the conference.

The Russians have already raised the question of giving White Russia and the Ukraine original voting membership in the organization, and this question, about which there is considerable controversy, may come up sooner than is expected.

The Latin-American countries are taking the line that Argentina has now qualified for

Delegates newly arrived at the San Francisco Conference queue to pick up their credentials on the day before the opening session.

membership in the United Nations and should be represented here, and this proposal has the backing of the United States. The first plenary session of the conference will be held tomorrow afternoon.

President Truman made it clear in his speech to the delegates that he had every confidence in the American delegation, which was appointed by the late President Roosevelt, and that he would back the delegates in their work here. He also took occasion on this opening meeting to say that he had confidence in Secretary Stettinius—a remark which was interpreted as an effort to temper published reports that Mr. Stettinius would be displaced as Secretary of State.

Many millions of men had died to achieve the ideals which this conference was called upon to perpetuate, President Truman said. Among these, he added, was the late President Roo-

sevelt, whose hopes and labors had done much to bring about the United Nations Conference at this time and place.

"In the name of a great humanitarian," he said, "one who is surely with us today in spirit, I earnestly appeal to each and every one of you to rise above personal interests and adhere to those lofty principles which benefit all mankind."

The magnitude of the problem of outlawing war was great, but the penalties of failing to outlaw it with justice and to reverse the ancient doctrine that might made right were equally as great, the President said. With ever-increasing brutality and destruction, he emphasized, modern warfare, if unchecked, would ultimately crush all civilization.

This conference, he said, was, of course, called to concentrate on the specific problem of creating an international security organization based on justice to keep the peace. And that, he added, was in some ways even more difficult than redrawing boundary lines on a map.

Following the President's address, Mr. Stettinius told the delegates that the United States was united with both the large countries and the small countries in the attempt to create an effective organization, and he added that, in his judgment, "no one of the large nations, no one of the small nations, can afford anything less than the success of this endeavor."

Mr. Stettinius compared the job ahead of the delegates here to the job of the American pioneers who had conquered the West. Both faced great difficulties, but the American pioneers who reached the great Western ocean had believed all things were possible, and the task of creating an effective peace organization must be met in the same spirit, he declared.

"The deepest hope and highest purpose of all mankind, enduring peace," he said, "is here committed to our hands. We, too, are pioneers on a new road."

Governor Warren, in welcoming the delegates, noted that the conference had been held on time despite the fact that it had been called only recently and had had to overcome many difficulties, including the death of Franklin D. Roosevelt.

"Unity," he said, "has created the strength to win the war. It is bringing us ever closer to the end of the world conflict. This same strength of unity, continued and cultivated here, can be made to develop a sound pattern of world affairs with a new measure of security for all nations."

Mayor Lapham reminded the delegates that they were meeting at the gateway to the Pacific and that this port still had a great wartime duty to perform. He reminded them, also, that they were meeting in a building which was a memorial to the men who died in the first World War, and that they had an obligation to succeed for the veterans of the two wars.

The audience was undemonstrative at the opening meeting of the conference.

"There is only one delegation that can make big news."

John F. Kennedy reports on the San Francisco Conference

Following his discharge from the navy in April 1945, Lt. John F. Kennedy, the hero of PT-109, prepared to enter politics. Before launching his campaign for Congress in 1946, however, he worked as a freelance journalist, covering the San Francisco Conference for Hearst's *Chicago Herald-American* and Potsdam for the International News Service.

Kennedy Tells Parley Trends
By Lt. John F. Kennedy

SAN FRANCISCO, April 28—It is still too early to judge how the united nations conference is going to work out—but there are certain definite trends already discernible.

In the first place, it is becoming increasingly obvious that this conference has been given too big a buildup. There is an impression that this is the conference to end wars and introduce peace on earth and good-will toward nations—excluding of course, Germany and Japan.

Well, it's not going to do that.

The best that can be hoped for is some changes in the voting procedure of the security council as set up at Dumbarton Oaks and that the Rusians can be persuaded to make some compromises on their stiff-necked attitude toward the Polish question. If we can gain those two points, we shall be doing well. And the old hands out here know this.

Secondly, while this is the most reported event in history—it looks like a newspaper men's convention—and in spite of the thousands of words going out daily—there is very little real news.

There is only one delegation that can make big news at the conference and that's the Soviet and they don't talk—never to the press and seldom to each other.

Vyacheslav Molotov deviated from the party line of strict silence for a few minutes at a press conference Thursday but he was singularly uninformative.

It was all handled so smoothly and smilingly though that no one realized until they read transcripts of the conference afterwards how uninformative an uninformative Russian can be.

Molotov's apparent readiness to pick a fight over the comparatively small question of who was to be permanent chairman of the Security Conference—job ordinarily given to the foreign minister of the host nation—was the tip-off that the Russians are going to make a fight on all of the little issues in the hope they can write their own terms on the big ones.

The average GI in the street, and the streets of San Francisco are crowded with them, doesn't seem to have a very clear-cut conception of what this meeting is all about. But one demedaled marine sergeant gave the general reaction when he said:

"I don't know much about what's going on—but if they just fix it so that we don't have to fight any more—they can count me in."

Me, too, sarge.

43.

The Link-up on the Elbe

April 1945

The Wehrmacht's strength on the eastern front was broken in July 1943 during an epic tank battle with the Soviets at Kursk. Thereafter, stripped of its offensive capability, the German army defended itself as best it could during a slow, bloody, twenty-month retreat to Berlin. The Red Army recrossed the Dnieper in September 1943, relieved a besieged Leningrad in January 1944, and six months later reached the

Vistula in central Poland. There, just eight miles from Warsaw, the Soviets tarried while the Germans brutally crushed an uprising in the capital staged by the Polish Home Army, a paramilitary group associated with the London government-in-exile. (It has since been suggested that Stalin intentionally held up the Red Army advance so that the Germans might have time to eliminate the leaders of what would likely be future opposition to the Lublin government that he backed.)

In the fall of 1944, Hitler's transfer of armor and troops to the west (for the Ardennes counteroffensive) weakened German defenses sufficiently in the east to cause Stalin to accelerate the winter offensive he had already planned to launch in cooperation with an Anglo-American offensive in the west. The force that the Red Army assembled was overwhelming—1.5 million men, 3,300 tanks, and 10,000 aircraft, compared to 600,000 men, 700 tanks, and 1,300 planes available to the Germans. Beginning on January 12, the strike carried the Soviets all the way from the Vistula to the Oder, where by the

end of the month Marshal Ivan Konev's First Ukrainian Front had established several bridgeheads within sixty-five miles of Berlin.

Meanwhile, the western Allies advanced from the Rhine toward the Elbe. The Germans who had escaped across the Rhine were too few, too disorganized, and too demoralized to put up much of a resistance, and by March 27 all seven armies (four American, one British, one Canadian, and one French) were across. Now Eisenhower's goals became threefold: to capture the Ruhr, Germany's industrial heartland; to prevent a Nazi withdrawal to the Bavarian Alps, where fanatical units might hold out for months; and to avoid a potential clash with Soviet troops pushing west. To this latter end, Eisenhower sent a cable to Stalin on March 28 informing him of the western Allies' plans and requesting similar information on Red Army intentions. Recalling the heavy fighting that had occurred when German and Soviet troops met unexpectedly in Poland during the 1939 partition of that country, Eisenhower wanted to avoid similar circumstances if at all possible.

First Army infantrymen make their way across a broken Elbe bridge near Torgau to greet Soviet troops on April 27, 1945.

U. S. AND RED ARMIES JOIN, SPLIT GERMANY

Firm Link Formed; Junction of Two Armies Splits Rest of Reich Into Huge Pockets

By DREW MIDDLETON

PARIS, April 27—Two armies of plain men who had marched and fought from the blood-splashed beaches of Normandy and the shattered streets of Stalingrad have met on the Elbe River in the heart of Germany, splitting the Third Reich and sealing the doom of the German Army, whose tread shook the world only three short years ago.

The junction on the Elbe River of Gen. Courtney H. Hodges' United States First Army and Marshal Ivan S. Koneff's First Ukrainian Army transcends all other developments on the Western Front, even a thrust across the Austrian border by an armored column of Gen. George S. Patton's United States Third Army, which is diving eastward toward Marshal Fedor J. Tolbukhin's Soviet forces smashing westward eighty miles away.

The first official contact between the Red Army and the Allies' Expeditionary Forces was made at 4:40 P.M. on Wednesday, when a second lieutenant and three men of an intelligence and reconnaissance platoon of the 273d Regiment of the Sixty-ninth Infantry Division of the First Army met elements of the 173d Regiment of the Fifty-eighth Guards Division of the First Ukrainian Army on the girders of a demolished bridge at Torgau on the Elbe, twenty-eight miles northeast of Leipzig. Yesterday afternoon at 4 o'clock Maj. Gen. Emil F. Reinhardt, commanding the Sixty-ninth Division, conferred with the commander of the Soviet Guards Division at Torgau the mutual exchange of liberated prisoners of war.

Tonight the meeting of the East and West is sealed and details of both armies are guarding the roads between the two fronts while senior officers of both sides pay their respects to their comrades in arms.

The German front was split after a junction that ended a drive of 1,400 miles to the west by the Red Armies starting from Stalingrad and 700 miles to the east by the First Army, whose first elements came ashore in Normandy last June.

From now on pockets and redoubts of varying sizes and strengths are the main tactical objectives of the Anglo-American and Red Armies and the advances will be to the north and south rather than to the east and west, as so long has been the case.

With the American and Red Armies now in firm contact to the north, the United States Third Army and Marshal Tolbukhin's Third Ukrainian Army are moving swiftly toward each other and another junction in Austria which would isolate the Bohemian redoubt in western Czechoslovakia. At the same time the United States Seventh Army and the French First Army have broken German defenses in the western part of the Bavarian foreland and are rolling down on the northern boundary of Hitler's Alpine redoubt.

At last reports tonight columns of both the United States Seventh and Third Armies were less than forty miles from Munich, key to the outer defenses of the redoubt, and tanks of the Tenth Armored Division on the Seventh Army's right flank were only twenty-seven miles north of the Austrian frontier at the western end of the redoubt.

The swift advances of the last two days have now cut all but one of the main railroad lines running to the Alpine redoubt, and General Patton's armored columns pounding down from the northwest toward Linz are less than twenty-five miles from this railroad center on the last railway route into the enemy stronghold.

Farther west Third Army forces have captured the fortified cities of Regensburg and Ingolstadt and are sweeping southward toward Munich.

The Eleventh Armored Division, which paced the drive into Austria, advanced two columns that covered nine and twelve miles respectively in the latest advances reported here.

One column made the first American advance in history into Austria at 6 P.M. yesterday, crossing the frontier two miles south of the point where Germany, Austria and Czechoslovakia meet. [Press service dispatches said this column took Schwarzenberg and met no opposition.] Another column entered Gegenbach, a mile west of the frontier.

According to reports from the front the two columns bit deeper into Austria today and were less than twenty-five miles from Linz at noon.

Regensburg, site of two Messerschmitt aircraft factories, was captured in a joint operation by the Seventy-first and Sixty-fifth Infantry Divisions of the Third Army, which crossed the Danube east and west of the city and then expanded their crossings to form bridgeheads of thirty-two and fifty square miles respectively.

The Eighty-sixth Infantry Division on the right flank took Ingolstadt and then advanced southward along a superhighway, reaching positions three and a half miles south of the town and thirty-seven and a half miles from the northern outskirts of Munich.

Doughboys of the Ninety-ninth Infantry Division poured across the Danube in an area thirteen miles from Ingolstadt today while the Fourteenth Armored Division reached the Danube on a ten-mile front west of Ingolstadt today and prepared to cross and join in the final dash toward the redoubt.

U.S. and Soviet officers at the official meeting of their respective forces on April 26. In the center, wearing two stars on his helmet, is Maj. Gen. Emil F. Reinhardt of the First Army.

Lieut. Gen. Alexander M. Patch broke two of this Seventh Army armored and two infantry divisions loose today. By tonight Seventh Army troops were closing in on Augsburg from the west and were rolling south toward Munich and the Austrian frontier.

German resistance in the Dillingen bridgehead, which has been stubborn, gave way. The Twelfth Armored Division, which had made the original crossing, smashed southward, crossing the Wertach River over a captured bridge to positions fifteen miles southwest of Augsburg and thirty-eight miles west of Munich.

While the tanks rolled due south, veteran doughboys of the Third Infantry Division smashed heavy German resistance late yesterday and today and captured Feigenhofen, eight miles northwest of Augsburg after a five-mile gain. Another column pushed to positions twelve miles north of Augsburg. Augsburg was the site of Messerschmitt aircraft and Diesel engine plants.

The Fourth Infantry Division also thrust through broken enemy defenses out of the bridgehead capturing Dinkelscherben, twelve miles west of Augsburg. The 101st Cavalry Group is operating between the Fourth and Third Divisions.

The Tenth Armored Division, on the right of General Patch's line, smashed out of its bridgehead over the Iller for a six-mile gain, capturing Memmingen, twenty-eight miles south, southeast of Ulm, where 4,000 Allied prisoners of war were liberated.

The Forty-fourth Infantry Division also pushed eastward, reaching Sontheimmand Bad Woerishafen and Schwabmuenchen, southwest of Augsburg.

All of General Patch's divisions engaged in the present operation are over the Danube. Doughboys of the Forty-second Infantry Division advanced southeast from Donauwoerth, twenty miles north of Augsburg today, while the Forty-fifth Infantry Division crossed the river and captured Burgheim, twenty miles west of Ingolstadt.

The main French advance today was in the area northwest of Constance, where the French captured Radolzell. Constance fell to the First French Corps late yesterday after a stiff fight outside the lakeside city.

French troops have now reduced the Black Forest pocket south of Stuttgart to 250 square miles, half its original size. [Later press service reports said the pocket had been virtually wiped out when French forces reached the center of it and found out.]

The southern exits along the Swiss frontier have been blocked and mopping-up operations are proceeding satisfactorily, although some brisk local actions have been reported. A small area fifteen miles southwest of Reutlingen is still holding out.

The French advance in the Maritime Alps continued with the forces capturing Bordighera, five miles east of the Italian frontier.

Gen. Jean de Lattre's forces took 6,500 prisoners, including two generals, yesterday. Since entering Germany the French First Army has liberated 60,000 prisoners of war and slave laborers.

The British Second Army has completed its businesslike job on Bremen with advance of the Third Infantry Division through the southern suburbs where a radar station was taken. At the same time tanks of the Guards Armored Division continued to advance from Zeven, against slackening resistance today. Elsewhere there was little activity on Lieut. Gen. Sir Miles C. Dempsey's front. The Guards are now seven miles southwest and six miles northwest of Zeven.

Most of the activity on the front of Lieut. Gen. H. D. G. Crerar's Canadian First Army is centered in the sector between the Ems and Weser Rivers. Elements of the Canadian Second Infantry Division pushed north to cut the highway and railroad between Oldenburg and Delmenhorst today.

Tanks of the Canadian Fourth Armored Division pushed forward slowly against stiff resistance to expand the bridgehead north of the Kuesten canal, west of the Ems. Farther east the Polish Armored Division is only three miles southeast of Emden, German naval base.

There was no activity in the Amersfoort sector or along the Grebbe River line.

"I regard it as essential that we co-ordinate our action."

Dwight D. Eisenhower's March 28, 1945, message to Joseph Stalin

The political subtext of Eisenhower's cable to Stalin was unmistakable: Berlin was being ceded to the Soviets. This infuriated the British, but, with U.S. troops making up the bulk of the advancing forces, Churchill had scant leverage. As it turned out, the failure to reach Berlin in 1945 was regretted by the western Allies for decades to come. However, in Eisenhower's defense, he had other considerations. First, given his primary duty to end the war as quickly as possible, with as few casualties as possible, he tended to discount political objectives. Second, he wanted to consolidate his control of the Ruhr, so that the British and Americans could manage the region's wealth without any Soviet interference (possession having been shown by the Soviets to be the determining factor). And, third, he believed that Hitler was planning a last stand in the Bavarian Alps. For months, intelligence reports had described construction of a National Redoubt centered on Berchtesgaden. Had the Nazis withdrawn to such a place, the war might have dragged on for yet another year. In reality, though, there was no such Alpine fortress. "The Redoubt existed largely in the imagination of a few fanatical Nazis," Bradley later admitted. "It grew into so exaggerated a scheme that I am astonished we could have believed it as innocently as we did. But while it persisted, this legend…shaped our tactical thinking."

1. My immediate operations are designed to encircle and destroy the enemy forces defending the Ruhr, and to isolate that area from the rest of Germany. This will be accomplished by developing around north of the Ruhr and from Frankfurt through Kassel line until I close the ring. The enemy thus enclosed will then be mopped up.

2. I estimate that this phase of operations will end late in April or even earlier, and my next task will be to divide the remaining enemy forces by joining hands with your forces.

3. For my forces the best axis on which to effect this junction would be Erfurt-Leipzig-Dresden. I believe, moreover, that this is the area to which main German governmental departments are being moved. It is along this axis that I propose to make my main effort. In addition, as soon as the situation allows, a secondary advance will be made to effect a junction with your forces in the area of Regensburg-Linz, thereby preventing the consolidation of German resistance in Redoubt in Southern Germany.

4. Before deciding firmly on my plans, it is, I think, most important they should be co-ordinated as closely as possible with yours both as to direction and timing. Could you, therefore, tell me your intentions and let me know how far the proposals outlined in this message conform to your probable action.

5. If we are to complete the destruction of German armies without delay, I regard it as essential that we co-ordinate our action and make every effort to perfect the liaison between our advancing forces. I am prepared to send officers to you for this purpose.

44.

The Battle of Berlin

April 1945

Once the Red Army reached the Oder in late January 1945, Hitler turned his primary attention to the defense of his capital. During February and March, he established three formidable lines, the first two running north–south from the Baltic Sea to the Sudeten Mountains on the Czechoslovakian border and the third ringing Berlin itself. These lines were manned by about a million German soldiers. Even so, the

Soviets had a significant advantage in manpower. Together, Zhukov and Konev had 2.5 million men under arms, none of whom were Home Guard units with inferior equipment and questionable training. Shortly before dawn on April 16, the Soviets began their main attack, with Zhukov's First Belorussian Front pushing west from its bridgehead at Küstrin. "For the last time, the deadly Jewish-Bolshevik enemy has started a mass attack," Hitler declared in a written order to the troops in Berlin. "He is trying to reduce Germany to rubble and to exterminate our people."

The German resistance on the Seelow Heights—the heart of Hitler's first defensive line, about five miles from the Oder—was fierce enough to delay Zhukov's army for nearly two days. Similar difficulties at the second defensive line cost Zhukov another two days and postponed his arrival at Berlin's northern suburbs until April 19. Driving up from the south, Konev's First Ukrainian Front reached the outskirts of the capital on April 20. Five days later—as the U.S. and Soviet armies met on the Elbe, splitting Germany in half—Zhukov and Konev linked up themselves, completing their encirclement of the city. Recognizing the trap, Hitler ordered his troops on the Elbe to disengage and move east relieve Berlin, but his order came too late to break through the Soviet stranglehold.

The Red Army began the last phase of the battle of Berlin on April 26. During the week of savage street fighting that followed, SS units roamed the city, summarily executing any soldier who left his post. Meanwhile, civilians retreated to their cellars and waited anxiously for the arrival of the enemy, fearful of the revenge he would exact for German violence to the Russian homeland. (For the most part, this retaliation was limited to rape and looting.) Not surprisingly, the worst fighting took place at the Reichstag, where some five thousand Nazi diehards held out for two days, forcing the Soviets to clear them from the building room by room and corridor by corridor.

Berlin's Wittenberg Platz during the last days of Nazi rule. The signs indicate the new locations of bombed-out tenants.

ALLIES BAR PEACE PLEA THAT OMITS RUSSIA; SURRENDER REPORT UNTRUE, TRUMAN SAYS

Nazis' End Near; But President on Word From Eisenhower Corrects Rumor

WASHINGTON, April 28—Truman announced at 9:36 o'clock tonight that there was no foundation for a report that Nazi Germany had surrendered unconditionally.

The report was circulated from San Francisco, after information had been received that Heinrich Himmler had offered a German surrender to the United States and Britain. The Western Allies stood on the terms that Germany must surrender unconditionally to the three great powers, including the Soviet Union.

The fact that there was no foundation for the full-surrender rumor was established by Fleet Admiral William D. Leahy, the President's Chief of Staff, through a telephone call to General Dwight D. Eisenhower.

President Truman summoned reporters to his office in the White House and stated that he had heard the rumor while working in his office this evening.

The White House permitted direct quotation of President Truman's announcement. This is it:

"Well, I was over here as you can see doing a little work, and this rumor got started.

"I had a call from San Francisco and the State Department called me.

"I just got in touch with Admiral Leahy and had him call our headquarters Commander in Chief in Europe, and there is no foundation for the rumor. That is all I have to say."

Earlier in the evening the report had been generally accredited in White House circles, and members of the secretariat and other officials returned to the Executive Offices.

In case the rumor should have been verified, President Truman started preparation of a proclamation to be read to the American people over all the radio networks to announce the fall of Germany.

[The Moscow radio said it had been "confirmed by responsible Soviet circles" that Himmler had made an offer to surrender Germany unconditionally to the United States and Britain and that the Western Allies had rejected the proposal.

[Himmler, who transmitted his offer through Sweden, is understood to have told London and Washington Adolf Hitler was dying and that he was acting as next in command, The Associated Press reported.

[A United Press dispatch from San Francisco said Allied diplomatic quarters there suggested that Himmler had put Hitler to death to give cynical evidence to the Allies of his "good faith" in offering to surrender Germany unconditionally.

[These quarters said Himmler had advised the Allies through Stockholm that Hitler "may not live another twenty-four hours." The timing of the Himmler message was such, it was believed, that Hitler may already be dead at the hands of the man who was his lieutenant in terrorism, The United Press added.]

The President told White House reporters that he had returned to his office after dinner from Blair House, his temporary residence, and it was about that time, 7:35 P.M., that the report of the German surrender got started.

The President held his press conference with many officials of the White House standing

The commander of a Hitler Youth company gives directions for the defense of Berlin in late February 1945.

around him, including Stephen Early, his special assistant; William D. Hassett and Jonathan Daniels, secretaries; Elmer Davis, director of the Office of War Information, and others.

He waited until all the reporters had assembled and then gave them his brief announcement. In less than a minute the whole room was completely cleared, as the newsmen broke for telephones.

[President Truman remained at the White House until 12:20 A.M., Sunday, and then walked back to Blair House, The Associated Press stated.]

"No rest, no relief. No regular food."

The last days in Berlin from the viewpoint of a German tank officer

An administrative officer in one of the tank divisions defending Berlin kept a diary of his unit's final days in action. This entry was one of the last.

April 27

Continuous attack throughout the night. Increasing signs of dissolution. But that's no use—one must not give up at the last moment, and then regret it for the rest of one's life. K. brings information that American tank divisions are on their way to Berlin. In the Chancellery, they say, everybody is more certain of final victory than ever before. Hardly any communications among troops, excepting a few regular battalions equipped with radio posts. Telephone cables are shot to pieces. Physical conditions are indescribable. No rest, no relief. No regular food, hardly any bread. We get water from the tunnels and filter it. Nervous breakdowns. The wounded that are not simply torn apart are hardly taken in anywhere. The civilians in their cellars are afraid of them. Too many of them have been hanged as deserters. And the flying courts-martial drive the civilians out of cellars where they pick up deserters because they are accessories to the crime.

These courts-martial appear in our sector particularly often today. Most of them are very young SS officers. Hardly a medal or decoration on them. Blind and fanatical. The hope of relief and the fear of the courts-martial bring our men back to the fighting pitch.

General Mummert requests that no more courts-martial visit the sector. A division made up of the largest number of men with some of the highest decorations does not deserve to be persecuted by such babies. He is resolved to shoot down any court-martial that takes action in our sector.

The whole large expanse of Potsdamer Platz is a waste of ruins. Masses of damaged vehicles, half-smashed trailers of the ambulances with the wounded still in them. Dead people everywhere, many of them frightfully cut up by tanks and trucks.

At night, we try to reach the Propaganda Ministry for news about Wenck and the American divisions. Rumors that the Ninth Army is also on the way to Berlin. In the west, general peace treaties are being signed. Violent shelling of the center of town.

We cannot hold our present position. Around four o'clock in the morning, we retreat through the subway tunnels. In the tunnels next to ours, the Russians march in the opposite direction to the positions we have just lost.

45.

The Death of Hitler

April 1945

During the night of April 29–30, 1945, Gen. Karl Weidling, commanding the defense forces in Berlin, reported to Hitler that the army's ammunition was running out and there was no longer any chance of relief arriving from the west. Already, Hitler knew that the end was near. Earlier that day, he had married his longtime mistress, Eva Braun, and prepared both a personal and a political will. The next day, April 30,

he attended an early-afternoon conference with his staff and then sent his chauffeur to fetch some gasoline. Meanwhile, he and Braun said their good-byes to Propaganda Minister Goebbels, Secretary to the Führer Martin Bormann, and others who had remained behind in the Führerbunker, where Hitler had been living an eerily sequestered existence since January 1945. At 3:30 P.M., alone with Braun in his suite, the German dictator shot himself, while his new wife took her own life with cyanide. Their bodies were carried up to the rubble-strewn courtyard of the Chancellery, doused with the gasoline the chauffeur had obtained, and cremated.

The next day, German radio announced Hitler's death, reporting that he had fallen while leading the defense of the capital. Few accepted this story, and many, in fact, believed that Hitler was still alive. Without a corpse to disprove such speculation, rumors of the Führer's escape spread throughout the summer of 1945. Even as sober a man as Eisenhower admitted at a press conference in June that he harbored some doubts concerning

Hitler's death. Meanwhile, European newspapers printed stories of numerous Führer sightings, including one that asserted Hitler was working as a croupier at an Evian casino and another that he was disguising himself as a shepherd in the Swiss Alps. Later, the Soviet newspaper *Izvestia* reported that Hitler and Braun were living unmolested in a Westphalian castle, thereby implying Western complicity because Westphalia lay in the British zone of occupation.

Outraged by this charge, the British opened an official inquiry into Hitler's fate. Maj. Hugh Trevor-Roper, an Oxford history don in civilian life, spent September and October tracking down anyone who might have been present in the Führerbunker during Hitler's last days. Most witnesses had either died or fled, but Trevor-Roper was still able to speak with two secretaries who—while not eyewitnesses themselves—had received contemporaneous accounts from others who had been present at Hitler's death. At a November 1 press conference, Trevor-Roper outlined his findings, which are still considered accurate today.

HITLER DEAD IN CHANCELLERY, NAZIS SAY; DOENITZ, SUCCESSOR, ORDERS WAR TO GO ON

Admiral in Charge; Proclaims Designation to Rule—Appeals to People and Army

By SYDNEY GRUSON

LONDON, May 1—Adolf Hitler died this afternoon, the Hamburg radio announced tonight, and Grand Admiral Karl Doenitz, proclaiming himself the new Fuehrer by Hitler's appointment, said that the war would continue.

Crowning days of rumors about Hitler's health and whereabouts, the Hamburg radio said that he had fallen in the battle of Berlin at his command post in the Chancellery just three days after Benito Mussolini, the first of the dictators, had been killed by Italian Partisans. Doenitz, a 53-year-old U-boat specialist, broadcast an address to the German people and the surviving armed forces immediately after the announcer had given the news of Hitler's death.

[The British Foreign Office said that it would demand the production of Hitler's body after the end of hostilities, The Associated Press reported.]

First addressing the German people, Doenitz said that they would continue to fight only to save themselves from the Russians but that they would oppose the western Allies as long as they helped the Russians. In an order of the day to the German forces he repeated his thinly veiled attempt to split the Allies.

Early this evening the Germans were told that an important announcement would be broadcast tonight. There was no hint of what was coming. The stand-by announcement was repeated at 9:40 P.M., followed by the playing of excerpts from Wagner's "Goetterdaemmerung."

A few minutes later the announcer said: "Achtung! Achtung! In a few moments you will hear a serious and important message to the German people." Then the news was given to the Germans and the world after the playing of the slow movement from Bruckner's Seventh Symphony, commemorating Wagner's death.

Appealing to the German people for help, order and discipline, Doenitz eulogized Hitler as the hero of a lifetime of service to the nation whose "fight against the Bolshevik storm flood concerned not only Europe but the entire civilized world....It is my first task," Doenitz added, "to save Germany from destruction by the advancing Bolshevist enemy. For this aim alone the military struggle continues."

Clinging to the line of all recent German propaganda, reflected in Heinrich Himmler's reported offer to surrender to the western Allies but not to Russia, Doenitz said that the British and Americans were fighting not for their own interests but for the spreading of Bolshevism. He demanded of the armed forces the same allegiance that they had pledged to Hitler and he assured them that he took supreme command "resolved to continue the struggle against the Bolsheviks until the fighting men, until the hundreds of thousands of German families of the German east are saved from bondage and extermination." To the armed forces he described Hitler as "one of the greatest heroes of German history," who "gave his life and met a hero's death."

News tickers in the House of Commons lobby carried the news of Hitler's death just before the House rose tonight. The reaction of members and of the general public was much the

Hitler and his adjutant, Julius Schaub, survey damage to the Chancellery on April 20, 1945, in the last known photograph of the dictator.

same. Some doubted the truth of the announcement altogether, while others argued that there would have been no sense of making it if it were not true, since Hitler was perhaps the last person around whom the Germans still in unconquered territory would rally.

But there was an almost complete lack of excitement here. Those who believed the report seemed to accept it as a matter of course that Hitler would die. There was no official reaction.

The last reference to Hitler before tonight's announcement came in this afternoon's German communiqué, which said that the Berlin garrison had "gathered around the Fuehrer and, herded together in a very narrow space, is defending itself heroically." When Himmler offered his surrender to the Americans and British, it is reported, he told Count Folke Bernadotte, his Swedish emissary, that Hitler was dying of a cerebral hemorrhage. During the past week, Hitler was variously reported

dead, dying or insane in Berlin, Salzburg or the Bavarian mountains.

Doenitz' self-proclaimed accession was believed in some quarters here to bear out reports of a recent split in the German hierarchy between the supporters of an immediate peace gathered around Himmler and the die-hard clique clinging to Hitler and his determination to fight to the very end.

It was noted that Doenitz commanded the last arm of the German military machine that could cause the Allies major difficulties, and his ability as an expert on submarine tactics is not belittled here.

He was one of the first military men to join the Nazis and his loyalty to the party and its ideology never wavered. Known as one of the most ruthless men in Germany, he has been a bitter enemy of Britain since his imprisonment during World War I, when he was confined to a Manchester asylum as a lunatic.

"I die with a happy heart."

Adolf Hitler's personal and political testaments

Even after Trevor-Roper's press conference, the Soviets, among others, continued to voice skepticism because the British had offered no physical evidence to support their suicide story. Soon, however, Trevor-Roper learned that Bormann's adjutant, Wilhelm Zander, had been spotted in Bavaria, living under the assumed name of Paustin. Tracking Zander to a house in Tegernsee, Trevor-Roper discovered a suitcase containing a secret compartment. Inside were several remarkable documents, including Hitler and Braun's marriage contract and Hitler's personal and political wills. Authenticated by the FBI lab in Washington, these papers provided the corroborating evidence that Trevor-Roper had been seeking and persuaded most people of the Führer's death, although some rumors of Hitler's survival persisted for many years.

My Private Will and Testament

As I did not consider that I could take responsibility, during the years of struggle, of contracting a marriage, I have now decided, before the closing of my earthly career, to take as my wife that girl who, after many years of faithful friendship, entered, of her own free will, the practically besieged town in order to share her destiny with me. At her own desire she goes as my wife with me into death. It will compensate us for what we both lost through my work in the service of my people.

What I possess belongs—in so far as it has any value—to the Party. Should this no longer exist, to the State, should the State also be destroyed, no further decision of mine is necessary.

My pictures, in the collections which I have bought in the course of years, have never been collected for private purposes, but only for the extension of a gallery in my home town of Linz a.d. Donau.

It is my most sincere wish that this bequest may be duly executed.

I nominate as my Executor my most faithful Party comrade, Martin Bormann.

He is given full legal authority to make all decisions. He is permitted to take out everything that has a sentimental value or is necessary for the maintenance of a modest simple life, for my brothers and sisters, also above all for the mother of my wife and my faithful coworkers who are well known to him, principally my old Secretaries Frau Winter etc. who have for many years aided me by their work.

I myself and my wife—in order to escape the disgrace of deposition or capitulation—choose death. It is our wish to be burnt immediately on the spot where I have carried out the greatest part of my daily work in the course of a twelve years' service to my people.

Given in Berlin, 29th April 1945, 4:00 o'clock.
A. Hitler

As Witnesses: Martin Bormann, Dr. Fuhr
As Witness: Nicolaus von Below

My Political Testament

More than thirty years have now passed since I in 1914 made my modest contribution as a volunteer in the first world-war that was forced upon the Reich.

In these three decades I have been actuated solely by love and loyalty to my people in all my thoughts, acts, and life. They gave me the strength to make the most difficult decisions which have ever confronted to mortal man. I have spent my time, my working strength, and my health in these three decades.

It is untrue that I or anyone else in Germany wanted the war in 1939. It was desired and instigated exclusively by those international statesmen who were either of Jewish descent or worked for Jewish interests. I have made too many offers for the control and limitation of armaments, which posterity will not for all time be able to disregard for the responsibility for the outbreak of this war to be laid on me. I have further never wished that after the first fatal world war a second against England, or even against America, should break out. Centuries will pass away, but out of the ruins of our towns and monuments the hatred against those finally responsible whom we have to thank for everything, International Jewry and its helpers, will grow.

Three days before the outbreak of the German-Polish war I again proposed to the British ambassador in Berlin a solution to the German-Polish problem—similar to that in the case of the Saar district, under international control. This offer also cannot be denied. It was only rejected because the leading circles in English politics wanted the war, partly on account of the business hoped for and partly under influence of propaganda organized by international Jewry.

I also made it quite plain that, if the nations of Europe are again to be regarded as mere shares to be bought and sold by these international conspirators in money and finance, then that race, Jewry, which is the real criminal of this murderous struggle, will be saddled with the responsibility. I further left no one in doubt that this time not only would millions of children of Europe's Aryan peoples die of hunger, not only would millions of grown men suffer death, and not only hundreds of thousands of women and children be burnt and bombed to death in the towns, without the real criminal having to atone for this guilt, even if by more humane means.

After six years of war, which in spite of all set-backs, will go down one day in history as the most glorious and valiant demonstration of a nation's life purpose, I cannot forsake the city which is the capital of this Reich. As the forces are too small to make any further stand against the enemy attack at this place and our resistance is gradually being weakened by men who are as deluded as they are lacking in initiative, I should like, by remaining in this town, to share my fate with those, the millions of others, who have also taken upon themselves to do so. Moreover I do not wish to fall into the hands of an enemy who requires a new spectacle organized by the Jews for the amusement of their hysterical masses.

I have decided therefore to remain in Berlin and there of my own free will to choose death at the moment when I believe the position of the Fuehrer and Chancellor itself can no longer be held.

I die with a happy heart, aware of the immeasurable deeds and achievements of our soldiers at the front, our women at home, the achievements of our farmers and workers and the work, unique in history, of our youth who bear my name.

That from the bottom of my heart I express my thanks to you all, is just as self-evident as my wish that you should, because of that, on no account give up the struggle, but rather continue it against the enemies of the Fatherland, no matter where, true to the creed of a great Clausewitz. From the sacrifice of our soldiers and from my own unity with them unto death, will in any case spring up in the history of Germany, the seed of a radiant renaissance of the National-Socialist movement and thus of the realization of a true community of nations.

Many of the most courageous men and women have decided to unite their lives with mine until the very last. I have begged and finally ordered them not to do this, but to take part in the further battle of the Nation. I beg the heads of the Armies, the Navy and the Air Force to strengthen by all possible means the spirit of resistance of our soldiers in the National-Socialist sense, with special reference to the fact that also I myself, as founder and creator of this movement, have preferred death to cowardly abdication or even capitulation.

May it, at some future time, become part of the code of honour of the German officer—as is already the case in our Navy—that the surrender of a district or of a town is impossible, and that above all the leaders here must march ahead as shining examples, faithfully fulfilling their duty unto death.

Second Part of the Political Testament

Before my death I expel the former Reichsmarschall Hermann Goering from the party and deprive him of all rights which he may enjoy by virtue of the decree of June 29th, 1941, and also by virtue of my statement in the Reichstag on September 1st, 1939, I appoint in his place Grossadmiral Doenitz, President of the Reich and Supreme Commander of the Armed Forces.

Before my death I expel the former Reichsfuehrer-SS and Minister of the Interior, Heinrich Himmler, from the party and from all offices of State. In his stead I appoint Gauleiter Karl Hanke as Reichsfuehrer-SS and Chief of the German Police, and Gauleiter Paul Giesler as Reich Minister of the Interior.

Goering and Himmler, quite apart from their disloyalty to my person, have done immeasurable harm to the country and the whole nation by secret negotiations with the enemy, which they conducted without my knowledge and against my wishes, and by illegally attempting to seize power in the State for themselves.

In order to give the German people a government composed of honourable men,—a government which will fulfill its pledge to continue the war by every means—I appoint the following members of the new Cabinet as leaders of the nation:

President of the Reich: Doenitz.
Chancellor of the Reich: Dr. Goebbels.
Party Minister: Bormann.
Foreign Minister: Seyss-Inquart.
Minister of the Interior: Gauleiter Giesler.
Minister for War: Doenitz.
C-in-C of the Army: Schoerner.
C-in-C of the Navy: Doenitz.
C-in-C of the Air Force: Greim.
Reichsfuehrer-SS and Chief of the German Police: Gauleiter Hanke.
Economics: Funk.
Agriculture: Backe.
Justice: Thierack.
Education and Public Worship: Dr. Scheel.

Propaganda: Dr. Naumann.
Finance: Schwerin-Grossigk.
Labour: Dr. Hupfauer.
Munitions: Saur.
Leader of the German Labour Front and Member of the Reich Cabinet: Reich Minister Dr. Ley.

Although a number of these men, such as Martin Bormann, Dr. Goebbels etc., together with their wives, have joined me of their own free will and did not wish to leave the capital of the Reich under any circumstances, but were willing to perish with me here, I must nevertheless ask them to obey my request, and in this case set the interests of the nation above their own feelings. By their work and loyalty as comrades they will be just as close to me after death, as I hope that my spirit will linger among them and always go with them. Let them be hard, but never unjust, above all let them never allow fear to influence their actions, and set the honour of the nation above everything in the world. Finally, let them be conscious of the fact that our task, that of continuing the building of a National Socialist State, represents the work of the coming centuries, which places every single person under an obligation always to serve the common interest and to subordinate his own advantage to this end. I demand of all Germans, all National Socialists, men, women and all the men of the Armed Forces, that they be faithful and obedient unto death to the new government and its President.

Above all I charge the leaders of the nation and those under them to scrupulous observance of the laws of race and to merciless opposition to the universal poisoner of all peoples, international Jewry.

Given in Berlin, this 29th day of April 1945. 4:00 A.M.
Adolf Hitler

Witnessed by Dr. Josef Fuhr, Martin Bormann,
Wilhelm Buergdorf, Hans Krebs.

46.

V-E Day

May 1945

On May 1, 1945, the day after Hitler's suicide, Goebbels and Bormann sent Gen. Hans Krebs, the Wehrmacht chief of staff since March, to meet with Zhukov in the hope that he might be able to arrange a cease-fire now that Hitler was gone. Zhukov wouldn't bargain, however, and insisted on an unconditional surrender, which Goebbels and Bormann refused, prompting the Red Army to resume its attacks.

Back in the Führerbunker, Goebbels and his wife poisoned their six children before taking cyanide themselves. Bormann tried to escape, and there the record ends. Some reports suggest that he was killed in the streets outside the Chancellery, but his body was never found. The next day, May 2, General Weidling surrendered Berlin, and by 3 P.M. the fighting in the capital was over.

That same day, Admiral Dönitz, Hitler's successor as German head of state, offered to conclude a separate peace with the western Allies so that his armed forces, presumably with Anglo-American help, could continue fighting the Soviets in the east. Now that Hitler was out of the way, Dönitz reasoned, such an anti-Communist alliance made obvious sense, yet President Truman disappointed the admiral by insisting that the Germans surrender simultaneously on all fronts. Meanwhile, the war continued, as American troops pushed into southern Germany and Austria, rounding up Hermann Göring and other important Nazi leaders, while the Soviets continued to face stiff

opposition from German soldiers who feared above all else capture by the Red Army.

During the next four days, Dönitz made additional efforts to split the Grand Alliance, sending first Adm. Hans von Freideburg and then Chief of Staff Alfred Jodl to persuade Eisenhower to accept the surrender of German troops in the west, but the American commander refused to meet with any German officer until the unconditional surrender documents had been signed. Meanwhile, Eisenhower had his own chief of staff, Lt. Gen. Walter Bedell "Beetle" Smith, show Freideburg and Jodl maps demonstrating the hopelessness of the German position. Finally, Dönitz realized that his efforts were hopeless and, late on May 6, began negotiating the formalities of German capitulation. Dönitz was, however, able to win one concession from Eisenhower: a forty-eight-hour delay in the announcement of the surrender—"in order," Jodl said, "to get the necessary instructions to all the outlying units," but in reality to allow more time for German troops to cross the Elbe and escape the Russians.

GIs at an American Red Cross club in London celebrate the end of the war after hearing first Dönitz's broadcast order that all U-boats cease fire immediately and then the announcement of unconditional surrender made by newly appointed German foreign minister Lutz Schwerin von Krosigk.

THE WAR IN EUROPE IS ENDED! SURRENDER IS UNCONDITIONAL; V-E WILL BE PROCLAIMED TODAY

Germans Capitulate on All Fronts

By EDWARD KENNEDY

REIMS, France, May 7—Germany surrendered unconditionally to the Western Allies and the Soviet Union at 2:41 A.M. French time today. [This was at 8:41 P.M., Eastern war time Sunday.]

The surrender took place at a little red schoolhouse that is the headquarters of Gen. Dwight D. Eisenhower.

The surrender, which brought the war in Europe to a formal end after five years, eight months and six days of bloodshed and destruction, was signed for Germany by Col. Gen. Gustav Jodl. General Jodl is the new Chief of Staff of the German Army.

The surrender was signed for the Supreme Allied Command by Lieut. Gen. Walter Bedell Smith, Chief of Staff for General Eisenhower.

It was also signed by Gen. Ivan Susloparoff for the Soviet Union and by Gen. Francois Sevez for France.

[The official Allied announcement will be made at 9 o'clock Tuesday morning when President Truman will broadcast a statement and Prime Minister Churchill will issue a V-E Day proclamation. Gen. Charles de Gaulle also will address the French at the same time.]

General Eisenhower was not present at the signing, but immediately afterward General Jodl and his fellow delegate, Gen. Admiral Hans Georg Friedeburg, were received by the Supreme Commander.

They were asked sternly if they understood the surrender terms imposed upon Germany and if they would be carried out by Germany.

They answered Yes.

Germany, which began the war with a ruthless attack upon Poland, followed by successive aggressions and brutality in internment camps, surrendered with an appeal to the victors for mercy toward the German people and armed forces.

After having signed the full surrender, General Jodl said he wanted to speak and received leave to do so.

"With this signature," he said in soft-spoken German, "the German people and armed forces are for better or worse delivered into the victors' hands.

"In this war, which has lasted more than five years, both have achieved and suffered more than perhaps any other people in the world."

"The announcement of V-E Day was terribly confused."

Memorandum of a telephone conversation made by
Acting Secretary of State Joseph C. Grew

"In every move we make these days," Eisenhower wrote to Marshall on April 27 concerning the maintenance of good relations with the Soviets, "we are trying to be meticulously careful in this regard." So, too, were U.S. officials in Washington, who had to scramble when Churchill insisted on moving up by nearly twenty-four hours the agreed-upon announcement time of Germany's surrender. Truman managed to stop Churchill, but then he had to weather Stalin's own last-minute request for a delay. "Please inform Marshal Stalin," the president wrote in a note that he handed to Soviet ambassador Andrei Gromyko later on May 8, "that his message to me was received in the White House at 1 o'clock this morning. However, by the time the message reached me, preparations had proceeded to such an extent that it was not possible to give consideration to a postponement of my announcement of the German surrender," which Truman had already made at 8:15 Washington time that morning.

May 7, 1945—1:45 P.M.

Admiral Leahy telephoned me and said that the situation on the announcement of V-E Day was terribly confused and he wanted me to know the background of the latest information. He stated that we have an agreement with Stalin and Churchill to make the announcement at 9 o'clock tomorrow morning but Churchill today raised the devil because he said he had to make the announcement right away and wanted to make it at noon today. Admiral Leahy said the President declined to do it then and said that he had arranged with Stalin and Churchill to announce it at 9 o'clock and he could not violate his agreement without the assent of Stalin. Admiral Leahy said they had been trying to get in touch with Stalin but so far have had nothing from him except the vague thought that he doesn't know the terms and can't make an announcement as yet. Admiral Leahy said he had heard later through BBC that Churchill was going to make the announcement at 3 o'clock. He said that he also had heard that de Gaulle is going to announce it at 2 o'clock. He stated that nobody has any control over de Gaulle and that this action was typical of him. I agreed with Admiral Leahy and remarked that de Gaulle was acting just like a naughty boy. Admiral Leahy said he spoke to the President about 20 minutes ago and thought it was definite for 9 o'clock tomorrow morning. He said that the only way the thing would be stopped would be for Stalin to ask us not to announce it yet. Admiral Leahy also said that he had been in touch with Eisenhower who said he had made no announcement and has kept it as secret as it could be kept. He said he would not make any announcement until it was released here. I said I understood it had leaked through AP. Admiral Leahy said the Germans are talking freely in plain language about it so everyone knows it. I said at any rate the only people who would be displeased about the whole thing would be the newspapermen.

VICTORY IN THE PACIFIC

47.

The Fall of Okinawa

June 1945

The next stop for the Americans after Iwo Jima was Okinawa in the Ryukyus. Sixty-seven miles long and eighteen miles wide at its broadest point, Okinawa lay only 330 miles from Kyushu, the southernmost of the Japanese home islands. Okinawa had two useful airfields, but more important were its pair of excellent anchorages. These made the island an ideal staging point for Olympic, the November 1945

invasion of Kyushu, for which planning was already under way. Following a naval and air bombardment that may have been the heaviest of the Pacific war but did little to soften the well-constructed Japanese defenses, the Tenth Army landed on the southwestern coast of Okinawa on Easter Sunday, April 1. Commanding its 172,000 soldiers and marines was Lt. Gen. Simon Bolivar Buckner Jr., son of the famous Confederate general.

Opposing Buckner was Lt. Gen. Ushijima Mitsuru, who led the hundred-thousand-man Okinawa garrison. Like the Japanese commander on Iwo Jima, Ushijima knew that he couldn't prevent the American landing, so he didn't try. He also knew that he couldn't defend the entire island, so he concentrated his forces on its southern quarter around the castle town of Shuri. There, he waited for the Americans to come to him. Ushijima's overall goal wasn't to defeat the Tenth Army, which he knew was impossible; rather, he wanted to delay the fall of Okinawa long enough to allow for additional defense preparations at home—and, if possible,

to inflict such heavy casualties on the Americans that they would give up their demand for an unconditional surrender and consider a negotiated peace instead.

The terrain around Shuri featured steep limestone ridges honeycombed with caves that the Japanese had reinforced with concrete and interconnected with tunnels. On April 9, U.S. troops reached the first of Ushijima's defensive lines along the Kakazu Ridge. It took them six days to break through this line and six weeks in all to penetrate the last defensive ring around Shuri. By that time, Ushijima had ordered his troops to fall back for a last stand in a group of ravines at the island's extreme southern tip. When eighty-two days of desperate fighting finally ended on June 21, the Tenth Army had suffered nearly eight thousand fatalities, thirty-two thousand injuries, and twenty-six thousand nonbattle losses for an overall casualty rate of some 35 percent. At that pace, Admiral Leahy estimated, Operation Olympic would cost the United States some 268,000 soldiers and marines.

Pfc. Galen A. Brehm of the Sixth Marine Division uses his flamethrower against an enemy cave on Okinawa. Nearby a rifleman waits for any Japanese soldier who might try to escape the enveloping flames.

JAPAN, LIKE OKINAWA, WILL COST HIGH PRICE

Our Soldiers, Sure of Final Victory, Expect Harder and Greater Battles

By W. H. LAWRENCE

OKINAWA, June 23—Out here in Okinawa where this week we won our greatest victory but paid the highest price for any island yet taken in the Pacific war the soldiers and marines who fought the action, and with whom this correspondent has talked, believe that several truths are self-evident from any reading of the eighty-two-day record of this campaign.

These, in the order of their importance, are:

(1) The war with Japan may well last for years, instead of months as some optimists hope. However soon it is won the cost in life blood and money will be high.

(2) Final victory over the Japanese can be achieved only by ground action. Large-scale bombing and fleet action unquestionably will reduce the enemy's power of resistance, they believe, but when his soldiers and sailors hole up in caves, as they did on this island, they can be flushed out and killed only by foot soldiers supported by tank and flamethrowers.

(3) There is virtually no evidence, soldiers and marines have told me, that the will to resist of the average individual Japanese soldier is weakening. The record number of prisoners taken in the final days of this campaign can be considered only a minor gain for our psychological warfare efforts when it is measured against the unabated fanaticism with which the enemy fought.

When the time factor is considered, and when it is remembered that warlike as the Nazis were when the Wehrmacht was at its peak, the German commanders when they knew they were beaten, would surrender their troops by the tens of thousands, hope for quick victory dims.

Our troops believe we need bigger tanks, sacrificing speed, if necessary, to maintain a mobile artillery or flame-throwing weapon that can bring the Japanese out of their holes or exterminate them inside their hiding places.

One Japanese word is heard again and again in the conversation of everybody who has seen frontline action here. It is the word "Kamikaze," which, translated, literally means "Divine Wind." That is the name we have given the pilots of enemy aircraft who dive their planes and bombload squarely into American naval and merchant vessels in an effort to sink or damage them. It is a tactic that has been used before but never with such frequency as at Okinawa.

No American regards it as a potential victory-producing weapon for the enemy. No country can win a war when it loses pilots and planes literally by the thousands in a vain effort to knock out the naval craft supporting and supplying a ground operation, but likewise, nobody who has been at Okinawa is inclined to write off the "Kamikaze kids" as a complete failure.

But people out here attach more importance to the Kamikaze method of attack as an illustration of the Japanese state of mind than as a weapon of destruction. Considered carefully, the fact that literally thousands of men, many of them young and in their prime, will go out alone on missions of certain death to achieve results that even at best would not be commensurate with the sacrifice, is certainly not one calculated to breed optimism.

The continuing attacks by the "suicide" planes throughout this campaign, with as many

The bodies of two Japanese marines on Tarawa in the Gilbert Islands who shot themselves in November 1943 rather than surrender.

as fifty ganging up on two destroyers which they couldn't sink, are, in the opinion of this correspondent, more demonstrative than the last-ditch fight waged by the Japanese infantrymen in the hills of southern Okinawa.

Both, in their own way, are examples of the fanaticism of the Japanese warrior and his willingness to die for little, if any, gain on behalf of his country. The pilot, after he was off the ground, knew that his next landing, if his mission was successful, would be to a death into the side of an American ship.

The infantryman on the beach always hoped that his country might, from somewhere, summon the resources to land reinforcements to turn the tide of battle against the attacking American forces.

This complete disregard of the individual for his own life, never demonstrated more vividly than at Okinawa, is the factor that must be taken into account when the case of a long versus a short war with Japan is being considered.

There is no doubt in the mind of this correspondent that our air force can bomb Japanese cities off the map. There likewise is no doubt that the small remnants of the Japanese Fleet would be easy targets for our powerful fleet and its aircraft carriers if they came within range by venturing out to fight.

It has been evident for a long time that Japan can't win the war. After our victory on Okinawa and in the Philippines, it is clear that the Japanese can't hold any of the empire they started to conquer in 1941.

The Japanese position as of today is, therefore, hopeless, and in time it certainly will be helpless.

But these conditions do not bring about the state of defeat contemplated in the "unconditional surrender" goal of the Allied nations fighting Japan.

The campaign on Okinawa, admittedly small when compared to the later actions that must be fought, was a vivid illustration of the length of time it takes to subdue a beaten enemy, and the cost that must be paid by the attacking force even after victory is assured.

The "cave warfare" in which the Japanese engaged here, is not one that holds any promise of victory, for the defender, but it is one calculated to conserve the defense force as long as possible.

When the soldier and marine here talks about potential future battlegrounds, he asks at once about the terrain.

"Are there caves?"

That is all he wants to know. He is sure there will be, judging by the terrain throughout the Japanese home islands, if those men I have talked with are representative, he thinks it will take a long time to dig all the Japanese out of their caves throughout Japan. On Okinawa there was no victory until practically all of the Japanese caves had been sealed and their occupants killed.

Soldiers and marines out here believe that the great power of the American Army and air force, released by the victory in Europe, soon will be making itself felt out here. They know that their victory on Okinawa speeded that day, for this island already is well on its way to becoming our most powerful Pacific airbase.

In debating the oft-propounded question of whether air power alone could knock out Japan, the infantrymen believe the Battle of Okinawa affords good first-hand information on this issue.

Never before in any Pacific island campaign have we had the airfields and the aircraft with which to subject the enemy's forces to a continuous heavy pounding from the air. We threw everything we had at him from the air. The assault from the air helped to soften the enemy up but it was the flame-throwing tank and the riflemen marching beside it who finally cleared out the caves.

There are too many crosses in the seven Divisional cemeteries on Okinawa for anyone to say that disposing of the Japanese is a one-handed job requiring only a 50 percent home-front effort, now that Germany is out of the way.

"Tears fall upon ragged uniforms...."

An eyewitness account of Okinawa commander Ushijima Mitsuru's suicide

Before arriving on Okinawa, Lieutenant General Ushijima participated in the 1942 invasion of Burma and commanded the Japanese military academy. As the Seventh Infantry Division closed in around his command cave on the evening of June 21, Ushijima and his chief of staff ate a lavish dinner. Then, during the early-morning hours of June 22, they put on their full field uniforms and committed ritual suicide together, as described by a Japanese eyewitness.

Alas! The stars of the generals have fallen with the setting of the waning moon....

Gathered around their chiefs, members of each section bow in veneration toward the eastern sky and the cheer of 'Long Live the Emperor' echoes among the boulders....The faces of all are flushed with deep emotion and tears fall upon ragged uniforms, soiled with the dirt and grime of battle....

Four o'clock, the final hour of *hara-kiri;* the Commanding General, dressed in full field uniform, and the Chief of Staff in a white kimono appeared....The Chief of Staff says as he leaves the cave first:

"Well, Commanding General Ushijima, as the way may be dark, I, Cho, will lead the way."

The Commanding General replies, "Please do so, and I'll take along my fan since it is getting warm." Saying this he picked up his Okinawa-made fan and walked out quietly fanning himself....

The moon, which had been shining until now, sinks below the waves of the western sea. Dawn has not yet arrived and, at 0410, the generals appeared at the mouth of the cave. The American forces were only three meters away.

A sheet of white cloth is placed on a quilt....The Commanding General and the Chief of Staff sit down on the quilt, bow in reverence to the eastern sky, and Adjutant J——— respectfully presents the sword....

At this time several grenades were hurled near this solemn scene by the enemy troops who observed movements taking place beneath them. A simultaneous shout and a flash of a sword, then another repeated shout and a flash, and both generals had nobly accomplished their last duty to their Emperor....

48.

The Potsdam Conference

July–August 1945

In mid-July 1945, President Truman traveled to the Berlin suburb of Potsdam for his first Big Three summit. Most of the items on the agenda involved finalizing the details of the German occupation. However, two other topics, left off the public agenda, had much greater political significance—the Soviet entry into the Pacific war and the Manhattan Project, which was the code name given to the secret Anglo-American effort to develop an atomic bomb.

At Yalta, President Roosevelt had made several territorial concessions to Stalin in order to win Stalin's promise that the Soviets would enter the war against Japan within three months of Germany's surrender. It was generally believed by Roosevelt's top military advisers that a Soviet declaration of war would shock the Japanese into surrender, thus avoiding the necessity of an invasion. Truman accepted this view and was therefore elated when Stalin told him on July 17, the first day of the two-week conference, that the Soviets would be declaring war on August 15. "Fini Japs when that comes about," the president wrote in his diary. However, early on July 18, Truman received a brief coded cable indicating that the July 16 atomic-bomb test at Alamogordo, New Mexico, had proven much more successful than initially imagined. This changed Truman's thinking entirely, because he now had a way to end the war quickly without Soviet involvement.

On July 26, the United States, Great Britain, and China issued (without the Soviet Union) a joint proclamation demanding Japan's immediate, unconditional surrender. Aware that the Japanese would accept only terms that guaranteed the perpetuation of the imperial dynasty, U.S. officials had included in their draft a sentence offering the possibility that Japan might be governed in the future by "a constitutional monarchy under the present dynasty." However, Truman's new secretary of state, James F. Byrnes, subsequently persuaded the president to delete this sentence. Perhaps Byrnes believed it unwise to abandon Roosevelt's "unconditional surrender" policy, or possibly he didn't want to compromise Allied postwar options. Yet, as historian John W. Dower has observed, "It is also possible—and this is the most cynical reading of the decision—that he wished to make the bomb known to the world in the most dramatic fashion and thus deliberately chose to render the warning statement unacceptable to the Japanese leadership." In fact, on July 28, Japanese prime minister Suzuki Kantaro dismissed the Potsdam Proclamation as nothing new and indicated that it would be ignored.

Truman chats privately with Secretary of State James F. Byrnes aboard the Augusta *during their voyage to Europe for the Potsdam Conference.*

GERMANY STRIPPED OF INDUSTRY BY BIG 3; 5 POWERS TO PLAN PEACE; FRANCO BARRED

No Word on Japan; Russia Gets Majority of Reparations, Sharing in Western Zones

By FELIX BELAIR JR.

WASHINGTON, Aug. 2—The broad outlines of a post-war Germany reduced to a third-rate industrial power with all its economy operating at subsistence levels, incapable of waging war and stripped of East Prussia and a large area along the Oder River, were laid down in a joint communiqué today by the Big Three, reporting on the meeting in Berlin.

Bearing the signatures of J. V. Stalin, Harry S. Truman and C. R. Attlee, the document, released simultaneously at 5:30 P.M. in Washington, London and Moscow, ended any further debate whether Germany was to have a "hard" or "soft" peace. That peace, in the language of the communiqué, will be designed "to convince the German people that they have suffered a total military defeat and that they cannot escape responsibility for what they have brought upon themselves since their own ruthless warfare and the fanatical Nazi resistance have destroyed German economy and made chaos and suffering inevitable."

The document did not mention Russia's intentions on the Pacific war but it ended on the significant note that "during the conference there were meetings between the Chiefs of Staff of the three Governments on military matters of common interest." If these "matters" went beyond European zones of occupation, the communiqué did not explain.

The conference warned the present Government of Spain that it need not apply for admission to the United Nations' organization. That Government, according to the communiqué, "having been founded with the support of the Axis powers, does not, in view of its origin, its nature, its record and its close association with the aggressor states, possess the qualifications necessary to justify such membership." But the Big Three agreed on at least temporary territorial accessions by Russia and Poland.

The conference decided to create a new Council of Foreign Ministers to succeed the European Advisory Commission. It will have headquarters in London and meet for the first time on Sept. 1. It will draw peace settlements with Germany and her satellites, including Italy, Finland, Bulgaria, Hungary and Rumania, for submission to the United Nations.

China and France were invited to adopt the text of the communiqué and to join in the establishment of the Foreign Ministers' Council, but it was stipulated here that the creation of the new Council was without prejudice to the Yalta Conference plan for periodical meetings of the Foreign Secretaries of the Big Three on questions of primary concern to themselves.

The preparation of the peace treaty with Italy was suggested as "first" among the immediate important tasks of the new council. Having rid herself of the Fascist regime, the communiqué said, Italy has made good progress toward the establishment of democratic government and institutions and the Big Three are therefore willing to support her application from Italy to join the United Nations.

The main body of the communiqué was devoted to the decisions on Germany, the political and economic principles to govern her treatment in the initial control period and a formula for German reparations based not on cash payments but on removals of capital equipment, war materials and finished products from defeated Germany.

Under the formula Russia will receive from the western zones of occupation 15 per cent of all industrial equipment removed as surplus by other Allies, in exchange for an equivalent value of food, coal, potash, zinc, timber, clay, petroleum and other products. Russia will also receive 10 per cent of such capital equipment removed from western zones without payment or exchange in return to the other occupying Allies.

Reparations to the United States and Great Britain, under the agreement, will come exclusivly from their own zones of occupation and from Germany's remaining external assets. Meanwhile, the United States and Britain renounced any claims to shares of German enterprises in the eastern zone as well as to German foreign assets in the eastern European satellite countries, while Russia renounced any claim to gold captured by the western Allies in Germany.

Leaving no doubt of their intention to control the German economy lock, stock and barrel, the Big Three said that "in organizing the German economy primary emphasis shall be given to the development of agriculture and peaceful domestic industries." They added: "At the earliest practicable date, the German economy shall be decentralized for the purpose of eliminating the present excessive concentration of economic power as exemplified in particular by cartels, syndicates, trusts and other monopolistic arrangments."

Reaffirming the political principles laid down at Yalta, the Big Three served notice that they did not intend "to destroy or enslave the German people." Rather they intended to give them an opportunity "to prepare for the eventual reconstruction of their life on a democratic and peaceful basis."

On the other hand, the Allies reiterated their determination to wipe out German militarism

During the opening session at Potsdam, Truman sits with his back to the camera, aides on either side. Stalin is seated on the right; Churchill and his staff on the left.

and Nazism without destroying or enslaving. This section set forth in detail the purposes of the occupation of Germany by which the Allied Control Council will be guided in accomplishing the destruction of the National Socialist party and its affiliates, the handling of war criminals, the control of German education, the reorganization of the judicial system and the direction of German administrative affairs.

It was decided that for the time being, at least, there would be no central German government. However, once the mechanisms of political and economic control have been applied by the control council in Berlin, their administration will be placed in German hands and German authorities will assume full responsibility for their successful operation.

Among the measures to be taken promptly the agreement listed the essential repair of transport, the expansion of coal production, maximizing agricultural output and the emergancy repair of housing and essential utilities. To safeguard against German external assets slipping through the hands of the Control

Council through pre-armistice investment or transfer to Argentina, Switzerland or other neutral countries, that body was empowered to control and dispose of external assets not already under control of the United Nations "which have taken part in the war against Germany."

Several important political decisions, including the ultimate disposition of former Italian territory and the final decision on the Polish boundary question, were left to be decided at the forthcoming peace settlement. One of these was a Russian proposal that the Soviet Union's western frontier, adjacent to the Baltic Sea, should pass from a point on the eastern shore of the Bay of Danzig to the east, north of Braunsberg-Goldap, to the meeting point of the frontiers of Lithuania, Poland and East Prussia.

Agreement in principle was reached on the transfer of the city of Koenigsberg and the area adjacent to it to Russsia, subject to expert examination of the actual frontier. Both President Truman and Prime Minister Attlee agreed to support the Russian proposal at the peace conference.

The three powers put off a Russian proposal that the Austrian Provisional Government's authority be extended to all Austria. It was agreed to postpone consideration of this plan until British and American troops had entered Vienna.

Pending a final determination of Poland's western frontier at the peace settlement, it was agreed that Poland should take over the Free City of Danzig and the former German territories east of a line running from the Baltic Sea immediately west of Swinemuende, along the Oder River to the confluence of the western Neisse River and along the western Neisse to the Czechoslovak frontier, including the portion of east Prussia not placed under Russian administration.

In an apparent concession to the Western powers and to assure the holding of free elections under universal suffrage and a secret ballot in Poland, it was agreed that "the Allied press shall enjoy full freedom to report to the world upon developments in Poland before and during the elections." A similar stipulation was put into the provisions for the admission of Finland, Bulgaria, Rumania and Hungary to the United Nations and the three powers expressed confidence that "representatives of the Allied press will enjoy full freedom to report to the world upon developments" in these countries.

The eventual transfer of Germans from Poland, Czechoslovakia and Hungary was a matter that the Big Three said, "will have to be undertaken" but in an orderly and humane manner. Since an influx of a large number of Germans would increase the occupying authorities' burden, the Control Council was directed to examine the problem to learn how many Germans had already been repatriated and to recommend a time and rate at which further transfers might be carried out.

"I can deal with Stalin. He is honest, but smart as hell."

Entries from Harry Truman's Potsdam diary

Truman's handwritten diary of the Potsdam Conference—containing his most intimate, unmediated thoughts—languished in an archive for more than three decades until it was rediscovered by scholars in 1979.

July 17, 1945

Just spent a couple of hours with Stalin. Joe Davies called on Maisky and made the date last night for noon today. Promptly at a few minutes before twelve I looked up from my desk and there stood Stalin in the doorway. I got to my feet and advanced to meet him. He put out his hand and smiled. I did the same, we shook, I greeted Molotov and the interpreter and we sat down.

After the usual polite remarks we got down to business. I told Stalin that I am no diplomat but usually said yes and no to questions after hearing all the argument. It pleased him. I asked him if he had the agenda for the meeting. He said he had and that he had some more questions to present. I told him to fire away. He did and it is dynamite—but I have some dynamite too which I am not exploding now. He wants to fire Franco, to which I wouldn't object and divide up the Italian colonies and other mandates, some no doubt that the British have. Then he got on the Chinese situation told us what agreements had been reached and what was in abeyance. Most of the big points are settled. He'll be in the Jap war on August 15. Fini Japs when that comes about.

We had lunch, talked socially, put on a real show, drinking toasts to everyone. Then had pictures made in the backyard.

I can deal with Stalin. He is honest, but smart as hell.

July 18, 1945

Ate breakfast with nephew Harry, a sergeant in the field artillery. He is a good soldier and a nice boy. They took him off *Queen Elizabeth* at Glasgow and flew him here. Sending him home Friday. Went to lunch with P.M. at 1:30, walked around to British headquarters. Met at the gate by Mr. Churchill. Guards of honor drawn up. Fine body of men—Scottish Guards. Band played "Star-Spangled Banner." Inspected guard and went in for lunch. P.M. and I ate alone. Discussed Manhattan (it is a success). Decided to tell Stalin about it. Stalin had told P.M. of telegram from Jap emperor asking for peace. Stalin also read his answer to me. It was satisfactory. Believe Japs will fold up before Russia comes in. I am sure they will when Manhattan appears over their homeland. I shall inform Stalin about it at an opportune time.

Stalin's luncheon was a most satisfactory meeting. I invited him to come to the U.S. Told him I'd send the battleship Missouri for him if he'd come. He said he wanted to cooperate with the U.S. in peace as we had cooperated in war, but it would be harder. Said he was grossly misunderstood in the U.S. and I was misunderstood in Russia. I told him that we each could help to remedy that situation in our home countries and that I intended to with all I had to do my part at home. He gave me a most cordial smile and said he would do as much in Russia.

We then went to the conference and it was my job to present the ministers' proposed agenda. There were three proposals, and I banged them through in short order, much to the surprise of Mr. Churchill. Stalin was very much pleased. Churchill was too, after he had recovered. I'm not going to stay around this terrible place all summer just to listen to speeches. I'll go home to the senate for that.

July 25, 1945

We met at 11:00 A.M. today. That is, Stalin, Churchill and the U.S. president. But I had a most important session with Lord Mountbatten and General Marshall before that. We have discovered the most terrible bomb in the history of the world. It may be the fire destruction prophesied in the Euphrates Valley era, after Noah and his fabulous ark. Anyway, we think we have found the way to cause a disintegration of the atom. An experiment in the New Mexico desert was startling—to put it mildly. Thirteen pounds of the explosive caused a crater six feet deep and twelve hundred feet in diameter, knocked over a steel tower a half mile away, and knocked men down ten thousand yards away. The explosion was visible for more than two hundred miles and audible for forty miles and more.

This weapon is to be used against Japan between now and August 10. I have told the secretary of war, Mr. Stimson, to use it so that military objectives and soldiers and sailors are the target and not women and children. Even if Japs are savages, ruthless, merciless and fanatic, we as the leader of the world for the common welfare cannot drop this terrible bomb on the old capital or the new. He and I are in accord. The target will be a purely military one and we will issue a warning statement asking the Japs to surrender and save lives. I'm sure they will not do that, but we will have given them the chance. It is certainly a good thing for the world that Hitler's crowd or Stalin's did not discover this atomic bomb. It seems to be the most terrible thing ever discovered, but it can be made the most useful.

49.

Churchill Leaves Office

July 1945

Halfway through the Potsdam Conference, Churchill returned home to London to await the results of the July 5 general election, the first held in Britain since the formation of the current union government in May 1940. As head of the Conservative party, he was opposed by Labor leader Clement R. Attlee, who had taken control of Labor in 1935 after the previous leader was forced to step down because of his

uncompromising pacifism. Although Attlee refused to enter Neville Chamberlain's government when war broke out in 1939, he did agree to join Churchill's cabinet after Chamberlain's ouster. Serving first as lord privy seal (1940–1942) and then as deputy prime minister (1942–1945), Attlee supported Churchill loyally throughout the war, yet in May 1945, following the defeat of Nazi Germany, he nevertheless pulled his party out of the governing coalition and called for new, contested elections.

During the campaign that followed, the Conservatives praised Britain's wartime success and tried to tar the Labor leadership as dangerously socialist. Meanwhile, Attlee spoke of the future, emphasizing the need for social as well as national security. And while Labor had a comprehensive plan for the reconstruction of the British economy (through the nationalization of key industries) and the transformation of its crumbling empire (by granting colonial independence), the Conservatives had none. In fact, their leaders, as well as their ideas, seemed exhausted.

Churchill bitterly resented being forced to contest a general election so soon after V-E Day, believing that Attlee could at least have waited for the defeat of Japan. Not that Churchill was terribly worried about losing the election: Most pundits agreed that the prime minister's heroic status as wartime leader would make his party unbeatable. Yet, on the campaign trail, Churchill turned out to be his own worst enemy. His extravagant, inflated rhetoric concerning the disasters that would surely befall the country should Labor win the election turned off many voters and made his own more reasonable policies seem too closely identified with unpopular Conservative orthodoxy. Enormous crowds cheered his every appearance, supporting the conventional wisdom of a Conservative sweep, yet the applause was for the war leader, not the party chief. In the end, the Conservatives won 213 of the 640 seats in Parliament—180 fewer than Labor—and it was Attlee, not Churchill, who returned to the British seat of power at Potsdam.

BRITISH VOTE REFLECTS DEEP-SEATED FORCES

Labor's Victory Seemingly Indicates Desire for Clean Break With Past

By CLIFTON DANIEL

LONDON, July 28—British voters had a choice between Churchill and change. When the ballot boxes were opened this week they had chosen change and Britain had joined the European swing to the Left. Britain had been in the swing all along, but during ten years without a general election no one had been able to gauge the extent of the fact.

If Americans now wish to understand why the British people with seeming ingratitude turned Winston Churchill out of office, they must first appreciate the depth of the yearning here for a change in the conception, functions and performance of government. That urge overrode all other considerations.

To its own undoing the Conservative party underestimated the popular impulse. Beguiled by the personality of Mr. Churchill and deceived by the outward apathy of the voters, disinterested observers, including this writer, failed to perceive the irresistibility of that impulse in the English people.

But it is now apparent that by installing a Labor Government at Westminster the British people intended to make a clean break with the past—the past of unemployment and doles, the past of appeasement and unpreparedness, the past of war and suffering, the past of unfulfilled promises and national frustration.

Whatever they may have gained or failed to gain by their votes, it is plain most of the British people were seeking somehow a guarantee for the future, a guarantee for the fulfillment of post-war hopes and schemes that have no relation to the muddling uncertainty that characterized years between the wars.

There is no question of the new Attlee Government's repudiating any of the broad international agreements undertaken by Britain in the five war years under Mr. Churchill, for the leaders of the Labor party participated in them all, as they have participated in the San Francisco and Potsdam conferences.

The victorious Labor party, which its opponents try to stigmatize with the label of "socialist," is by no means a party of working-class revolution. Its domestic and foreign policies are not so alien to the modern British mind as the Conservatives would have had the voters believe.

But the British vote for Labor does represent a profound and fundamental change in political trends. For the ballots cast have turned out of office not only a party but a class.

A confirmed but candid Conservative, who learned that one of his rich friends was voting against the party, remarked, "The Conservative party is the party of privilege. If in your position you don't believe in privilege, what do you believe in?"

Whatever its aims and accomplishments, the Conservative party was certainly regarded as a natural ally by those who enjoyed or sought special privilege.

While there are renegades and "class traitors" in both parties, it is broadly true that the Conservative party speaks with the accent of Eton and Oxford while Labor speaks the tongue of the people. Notwithstanding—or perhaps because of—that fact, the Conservative party drew its mass strength, year after year, not from the upper class but from the great aspiring British middle class.

It was a revolt of the middle class led by servicemen and millions of first voters that put Clement R. Attlee into 10 Downing Street this week. Britain has had Labor party governments before, but none with such a majority as this.

In 1923 Labor gained power with 191 seats in Parliament and an uneasy coalition with the Liberals, who in this election have been all but extinguished and left with only eleven seats in Parliament.

In 1929 Labor held 288 seats, twenty-eight more than the Conservatives. This time the Labor party holds 390 seats in the House of Commons and an undisputed majority.

For the first time Labor has a plain mandate from the people, directly backed by nearly 12,000,000 of them out of a voting population of some 25,000,000. It is a national mandate, not a mandate only from the workers as represented by the trade unions or the Socialist intellectuals, but from the electorate.

In his first campaign broadcast Mr. Churchill stated that the basic issue was "Socialism versus the rest." If his analysis was correct, it can only be concluded that the Labor party has now received a commission to introduce socialism here and now—at least that degree of socialism put forward in its platforms for the past half century.

It is fair to say that even the leaders of the Labor party did not expect to have this opportunity so soon and in such full measure. Probably the voters themselves did not expect so.

This is Labor's great chance, as Herbert Morrison, the new leader of the House of Commons, remarked on Thursday night. If the job is well done, he said Labor may stay in office for two decades or more. It probably would take that long to do all that the party proposes.

"There is no reason, however, why the world should look for any revolutionary change in foreign—or indeed—domestic policy," The Times of London said Friday morning. "No violent

Churchill, Truman, and Stalin pose for photographers in the garden of the Cecilienhof Palace during the Potsdam Conference.

reversal," was the way The Times expressed it.

From afar and indeed near by, there seems to be no radical difference betwen the programs of the two main parties except on the issue of nationalization. After all, the two parties were associated with each other in the Government for five war years, and some of the most controversial of the reconstruction projects now outstanding were jointly contrived during that period.

Labor has proposed to socialize such public utilities and basic industries as iron and steel, fuel, power, transport and banking. The party unquestionably intends to proceed with those projects.

By reason of its comfortable parliamentary margin of some 200 votes (the exact number depends on the support it gets from smaller parties and independents) the Labor Government has a guarantee of a full five years in which to accomplish its basic reforms.

It is in the spirit and personnel of its administration and not the outward aspects of written policy, however, that the Labor Government is likely to differ most from its predecessors. To the world beyond Britain's shores the most startling immediate change in the Government was the overnight disappearance of the towering personality of Winston Churchill from the world scene.

It is surely without precedent in history that a great and victorious leader should be removed from office on the morrow of victory and in the midst of a critical conference of the triumphant powers. A game of musical chairs is being played at Potsdam with Mr. Attlee and his Foreign Secretary, Ernest Bevin, moving into the seats occupied until Wednesday by Mr. Churchill and Anthony Eden.

Mr. Churchill had not excluded that possibility, however, as shown by the fact that he took Mr. Attlee with him to Potsdam in the first place. Mr. Attlee now returns to Potsdam with an assurance of authority that even Mr. Churchill did not possess—the recorded backing of the nation's electorate.

Still, no one can doubt that the greatest regret of the electorate this week—and of many Labor leaders as well—was to lose the high talents of Winston Churchill as Minister of Defense and Anthony Eden as Foreign Secretary. But it could not be helped.

Having made himself the main issue of the election Mr. Churchill had to accept the full consequences of the voters' decision. As The Daily Herald said, they cheered Churchill and voted Labor, grateful for his war leadership but not grateful enough to return his unpopular party to power.

Although Churchill the war leader left office with Churchill the politician, it was he, himself, who was the first to say that plans for finishing the Japanese war, perhaps quicker than expected, had already been made.

Nobody here seems to have given the Pacific a second thought, its victorious conclusion being assumed. As in the election, domestic issues are still foremost.

Although Labor's Ministers are experienced and their policy has electoral endorsement, the Conservative Daily Telegraph remarked that "Socialists in office will find it no easier than it was for the coalition Government to satisfy the critics."

"The people will be no more tolerant of a Labor Government which does not fully and effectively mobilize national resources to provide homes, jobs and security than it would be of an incompetent Conservative administration," the paper added.

As for foreign affairs it was Mr. Bevin, the new Foreign Secretary, who said some weeks ago that "revolutions do not change geography." What he was saying was that the fundamental objectives of British foreign policy are not altered by a Labor victory. Only the methods of achieving them may be different.

As in domestic policy, Labor has the same broad aims as the Conservatives—solidarity with the Soviet Union and United States, a workable world order for the prevention of war, a world economic policy to raise the standards of living everywhere, and above all security for Britain.

Broadly speaking the Labor party feels that it can achieve a warmer rapprochement than the Conservatives with the left-wing governments of post-war Europe.

Supporters of the new Government believe that Labor's victory will bring hope to the common man everywhere and overdue discouragement to what Professor Harold Laski, chairman of the Labor party, called "decaying monarchs of obsolete social systems." In its specific application this policy awaits the definition of time and experience.

"Socialist policy is abhorrent to the British ideas of freedom."

Winston Churchill's defense of Conservative party rule

The heart of the 1945 British election campaign was a series of party political broadcasts made in the evening on radio. On average, an estimated 45 percent of the adult population tuned in. This broadcast, Churchill's first, was aired on June 4.

My friends, I must tell you that a Socialist policy is abhorrent to the British ideas of freedom. Although it is now put forward in the main by people who have a good grounding in the Liberalism and Radicalism of the early part of this century, there can be no doubt that Socialism is inseparably interwoven with Totalitarianism and the abject worship of the State. It is not alone that property, in all its forms, is struck at, but that liberty, in all its forms, is challenged by the fundamental conceptions of Socialism.

Look how even today they hunger for controls of every kind, as if these were delectable foods instead of wartime inflictions and monstrosities. There is to be one State to which all are to be obedient in every act of their lives. This State is to be the arch-employer, the arch-planner, the arch-administrator and ruler, and the arch–caucus boss.

How is an ordinary citizen or subject of the King to stand up against this formidable machine, which, once it is in power, will prescribe for every one of them where they are to work, what they are to work at, where they may go and what they may say, what views they are to hold and within what limits they may express them, where their wives are to go to queue up for the State ration, and what education their children are to receive to mould their views of human liberty and conduct in the future?

A Socialist State once thoroughly completed in all its details and its aspects—and that is what I am speaking of—could not afford to suffer opposition. Here in old England, in Great Britain, of which old England forms no inconspicuous part, in this glorious island, the cradle and citadel of free democracy throughout the world, we do not like to be regimented and ordered about and have every action of our lives prescribed for us. In fact, we punish criminals by sending them to Wormwood Scrubs and Dartmoor, where they get full employment and whatever board and lodging is appointed by the Home Secretary.

Socialism is, in its essence, an attack not only upon British enterprise but upon the right of the ordinary man or woman to breathe freely without having a harsh, clumsy, tyrannical hand clapped across their mouths and nostrils. A Free Parliament—look at that—a Free Parliament is odious to the Socialist doctrinaire. Have we not heard Mr. Herbert Morrison descant upon his plans to curtail Parliamentary procedure and pass laws simply by resolutions of broad principle in the House of Commons, afterwards to be left by Parliament to the executive and to the bureaucrats to elaborate and enforce by departmental regulations? As for Sir Stafford Cripps on "Parliament in the Socialist State," I have not time to read you what he said, but perhaps it will meet the public eye during the election campaign.

But I will go farther. I declare to you, from the bottom of my heart, that no Socialist system can be established without a political police. Many of those who are advocating Socialism or voting Socialist today will be horrified at this idea. That is because they are shortsighted; that is because they do not see where their theories are leading them.

No Socialist Government conducting the entire life and industry of the country could afford to allow free, sharp, or violently worded expressions of public discontent. They would have to fall back on some form of Gestapo, no doubt very humanely directed in the first instance. And this would nip in the bud opinion and its forms; it would stop criticism as it reared its head, and it would gather all the power to the supreme party and the party leaders, rising like stately pinnacles above their vast bureaucracies of civil servants, no longer servants and no longer civil. And where would the ordinary simple folk—the common people, as they like to call them in America—where would they be, once this mighty organism had got them in its grip?

I stand for the sovereign freedom of the individual within the laws which freely elected Parliaments have freely passed. I stand for the rights of the ordinary man to say what he thinks of the Government of the day, however powerful, and to turn them out, neck and crop, if he thinks he can better his temper or his home thereby, and if he can persuade enough others to vote with him.

But, you will say, look at what has been done in the war. Have not many of those evils which you have depicted been the constant companions of our daily life? It is quite true that the horrors of war do not end with the fighting line. They spread far away to the base and the homeland, and everywhere people give up their rights and liberties for the common cause. But this is because the life of their country is in mortal peril or for the sake of the cause of freedom in some other land. They give them freely as a sacrifice. It is quite true that the conditions of Socialism play a great part in wartime. We all submit to being ordered about to save our country. But when the war is over and the imminent danger to our existence is removed, we cast off these shackles and burdens which we imposed upon ourselves in times of dire and mortal peril and quit the gloomy caverns of war and march out into the breezy fields, where the sun is shining and where all may walk joyfully in its warm and golden rays.

50.

Hiroshima

August 1945

By July 31, 1945, the day that President Truman gave the final go-ahead for the dropping of the atomic bomb on Hiroshima, whatever qualms most American leaders may have had about the morality of the bomb's use had largely disappeared. The firebombings of Dresden and Tokyo, for instance, had already demonstrated the willingness of the Allies to use weapons of mass destruction against civilian targets,

if such use might produce a shorter war. Truman was especially interested in shortening the Pacific war because of the high death toll that any invasion of Japan would surely exact. During an important June 18 planning session with the Joint Chiefs of Staff, Truman repeatedly pressed for casualty estimates for Olympic, the invasion of Kyushu planned for November 1945, and Coronet, the invasion of Japan's main island, Honshu, scheduled for March 1946. The responses he received were mostly vague, but Admiral Leahy did point out that, if Okinawa's 35 percent casualty rate were extrapolated, the 766,000-man Olympic invasion force would suffer 268,000 casualties—an unacceptable number in Truman's judgment.

Even worse, most of the joint chiefs acknowledged that the Japanese would likely fight even harder to defend their homeland than they had fought in the Ryukyus. There were still two million Japanese under arms and another four million reservists who could be called up. The number of American fatalities necessary to subdue these men would no doubt reach into the

hundreds of thousands. The president thus had two options: revise the Allies' demand for an unconditional surrender or use the atomic bomb.

The target chosen for the first bomb was one of several Japanese cities intentionally spared the devastation of LeMay's incendiary attacks so that the bomb's immense destructive power could be demonstrated against a relatively unscathed urban landscape. Although Truman had, in his July 25 Potsdam diary entry, written that "military objective and soldiers and sailors are the target and not women and children," this was a comforting rationalization on his part. On May 31, the top-secret Interim Committee, charged with creating atomic policy, had already advised the president that "the most desirable target would be a vital war plant employing a large number of workers and closely surrounded by workers' houses." An isolated military target was specifically rejected because one of the primary U.S. goals was to "make a profound psychological impression on as many inhabitants as possible." Truman had accepted this recommendation, and Hiroshima was, in fact, just such a place.

FIRST ATOMIC BOMB DROPPED ON JAPAN; MISSILE IS EQUAL TO 20,000 TONS OF TNT; TRUMAN WARNS FOE OF A 'RAIN OF RUIN'

New Age Ushered; Day of Atomic Energy Hailed by President, Revealing Weapon

By SIDNEY SHALETT

WASHINGTON, Aug. 6—The White House and War Department announced today that an atomic bomb, possessing more power than 20,000 tons of TNT, a destructive force equal to the load of 2,000 B-29's and more than 2,000 times the blast power of what previously was the world's most devastating bomb, had been dropped on Japan.

The announcement, first given to the world in utmost solemnity by President Truman, made it plain that one of the scientific landmarks of the century had been passed, and that the "age of atomic energy," which can be a tremendous force for the advancement of civilization as well as for destruction, was at hand.

At 10:45 o'clock this morning, a statement by the President was issued at the White House that sixteen hours earlier—about the time that citizens on the Eastern seaboard were sitting down to their Sunday suppers—an American plane had dropped the single atomic bomb on the Japanese city of Hiroshima, an important army center.

What happened at Hiroshima is not yet known. The War Department said it "as yet was unable to make an accurate report" because "an impenetrable cloud of dust and smoke" masked the target area from reconnaissance planes. The Secretary of War will release the story "a soon as accurate details of the results of the bombing become available."

But in a statement vividly describing the results of the first test of the atomic bomb in New Mexico, the War Department told how an immense steel tower had been "vaporized" by the tremendous explosion, how a 40,000-foot cloud rushed into the sky, and two observers were knocked down at a point 10,000 yards away. And President Truman solemnly warned:

"It was to spare the Japanese people from utter destruction that the ultimatum of July 26 was issued at Postdam. Their leaders promptly rejected that ultimatum. If they do not now accept our terms, they may expect a rain of ruin from the air the like of which has never been seen on this earth."

The President referred to the joint statement issued by the heads of the American, British and Chinese Governments, in which terms of surrender were outlined to the Japanese and warning given that rejection would mean complete destruction of Japan's power to make war.

[The atomic bomb weighs about 400 pounds and is capable of utterly destroying a town, a representative of the British Ministry of Aircraft Production said in London, The United Press reported.]

What is this terrible new weapon, which the War Department also calls the "Cosmic Bomb"? It is the harnessing of the energy of the atom, which is the basic power of the universe. As President Truman said, "The force from which the sun draws its power has been loosed against those who brought war to the Far East."

A Japanese soldier walks in September 1945 through an area of Hiroshima leveled by the atomic bomb.

"Atomic fission"—in other words, the scientists' long-held dream of splitting the atom—is the secret of the atomic bomb. Uranium, a rare, heavy metallic element, which is radioactive and akin to radium, is the source essential to its production. Secretary of War Henry L. Stimson, in a statement closely following that of the president, promised that "steps have been taken, and continue to be taken, to assure us of adequate supplies of this mineral."

The imagination-sweeping experiment in harnessing the power of the atom has been the most closely guarded secret of the war. America to date has spent nearly $2,000,000,000 in advancing its research. Since 1939, American, British and Canadian scientists have worked on it. The experiments have been conducted in the United States, both for reasons of achieving concentrated efficiency and for security; the consequences of having the material fall into the hands of the enemy, in case Great Britain should have been successfully invaded, were too awful for the Allies to risk.

All along, it has been a race with the enemy. Ironically enough, Germany started the experiments, but we finished them. Germany made the mistake of expelling, because she was a "non-Aryan," a woman scientist who held one of the keys to the mystery, and she made her knowledge available to those who brought it to the United States. Germany never quite mastered the riddle, and the United States, Secretary Stimson declared, is "convinced that Japan will not be in a position to use an atomic bomb in this war."

Not the slightest spirit of braggadocio is discernable either in the wording of the official announcements or in the mien of the officials who gave out the news. There was an element of elation in the realization that we had perfected this devastating weapon for employment against an enemy who started the war and has told us she would rather be destroyed than surrender, but it was grim elation. There was sobering awareness of the tremendous responsibility involved.

Secretary Stimson said that this new weapon "should prove a tremendous aid in the shortening of the war against Japan," and there were other responsible officials who privately thought that this was an extreme understatement, and that Japan might find herself unable to stay in the war under the coming rain of atom bombs.

It was obvious that officials at the highest levels made the important decision to release news of the atomic bomb because of the psychological effect it may have in forcing Japan to surrender. However, there are some officials who feel privately it might have been well to keep this completely secret. Their opinion can be summed up in the comment by one spokesman: "Why bother with psychological warfare against an enemy that already is beaten and hasn't sense enough to quit and save herself from utter doom?"

The first news came from President Truman's office. Newsmen were summoned and the historic statement from the Chief Executive, who still is on the high seas, was given to them.

"That bomb," Mr. Truman said, "had more power than 20,000 tons of TNT. It had more than 2,000 times the blast power of the British 'Grand Slam,' which is the largest bomb (22,000 pounds) ever yet used in the history of warfare."

No details were given on the plane that carried the bomb. Nor was it stated whether the bomb was large or small. The president, however, said the explosive charge was "exceedingly small." It is known that tremendous force is packed into tiny quantities of the element that constitutes these bombs. Scientists, looking to the peacetime uses of atomic power, envisage submarines, ocean liners and planes traveling around the world on a few pounds of the element. Yet, for various reasons, the bomb used against Japan could have been extremely large.

Hiroshima, first city on earth to be the target of the "Cosmic Bomb," is a city of 318,000, which is—or was—a major quartermaster depot and port of embarkation for the Japanese. In addition to large military supply depots, it manufactured ordnance, mainly large guns and tanks, and machine tools and aircraft-ordnance parts.

President Truman grimly told the Japanese that "the end is not yet."

"In their own present form these bombs are now in production," he said, "and even more powerful forms are in development."

He sketched the story of how the late President Roosevelt and Prime Minister Churchill agreed that it was wise to concentrate research in America, and how great, secret cities sprang up in this country, where, at one time, 125,000 men and women labored to harness the atom. Even today more than 65,000 workers are employed.

"What has been done," he said "is the greatest achievement of organized science in history.

"We are now prepared to obliterate more rapidly and completely every productive enterprise the Japanese have above ground in any city. We shall destroy their docks, their factories and their communications. Let there be no mistake; we shall completely destroy Japan's power to make war."

The President emphasized that the atomic discoveries were so important, both for the war and for the peace, that he would recommend to Congress that it consider promptly establishing "an appropriate commission to control the production and use of atomic power within the United States."

"I shall give further consideration and make further recomendations to the Congress as to how atomic power can become a powerful and forceful influence toward the maintenance of world peace," he said.

Secretary Stimson called the atomic bomb "the culmination of years of herculean effort on the part of science and industry, working in cooperation with the military authorities." He promised that "improvements will be forthcoming shortly which will increase by several fold the present effectiveness."

"But more important for the long-range implications of this new weapon," he said, "is the possibility that another scale of magnitude will be developed after considerable research and development. The scientists are confident that over a period of many years atomic bombs may well be developed which will be very much more powerful than the atomic bombs now at hand."

It was late in 1939 that President Roosevelt appointed a commisssion to investigate use of atomic energy for military purposes. Until then only small-scale research with Navy funds had taken place. The program went into high gear.

By the end of 1941 the projecct was put under direction of a group of eminent American scientists in the Office of Scientific Research and Development, under Dr. Vannevar Bush, who reported directly to Mr. Roosevelt. The President also appointed a General Policy Group, consisting of former Vice President Henry A. Wallace, Secretary Stimson, Gen. George C. Marshall, Dr. James B. Conant, president of Harvard, and Dr. Bush. In June, 1942, this group recommended vast expansion of the work and transfer of the major part of the program to the War Department.

Maj. Gen. Leslie R. Groves, a native of Albany, N. Y., and a 48-year-old graduate of the 1918 class at West Point, was appointed by Mr. Stimson to take complete executive charge of the program. General Groves, an engineer, holding the permanent Army rank of lieutenant colonel, received the highest praise from the War Department for the way he "fitted together the multifarious pieces of the vast country-wide jigsaw," and, at the same time, organized the virtually air-tight security system that kept the project a secret.

A military policy committee also was appointed, consisting of Dr. Bush, chairman; Dr. Conant, Lieut. Gen. Wilhelm D. Styer and Rear Admiral William R. Purnell.

In December, 1942, the decision was made to proceed with construction of large-scale plants. Two are situated at the Clinton Engineer Works in Tennessee and a third at the Hanford Engineer Works in the State of Washington.

These plants were amazing phenomena in themselves. They grew into large, self-sustaining cities, employing thousands upon thousands of workers. Yet, so close was the secrecy that not only were the citizens of the area kept in darkness about the nature of the project, but the workers themselves had only the sketchiest ideas—if any—as to what they were doing. This was accomplished, Mr. Stimson said, by "compartmentalizing" the work so "that no one has been given more information than was absolutely necessary to his particular job."

The Tennessee reservation consists of 59,000 acres, eighteen miles west of Knoxville; it is known as Oak Ridge and has become a modern small city of 78,000, fifth largest in Tennessee.

In the state of Washington the Government has 430,000 acres in an isolated area, fifteen miles northwest of Pasco. The settlement there, which now has a population of 17,000, consisting of plant operators and their immediate families, is known as Richland.

A special laboratory also has been set up near Santa Fe, N. M., under dirction of Dr. J. Robert Oppenheimer of the University of California. Dr. Oppenheimer also supervised the first test of the atomic bomb on July 16, 1945. This took place in a remote section of the New Mexico desert lands, with a group of eminent scientists gathered, frankly fearful to witness the results of the invention, which might turn out to be either the salvation or the Frankenstein's monster of the world.

Mr. Stimson also gave full credit to the many industrial corporations and educational institutions which worked with the War Department in bringing this titanic undertaking to fruition.

In August, 1943, a combined policy committee was appointed, consisting of Secretary Stimson, Drs. Bush and Conant for the United States;

The atomic explosion at Hiroshima photographed at ground level by a cameraman in Kure.

the late Field Marshal Sir John Dill (now replaced by Field Marshall Sir Henry Maitland Wilson) and Col. J. J. Llewellin (since replaced by Sir Ronald Campbell) for the United Kingdom, and C. D. Howe for Canada.

"Atomic fission holds great promise for sweeping developments by which our civilization may be enriched when peace comes, but the overriding necessities of war have precluded the full exploration of peacetime applications of this new knowledge," Mr. Stimson said. "However, it appears inevitable that many useful contributions to the well-being of mankind will ultimately flow from these discoveries when the world situation makes it possible for science and industry to concentrate on these aspects."

Although warning that many economic factors will have to be considered "before we can say to what extent atomic energy will supplement coal, oil and water as fundamental sources of power," Mr. Stimson acknowleged that "we are at the threshold of a new industrial art which will take many years and much expenditure of money to develop."

The Secretary of War disclosed that he had appointed an interim committee to study post-war control and development of atomic energy. Mr. Stimson is serving as chairman, and other members include James F. Byrnes, Secretary of State; Ralph A. Bard, former Under-Secretary of the Navy; William L. Clayton, Assistant Secretary of State; Dr. Bush, Dr. Conant, Dr. Carl T. Compton, chief of the Office of Field Service in OSRD and president of Massachusetts Institue of Technology, and George L. Harrison, special consultant to the Secretary of War and president of the New York Life Insurance Company. Mr. Harrison is alternate chairman of the committee.

The committee also has the assistance of an advisory group of some of the country's leading physicists, including Dr. Oppenheimer, Dr. E. O. Lawrence, Dr. A. H. Compton and Dr. Enrico Fermi.

The War Department gave this supplementary background on the devlopment of the atomic bomb:

"The series of discoveries which led to development of the atomic bomb started at the turn of the century when radioactivity became known to science. Prior to 1939 the scientific work in this field was world-wide, but more particularly so in the United States, the United Kingdom, Germany, France, Italy and Denmark. One of Denmark's great scientists, Dr. Niels Bohr, a Nobel Prize winner, was whisked from the grasp of the Nazis in his occupied homeland and later assisted in developing the atomic bomb.

"It is known that Germany worked desperately to solve the problem of controlling atomic energy."

"We were reaching into the unknown."

Leslie R. Groves's July 18, 1945, report on the Trinity test

The first word of the July 16 atomic-bomb test to reach Truman at Potsdam arrived that evening but indicated only that the bomb had detonated successfully. It wasn't until five days later that the president received a full, detailed accounting of the test, code-named Trinity, in this vivid report prepared by General Groves.

Memorandum for the Secretary of War
Subject: The Test.

1. This is not a concise, formal military report but an attempt to recite what I would have told you if you had been here on my return from New Mexico.

2. At 0530, 16 July 1945, in a remote section of the Alamogordo Air Base, New Mexico, the first full scale test was made of the implosion type atomic fission bomb. For the first time in history there was a nuclear explosion. <u>And what an explosion!</u> The bomb was not dropped from an airplane but was exploded on a platform on top of a 100-foot high steel tower.

3. The test was successful beyond the most optimistic expectations of anyone. Based on the data which it has been possible to work up to date, I estimate the energy generated to be in excess of the equivalent of 15,000 to 20,000 tons of TNT; and this is a conservative estimate. Data based on measurements which we have not yet been able to reconcile would make the energy release several times the conservative figure. There were tremendous blast effects. For a brief period there was a lighting effect within a radius of 20 miles equal to several suns in midday; a huge ball of fire was formed which lasted for several seconds. This ball mushroomed and rose to a height of over ten thousand feet before it dimmed. The light from the explosion was seen clearly at Albuquerque, Santa Fe, Silver City, El Paso and other points generally to about 180 miles away. The sound was heard to the same distance in a few instances but generally to about 100 miles. Only a few windows were broken although one was some 125 miles away. A massive cloud was formed which surged and billowed upward with tremendous power, reaching the substratosphere at an elevation of 41,000 feet, 36,000 feet above the ground, in about five minutes, breaking without interruption through a temperature inversion at 17,000 feet which most of the scientists thought would stop it. Two supplementary explosions occurred in the cloud shortly after the main explosion. The cloud contained several thousand tons of dust picked up from the ground and a considerable amount of iron in the gaseous form. Our present thought is that this iron ignited when it mixed with the oxygen in the air to cause these supplementary explosions. Huge concentrations of highly radioactive materials resulted from the fission and were contained in this cloud.

4. A crater from which all vegetation had vanished, with a diameter of 1200 feet and a slight slope toward the center, was formed. In the center was a shallow bowl 130 feet in diameter and 6 feet in depth. The material within the crater was deeply pulverized dirt. The material within the outer circle is greenish and can be distinctly seen from as much as 5 miles away. The steel from the tower was evaporated. 1500 feet away there was a four-inch iron pipe 16 feet high set in concrete and strongly guyed. It disappeared completely.

5. One-half mile from the explosion there was a massive steel test cylinder weighing 220 tons. The base of the cylinder was solidly encased in concrete. Surrounding the cylinder was a strong steel tower 70 feet high, firmly anchored to concrete foundations. This tower is comparable to a steel building bay that would be found in typical 15 or 20 story skyscraper or in warehouse construction. Forty tons of steel were used to fabricate the tower which was 70 feet high, the height of a six story building. The cross bracing was much stronger than that normally used in ordinary steel construction. The absence of the solid walls of a building gave the blast a much less effective surface to push against. The blast tore the tower from its foundation, twisted it, ripped it apart and left it flat on the ground. The effects on the tower indicate that, at that distance, unshielded permanent steel and masonry buildings would have been destroyed. I no longer consider the Pentagon a sage shelter from such a bomb. Enclosed are a sketch showing the tower before the explosion and a telephotograph showing what it looked like afterwards. None of us had expected it to be damaged.

6. The cloud traveled to a great height first in the form of a ball, then mushroomed, then changed into a long trailing chimney-shaped column and finally was sent in several directions by the variable winds at the different elevations. It deposited its dust and radioactive materials over a wide area. It was followed and monitored by medical doctors and scientists with instruments to check its radioactive effects. While here and there the activity on the ground was fairly high, at no place did it reach a concentration which required evacuation of the population. Radioactive material in small quantities was located as much as 120 miles away. The measurements are being continued in order to have adequate data with which to protect the Government's interests in case of future claims. For a few hours I was none too comfortable about the situation.

7. For distances as much as 200 miles away, observers were stationed to check on blast effects, property damage, radioactivity and reactions of the population. While complete reports have not yet been received, I now know that no persons were injured nor was there any real property damage outside our Government area. As soon as all the voluminous data can be checked and correlated, full technical studies will be possible.

8. Our long range weather predictions had indicated that we could expect weather favorable for our test beginning on the morning of the 17th and continuing for four days. This was almost a certainty if we were to believe our long range forecasters. The prediction for the morning of the 16th was not so certain but there was about an 80% chance of the conditions being suitable. During the night there were thunder storms with lightning flashes all over the area. The test had been originally set for 0400 hours and all the night through, because of the bad weather, there were urgings from many of the scientists to postpone the test. Such a delay might well have crippling results due to mechanical difficulties in our complicated test set-up. Fortunately, we disregarded the urgings. We held firm and waited

the night through hoping for suitable weather. We had to delay an hour and a half, to 0530, before we could fire. This was 30 minutes before sunrise.

9. Because of bad weather, our two B-29 observation airplanes were unable to take off as scheduled from Kirtland Field at Albuquerque and when they finally did get off, they found it impossible to get over the target because of the heavy clouds and the thunder storms. Certain desired observations could not be made and while the people in the airplanes saw the explosion from a distance, they were not as close as they will be in action. We still have no reason to anticipate the loss of our planes in an actual operation although we cannot guarantee safety.

10. Just before 1100 the news stories from all over the state started to flow into the Albuquerque Associated Press. I then directed the issuance by the Commanding Officer, Alamogordo Air Base of a news release as shown on the inclosure. With the assistance of the Office of Censorship we were able to limit the news stories to the approved release supplemented in the local papers by brief stories from the many eyewitnesses not connected with our project. One of these was a blind woman who saw the light.

11. Brigadier General Thomas F. Farrell was at the control shelter located 10,000 yards south of the point of explosion. His impressions are given below:

"The scene inside the shelter was dramatic beyond words. In and around the shelter were some twenty-odd people concerned with last minute arrangements prior to firing the shot. Included were: Dr. Oppenheimer, the Director who had borne the great scientific burden of developing the weapon from the raw materials made in Tennessee and Washington and a dozen of his key assistants—Dr. Kistiskowsky, who developed the highly special explosive; Dr. Bainbridge, who supervised all the detailed arrangements for the test; Dr. Hubbard, the weather expert, and several others. Besides these, there were a handful of soldiers, two or three Army officers and one Naval officer. The shelter was cluttered with a great variety of instruments and radios.

"For some hectic two hours preceding the blast, General Groves stayed with the Director, walking with him and steadying his tense excitement. Every time the director would be about to explode because of some untoward happening, General Groves would take him off and walk with him in the rain, counselling with him and reassuring him that everything would be all right. At twenty minutes before zero hour, General Groves left for his station at the base camp, first because it provided a better observation point and second, because of our rule that he and I must not be together in situations where there is an element of danger, which existed at both points.

"Just after General Groves left, announcements began to be broadcast of the interval remaining before the blast. They were sent by radio to the other groups participating in and observing the test. As the time interval grew smaller and changed from minutes to seconds, the tension increased by leaps and bounds. Everyone in that room knew the awful potentialities of the thing that they thought was about to happen. The scientists felt that their figuring must be right and that the bomb had to go off but there was in everyone's mind a strong measure of doubt. The feeling of many could be expressed by "Lord, I believe; help Thou mine unbelief." We were reaching into the unknown and we did not know what might come of it. It can be safely said that most of those present—Christian, Jew and Atheist—were praying and praying harder than they had ever prayed before. If the shot were successful, it was a justification of the several years of intensive effort of tens of thousands of people—statesmen, scientists, engineers, manufacturers, soldiers, and many others in every walk of life.

"In that brief instant in the remote New Mexico desert the tremendous effort of the brains and brawn of all these people came suddenly and startingly to the fullest fruition. Dr. Oppenheimer, on whom had rested a very heavy burden, grew tenser as the last seconds ticked off. He scarcely breathed. He held on to a post to steady himself. For the last few seconds, he started directly ahead and then when the announcer shouted "Now!" and there came this tremendous burst of light followed shortly thereafter by the deep growing roar of the explosion, his face relaxed into an expression of tremendous relief. Several of the observers standing back of the shelter to watch the lighting effects were knocked flat by the blast.

"The tension in the room let up and all started congratulating each other. Everyone sensed 'This is it!' No matter what might happen now all knew that the impossible scientific job had been done. Atomic fission would no longer be hidden in the cloisters of the theoretical physicists' dreams. It was almost full grown at birth. It was a great new force to be used for good or for evil. There was a feeling in that shelter that those concerned with its nativity should dedicate their lives to the mission that it would always be used for good and never for evil.

"Dr. Kistiakowsky, the impulsive Russian, threw his arms around Dr. Oppenheimer and embraced him with shouts of glee. Others were equally enthusiastic. All the pent-up emotions were released in those few minutes and all seemed to sense immediately that the explosion had far exceeded the most optimistic expectations and wildest hopes of the scientists. All seemed to feel that they had been present at the birth of a new age—The Age of Atomic Energy—and felt their profound responsibility to help in guiding into right channels the tremendous forces which had been unlocked for the first time in history.

Gen. Leslie R. Groves (foreground) walks over sand crystallized by the Trinity test at Alamogordo, New Mexico.

"As to the present war, there was a feeling that no matter what else might happen, we now had the means to insure its speedy conclusion and save thousands of American lives. As to the future, there had been brought into being something big and something new that would prove to be immeasurably more important than the discovery of electricity or any of the other great discoveries which have so affected our existence.

"The effects could well be called unprecedented, magnificent, beautiful, stupendous and terrifying. No man-made phenomenon of such tremendous power had ever occurred before. The lighting effects beggared description. The whole country was lighted by a searing light with the intensity many times that of the midday sun. It was golden, purple, violet, gray and blue. It lighted every peak, crevasse and ridge of the nearby mountain range with a clarity and beauty that cannot be described but must be seen to be imagined. It was that beauty the great poets dream about but describe most poorly and inadequately. Thirty seconds after the explosion came first, the air blast pressing hard against the people and things, to be followed almost immediately by the strong, sustained, awesome roar which warned of doomsday and made us feel that we puny things were blasphemous to dare tamper with the forces heretofore reserved to The Almighty. Words are inadequate tools for the job of acquainting those not present with the physical, mental and psychological effects. It had to be witnessed to be realized."

12. My impressions of the night's high points follow:

After about an hour's sleep I got up at 0100 and from that time on until about five I was with Dr. Oppenheimer constantly. Naturally he was nervous, although his mind was working at its usual extraordinary efficiency. I devoted my entire attention to shielding him from the excited and generally faulty advice of his assistants who were more than disturbed by their excitement and the uncertain weather conditions. By 0330 we decided that we could probably fire at 0530. By 0400 the rain had stopped but the sky was heavily overcast. Our decision became firmer as time went on. During most of these hours the two of us journeyed from the control house out into the darkness to look at the stars and to assure each other that the one or two visible stars were becoming brighter. At 0510 I left Dr. Oppenheimer and returned to the main observation point which was 17,000 yards from the point of explosion. In accordance with our orders I found all personnel not otherwise occupied massed on a bit of high ground.

At about two minutes of the scheduled firing time all persons lay face down with their feet pointing towards the explosion. As the remaining time was called from the loud speaker from the 10,000 yard control station there was complete silence. Dr. Conant said he had never imagined seconds could be so long. Most of the individuals in accordance with orders shielded their eyes in one way or another. There was then this burst of light of a brilliance beyond any comparison. We all rolled over and looked through dark glasses at the ball of fire. About forty seconds later came the shock wave followed by the sound, neither of which seemed startling after our complete astonishment at the extraordinary lighting intensity. Dr. Conant reached over and we shook hands in mutual congratulations. Dr. Bush, who was on the other side of me, did likewise. The feeling of the entire assembly was similar to that described by General Farrell, with even the uninitiated feeling profound awe. Drs. Conant and Bush and myself were struck by an even stronger feeling that the faith of those who had been responsible for the initiation and the carrying on of this Herculean project had been justified. I personally thought of Blondin crossing Niagara Falls on his tight rope, only to me this tight rope had lasted for almost three years and of my repeated confident-appearing assurances that such a thing was possible and that we would do it.

13. A large group of observers were stationed at a point about 27 miles north of the point of explosion. Attached is a memorandum written shortly after the explosion by Dr. E. O. Lawrence which may be of interest.

14. While General Farrell was waiting about midnight for a commercial airplane to Washington at Albuquerque—120 miles away from the site—he overheard several airport employees discussing their reaction to the blast. One said that he was out on the parking apron; it was quite dark; then the whole southern sky was lighted as though by a bright sun; the light lasted several seconds. Another remarked that if a few exploding bombs could have such an effect, it must be terrible to have them drop on a city.

15. My liaison officer at the Alamogordo Air Base, 60 miles away, made the following report:

"There was a blinding flash of light that lighted the entire northwestern sky. In the center of the flash, there appeared to be a huge billow of smoke. The original flash lasted approximately 10 to 15 seconds. As the first flash died down, there arose in the approximate center of where the original flash had occurred an enormous ball of what appeared to be fire and closely resembled a rising sun that was three-fourths above a mountain. The ball of fire lasted approximately 15 seconds, then died down and the sky resumed an almost normal appearance.

"Almost immediately, a third, but much smaller, flash and billow of smoke of a whiteish-orange color appeared in the sky, again lighting the sky for approximately 4 seconds. At the time of the original flash, the field was lighted well enough so that a newspaper could easily have been read. The second and third flashes were of much lesser intensity.

"We were in a glass-enclosed control tower some 70 feet above the ground and felt no concussion or air compression. There was no noticeable earth tremor although reports overheard at the Field during the following 24 hours indicated that some believed that they had both heard the explosion and felt some earth tremor."

16. I have not written a separate report for General Marshall as I feel you will want to show this to him. I have informed the necessary people here of our results. Lord Halifax after discussion with Mr. Harrison and myself stated that he was not sending a full report to his government at this time. I informed him that I was sending this to you and that you might wish to show it to the proper British representatives.

17. We are all fully conscious that our real goal is still before us. The battle test is what counts in the war with Japan.

18. May I express my deep personal appreciation for your congratulatory cable to us and for the support and confidence which I have received from you ever since I have had this work under my charge.

19. I know that Colonel Wyle will guard these papers with his customary extraordinary care.

51

Nagasaki

August 1945

On August 6, 1945, the *Enola Gay* dropped an atomic bomb containing a fissionable core of uranium-235 on Hiroshima, Japan, killing about 80,000 people immediately and 140,000 by the end of 1945. (Tens of thousand more died lingering deaths in the years afterward.) Three days later, the *Grand Artiste* dropped a plutonium bomb on Nagasaki, killing about half as many people. Many have since questioned

why the second bomb was dropped, and whether three days was sufficient time for the Japanese government to come to terms with what had happened at Hiroshima. "The first bomb might have been justifiable," physicist Victor Weisskopf, a member of the Manhattan Project team, declared in his memoirs, "but the second was a crime."

The reason most often given for the use of a second bomb so soon after the first was that the United States had to show Japan that it possessed more than one atomic weapon and could continue the devastation of Japanese cities until the empire surrendered. In reality, however, it's unlikely that such proof was necessary. Only the day before the bombing of Nagasaki, the Soviet Union had hastily declared war on Japan, creating an immense new front in mainland Asia. Emperor Hirohito had been hoping for several months that the erstwhile neutral Soviets might agree to act as intermediaries with the British and Americans. Therefore, their August 8 declaration of war must have shaken him severely, probably severely enough to induce his submis-

sion without the subsequent destruction of Nagasaki. Yet the momentum for the bombs' development and use had become irresistible, and once Truman gave his approval for the use of both bombs, there was little chance that either would be withheld.

Furthermore, Japan was not the only audience for these weapons—as Stalin well understood. In July 1944, physicist Niels Bohr had urged Roosevelt and Churchill to inform the Soviets of the Manhattan Project, arguing that the future security of the world depended on shared postwar atomic controls. Although the two leaders chose to reject this advice, Stalin, through a spy ring, found out about the project anyway, and it was with this knowledge that he assessed the situation at Potsdam, where Truman urged the Soviets to enter the war yet kept secret from them the upcoming atomic strikes that would preclude any such involvement. Had Truman chosen a different course and heeded Bohr's advice to share his knowledge of the Manhattan Project, the postwar nuclear arms race might well have been greatly ameliorated.

Nagasaki, near Ground Zero, in September 1945. The city was so devastated that only a few shacks could be rebuilt from the debris.

ATOMIC BOMBING OF NAGASAKI TOLD BY FLIGHT MEMBER

Seething Pillar of Fire Rose 60,000 Feet From Blast—Planes High Up Rocked

By WILLIAM L. LAURENCE

WITH THE ATOMIC BOMB MISSION TO JAPAN, Aug. 9 (Delayed)—We are on our way to bomb the mainland of Japan. Our flying contingent consists of three specially designed B-29 "Superforts," and two of these carry no bombs. But our lead plane is on its way with another atomic bomb, the second in three days, concentrating in its active substance an explosive energy equivalent to 20,000 and, under favorable conditions, 40,000 tons of TNT.

We have several chosen targets. One of these is the great industrial and shipping center of Nagasaki, on the western shore of Kyushu, one of the main islands of the Japanese homeland.

I watched the assembly of this man-made meteor during the past two days, and was among the small group of scientists and Army and Navy representatives privileged to be present at the ritual of its loading in the "Superfort" last night, against a background of threatening black skies torn open at intervals by great lightning flashes.

It is a thing of beauty to behold, this "gadget." In its design went millions of man-hours of what is without doubt the most concentrated intellectual effort in history. Never before had so much brainpower been focused on a single problem.

This atomic bomb is different from the bomb used three days ago with such devastating results on Hiroshima.

I saw the atomic substance before it was placed inside the bomb. By itself it is not at all dangerous to handle. It is only under certain conditions, produced in the bomb assembly, that it can be made to yield up its energy, and even then it gives only a small fraction of its total contents—a fraction, however, large enough to produce the greatest explosion on earth.

The briefing at midnight revealed the extreme care and the tremendous amount of preparation that had been made to take care of every detail of the mission, to make certain that the atomic bomb fully served the purpose for which it was intended. Each target in turn was shown in detailed maps and in aerial photographs. Every detail of the course was rehearsed—navigation, altitude, weather, where to land in emergencies. It came out that the Navy had submarines and rescue craft, known as Dumbos and Superdumbos, stationed at various strategic points in the vicinity of the targets, ready to rescue the fliers in case they were forced to bail out.

The briefing period ended with a moving prayer by the chaplain. We then proceeded to the mess hall for the traditional early morning breakfast before departure on a bombing mission.

A convoy of trucks took us to the supply building for the special equipment carried on combat missions. This included the "Mae West," a parachute, a lifeboat, an oxygen mask, a flak suit and a survival vest. We still had a few hours before take-off time, but we all went to the flying field and stood around in little groups or sat in jeeps talking rather casually about our mission to the Empire, as the Japanese home islands are known hereabouts.

In command of our mission is Maj. Charles W. Seeney, 25, of 124 Hamilton Avenue, North Quincy, Mass. His flagship, carrying the atomic

An aerial view of the dropping of the second atomic bomb on Nagasaki.

bomb, is named The Great Artiste, but the name does not appear on the body of the great silver ship, with its unusually long, four-bladed, orange-tipped propellers. Instead it carried the number 77, and someone remarks that it was "Red" Grange's winning number on the gridiron.

Major Seeney's co-pilot is First Lieut. Charles D. Albury, 24 , of 252 Northwest Fourth Street, Miami, Fla. The bombardier, upon whose shoulders rests the responsibility of depositing the atomic bomb square on its target, is Capt. Kermit K. Beahan of 1004 Telephone Road, Houston, Tex., who is celebrating his twenty-seventh birthday today.

Captain Beahan has the awards of the Distinguished Flying Cross, the Air Medal and one Silver Oak Leaf Cluster, the Purple Heart, the Western Hemisphere Ribbon, the European Theatre Ribbon and two battle stars. He participated in the first Eighth Air Force heavy bombardment mission against the Germans from England on Aug. 17, 1942, and was on the plane that transported Gen. Dwight D. Eisenhower from Gibraltar to Oran at the beginning of the North African invasion. He has had a number of hair-raising escapes in combat.

The navigator on The Great Artiste is Capt. James F. Van Pelt Jr., 27, of Oak Hill, W. Va. The flight engineer is M/Sgt. John D. Kuharek, 32, of 1054 Twenty-second Avenue, Columbus, Neb.; S/Sgt. Albert T. De Hart of Plainview, Tex., who celebrated his thirtieth birthday yesterday, is the tail gunner; the radar operator is S/Sgt. Edward K. Buckley, 32, of 529 E. Washington Street, Lisbon, Ohio. The radio operator is Sgt. Abe M. Spitzer, 33, of 655 Pelham Parkway, North Bronx, N. Y.; Sgt. Raymond Gallagher, 23, of 572 South Mozart Street, Chicago, is assistant flight engineer.

The lead ship is also carrying a group of scientific personnel, headed by Comdr. Frederick

L. Ashworth, USN, one of the leaders in the development of the bomb. The group includes Lieut. Jacob Beser, 24, of Baltimore, Md., an expert on airborne radar.

The other two Superfortresses in our formation are instrument planes, carrying special apparatus to measure the power of the bomb at the time of explosion, high speed cameras and other photographic equipment.

Our "Superfort" is the second in line. Its commander is Capt. Frederick C. Bock, 27, of 300 West Washington Street, Greenville, Mich. Its other officers are Second Lieut. Hugh C. Ferguson, 21, of 247 Windermere Avenue, Highland Park, Mich., pilot; Second Lieut. Leonard A. Godfrey, 24, of 72 Lincoln Street, Greenfield, Mass., navigator; and First Lieut. Charles Levy, 26, of 1954 Spencer Street, Philadelphia, bombardier.

The enlisted personnel of this "Superfort" are: T/Sgt. Roderick F. Arnold, 28, of 130 South Street, Rochester, Mich., flight engineer; Sgt. Ralph D. Curry, 20, of 1101 South Second Avenue, Hoopeston, Ill., radio operator; Sgt. William C. Barney, 22, of Columbia City, Ind., radar operator; Corp. Robert J. Stock, 21, of 415 Downing Street, Fort Wayne, Ind., assistant flight engineer, and Corp. Ralph D. Belanger, 19, of Thendara, N. Y., tail gunner.

The scientific personnel of our "Superfort" includes S/Sgt. Walter Goodman, 22, of 1956 Seventy-fourth Street, Brooklyn, N. Y., and Lawrence Johnson, graduate student at the University of California, whose home is at Hollywood, Calif.

The third "Superfort" is commanded by Maj. James Hopkins, 1311 North Queen Street, Palestine, Tex. His officers are Second Lieut. John E. Cantlon, of 516 North Takima Street, Tacoma, Wash., pilot; Second Lieut. Stanley C. Steinke, 604 West Chestnut Street, West Chester, Pa., navigator; and Second Lieut. Myron Faryna, 16 Elgin Street, Rochester, N. Y., bombardier.

The crew are T/Sgt. George K. Brabenec, 9717 South Lawndale Avenue, Evergreen, Ill.; Sgt. Francis X. Dolan, 30-60 Warren Street, Elmhurst, Queens, N. Y.; Corp. Richard F. Cannon, 160 Carmel Road, Buffalo, N. Y.; Corp. Martin G. Murray, 7356 Dexter Street, Detroit, Mich., and Corp. Sidney J. Bellamy, 529 Johnson Avenue, Trenton, N. J.

On this "Superfort" are also two distinguished observers from Britain, whose scientists played an important role in the development of the atomic bomb. One of these is Group Capt. G. Leonard Chesire, famous Royal Air Force pilot, who is now a member of the British military mission to the United States. The other is Dr. William G. Denny, Professor of Applied Mathematics, London University, one of the group of eminent British scientists that has been working at the "Y-Site" near Santa Fe, N. M., on the enormous problems involved in taming the atom.

Group Captain Cheshire, whose rank is the equivalent to that of colonel in the United States Army Air Forces, was designated as an observer of the atomic bomb in action by Winston Churchill when he was still Prime Minister. He is now the official representative of Prime Minister Clement R. Attlee.

We took off at 3:50 this morning and headed northwest on a straight line for the Empire. The night was cloudy and threatening, with only a few stars here and there breaking through the overcast. The weather report had predicted storms ahead part of the way but clear sailing for the final and climatic stages of our odyssey.

We were about an hour away from our base when the storm broke. Our great ship took some heavy dips through the abysmal darkness around us but it took these dips much more gracefully than a large commercial airliner, producing a sensation more in the nature of a glide than a "bump," like a great ocean liner riding the waves, except that in this case the air waves were much higher and the rhythmic tempo of the glide much faster.

I noticed a strange eerie light coming through the window high above the navigator's cabin and as I peered through the dark all around us I saw a

startling phenomenon. The whirling giant propellers had somehow become great luminous
disks of blue flame. The same luminous blue
flame appeared on the plexiglass windows in the
nose of the ship, and on the tips of the giant
wings it looked as though we were riding the
whirlwind through space on a chariot of blue fire.

It was, I surmised, a surcharge of static electricity that had accumulated on the tips of the
propellers and on the di-electric material in the
plastic windows. One's thoughts dwelt anxiously
on the precious cargo in the invisible ship ahead
of us. Was there any likelihood of danger that
this heavy electric tension in the atmosphere all
about us might set it off?

I expressed my fears to Captain Bock, who
seems nonchalant and imperturbed at the controls. He quickly reassures me:

"It is a familiar phenomenon seen often on
ships. I have seen it many times on bombing missions. It is known as St. Elmo's Fire."

On we went through the night. We soon rode
out the storm and our ship was once again sailing
on a smooth course straight ahead, on a direct
line to the Empire.

Our altimeter showed that we were traveling
through space at a height of 17,000 feet. The
thermometer registered an outside temperature
of 33 degrees below zero centigrade, about 30
below Fahrenheit. Inside our pressurized cabin
the temperature was that of a comfortable air-
conditioned room, and a pressure corresponding
to an altitude of 8,000 feet. Captain Bock cau-
tioned me, however, to keep my oxygen mask
handy in case of emergency. This, he explained,
might mean either something going wrong with
the pressure equipment inside the ship or a hole
through the cabin by flak.

The first signs of dawn came shortly after 5
o'clock. Sergeant Curry, who had been listening steadily on his earphones for radio reports,
while maintaining a strict radio silence himself, greeted it by rising to his feet and gazing
out the window.

"It's good to see the day," he told me. "I get a
feeling of claustrophobia hemmed in in this
cabin at night."

He is a typical American youth, looking even
younger than his 20 years. It takes no mind-
reader to read his thoughts.

"It's a long way from Hoopeston, Ill.," I find
myself remarking.

"Yep," he replies, as he busies himself decoding a message from outer space.

"Think this atomic bomb will end the war?"
he asks hopefully.

"There is a very good chance that this one
may do the trick," I assure him, "but if not, then
the next one or two surely will. Its power is such
that no nation can stand up against it very long."

This was not my own view. I had heard it
expressed all around a few hours earlier, before
we took off. To anyone who had seen this man-
made fireball in action, as I had less than a month
ago in the desert of New Mexico, this view did
not sound overoptimistic.

By 5:50 it was real light outside. We had lost
our lead ship, but Lieutenant Godfrey, our navigator, informs me that we had arranged for that
contingency. We have an assembly point in the
sky above the little island of Yakoshima, southeast of Kyushu, at 9:10. We are to circle there
and wait for the rest of our formation.

Our genial bombardier, Lieutenant Levy,
comes over to invite me to take his front-row
seat in the transparent nose of the ship and I
accept eagerly. From that vantage point in
space, 17,000 feet above the Pacific, one gets a
view of a hundred miles on all sides, horizon-
tally and vertically. At that height the vast
ocean below and the sky above seem to merge
into one great sphere.

I was on the inside of that firmament, riding
above the giant mountains of white cumulous
clouds, letting myself be suspended in infinite
space. One hears the whirl of the motors behind
one, but it soon becomes insignificant against the
immensity all around and is before long swallowed

by it. There comes a point where space also swallows time and one lives through eternal moments filled with oppressive loneliness, as though all life had suddenly vanished from the earth and you are the only one left, a lone survivor traveling endlessly through interplanetary space.

My mind soon returns to the mission I am on. Somewhere beyond these vast mountains of white clouds ahead of me there lies Japan, the land of our enemy. In about four hours from now one of

A mother and son carry boiled rice balls distributed by an emergency relief party one mile southeast of Ground Zero in Nagasaki on the morning after the atomic explosion there.

its cities, making weapons of war for use against us, will be wiped off the map by the greatest weapon ever made by man. In one-tenth of a millionth of a second, a fraction of time immeasurable by any clock, a whirlwind from the skies will pulverize thousands of its buildings and tens of thousands of its inhabitants.

Our weather planes ahead of us are on their way to find out where the wind blows. Half an hour before target time we will know what the winds have decided.

Does one feel any pity or compassion for the poor devils about to die? Not when one thinks of Pearl Harbor and of the Death March on Bataan.

Captain Bock informs me that we are about to start our climb to bombing altitude.

He manipulates a few knobs on his control panel to the right of him and I alternately watch the white clouds and the ocean below me and the altimeter on the bombardier's panel. We reached our altitude at 9 o'clock. We were then over Japanese waters, close to their mainland. Lieutenant Godfrey motioned to me to look through his radar scope. Before me was the outline of our assembly point. We shall soon meet our lead ship and proceed to the final stage of our journey.

We reached Yakoshima at 9:12 and there, about 4,000 feet ahead of us, was The Great Artiste with its precious load. I saw Lieutenant Godfrey and Sergeant Curry strap on their parachutes and I decided to do likewise.

We started circling. We saw little towns on the coastline, heedless of our presence. We kept on circling, waiting for the third ship in our formation.

It was 9:56 when we began heading for the coastline. Our weather scouts had sent us code messages, deciphered by Sergeant Curry, informing us that both the primary target as well as the secondary were clearly visible.

The winds of density seemed to favor certain Japanese cities that must remain nameless. We circled about them again and again and found no opening in the thick umbrella of clouds that covered them. Destiny chose Nagasaki as the ultimate target.

We had been circling for some time when we noticed black puffs of smoke coming through the white clouds directly at us. There were fifteen bursts of flak in rapid succession, all too low. Captain Bock changed his course. There soon followed eight more bursts of flak, right up to our altitude, but by this time were too far to the left.

We flew southward down the channel and at 11:33 crossed the coastline and headed straight for Nagasaki about 100 miles to the west. Here again we circled until we found an opening in the clouds. It was 12:01 and the goal of our mission had arrived.

We heard the prearranged signal on our radio, put on our arc-welder's glasses and watched tensely the maneuverings of the strike ship about half a mile in front of us.

"There she goes!" someone said.

Out of the belly of The Great Artiste what looked like a black object went downward.

Captain Bock swung around to get out of range; but even though we were turning away in the opposite direction, and despite the fact that it was broad daylight in our cabin, all of us became aware of a giant flash that broke through the dark barrier of our arc-welder's lenses and flooded our cabin with intense light.

We removed our glasses after the first flash, but the light still lingered on, a bluish-green light that illuminated the entire sky all around. A tremendous blast wave struck our ship and made it tremble from nose to tail. This was followed by four more blasts in rapid succession, each resounding like the boom of cannon fire hitting our plane from all directions.

Observers in the tail of our ship saw a giant ball of fire rise as though from the bowels of the earth, belching forth enormous white smoke rings. Next they saw a giant pillar of purple fire, 10,000 feet high, shooting skyward with enormous speed.

By the time our ship had made another turn in the direction of the atomic explosion the pillar of purple fire had reached the level of our altitude. Only about forty-five seconds had passed. Awe-struck, we watched it shoot upward like a meteor coming from earth instead of from outer space, becoming ever more alive as it climbed skyward throughout the white clouds. It was no longer smoke, or dust, or even a cloud of fire. It was a living thing, a new species of being, born right before our incredulous eyes.

At one stage of its evolution, covering millions of years in terms of seconds, the entity assumed the form of a giant square totem pole, with its base about three miles long, tapering off to about a mile at the top. Its bottom was brown, its center was amber, its top white. But it was a living totem pole, carved with many grotesque masks grimacing at the earth.

Then, just when it appeared as though the thing has settled down into a state of permanence, there came shooting out of the top a giant mushroom that increased the height of the pillar to a total of 45,000 feet. The mushroom top was even more alive than the pillar, seething and boiling in a white fury of creamy foam, sizzling upward and then descending earthward, a thousand Old Faithful geysers rolled into one.

It kept struggling in an elemental fury, like a creature in the act of breaking the bonds that held it down. In a few seconds it had freed itself from its gigantic stem and floated upward with tremendous speed, its momentum carrying into stratosphere to a height of about 60,000 feet.

But no sooner did this happen when another mushroom, smaller in size than the first one, began emerging out of the pillar. It was as though the decapitated monster was growing a new head.

As the first mushroom floated off into the blue it changed its shape into a flowerlike form, its giant petal curving downward, creamy white outside, rose-colored inside. It still retained that shape when we last gazed at it from a distance of about 200 miles.

"Suddenly a glaring whitish-pink light appeared in the sky."

A ground-level account of the Hiroshima blast

In September 1945, Dr. Marcel Junod traveled to Hiroshima as part of an investigating commission sponsored by the International Committee of the Red Cross. One of his interpreters, a Japanese journalist who had spent two decades in the United States, gave him this ground-level description of the atomic explosion there.

The town was not much damaged. It had suffered very little from bombing. There were only two minor raids: one on March 19th last by a squadron of American naval planes, and one on April 30th by a Flying Fortress.

On August 6th there wasn't a cloud in the sky above Hiroshima, and a mild, hardly perceptible wind, blew from the south. Visibility was almost perfect for ten or twelve miles.

At nine minutes past seven in the morning an air-raid warning sounded and four American B-29 planes appeared. To the north of the town two of them turned and made off to the south and disappeared in the direction of the Shoho Sea. The other two, after having circled the neighborhood of Shukai, flew off at high speed southward in the direction of the Bingo Sea.

At seven thirty-one the all clear was given. Feeling themselves safe, people came out of their shelters and went about their affairs and the work of the day began.

Suddenly a glaring whitish-pink light appeared in the sky accompanied by an unnatural tremor that was followed almost immediately by a wave of suffocating heat and a wind that swept away everything in its path.

Within a few seconds the thousands of people in the streets and the gardens in the center of the town were scorched by a wave of searing heat. Many were killed instantly, others lay writhing on the ground, screaming in agony from the intolerable pain of their burns. Everything standing upright in the way of the blast, walls, houses, factories, and other buildings, was annihilated; and the débris spun round in a whirlwind and was carried up into the air. Trams were picked up and tossed aside as though they had neither weight nor solidity. Trains were flung off the rails as though they were toys. Horses, dogs, and cattle suffered the same fate as human beings. Every living thing was petrified in an attitude of indescribable suffering. Even the vegetation did not escape. Trees went up in flames, the rice plants lost their greenness, the grass burned on the ground like dry straw.

Beyond the zone of utter death in which nothing remained alive, houses collapsed in a whirl of beams, bricks, and girders. Up to about three miles from the center of the explosion, lightly built houses were flattened as though they had been built of cardboard. Those who were inside were either killed or wounded. Those who managed to extricate themselves by some miracle found themselves surrounded by a ring of fire. And the few who succeeded in making their way to safety generally died twenty or thirty days later from the delayed effects of the deadly gamma rays. Some of the reinforced concrete or stone buildings remained standing, but their interiors were completely gutted by the blast.

About half an hour after the explosion, while the sky all around Hiroshima was still cloudless, a fine rain began to fall on the town and continued for about five minutes. It was caused by the sudden rise of overheated air to a great height, where it condensed and fell back as rain. Then a violent wind rose, and the fires extended with terrible rapidity because most Japanese houses are built only of timber and straw.

By the evening the fire began to die down and then it went out. There was nothing left to burn, Hiroshima had ceased to exist.

52.

V-J Day
August 1945

The day after the bombing of Nagasaki, the Japanese government announced its willingness to accept the terms of the Potsdam Proclamation "with the understanding that the said declaration does not comprise any demand which prejudices the prerogatives of His Majesty as a Sovereign Ruler." To this communication, Secretary of State Byrnes replied ambiguously (in a statement approved by the British,

Chinese, and Soviets) that "from the moment of surrender the authority of the emperor and the Japanese Government to rule the state shall be subject to the Supreme Commander of the Allied Powers who will take such steps as he deems proper to effectuate the surrender terms." This was sufficient for Foreign Minister Togo Shigenori to persuade Hirohito that the Allies had recognized the legitimacy of his dynasty, and so Japan's capitulation followed.

The emperor sent his written submission to the Allies late on August 14, but the Japanese population wasn't informed until the next afternoon. Early on the morning of August 15, radio stations throughout Japan alerted citizens to an important broadcast scheduled for noon. In the meantime, loudspeakers were set up in various public places to ensure as large an audience as possible. Most Japanese knew that defeat was not far off and expected to hear another exhortation to fight to the death for the national honor. Instead, according to Rear Adm. Nakamura Katsuhei, "The strident note of the noontime signal was followed by the muted strains of the national anthem. Then, listeners heard State Minister Shimomura, President of the Cabinet Information Board, announce that the next voice would be that of His Majesty the Emperor. People caught their breaths in quick surprise for never before had the Emperor spoken directly to his subjects by radio. They listened in tense silence as the Emperor's voice came over the air, reading the solemn and fateful words of the Imperial Rescript."

A Japanese prisoner of war on Guam bows his head after hearing Hirohito's surrender announcement.

JAPAN SURRENDERS, END OF WAR! EMPEROR ACCEPTS ALLIED RULE; M'ARTHUR SUPREME COMMANDER

Yielding Unqualified, Truman Says

By ARTHUR KROCK

WASHINGTON, Aug. 14—Japan today unconditionally surrendered the hemispheric empire taken by force and held almost intact for more than two years against the rising power of the United States and its Allies in the Pacific war.

The bloody dream of the Japanese military caste vanished in the text of a note to the Four Powers accepting the terms of the Potsdam Declaration of July 26, 1945, which amplified the Cairo Declaration of 1943.

Like the previous items in the surrender correspondence, today's Japanese document was forwarded through the Swiss Foreign Office at Berne and the Swiss Legation in Washington. The note of total capitulation was delivered to the State Department by the Legation Charge d'Affaires at 6:10 P.M., after the third and most anxious day of waiting on Tokyo, the anxiety intensified by several premature or false reports of the finale of World War II.

The Department responded with a note to Tokyo through the same channel, ordering the immediate end of hostilities by the Japanese, requiring that the Supreme Allied Commander—who, the President announced, will be Gen. Douglas MacArthur—be notified of the date and hour of the order, and instructing that emissaries of Japan be sent to him at once—at the time and place selected by him—"with full information of the disposition of the Japanese forces and commanders."

President Truman summoned a special press conference in the Executive offices at 7 P.M. He handed to the reporters three texts.

The first—the only one he read aloud—was that he had received the Japanese note and deemed it full acceptance of the Potsdam Declaration, containing no qualification whatsoever; that arrangements for the formal signing of the peace would be made for the "earliest possible moment"; that the Japanese surrender would be made to General MacArthur in his capacity as Supreme Allied Commander in Chief; that Allied military commanders had been instructed to cease hostilities, but that the formal proclamation of V-J Day must await the formal signing.

The text ended with the Japanese note, in which the Four Powers (the United States, Great Britain, China and Russia) were officially informed that the Emperor of Japan had issued an imperial rescript of surrender, was prepared to guarantee the necessary signatures to the terms as prescribed by the Allies, and had instructed all his commanders to cease active operations, to surrender all arms and to disband all forces under their control and within their reach.

The President's second announcement was that he had instructed the Selective Service to reduce the monthly military draft from 80,000 to 50,000 men, permitting a constant flow of replacements for the occupation forces and other necessary military units, with the draft held to

GIs and WACs gather in front of an American Red Cross club in Paris to celebrate the announcement of Japan's unconditional surrender.

low-age groups and first discharges given on the basis of long, arduous and faithful war service. He said he hoped to release 5,000,000 to 5,500,000 men in the subsequent year or eighteen months, the ratio governed in some degree by transportation facilities and the world situation.

The President's final announcement was to decree holidays tomorrow and Thursday for all Federal workers, who, he said, were the "hardest working and perhaps the least appreciated" by the public of all who had helped to wage the war.

Mr. Truman spoke calmly to the reporters, but when he had finished reading his face broke into a smile. Also present were Secretary of State James F. Byrnes and Admiral William D. Leahy, the President's personal Chief of Staff, and two other members of the Cabinet—Henry A. Wallace, Secretary of Commerce, and James V. Forrestal, Secretary of the Navy—managed

to respond to a hurry call in time to be there. The agreement to issue the statements simultaneously in all the Allied capitals, and the brief period between the call to the Cabinet and the announcement, were responsible. Later the chief war administrators and Cordell Hull, former Secretary of State, arrived to congratulate the President.

After the press conference, while usually bored Washington launched upon a noisy victory demonstration, the President with Mrs. Truman walked out to the fountain in the White House grounds that face on Pennsylvania Avenue and made the V sign to the shouting crowds.

But this did not satisfy the growing assemblage, or probably the President either, for, in response to clamor, he came back and made a speech from the north portico, in which he said that the present emergency was as great as that of Pearl Harbor Day and must and would be met in the same spirit. Later in the evening he appeared to the crowds and spoke again.

He then returned to the executive mansion to begin work at once on problems of peace, including domestic ones affecting reconversion, unemployment, wage-and-hour scales and industrial cut-backs, which are more complex and difficult than any he has faced and call for plans and measures that were necessarily held in abeyance by the exacting fact of war.

But certain immediate steps to deal with these problems and restore peacetime conditions were taken or announced as follows:

1. The War Manpower Commission abolished all controls, effective immediately, creating a free labor market for the first time in three years. The commission also set up a plan to help displaced workers and veterans find jobs.

2. The Navy canceled nearly $6,000,000,000 of prime contracts.

The Japanese offer to surrender, confirmed by the note received through Switzerland today, came in the week after the United States Air Forces obliterated Hiroshima with the first atomic bomb in history and the Union of Soviet Socialist Republics declared war on Japan. At the time the document was received in Washington Russian armies were pushing back the Japanese armies in Asia and on Sakhalin Island, and the Army and Navy of the United States with their air forces—aided by the British—were relentlessly bombarding the home islands.

When the President made his announcements tonight it was three years and 250 days after the bombing of Pearl Harbor, which put the United States at war with Japan. This was followed immediately by the declarations of war on this country by Germany and Italy, the other Axis partners, which engaged the United States in the global conflict that now, in its military phases, is wholly won.

If the note had not come today the President was ready, though reluctant, to give the order that would have spread throughout Japan the hideous death and destruction that are the toll of the atomic bomb.

Officially the Japanese note was a response to the communication to Tokyo, written on behalf of the Allies Aug. 11 by Secretary Byrnes, which was itself a reply to a Japanese offer on Aug. 10 to surrender on the understanding of the Japanese Government that the Potsdam Declaration did not "prejudice the prerogatives" of the Emperor of Japan as its "sovereign ruler."

Mr. Byrnes wrote, in effect, that the Japanese might keep their Emperor if they chose to do so of their own free-will, but that he would be placed under the authority of the Allied Commander-in-Chief in Tokyo and would be responsible to that commander for his official and public activities.

Relief rather than jubilation that the grim and costly task of conquering the Axis is done was the emotion of officials, from the President down, who have traversed the long and agonizing road to victory since Dec. 7, 1941, when the Japanese attacked Pearl Harbor while Tokyo's "peace" envoys—Admiral Kichisahura Nomura and Ambassador Saburo Kurusu—were still continuing their negotiations with Secretary of State Hull. The road is piled high with the bodies of American soldiers, sailors, airmen and civilians who gave their lives that the victory might be attained.

And, in a solemn hour of triumph, the men in Washington that were their military and civilian commanders could not be jubilant in the lasting memory of these human sacrifices. On the contrary, they seemed more than ever resolved to produce a system of world security which for a long time would obviate the necessity of such sacrifices to dictators and aggressive nations; and to impress on the Japanese—as on the Germans—their crimes, nor relax their punishments, until they learn to follow the ways of peace.

Though the victory over the Japanese as well as

the Nazis had always seemed assured to the American authorities, it did not become a certainty until the Allies—through United States invention and production, Allied military and scientific skills and the fortitude of the British, Chinese, Russian and American populations—were able to change from defense to attack. This change, so far as the Pacific was concerned, came after the Battle of Midway gathered force after the actions of the Coral Sea and the Philippines and came to crescendo with the captures of Saipan, Iwo Island and Okinawa, the perfection of radar and the discovery and use of the atomic bomb. But before these successes the story was very different.

The Japanese attack on Pearl Harbor found the Pacific Fleet divided, half of it crowded in the roadstead, the other half dispatched for Atlantic service for reasons of policy. These reasons grew out of President Roosevelt's decision that the Nazi menace required the fleet diversion to the Atlantic for immediate national defense, and out of his belief that, as he expressed it, he could "baby along Japan." This latter view was the foundation of the underlying policy by which the United States continued to furnish Japan with scrap iron, petrol and other materials transferable to war uses long after Japan by many officials was conceded to be bent on hemispheric and eventual world-wide aggression.

There followed the loss of the Philippines and Malaya, the death march of Bataan, the shelling of the coast of California, the desperate, costly invasion and divided struggle of Guadalcanal, the defense of the Antipodes and the slow process by which General MacArthur—necessarily long held to small resources—built up the force that won back the Philippines and whose commander will be the military ruler, civil supervisor and warden of the Japanese nation.

These are a few highlights in the violent chapter of unprecedented war that ended today, with the receipt of the note from Tokyo. It is not strange that, remembering all these things, the President and high officials were under a strain as acute as any mother, father or wife of a man in the Pacific combat could have been while waiting for the words that would bring the chapter to a present close.

The alternative for the Japanese would, of course, have been national suicide. But there are many in Washington, students of this strange race or baffled by the ways of the Orient, who have predicted that such would be the decision of the Japanese military leaders to which the people would submit. The Japanese, they contended, would commit mass suicide before they would yield their god, the Emperor, to an alien enemy as his overlord.

But now this god, in the person of an ordinary human being, representative of other human beings who were vanquished with him, is to take his orders from a mortal man who, above all others, symbolizes the spirit of the alien enemy that was foremost in crushing the myth of divinity and shattering the imperial dream. And the Emperor, with his Ministers and commanders, has been obliged to accept the condition that disproves the fanatical concept used by the militarists of Japan to produce unquestioned obedience to orders issued in the Emperor's name, however much or little he may have had to do with them.

"To Our good and loyal subjects, we hereby convey Our will."

The Imperial Rescript

Hirohito's ministers carefully crafted the emperor's August 15 broadcast so that the text softened the impact of surrender as much as possible. For instance, the word *surrender* was never uttered. However, the point of the statement was painfully clear to all. Even those who had never heard of the Joint Declaration of the Allied Powers understood that the emperor was accepting surrender terms laid down by the enemy.

After pondering deeply the general trend of the world situation and the actual state of Our Empire, We have decided to effect a settlement of the present crisis by resort to an extraordinary measure. To Our good and loyal subjects, we hereby convey Our will.

We have commanded Our Government to communicate to the Governments of the United States, Great Britain, China and the Soviet Union that Our Empire accepts the terms of their Joint Declaration.

To strive for the common prosperity and happiness of all nations as well as the security and well-being of Our subjects is the solemn obligation handed down to Us by Our Imperial Ancestors, and We keep it close to heart. Indeed, We declared war on America and Britain out of Our sincere desire to ensure Japan's self-preservation and the stabilization of East Asia. It was not Our intention either to infringe upon the sovereignty of other nations or to seek territorial aggrandizement.

The hostilities have now continued for nearly four years. Despite the gallant fighting of the Officers and Men of Our Army and Navy, the diligence and assiduity of Our servants of State, and the devoted service of Our hundred million subjects—despite the best efforts of all—the war has not necessarily developed in Our favor, and the general world situation also is not to Japan's advantage. Furthermore, the enemy has begun to employ a new and cruel bomb which kills and maims the innocent and the power of which to wreak destruction is truly incalculable.

Should We continue to fight, the ultimate result would be not only the obliteration of the race but the extinction of human civilization. Then, how should We be able to save the millions of Our subjects and make atonement to the hallowed spirits of Our Imperial Ancestors? That is why We have commanded the imperial Government to comply with the terms of the Joint Declaration of the Powers.

To those nations which, as Our allies, have steadfastly cooperated with the Empire for the emancipation of East Asia, We cannot but express Our deep regret. Also, the thought of Our subjects who have fallen on the field of battle or met untimely death while performing their appointed tasks, and the thought of their bereaved families, rends Our heart, and We feel profound solicitude for the wounded and for all war-sufferers who have lost their homes and livelihood.

The suffering and hardship which Our nation yet must undergo will certainly be great. We are keenly aware of the innermost feelings of all ye, Our subjects. However, it is according to the dictates of time and fate that We have resolved, by enduring the unendurable and bearing the unbearable, to pave the way for a grand peace for all generations to come.

Gen. Yoshijuro Umezu leads the Japanese delegation off the USS Missouri *after signing the formal surrender papers on September 2.*

Since it has been possible to preserve the structure of the Imperial State, We shall always be with ye, Our good and loyal subjects, placing Our trust in your sincerity and integrity. Beware most strictly of any outburst of emotion which may engender needless complications, and refrain from fraternal contention and strife which may create confusion, lead ye astray and cause ye to lose the confidence of the world. Let the nation continue as one family from generation to generation with unwavering faith in the imperishability of Our divine land and ever mindful of its heavy burden of responsibility and the long road ahead. Turn your full strength to the task of building a new future. Cultivate the ways of rectitude, foster nobility of spirit, and work with resolution so that ye may enhance the innate glory of the Imperial State and keep pace with the progress of the world. We charge ye, Our loyal subjects, to carry out faithfully Our will.

ACKNOWLEDGMENTS

We would like to acknowledge the contributions made to this project by Robin Dennis of Times Books; by Susan Chira, Mike Levitas, and Tomi Murata of *The New York Times;* and by Wendy Fuller and the staff of the Chatham Public Library.

PERMISSIONS

We would like to thank the copyright holders listed below for their permission to reprint some of the documents used in this book:

Excerpt from *Midway* by Mitsuo Fuchida reprinted with the permission of the Naval Institute Press and Cassell Military. Copyright ©1955.

Excerpt from *Churchill* by Lord Moran reprinted with the permission of Constable & Robinson Ltd.

Excerpts from "Gazala and Tobruk" in *The Rommel Papers*, copyright ©1953 by B. H. Liddell-Hart and renewed 1981 by Lady Kathleen Liddell-Hart, Fritz Bayerlein-Dittmar and Manfred Rommel, reprinted by permission of Harcourt, Inc., and David Higham Associates.

Translation of "The Drones" reprinted with the permission of Randall Bytwerk.

Excerpt from Mitchell Paige's account of his service on Guadalcanal reprinted with the permission of Mitchell Paige.

Excerpt from the *Mission to Moscow* screenplay in *Mission to Moscow* by David Culbert, copyright ©1980, reprinted with the permission of The University of Wisconsin Press.

Ernie Pyle's dispatches from Sicily reprinted with the permission of the Scripps Howard Foundation.

Excerpt from *My Three Years with Eisenhower: The Personal Diary of Captain Harry C. Butcher* by Harry C. Butcher reprinted with the permission of Simon & Schuster. Copyright ©1946 by Harry C. Butcher, renewed 1974 by Harry C. Butcher.

Excerpt from *Up Front* by Bill Mauldin reprinted with permission. Copyright ©1944 by Bill Mauldin.

"Working at the Navy Yard" by Susan B. Anthony II reprinted by permission of *The New Republic*. Copyright ©1944 by The New Republic, LLC. Originally published in *The New Republic*, May 1, 1944.

Excerpt from "Half a Day in Hell" by Erika Dienel reprinted with the permission of Independent Newspapers. Copyright ©1992 by *The Independent*. Originally published in *The Independent*, May 3, 1992.

Excerpt from *The Bloody Battle for Suribachi* by Richard Wheeler reprinted with the permission of McIntosh and Otis, Inc. Copyright ©1965 by Richard Wheeler.

Excerpt from *Private* by Lester Atwell reprinted with the permission of the Harold Matson Co.,

ILLUSTRATION CREDITS

Photographs from the Library of Congress are indicated with image numbers that begin LC. Those from the National Archives are indicated with image numbers that begin NA.

219: NA-208-AA-301HH-1;

222: NA-208-MO-31803;

225: NA-208-MO-33502;

229: NA-208-MO-31912;

230: NA-80-G-270710;

233: NA-208-PU-127A-13;

239: NA-208-WP-BOX23R-35340;

243: D.C. Public Library, *Washington Star* Collection;

246: NA-111-SC-199406;

249: NA-111-SC-198304;

255: Franklin D. Roosevelt Library;

257: NA-111-SC-199753;

260: Franklin D. Roosevelt Library;

271: LC-USZ62-15193;

275: LC-NYWTS;

278: LC-USZ62-93535;

281: NA-208-AA-249Z-14;

286: NA-208-YE-132;

289: NA-208-YE-133;

292: NA-208-AA-32CC-1;

294: NA-208-AA-206K-31;

297: NA-208-AA-206H-1;

302: NA-80-G-377562;

305: NA-80-G-377605;

309: Harry S. Truman Library;

312: NA-208-SF-10-40537;

315: NA-208-SF-1-40022;

318: NA-208-MNC-24-1;

321: NA-208-AMC-64316;

324: LC-NYWTS;

327: LC-USZ62-116110;

331: LC-NYWTS;

336: NA-111-SC-262185;

342: NA-127-GR-100-122160;

345: LC-USZ62-98191;

348: Harry S. Truman Library;

351: NA-208-PU-205G-21;

357: Harry S. Truman Library;

363: NA-80-G-473733;

366: LC-USZ62-113252;

371: LC-NYWTS;

374: NA-342-FHA-3614;

377: LC-USZ62-36452;

380: NA-434-OR-75(1);

384: NA-80-G-490317;

387: NA-111-SC-210241;

391: NA-80-G-472629

INDEX

About the Editors

DOUGLAS BRINKLEY currently serves as director of the Eisenhower Center for American Studies and is a professor of history at the University of New Orleans. Three of his biographies—*Dean Acheson: The Cold War Years* (1992), *Driven Patriot: The Life and Times of James Forrestal* (with Townsend Hoopes) (1992), and *The Unfinished Presidency: Jimmy Carter's Journey Beyond the White House* (1998)—were chosen as Notable Books of the Year by *The New York Times*.

Brinkley's recent publications include *Wheels for the World: Henry Ford, His Company and a Century of Progress*, *The Mississippi and the Making of a Nation*, *Rosa Parks* (in the Penguin Lives series), and *The American Heritage History of the United States*. He is also a regular contributor to *Newsweek*, *Time*, *American Heritage*, *The New Yorker*, *The New York Times*, *The Wall Street Journal*, *The Atlantic Monthly*, *Foreign Affairs*, *Foreign Policy*, and other journals.

DAVID RUBEL is the president of Agincourt Press, a book production company in Chatham, New York. Specializing in American history, Rubel has edited (with James M. McPherson) *To the Best of My Ability: The American Presidents* (2000) and (with James M. McPherson and Alan Brinkley) *Days of Destiny: Crossroads in American History* (2001). He is also the author (with Allen Weinstein) of *The Story of America: Freedom and Crisis from Settlement to Superpower* (2002). Rubel's books for children include *The Scholastic Encyclopedia of the Presidents and Their Times*, originally published in 1994 and now about to appear in its fourth edition.